CHURCH POTLUCK

BEST-LOVED SLOW COOKER AND CASSEROLE RECIPES

Homestyle recipes for church suppers,

family gatherings, and

community celebrations

LINDA LARSEN AND SUSIE SIEGFRIED

RODALE

Portions of the book were previously published as *Church Potluck Carry-Ins and Casseroles* © 2006 by Susie Siegfried;
and *Church Potluck Slow Cooker* © 2008 by F & W Publications, Inc. Exclusive direct mail edition published by Rodale Inc.
in September 2010 under license from Adams Media, a division of F & W Media, Inc., Cincinnati, Ohio.

Book design by Christina Gaugler

Library of Congress Cataloging-in-Publication Data

Larsen, Linda Johnson.
    Church potluck best-loved slow cooker and casserole recipes / Linda Larsen and Susie Siegfried.
        p.   cm.
    First work originally published: Church potluck slow cooker. Avon, Mass. : Adams Media, c2008; 2nd work: Church
potluck carry-ins and casseroles. Avon, Mass. : Adams Media, c2006.
    Includes index.
    ISBN 978–1–60529–297–7   hardcover
    1. Casserole cooking.   2. Electric cooking, Slow.   3. Cookbooks.   I. Siegfried, Susie.   II. Larsen, Linda. Church
potluck slow cooker.   III. Larsen, Linda. Church potluck carry-ins and casseroles.   IV. Title.
    TX693.L37   2010
    641.5'884—dc22   2010034052

2 4 6 8 10 9 7 5 3 1   hardcover

We inspire and enable people to improve their lives and the world around them
For more of our products visit **rodalestore.com** or call 800-848-4735

*To all of you who were so willing
to share your time, your favorite recipes,
and your love of cooking*

Contents

Give us this day our daily bread.

—Matthew 6:11

Introduction

✠

There's something really special about potlucks and carry-ins—the excitement of getting together with friends and family, meeting new people, enjoying good conversation; and then there's the food. We're always thrilled to find a fabulous new recipe at a potluck event. Not only do we love the anticipation of trying all the new and different dishes, we also love sharing some of our very favorite recipes with others and hope they will enjoy them as much as we do. Love of God, good food, and getting together with loved ones go hand in hand.

You will eat some of the best food anywhere at church potlucks. Everyone brings his or her best recipes, and reputations are made around the communal table. From delicate cakes to rich entrées to crisp salads, decadent desserts and hot and creamy soups, this food must be the best.

If you're cooking for your church family, you know the challenges and rewards that come with the job. These recipes will help, offering lots of easily prepared and delicious food that caters to a variety of tastes.

There are quite a few things to think about when you're staging a potluck in your church. The most important is food safety. Never let perishable food sit out at room temperature for longer than

2 hours. Always wash your hands before (and after) serving or preparing food, and after handling raw dairy or meat products. Keep raw meats away from foods to be served uncooked. Refrigerate cooked food after it's been sitting out for 2 hours (1 hour in hot weather). And always cook eggs and meat to the correct safe, final internal temperature, using a food thermometer to be sure.

These recipes use the best ingredients— real butter, heavy cream, beef, and fresh vegetables. For lower-fat versions, you can substitute half-and-half or milk for the cream, or use lower-fat or fat-free dairy products. Please don't use margarine in place of butter; butter adds an important flavor dimension to many of these recipes.

Slow Cooker Hints and Tips

The slow cooker can be an assistant in the kitchen, whether you're serving hundreds after Easter services or a small Bible study group that gathers in the evenings after work. They cook food perfectly while you work on other tasks, don't heat up the kitchen as much as the oven does, and are portable, too. In addition, a lot of the newer cookers are pretty enough to serve from once the food is cooked. You can double, triple, or quadruple these

recipes, keeping the proportions the same, to fill as many slow cookers as you need. Recipes can also be cut in half, as long as the appliance is filled correctly.

When you cook with the slow cooker, you'll get the best results if it is filled between $\frac{1}{2}$ and $\frac{3}{4}$ full. Because the recipes in this book call for "2 onions, chopped" or " 4 carrots, sliced," you may need to alter the amount of food you put in the slow cooker if your vegetables are very large or small. Just adhere to the $\frac{1}{2}$ to $\frac{3}{4}$ rule and everything will turn out beautifully. You may need to cut large roasts or pieces of meat in half, and do some experimenting to discover which size slow cooker best fits the cut of meat or food you are cooking.

The slow cookers recommended for these recipes range in size from 4 to 7 quarts. There are a few recipes for very small slow cookers, usually for sauces or condiments. For cooking large cuts of meat, the oval slow cookers work better. Their shape easily handles the bulk of these foods. Follow directions to the letter for cutting and trimming the meat.

Not all the food you serve from the slow cooker has to be hot! Use this versatile appliance to make fillings for sandwiches, as well as pie fillings. Leftover roast beef and poached chicken are ideal for making salads and appetizers.

Newer slow cookers, those which have been manufactured in the last 3 or 4 years, cook much hotter than did the slow cookers of 10 to 15 years ago. Many recipes do take this into account. In the newer slow cookers, raw boneless chicken breasts will cook in 5 to 6 hours, as opposed to the 7 to 8 hours called for in older recipes. Use a meat thermometer to check the internal temperature at the minimum cooking time. If it's already done, make a note that your slow cooker cooks at a higher temperature.

For easy cleanup, spray the slow cooker with nonstick cooking spray before you add the food. You could also use the cooking bags specifically made for slow cookers (don't use ordinary plastic bags)

for no cleanup at all. Soaking the ceramic or glass liners overnight with a little dish soap will help get rid of any food that doesn't come off with gentle scrubbing.

So many dear friends, new and old, were kind enough to share some of their favorite recipes for this book. Not everyone is willing to share his or her recipes, especially ones that have been handed down from generation to generation. So, it's particularly nice when others so generously share some of their very special recipes.

Many many thanks to each one of you who have provided your recipes for this cookbook. Without your willingness to bestow some of your unique recipes, this book could not have been possible. May God bless all of you, and also all of you who are enjoying these recipes.

—Linda Larsen and Susie Siegfried

Appertizers

❧

Whether you're serving dinner after a wedding or snacks before a hayride, appetizers made in the slow cooker are a great way to save time and effort. Appetizers not only help fill the time and whet the appetite until dinner is ready, they can *be* dinner! A collection of appetizers can be a meal replacement as long as you vary flavors and textures, and include some hearty recipes as well as light ones, with some simple sweets for dessert.

Offer lots of different dippers and bases for these recipes. Baby vegetables, carrot sticks, pepper strips, and cherry tomatoes are obvious choices. Also consider pita breads, cut into wedges; breadsticks; bubble bread; cheese toasts and party rye toast; warmed tortillas; and firm lettuces.

Because these recipes are going to be warm and creamy, think about contrast of texture and temperature in presentation. You can sprinkle a dip with crisp chopped green onions or fresh tomatoes, or use fresh apple or pear slices as dippers. All of these recipes are easily varied to suit your personal and local preferences. You can add or subtract ingredients easily or change the seasonings.

Timing is important when serving these foods. These hot appetizers can be kept warm on the low or warm setting for a few hours. For food safety reasons, when serving a crowd, remember to start a few batches of a recipe, each an hour apart. Then, every 2 hours, replace each older batch with a fresh one, in its own slow cooker. Do not transfer the fresh batch to the slow cooker that's already been on the serving table for 2 hours.

—Linda Larsen

Shrimp Cocktail Appetizer

Not only is this a great appetizer, but it makes a tasty meal as well. It's also good with imitation crab flakes or real crabmeat. Bring two of these when you go to a party, as one is never enough.

1 (8-ounce) package cream cheese, softened

½ cup mayonnaise

½ teaspoon garlic powder

1 teaspoon onion powder

¾–1 cup cocktail sauce

1 pound frozen cooked shrimp, thawed

2–3 tablespoons parsley

Assorted crackers

1. Blend cream cheese, mayonnaise, garlic powder, and onion powder in a small bowl, whisking until creamy.
2. Spread on serving plate, covering entire plate.
3. Spoon cocktail sauce over the mixture.
4. Rinse shrimp with cold water. Drain and pat dry with paper towels.
5. Place shrimp evenly over cocktail sauce. Sprinkle with parsley, and refrigerate until time to serve.
6. Serve with an assortment of crackers.

☙ **Makes 20–24 servings**

Crispy Chicken Strips

Finger foods are great to nibble on during Christmas parties. Sometimes young ones aren't so fond of some of these finger foods. But most love chicken fingers and you may have trouble making enough of them.

2 cups mashed potato flakes

½ teaspoon onion powder

2 cups seasoned bread crumbs

4 eggs, beaten

4 tablespoons milk

3 pounds chicken tenders

2–4 tablespoons vegetable oil

Honey mustard sauce or sweet and sour sauce

1. In a large bowl, combine potato flakes, onion powder, and bread crumbs.
2. In a smaller bowl, beat together eggs and milk.
3. Dip chicken into egg mixture, then into potato crumb mixture.
4. In a large skillet, over medium heat, cook chicken in oil, turning to avoid burning.
5. Cook 5 to 7 minutes until golden.
6. Serve with honey mustard sauce or sweet and sour sauce.

☙ **Makes 12–15 servings**

Sweet-and-Sour Chicken Bites

You can freeze these after cooking them—just reheat them at 350° for about 10 minutes.

1 egg
¼ cup flour
¼ cup cornstarch
¼ cup chicken broth
2 pounds chicken breasts, cubed
Vegetable oil for deep-frying

Sweet-and-Sour Sauce
1 cup cider vinegar
1 cup chicken broth
1 cup brown sugar
2 tablespoons cornstarch
4 tablespoons water

1. Beat egg with a fork. Using fork, blend in flour, cornstarch, and chicken broth.
2. Put chicken into cornstarch batter, stirring to coat.
3. Put oil in deep fryer. Deep-fry in small batches until golden brown. Drain on paper towels.
4. In saucepan, combine vinegar, broth, and brown sugar. Bring to a boil on low to medium heat.
5. In small cup, mix cornstarch with cold water.
6. Slowly pour into boiling vinegar mixture while stirring. Stir over medium heat until thickened.
7. Pour over chicken when time to serve.

❀ **Makes 10–12 servings**

Sweet-and-Sour Mini Sausages

The sausages you want for this recipe are called "Little Smokies." Kids and adults alike will gobble up this excellent appetizer.

1 (20-ounce) can pineapple tidbits in juice
2 pounds small fully cooked sausages
1 onion, chopped
¼ cup honey
¼ cup brown sugar
½ cup apple cider vinegar
½ cup applesauce
½ cup ketchup
¼ cup mustard
3 green bell peppers, chopped

1. Drain pineapple, reserving juice. In a 6-quart slow cooker, combine pineapple, sausages, and onion, and mix gently.
2. In medium bowl, combine ¼ cup reserved pineapple juice, honey, brown sugar, vinegar, applesauce, ketchup, and mustard, and mix well. Pour into slow cooker and stir.
3. Cover and cook on low for 4–5 hours until sausages are hot. Add green peppers. Cover and cook on low for 30 minutes longer, until peppers are tender. Stir and serve.

❀ **Makes 8–10 servings**

Slow Cooker Reuben Dip

Reuben sandwiches and dip are usually made with sauerkraut. This one is different; red cabbage is cooked until tender, then combined with the dip ingredients. It has less sodium and a fresher taste. You can omit the corned beef for a vegetarian version.

1 red cabbage, chopped

1 red onion, chopped

2 cloves garlic, minced

2 tablespoons apple cider vinegar

2 tablespoons honey

½ teaspoon salt

1 (8-ounce) package cream cheese, cubed

1 cup shredded Gruyère cheese

1 cup shredded Swiss cheese

½ cup Thousand Island dressing

1 (3-ounce) package thinly sliced corned beef, chopped

1. In a 5-quart slow cooker, combine cabbage, onion, garlic, vinegar, honey, and salt. Stir to combine, then cover and cook on low for 7 hours or until cabbage and onions are tender.
2. Drain the cabbage mixture; then return it to the slow cooker. Add remaining ingredients; stir to combine. Cover and cook on low for 2–3 hours longer or until cheeses melt. Stir to blend, and serve with crackers and breadsticks.

❀ **Makes 10–12 servings**

Apricot Slow Cooker "Wings"

Cutting dark meat into strips makes an excellent boneless appetizer, glazed with a sweet-and-sour sauce. Serve this recipe with lots of napkins!

3 pounds boneless, skinless chicken thighs

1 onion, chopped

¼ cup apple cider vinegar

½ cup apricot jam

2 tablespoons apple jelly

¼ cup honey

2 tablespoons soy sauce

4 cloves garlic, minced

1. Cut chicken into ½" × 3" strips. Place in 4-quart slow cooker with chopped onion, and stir gently to mix.
2. In small bowl, combine remaining ingredients and mix well. Pour into slow cooker. Cover and cook on low for 6–7 hours or until chicken is thoroughly cooked to an internal temperature of 165°F.

❀ **Makes 8–10**

Indian Chicken Drummies

These mildly spicy wings are glazed with a sweet and savory mixture. They are delicious at the start of a barbecue or any meal. Be sure to serve them with lots of napkins!

4 dozen chicken drummettes

1 (10-ounce) bottle mango chutney

2 tablespoons lime juice

1 onion, chopped

3 garlic cloves, minced

1 tablespoon grated fresh gingerroot

1 tablespoon curry powder

½ cup honey

2 tablespoons butter, melted

½ teaspoon salt

⅛ teaspoon pepper

1. Preheat broiler. Place the drummettes on a broiler pan. Broil 6" from heat, turning once, until browned, about 5–6 minutes. Place in a 4- or 5-quart slow cooker. In a medium bowl, combine remaining ingredients and mix well. Pour over wings.
2. Cover slow cooker and cook on low for 8–9 hours or until chicken is tender and glazed.

❦ **Makes 48**

Chicken and Artichoke Dip

Slice and toast French bread and rub with cut garlic to make crostini to serve with this fabulous warm and creamy dip.

1 (16-ounce) package frozen cut leaf spinach, thawed

2 (14-ounce) cans marinated artichoke hearts, drained

1 (10-ounce) jar four-cheese Alfredo sauce

½ cup mayonnaise

1 (8-ounce) package cream cheese, cubed

2 cups cubed cooked chicken

3 cloves garlic, minced

2 tablespoons lemon juice

1 cup shredded Monterey jack cheese

1 cup shredded Swiss cheese

½ cup grated Parmesan cheese

½ teaspoon paprika

1. Drain spinach thoroughly, pressing it between kitchen towels to remove as much moisture as possible. Rinse the artichoke hearts and cut into small pieces.
2. Combine all ingredients except Parmesan cheese and paprika in 3½ or 4-quart slow cooker. Cover and cook on low for 3–4 hours, until hot and bubbly. Sprinkle with Parmesan cheese and paprika and serve.

❦ **Makes 8–10 servings**

Curry Chicken Spread

This delicious spread is one of the terrific recipes prepared for guests at a bed and breakfast inn in Stowe, Vermont. Those you prepare it for will enjoy every bite as much as the B and B guests do.

2 cups shredded Monterey jack cheese

6 ounces cream cheese, softened

1 cup chopped green onions

2/3 cup Major Grey's chutney

1 tablespoon curry powder

1 teaspoon ginger

1/2 teaspoon salt

3 boneless skinless chicken breast halves, cooked and shredded

1 cup sour cream

1/2 teaspoon garlic powder

1/4 teaspoon paprika

1/4 teaspoon pepper

1/4 to 1/2 cup raisins

1/2 cup toasted slivered or sliced almonds

Wheat crackers

1. Beat Monterey jack cheese, cream cheese, 1/4 cup green onions, chutney, curry powder, ginger, and salt in a bowl until well mixed.
2. Spread thinly onto a large serving platter. Cover and chill.
3. Mix chicken, sour cream, garlic powder, paprika, and pepper in a bowl.
4. Spread over cheese layer. Cover and chill for 4 to 24 hours.
5. Sprinkle the remaining 3/4 cup chopped green onions around the edge of the cheese mixture when ready to serve.
6. Sprinkle the raisins and almonds over the center.
7. Serve with wheat crackers.

🐾 **Makes 18 servings**

And a basket of unleavened bread, cakes of fine flour mingled with oil, and wafers of unleavened bread anointed with oil, and their meat offering, and their drink offerings.

—Numbers 6:15

Garlic and Brie Spread

This elegant spread would be delicious for a wedding reception. The garlic and onions become very mellow and sweet, so there's no need to worry about garlic breath!

3 heads garlic

2 onions, chopped

1 tablespoon olive oil

½ teaspoon salt

½ teaspoon dried thyme leaves

2 (8-ounce) wedges Brie cheese, cubed

1. Carefully peel the garlic heads, separating them into cloves, and peel the cloves. Combine the garlic cloves with onion, olive oil, and salt in 2–quart slow cooker.
2. Cover and cook on low for 8–9 hours or until garlic and onion are soft and tender. Using a potato masher, mash the garlic and onion, leaving some pieces whole.
3. Stir in the thyme and cubed Brie. Cover the slow cooker again and cook on low for 30–40 minutes, or until Brie melts. Stir gently and serve.

❦ **Makes 10–12 servings**

Cranberries with Cream Cheese

This is such a festive-looking appetizer! Take it to holiday parties or make a batch of it and keep it in your fridge to share with any friends who may drop in. It's sure to become a holiday tradition.

1 cup water

1¼ cups sugar

1 (12-ounce) package fresh or frozen cranberries

½ cup orange marmalade

1 (11-ounce) can mandarin oranges, drained

1 tablespoon lemon juice

1 (8-ounce) package cream cheese at room temperature

Assorted crackers

1. In saucepan over medium heat, bring water and sugar to a boil without stirring. Boil for 5 minutes.
2. Add cranberries. Cook until berries pop and sauce is thickened, about 10 minutes. Remove from heat.
3. Add orange marmalade and mandarin oranges to cranberry mixture. Stir in lemon juice. Cool.
4. Spoon over cream cheese. Serve with crackers.

❦ **Makes 3 cups**

Pauline's Cheese Ball

When you first look at this recipe, you'll probably wonder about the number of jars of cheese. This recipe makes two cheese balls but you can make one HUGE one—great for a big crowd.

2 (8-ounce) packages cream cheese, softened
4 (5-ounce) jars pimiento and cheese
2 (5-ounce) jars cheese with chives
1 (4.25-ounce) jar finely chopped black olives
2 tablespoons grated onion
2 cups finely chopped nuts
Assorted crackers

1. In large bowl, combine all cheeses with electric beater and beat until smooth.
2. Blend in olives and onion.
3. Form into 2 cheese balls.
4. Put chopped nuts in a pie plate, and roll cheese balls in nuts.
5. Refrigerate for 24 hours. Serve with an assortment of crackers.

☙ **Makes 40–50 servings**

Slow Cooker Caponata

Caponata can be served as an appetizer with crackers and vegetables, as a sandwich spread, or as a side dish.

1 tablespoon olive oil
1 onion, chopped
3 cloves garlic, minced
1½ pounds plum tomatoes, chopped
2 eggplants, peeled and chopped
1 red bell pepper, chopped
1 cup chopped celery
1 (6-ounce) can tomato paste
1 teaspoon dried basil
½ teaspoon dried oregano
2 tablespoons sugar
1 tablespoon lemon juice
1 teaspoon salt
¼ teaspoon white pepper
2 tablespoons white wine vinegar
½ cup chopped black olives
2 tablespoons capers
½ cup chopped parsley
1 cup chopped smoked mozzarella cheese

1. In 4- or 5-quart slow cooker, combine all ingredients except parsley and cheese; mix well.
2. Cover and cook on low for 7–8 hours until vegetables are tender and mixture blends. Stir in parsley and cheese and place in serving dish. Let cool for 30 minutes. Serve warm or cold.

☙ **Makes 10–12 servings**

Onion Chutney over Brie

This chutney can be served warm or cold. If you let it cool for an hour or so, and then spoon it over any type of soft cheese, it will slightly melt the cheese. Yum.

1 (5-pound) bag yellow onions

8 cloves garlic, chopped

1 cup butter

1½ teaspoons seasoned salt

¼ teaspoon white pepper

1 cup brown sugar

½ cup apple cider vinegar

3 tablespoons minced fresh gingerroot

2 whole wheels Brie or Camembert cheese

1. Peel onions and coarsely chop. Combine in 5-quart slow cooker with garlic and butter.
2. Cover and cook on low for 8–10 hours, stirring once during cooking time, until onions are browned and caramelized.
3. Stir in seasoned salt, pepper, brown sugar, vinegar, and gingerroot. Cover and cook on high for 1–2 hours or until mixture is blended and hot.
4. Remove mixture from slow cooker to a large bowl. Cover loosely and let cool for 1–2 hours before serving over Brie or Camembert cheese. Serve with crackers and toasts for spreading.

❦ **Makes 10–12 servings**

Blueberry-Raisin Chutney

Serve this chutney hot or cold, plain or poured over Brie or Camembert cheese, along with fruit for dipping. It's also excellent as a sandwich spread or filling.

6 cups fresh blueberries

2 cups golden raisins

1 onion, minced

1 tart apple, cored, peeled and chopped

6 cloves garlic, minced

⅓ cup honey

⅓ cup white wine vinegar

¼ cup orange juice

¾ cup brown sugar

1 tablespoon curry powder

1 teaspoon salt

¼ teaspoon white pepper

2 tablespoons butter

¼ cup cornstarch

½ cup apple cider

1. Combine all ingredients except cornstarch and apple cider in 4-quart slow cooker. Stir to blend. Cover and cook on low for 5–7 hours or until blueberries pop and apple is very tender.
2. In small bowl combine cornstarch and apple cider; stir to blend. Stir into chutney mixture. Cover and cook on high for 20–30 minutes or until chutney has thickened. Serve hot or cold.

❦ **Makes 10–12 servings**

Hummus

Use this recipe for more than just an appetizer. Serve with gyros, as a sandwich spread, or as a dip for crudités.

2 (15-ounce) cans garbanzo beans, drained
6 tablespoons yogurt
¼ cup olive oil
2½ tablespoons toasted sesame seeds
3 garlic cloves, diced
2 tablespoons lemon juice
½ teaspoon onion powder
Salt and pepper to taste

1. Purée all ingredients in blender. Add extra oil if not smooth.
2. Refrigerate for 4 hours.
3. Serve cold with pita bread.

❦ **Makes 10 servings**

Bob's Won Tons

Won tons in a Chinese restaurant are usually skimpy on filling. Fill yours with a generous amount of meat, and then happily stuff yourselves with these outrageously delicious appetizers.

Won Tons
1 pound ground pork
¼ teaspoon salt
1 tablespoon vegetable oil
1 tablespoon white wine
1 egg
1 teaspoon Ac'cent
2 beaten eggs
1 package won ton wrappers
Vegetable oil for deep-frying

Sauce
½ cup water
2 tablespoons cornstarch
6 tablespoons sugar
2 tablespoons soy sauce
1 tablespoon white wine
3 tablespoons white vinegar
½ cup pineapple juice
3 tablespoons ketchup

For the won tons:
1. Mix together pork, salt, oil, wine, 1 egg, and Ac'cent.
2. Put a spoonful of mixture on won ton wrapper and bring opposite corners together forming a triangle. Overlap corners and seal edges with beaten egg.

(continued)

(Bob's Won Tons—continued)

3. Line a 9" × 13" baking dish with waxed paper and layer won tons.
4. Cover top layer with foil.
5. Cook immediately or freeze overnight.
6. Cook in hot oil at 375° until golden brown.
7. Drain and serve.

For the sauce:
1. In cup, mix together water and cornstarch.
2. In saucepan, mix sugar, soy sauce, wine, vinegar, pineapple juice, and ketchup. Bring to a boil and add cornstarch mixture, stirring until it thickens.
3. When thick, remove from heat and cool.

❦ **Makes 48**

David said to him, "Do not be afraid, for I will show you kindness for the sake of your father Jonathan, I will restore to you all the land of your grandfather Saul, and you yourself shall eat at my table always."

—2 Samuel 9:7

Best-Ever Snack Mix

Put out small bowls of this snack mix and replace them every hour to keep the mix fresh and crisp. You might want to make another batch of this delicious recipe.

2 cups small square cheese crackers

2 cups square corn cereal

2 cups pecan halves

2 cups cashews

2 cups garlic bagel chips

1 cup butter

¼ cup Worcestershire sauce

1 teaspoon garlic salt

1 teaspoon onion salt

¼ teaspoon pepper

½ cup finely grated Romano cheese

1. In 4-quart slow cooker, combine crackers, cereal, pecans, cashews, and bagel chips. Toss to mix.
2. In small saucepan, melt butter over medium heat. Remove from heat and stir in remaining ingredients except cheese. Drizzle over mixture in slow cooker. Stir gently to coat, then cover and cook on low for 2 hours.
3. Uncover slow cooker and cook for 1 hour, stirring occasionally. Then sprinkle with cheese, turn heat to high, and cook for 15 minutes longer, stirring once during cooking time.
4. Place mixture on cookie sheet to cool. Store covered in airtight container at room temperature.

❦ **Makes 10 cups**

Toasted Parmesan Nuts

You can use any combination of nuts in this simple appetizer. Substitute onion powder for the garlic powder for a slightly different taste.

3 cups small pecan halves

3 cups cashew halves

½ cup butter

½ teaspoon garlic powder

1 teaspoon salt

¼ teaspoon pepper

1½ cups grated Parmesan cheese

1. Combine nuts in a 3-quart slow cooker. In small saucepan, melt butter over low heat. Add garlic powder, salt, and pepper and mix well. Pour over nuts and stir to coat.
2. Cover and cook on low for 2 hours, then uncover slow cooker and turn heat to high. Stir in Parmesan cheese. Cook, uncovered, for 30 minutes, stirring every 10 minutes, until nuts are coated and glazed. Cool on cookie sheet, then store tightly covered in airtight container.

❦ **Makes 6 cups**

Rumaki

These hors d'oeuvres were used for a catering business. They're fantastic and will quickly become a favorite choice for entertaining.

1 cup teriyaki sauce

½ teaspoon minced jarred garlic

2 tablespoons brown sugar

2 (8-ounce) cans whole water chestnuts

1 pound bacon

1. In medium bowl, mix together teriyaki sauce, garlic, and brown sugar.
2. Put water chestnuts in marinade and marinate in refrigerator for 2 to 4 hours.
3. Slice bacon strips in half. Wrap 1 piece of bacon around each water chestnut and secure with toothpick.
4. Broil, turning frequently, until bacon is almost crisp, about 5 to 10 minutes. Drain on paper towel. Serve warm or cold.

❦ **Makes 48**

Giving Is Receiving

So many of these recipes that I've included in this cookbook are quick and easy to prepare but still full of flavor. Food is an integral part of our daily lives in so many ways. It's been that way since the beginning of time.

We celebrate with food, and we mourn with food. Whenever we have joyful events such as birthdays, weddings, anniversaries, church socials, office parties, and picnics, food takes on a major role. Conversely, whenever a family or friend loses a loved one, we then turn to food as well. One of the first things we do is prepare dinner to help comfort, console, and show our concern. We always put a little of ourselves into our cooking and add at least a cup of love.

The gift of food is always appropriate. You may need to make it sugar-free for your diabetic friend, low-calorie for those watching their weight, or otherwise tailor it to a special need. The act of giving is an outward sign that says, I care about you, I am here for you.

At potluck suppers and church events, everyone usually brings a dish they know others will enjoy. These are wonderful sources for good recipes. When we give to others, it always seems that we receive more than we give. I know how much I have appreciated the kindness and thoughtfulness of others for sharing these recipes and how much they warmed my heart. Don't wait for a special occasion or a time of need to take someone a dessert or casserole. Make someone's day—it will make your day a good one, too!

—Susie Siegfried

Cheese and Bacon Roll-Ups

This wonderfully tasty and super-easy recipe was donated especially for this cookbook. It's a favorite go-to recipe for many folks.

1 (24-ounce) loaf Earth Grains Honey Wheatberry Bread, sliced and partially frozen
1 (12-ounce) tub cream cheese with chives
1 pound bacon

1. Cut crust off bread.
2. Spread cream cheese on slices of bread.
3. Cut each slice of bread in half.
4. Cut raw bacon in thirds.
5. Roll up bread with cream cheese, wrap with bacon, and secure with toothpick.
6. Bake on cookie sheet at 350° for 35 to 40 minutes. Remove from cookie sheet and lay on paper towel to absorb any bacon drippings.
7. Serve warm or cold.

Makes 25 roll-ups

Aunt Margaret's Cranberry Meatballs

Two kinds of cranberry sauce make a wonderfully flavored sauce for meatballs in this delicious appetizer. This is a great choice for a Thanksgiving feast.

1 onion, chopped
3 cloves garlic, minced
3 pounds frozen cooked meatballs
1 (16-ounce) can jellied cranberry sauce
1 (16-ounce) can whole berry cranberry sauce
1 cup dried cranberries, chopped
½ cup brown sugar
¼ cup yellow mustard
1 cup chili sauce
1 cup ketchup

1. Layer onions and garlic in bottom of 5-quart slow cooker. Top with meatballs.
2. In large bowl, combine remaining ingredients and mix well, breaking up jellied cranberry sauce. Pour over meatballs.
3. Cover and cook on low for 6–7 hours or until sauce is bubbling and meatballs are hot.

Makes 14–16

Spicy Meatballs

You can make this recipe more or less spicy by varying the amounts and types of pepper you use.

1 tablespoon olive oil

2 tablespoons butter

1 onion, finely chopped

4 cloves garlic, minced

1 cup soft bread crumbs

2 eggs

1 tablespoon chili powder

¼ teaspoon hot sauce

1 teaspoon salt

¼ teaspoon pepper

⅛ teaspoon cayenne pepper

1½ pounds lean ground beef

1 pound bulk spicy pork sausage

1 (16-ounce) jar apricot preserves

1 (12-ounce) jar raspberry preserves

2 cups barbecue sauce

1 cup ketchup

1. In skillet, combine olive oil and butter over medium heat. When butter melts, add onion and garlic. Cook and stir until tender, about 6 minutes. Place in large mixing bowl. Add bread crumbs, eggs, chili powder, hot sauce, salt, pepper, and cayenne pepper; mix well. Add ground beef and pork sausage and mix gently until combined.

2. Preheat oven to 350°F. Form meat mixture into 1" meatballs and place on broiler pan. Bake in batches for 30–35 minutes or until meatballs are cooked to 165°F. Drain on paper towels.

3. In bowl, combine apricot preserves, raspberry preserves, barbecue sauce, and ketchup. Mix well. Layer with meatballs in a 5- to 6-quart slow cooker. Cover and cook on low for 5–6 hours or until heated. Provide toothpicks for serving.

❧ **Makes 24**

Mexican Cheesecake

This festive savory cheesecake will be great for any hungry crowd. It was created by Amy and Hap, who published it in their *Signature* cookbook highlighting some of their bed-and-breakfast guests' favorite recipes. Now you and others can savor it, too.

1½ cups finely crushed tortilla chips

¼ cup melted butter

1 (16-ounce) package cream cheese, softened

2 cups shredded Monterey jack cheese

2 cups sour cream

3 eggs

1 cup mild salsa

1 (4-ounce) can chopped green chilies

3 avocados

1 tomato, seeded and chopped

1 tablespoon lemon juice

1 teaspoon salt

1 teaspoon cumin

1 cup mild salsa, drained

Tortilla chips

1. Combine crushed tortilla chips and melted butter in a bowl. Stir to mix well. Press in the bottom of a lightly greased 9" springform pan. Bake at 350° for 10 minutes. Remove to cool on wire rack.
2. Combine cream cheese and Monterey jack cheese in a large bowl. Beat with an electric mixer until light and fluffy. Beat in 1 cup sour cream. Add eggs and beat at a low speed until the ingredients are just combined. Stir in 1 cup salsa and the green chilies.
3. Pour mixture over tortilla crust in the pan. Bake at 350° for 50 to 60 minutes or until center is almost set. Remove to wire rack.
4. Spread 1 cup sour cream over the top. Let cool to room temperature.
5. Cover and chill for 3 to 24 hours.
6. Peel, pit, and mash the avocados in a bowl 1 hour before serving time. Add tomato, lemon juice, salt, and cumin. Stir with a fork until combined. Cover and chill.
7. Loosen the cheesecake from the side of the pan with a sharp knife, and remove the side. Set cheesecake on a serving platter.
8. Dollop avocado mixture alternately with the drained salsa around the edge of the cheesecake.
9. Serve with tortilla chips.

❦ **Makes 20 servings**

Every moving thing that lives shall be food for you, and just as I gave you the green plants, I give you everything.

—Genesis 9:3

Spicy Scoops

You can make this recipe a lot easier by using tortilla scoops. These are very tasty, and you can make them spicier by using a medium to hot salsa.

1 (16-ounce) package spicy sausage

1 bag tortilla scoops

2 cups salsa

2 cups cubed American cheese

¼ cup scallions

Cherry tomatoes

1. Brown sausage in skillet and drain.
2. Preheat oven to 350°
3. Put one tortilla scoop in each muffin tin cup.
4. Mix together all remaining ingredients except tomatoes in bowl.
5. Spoon mixture into scoops until they are ⅔ full.
6. Bake for 5 minutes.
7. Remove and garnish with a cherry tomato.

 Makes 48

Beefy Cheese Dip

This dip has been a favorite at our family Christmas celebrations. We've all enjoyed it. You don't have to wait until Christmas—it's easy enough to whip up anytime.

1 2.75-ounce jar dried beef

½ cup sour cream

1 (8-ounce) package cream cheese, softened

¼ cup chopped onion

¼ cup chopped green peppers

¼ teaspoon garlic powder

Assorted crackers

1. Preheat oven to 350°.
2. Chop dried beef into small pieces.
3. Mix all ingredients together.
4. Place in greased 8" square baking dish and cook for 10 to 15 minutes or until warm.
5. Serve with crackers.

 Makes 6–8 servings

Now the feast of unleavened bread drew nigh, which is called the Passover.

—Luke 22:1

Spicy Nuts

If your crowd likes it spicy, increase the chili powder and cayenne pepper to taste. These nuts are great for snacking after a choir performance.

3 cups small pecan halves

2 cups walnut halves

3 cups salted cashews

½ cup butter, melted

¼ cup brown sugar

3 tablespoons chili powder

½ teaspoon cayenne pepper

1 teaspoon salt

1 teaspoon cinnamon

1. Turn 3½-quart slow cooker to high and let preheat for 15 minutes. Add all of the nuts; stir for 4–5 minutes until slightly toasted.
2. Meanwhile, in small bowl combine butter with remaining ingredients; mix well. Spoon mixture over the nuts and stir to coat. Cover and cook on low for 2 hours. Then uncover slow cooker, stir nuts, and cook on high for 20 minutes.
3. Spoon nuts onto a cookie sheet and let cool. Store covered in airtight containers at room temperature.

❧ **Makes 18–20 servings**

Sweet-and-Sour Nut Mix

Snack mixes are easy to make in the slow cooker. Use any combination of nuts and snack foods for a change of pace.

2 cups small pecan halves

2 cups whole almonds

2 cups hazelnuts

2 cups cashew halves

½ cup brown sugar

⅓ cup apple cider vinegar

1 teaspoon salt

3 tablespoons butter, melted

1 to 2 tablespoons curry powder

2 cups small pretzel rods

1. Turn 4-quart slow cooker to high and let preheat for 15 minutes. Add all of the nuts; stir for 4–5 minutes until slightly toasted.
2. Meanwhile, in small bowl combine brown sugar with remaining ingredients; mix well. Spoon mixture over the nuts and stir to coat. Cover and cook on low for 2 hours. Then uncover slow cooker, stir nuts, and cook on high for 1 hour longer, stirring occasionally.
3. Spoon nuts onto a cookie sheet and let cool. Store covered in airtight containers at room temperature.

❧ **Makes 20–30 servings**

Lois's Cheese Ball

Another cheese ball, but one well worth adding to your recipe box. It's a keeper.

1 (8-ounce) package cream cheese, softened

1 (5-ounce) jar Old English cheese

1 (5-ounce) jar Cheddar cheese

1 (5-ounce) jar pineapple cheese

1½ cups pecan pieces

Crackers or pita crisps

1. In large bowl, combine all cheeses and beat with electric mixer until smooth. Form into ball.
2. Place pecans in pie plate and roll cheese ball in nuts until well covered. Refrigerate until time to serve.
3. Serve with crackers or pita crisps.

❧ **Makes 25 servings**

Pam's Party Ryes

Everyone loves these tasty, cheesy ryes. Include them in your family holiday celebrations or offer them anytime friends and family gather. Keep them covered with foil until ready to serve. They're great for carry-in parties.

1 pound ground beef

1 pound sausage

1 pound Velveeta cheese

2 loaves Party Rye Bread

1 teaspoon garlic powder

1 teaspoon onion powder

1 tablespoon Worcestershire sauce

1. Brown ground beef and sausage together in skillet over medium heat. Drain on paper towels to remove grease.
2. In saucepan, put drained meat mixture and add cheese; cook over medium heat until cheese melts.
3. Remove from heat and spread over rye bread.
4. Bake at 350° for 3 to 5 minutes or until golden brown.

❧ **Makes 48 pieces**

Three-Cheese Dip

This creamy, melty cheese dip is delicious with crisp fresh vegetables. You could add meatballs, cooked chicken, or artichoke hearts for more interest.

2 pounds processed cheese, cubed

2 (8-ounce) packages garlic-flavored cream cheese, cubed

2 cups shredded Muenster cheese

1 tablespoon cornstarch

1 cup mayonnaise

½ cup sliced green onions, white and green parts

1. In a 4-quart slow cooker, combine processed cheese and cream cheese. Toss Muenster cheese with cornstarch and add to slow cooker along with mayonnaise; mix gently.
2. Cover and cook on low for 2–3 hours or until cheeses are melted, stirring twice during cooking time. Top with green onions and serve with fresh vegetables, crackers, and tortilla chips.

🕊 **Makes 12–14 servings**

My soul is satisfied as with a rich feast, and my mouth praises you with joyful lips.

—Psalms 63:5

Cheesy Taco Dip

Place bowls of chopped tomatoes, sour cream, and lettuce around so people can build their own nachos.

1½ pounds pork sausage

2 onions, chopped

4 cloves garlic, minced

2 jalapeño peppers, minced

1 (16-ounce) jar mild salsa

1 pound processed cheese, cubed

2 (8-ounce) cans sliced mushrooms, drained

4 tomatoes, chopped

2 tablespoons chili powder

2 tablespoons cornstarch

½ cup tomato juice

2 cups chopped tomatoes

2 cups shredded lettuce

1 cup sour cream

2 cups shredded CoJack cheese

1. In skillet, cook pork sausage until partially done. Add onions, garlic, and jalapeño pepper; continue cooking until sausage is cooked. Drain.
2. Place in 4-quart slow cooker along with salsa, cheese, mushrooms, tomatoes, and chili powder. Mix well. Cover and cook on low for 6–7 hours, stirring once during cooking time.
3. In small bowl, combine cornstarch and tomato juice. Add to slow cooker; cover and cook on high for 30 minutes. Serve with tortilla chips and the fresh topping ingredients.

🕊 **Makes 8–10 servings**

Hot Pepperoni Dip

This dip is sensational. Make two batches—one for the office picnic and one for everyone to enjoy at home.

1 (8-ounce) package cream cheese, softened
½ cup sour cream
1 teaspoon oregano
¼ teaspoon garlic powder
½ cup pizza sauce
¼ cup chopped green pepper
¼ cup chopped green onion
½ cup finely diced pepperoni
1 cup shredded mozzarella cheese
Crackers

1. Mix together cream cheese, sour cream, oregano, and garlic powder and spread on bottom of 10" pie plate.
2. Spread pizza sauce on top of cream cheese mixture. Top with green pepper, onions, and pepperoni.
3. Bake at 350° for 10 to 13 minutes.
4. Remove from oven and sprinkle with mozzarella cheese and bake 5 minutes longer.
5. Serve with Wheat Thins or other crackers.

❧ **Makes 10–15 servings**

Florentine Cups

If you are short of time, you could purchase mini phyllo cups in the frozen food section of your grocery store. Those are versatile and festive, but so easy to prepare.

3 eggs, slightly beaten
⅔ cup flour
½ teaspoon salt
1 cup milk
1½ cups sharp Cheddar cheese
3 tablespoons flour
3 eggs, slightly beaten
⅔ cup mayonnaise
1 (10-ounce) package frozen chopped spinach, thawed and drained
1 (4-ounce) can mushrooms, drained
6 bacon slices, fried, crisped, and crumbled

1. Combine eggs, ⅔ cups flour, salt, and milk and beat until smooth. Let stand 30 minutes.
2. Pour 2 tablespoons batter onto hot, lightly greased 8" griddle. Cook on one side only until underside is lightly browned. Place each mini crepe into a greased mini muffin tin cup.
3. In medium bowl, toss cheese with flour.
4. Add remaining ingredients, saving bacon for garnish and mix well. Fill cups with mixture.
5. Bake at 350° for 25 to 40 minutes or until set.
6. Top with bacon pieces.

❧ **Makes 12 cups**

Hot Lemon Cranberry Punch

If you're having a sleigh ride in the winter for your youth group, serve this hot punch to warm everybody up.

1 (48-ounce) bottle cranberry juice cocktail

1 (12-ounce) can frozen lemonade concentrate

½ cup sugar

1 cup water

1 teaspoon cinnamon

½ teaspoon nutmeg

1 (32-ounce) bottle apple juice

1. In 4- to 5-quart slow cooker, combine cranberry juice, lemonade concentrate, sugar, water, cinnamon, and nutmeg. Stir to blend. Cover and cook on low for 2 hours, stirring once during.

2. Stir in apple juice. Cover and cook on low for 1–2 hours longer, until hot and blended. Keep warm in slow cooker for 2 hours, stirring occasionally.

🌾 **Makes 24 servings**

For the Lord your God is bringing you into a good land, a land with flowing streams, a land of wheat and barley, of vines and fig trees and pomegranates, a land of olive trees and honey, a land where you may eat bread without scarcity, where you will lack nothing, a land whose stones are iron and from whose hills you may mine copper.

—Deuteronomy 8:7–10

Angel Sangria

Angel Sangria gives you the flavor of sangria with no alcohol. It's the perfect punch for an Advent or Christmas gathering.

1 (64-ounce) bottle red grape juice

2 cups pink grapefruit juice

2 tablespoons apple cider vinegar

½ cup sugar

1 teaspoon cinnamon

2 cups fresh cherries, pitted

2 (15-ounce) cans mandarin oranges, chopped

1. In 5-quart slow cooker, combine grape juice with pink grapefruit juice, vinegar, sugar, and cinnamon. Stir well. Cover and cook on high for 1 hour.
2. Stir mixture again, then stir in cherries and undrained mandarin oranges. Cover and cook on low for 1 hour longer. Punch can be kept warm for 2 hours on warm or low.

❦ **Makes 16 servings**

Pineapple Soother

If you use peach nectar or orange juice, this warm punch can be different, but still delicious. Freeze some pineapple juice in ring molds to add to the punch, so that as the "ice" melts, the mixture isn't diluted.

8 cups pineapple juice

½ cup sugar

1 teaspoon cinnamon

2 cups white grape juice

½ teaspoon nutmeg

⅓ cup lime juice

1. In 3½- or 4-quart slow cooker, combine pineapple juice with sugar and cinnamon. Stir, then cover and cook on low for 1 hour.
2. Stir mixture again and add grape juice, nutmeg, and lime juice. Cover and cook on low for 1 hour longer. Punch can be kept warm on warm or low setting for 2 hours.

❦ **Makes 18–20 servings**

Chai Tea

Chai is tea flavored with spices such as cardamom and cinnamon, and mellowed with heavy cream. It's a delicious drink that will warm you up after caroling.

10 cups boiling water

12 tea bags

1 teaspoon ground cardamom

1 teaspoon ground cinnamon

½ teaspoon ground ginger

½ cup sugar

2 cups pineapple juice

2 cups heavy cream

1. Combine boiling water and tea bags in a 5-quart slow cooker. Cover and let stand for 5–7 minutes, until tea is desired strength.
2. Remove tea bags, squeezing each one thoroughly. Stir in spices, sugar, and pineapple juice. Cover and cook on low for 2 hours.
3. Stir tea thoroughly. Add heavy cream. Cover and cook on low for 20 minutes or until hot. Turn slow cooker to warm, or off if warm setting is not available. Serve from the slow cooker. After 2 hours, discard leftovers.

❦ **Makes 16–20 servings**

Hot Cider

Cider is a classic hot drink after winter activities. Is your youth group having a skating party? This recipe will warm them up.

2 oranges

16 whole cloves

2 cinnamon sticks

½ cup sugar

1 gallon apple cider

¼ cup lemon juice

1. Roll the oranges gently on countertop, then stud with the whole cloves. Cut oranges in half and place in 6-quart slow cooker.
2. Add remaining ingredients and stir gently. Cover and cook on low for 2 hours. Remove cinnamon sticks and keep warm on low setting for 1 hour.

❦ **Makes 30 servings**

Grandpa's Hot Cocoa

Marshmallow crème in the bottom of each cup adds smooth richness to this praline-scented hot chocolate. How deliciously decadent!

½ cup sugar

⅓ cup brown sugar

1 cup unsweetened cocoa powder

½ teaspoon salt

2 tablespoons maple syrup

5 cups boiling water

4 cups nonfat dry milk powder

8 cups water

2 (13-ounce) cans evaporated milk

1 tablespoon vanilla

2 (7-ounce) jars marshmallow crème

1. In 6-quart slow cooker, combine sugar, brown sugar, cocoa powder, salt, maple syrup, and boiling water. Stir until sugar dissolves.
2. Add remaining ingredients except marshmallow crème and stir to blend. Cover and cook on low for 3–4 hours, until blended and hot.
3. Beat mixture with an eggbeater until frothy. Place a spoonful of marshmallow crème in each serving cup, then ladle in hot cocoa.

❧ **Makes 18–20 servings**

Spiced Mocha Coffee

Vary the spices in this easy recipe for a different taste. Multiply the recipe and have it brewing in several slow cookers at the same time.

12 cups brewed coffee

½ cup sugar

¼ cup maple syrup

⅓ cup unsweetened cocoa powder

4 cinnamon sticks

¼ teaspoon cardamom

1. In 4-quart slow cooker, combine all ingredients and mix well. Cover and cook on low for 2–3 hours or until hot and blended.
2. Remove cinnamon sticks and stir well with wire whisk. Serve immediately. Can be kept warm in slow cooker up to 1 hour. Stir occasionally.

❧ **Makes 12 servings**

I declare that I will bring you up out of the misery of Egypt, to the land of the Canaanites, the Hittites, the Amorites, the Perizzites, the Hivites, and the Jebusites, a land flowing with milk and honey.

—*Exodus 3:17*

Breakfast, Breads, and Brunch

⚜

Breakfast is the most important meal of the day. And when parishioners gather together, whether for an Easter service, a brunch on Christmas day, or just regular Sunday morning services, a meal is most welcome.

In college, I always liked attending the sunrise services held before Easter break. There's nothing like welcoming spring in the early morning hours with a worship service. My college had great breakfasts, too; their banana bread was spectacular, and I loved their fluffy and creamy scrambled eggs served with crisp, hot bacon.

With a couple of slow cookers on hand, you can have breakfast ready and waiting for a crowd with very little work. Bread puddings and stratas, which are a combination of bread layered with other ingredients and baked in a custard mixture, are warm and filling, and can even cook overnight while you sleep.

Be sure to follow food safety rules when you're working with eggs in the slow cooker. They should be fully cooked, and reach a temperature of 145°F. Eggs do cook well in the slow cooker, but they won't hold for more than an hour, so be sure to include that information in your planning.

Serve one of the beverages from the Appetizers chapter (page 1) for breakfast. Hot chocolate or a hot punch is welcome on cold mornings. And think about serving these foods with cold foods for contrast. Fresh fruit, in season, is a good choice, as is cold milk for the kids.

—Linda Larsen

Raspberry–Cream Cheese Coffeecake

Is there anything more delicious than the blending of raspberry and cream cheese? This luscious dish will definitely make your mouth water.

2¼ cups flour

¾ cup sugar

¾ cup chilled unsalted butter, cut into pieces

½ teaspoon baking powder

½ teaspoon baking soda

¼ teaspoon salt

¾ cup sour cream

1 egg

1 teaspoon almond extract

1 (8-ounce) package cream cheese, softened

¼ cup sugar

1 egg

½ cup raspberry preserves

½ cup sliced almonds

1. In a large bowl, mix together flour and ¾ cup sugar.
2. Cut in the butter with a pastry blender until crumbly.
3. Remove 1 cup of mixture and set aside for topping.
4. Add the baking powder, baking soda, salt, sour cream, 1 egg, and almond extract to the remaining mixture. Stir to mix well.
5. Spread evenly into the bottom and halfway up the sides of a greased 10" springform pan, using floured hands.
6. Combine the cream cheese, ¼ cup sugar, and 1 egg in a bowl. Beat with an electric mixer until smooth.
7. Spread over the crust in the pan. Top with the raspberry preserves.
8. Add the almonds to the reserved crumb mixture and sprinkle over the preserves.
9. Bake at 350° for 45–55 minutes or until the center is set and the crust is golden brown. Remove to a wire rack and let cool completely.
10. Loosen from the sides of the pan with a sharp knife and remove from pan.
11. Refrigerate until ready to serve.

Makes 12 servings

Feasts are made for laughter, wine gladdens life, and money meets every need.

—Ecclesiastes 10:19

Blueberry French Toast

Blueberries are a good healthy food. This recipe is delicious when made with peaches or raspberries in place of the blueberries. Put the sauce in a container that you can use when serving.

French Toast

12 slices day-old white bread

2 (8-ounce) packages cream cheese

1 cup fresh or frozen blueberries

12 eggs

2 cups milk

1/3 cup honey

Sauce

1 cup sugar

2 tablespoons cornstarch

1 cup water

1 cup blueberries

1 tablespoon butter

For the French toast:

1. Cut bread into 1" cubes and place half in a greased 9" × 13" baking dish.
2. Cut cream cheese into 1" cubes and place over bread.
3. Top with blueberries and remaining bread.
4. In a large bowl, beat eggs and add milk and honey, mixing well. Pour over blueberries. Cover and chill overnight.
5. Remove from refrigerator 30 minutes before baking.
6. Bake, covered with foil, at 350° for 30 minutes. Uncover and bake 25 to 30 minutes more until golden brown and center is set.

For the sauce:

1. In saucepan, combine sugar and cornstarch. Add water and bring to a boil over medium heat. Boil for 3 minutes, stirring constantly.
2. Stir in blueberries and reduce heat. Simmer for 8–10 minutes, stirring with whisk.
3. Stir in butter until melted.
4. Serve over French toast.

Makes 6–8 servings

Apple French Toast

What's more American than apple pie? This apple French toast will please a group of hungry breakfasters even more than apple pie. Serve with cinnamon sugar for a wonderful treat.

1 stick butter

1 cup packed brown sugar

2 tablespoons light Karo syrup

4 large apples, peeled and thinly sliced

3 eggs

1 cup milk

1 tablespoon vanilla

8 slices (¾" thick) French bread

1. In a saucepan, melt butter. Add brown sugar and syrup. Cook over medium heat until bubbly.
2. Pour mixture into a greased 9" × 13" baking pan. Layer apples on top.
3. In a bowl, beat eggs and add milk and vanilla and mix well.
4. Dip bread into egg mixture and layer over top of apples. Cover and put in refrigerator overnight.
5. Bake uncovered at 350° for 35 minutes.
6. To serve, invert each slice of bread onto a serving plate and spoon apples over the top.

❧ **Makes 8–10 servings**

Mother's Slow Cooker Oatmeal

Toasting the oats adds a depth of flavor, and helps keep some texture in this easy recipe. You could use chopped apples or strawberries instead of blueberries. If you substitute regular rolled oats for the steel cut oats, the oatmeal will be very soft.

3 tablespoons butter

1½ cups steel cut oats

2 cups water

1 cup milk

1½ cups apple juice

½ teaspoon salt

⅓ cup sugar

1 cup chopped walnuts, toasted

1 cup blueberries

1. Spray a 2-quart slow cooker with nonstick cooking spray and set aside. In skillet, melt butter. Add oats; cook and stir until oats are toasted, about 6–7 minutes. Place in slow cooker and add water, milk, apple juice, salt, and sugar, stirring to mix.
2. Cover and cook on low for 7–8 hours. Stir well, then add walnuts and blueberries; cook for another 30 minutes. Serve with cold cream and brown sugar, if desired.

❧ **Makes 6–8 servings**

Apple Oatmeal

Grated apple helps thicken the oatmeal a bit, and adds great flavor and a bit of texture. Top it with toasted walnuts or pecans for some crunch.

2 tablespoons butter

1½ cups steel cut oats

¼ cup brown sugar

1 cup applesauce

1½ cup apple juice

2 cups water

½ teaspoon salt

1 cup grated peeled apple

⅓ cup heavy cream

1. Spray a 2-quart slow cooker with nonstick cooking spray and set aside. In medium skillet, melt butter. Add oats; cook and stir until toasted, about 5–6 minutes. Combine with brown sugar, applesauce, apple juice, water, and salt in prepared slow cooker.
2. Cover and cook on low for 8–9 hours. Stir well, then add grated apple and cream. Cover and cook on low for 30 minutes longer. Serve with maple syrup and chopped apples, if desired.

❦ **Makes 6 servings**

Dried Fruit Oatmeal

Because the oats aren't toasted, this cereal is creamier than regular oatmeal, even with steel cut oats. Use your favorite combination of dried fruits and nuts.

2 cups steel cut oatmeal (not regular or quick-cooking oatmeal)

2 cups whole milk

3 cups water

2 cups apple juice

1 teaspoon cinnamon

⅓ cup brown sugar

⅛ teaspoon salt

1 cup chopped dried apricots

½ cup chopped dried cranberries

½ cup dried currants

1 cup chopped pecans

1. Spray a 4-quart slow cooker with nonstick baking spray containing flour. Combine all ingredients in slow cooker and stir well.
2. Cover and cook on low for 8–9 hours or until creamy, stirring once during cooking time. Serve immediately with maple syrup, heavy cream, and brown sugar, if desired.

❦ **Makes 8–10 servings**

Apple Pecan Strata

This delicious strata is perfect for brunch after morning services. The combination of flavors is perfect, and the aroma that will drift through the sanctuary is tempting. Serve with cold applesauce and heavy cream for a nice contrast.

½ cup light cream

¼ cup orange juice

4 eggs, beaten

3 tablespoons sugar

1 teaspoon cinnamon

1 teaspoon vanilla

6 cups cubed brioche or French bread

2 cups pecan crunch granola

1 cup toasted pecan pieces

2 Granny Smith apples, cored, peeled and cubed

1. To toast nuts, place in a dry skillet over medium heat and toss until fragrant and golden brown. Spray a 4- or 5-quart slow cooker with nonstick cooking spray. In medium bowl, combine cream, orange juice, eggs, sugar, cinnamon, and vanilla and blend well with whisk. Set aside.
2. Place ⅓ of the bread in the bottom of prepared slow cooker and sprinkle with ⅓ of the granola, pecans, and apples. Repeat layers. Pour egg mixture over all.
3. Cover and cook on high for 1½–2 hours or until just set. *Do not cook on low.*

❧ **Makes 8 servings**

Bacon and Waffle Strata

Crisp waffles, which bake into a wonderfully textured casserole in the slow cooker, make this version of strata unique.

8 slices bacon

8 frozen waffles, toasted

2 cups shredded Colby cheese

¼ cup chopped green onions, white and green parts

1 (13-ounce) can evaporated milk

1 (8-ounce) package cream cheese, softened

6 eggs

1 teaspoon dry mustard

½ cup maple syrup

1. In large skillet, cook bacon until crisp. Drain on paper towels, crumble, and set aside. Cut toasted waffles into cubes. Layer bacon and waffle cubes with cheese and green onions in 4- to 5-quart slow cooker.
2. Drain skillet, discarding bacon fat; do not wipe out. Add milk and cream cheese to skillet; cook over low heat, stirring frequently, until cheese melts and mixture is smooth.
3. Remove skillet from heat and beat in eggs, one at a time, until smooth. Stir in dry mustard and pour into slow cooker. Cover and cook on low for about 4–5 hours, until eggs are set. Serve with warmed maple syrup.

❧ **Makes 8–10 servings**

Ham and Egg Soufflé

Savor this recipe on Christmas morning. Just pop it into the oven after making it the day before, and ease into your day.

2½ cups cubed bread

1 pound deli ham, chipped

6 eggs

¼ teaspoon Worcestershire sauce

¾ teaspoon salt

¾ teaspoon pepper

¾ teaspoon dry mustard

⅛ teaspoon onion salt

1 cup half-and-half

1 cup milk

1½ cups shredded American and Cheddar cheeses

1. Spread bread and ham in bottom of greased 9" × 13" baking dish.
2. Blend together eggs, Worcestershire sauce, salt, pepper, dry mustard, onion salt, half-and-half, and milk in blender. Pour over bread and meat. Sprinkle shredded cheese over top of mixture.
3. Cover and refrigerate overnight.
4. Remove from refrigerator 30 minutes before baking.
5. Bake at 325° for 40–45 minutes.

🌿 **Makes 8–10 servings**

Sweet Potato Biscuits

If you like sweet potatoes, you'll like this down-home recipe from Tennessee. These biscuits would also be very good served with honey butter.

1 cup mashed sweet potatoes

1 cup milk

½ cup sugar

1 beaten egg

1 tablespoon butter, melted

3 cups self-rising flour

1 teaspoon baking powder

½ cup vegetable shortening

Butter

Cinnamon sugar

1. In a medium bowl, mix sweet potatoes, milk, sugar, egg, and butter until well blended.
2. In a large bowl, combine flour and baking powder. Use fork or pastry cutter to cut in the shortening.
3. Pour the sweet potato mixture into the flour mixture and mix well. Drop by large spoonfuls onto greased baking sheet. Bake at 400° for 15–17 minutes or until golden.
4. Serve with butter and cinnamon sugar.

🌿 **Makes 18–20 servings**

Tex-Mex Brunch Bake

Want something spicy for breakfast to wake up your taste buds? This easy casserole fills the bill. Serve it with sour cream and a fruit salad for a cooling contrast.

1 (32-ounce) package frozen hash brown potatoes, thawed and drained

1 (16-ounce) package spicy bulk pork sausage

1 onion, chopped

6 cloves garlic, minced

2 (4-ounce) jars sliced mushrooms, drained

2 jalapeño peppers, minced

14 eggs

½ cup whole milk

½ cup heavy cream

1 tablespoon chili powder

1 teaspoon salt

⅛ teaspoon cayenne pepper

⅛ teaspoon white pepper

2 cups shredded pepper jack cheese

¼ cup grated Parmesan cheese

½ teaspoon smoked paprika

1. Spray 5-quart slow cooker with nonstick cooking spray. Place drained potatoes in slow cooker.
2. In large skillet, cook pork sausage, stirring to break up meat, until almost cooked through. Add onion and garlic; cook and stir until sausage is thoroughly cooked. Drain well and add to slow cooker along with mushrooms and jalapeños.
3. In large bowl, beat eggs with milk, cream, chili powder, salt, cayenne and white pepper until blended. Stir in pepper jack cheese and pour into slow cooker; poke through ingredients with a knife to let egg mixture penetrate.
4. Sprinkle top with Parmesan cheese and paprika. Cover and cook on low for 8–9 hours or until casserole is set and internal temperature reaches 145°F. Serve immediately.

❦ **Makes 10–12 servings**

Then God said, "Let the earth put forth vegetation, plants yielding seed, and fruit trees of every kind that bear fruit with the seed in it." And it was so. The earth brought forth vegetation: plants yielding seed of every kind, and trees of every kind bearing fruit with the seed in it. And God saw that it was good.

—Genesis 1:11–12

Scrambled Eggs and Potatoes

Good for breakfast, brunch, even supper. Take this along to your next breakfast get-together. You can also use chicken and Mexican shredded cheese for a spicier flavor.

Butter cooking spray

1 (32-ounce) bag frozen hash brown potatoes, thawed

1 cup chopped onion

½ cup chopped green pepper

½ cup chopped yellow pepper

1 (16-ounce) package bacon, fried crisp

12 eggs

¾ cup milk

8 ounces shredded Cheddar cheese

1. Spray skillet with butter cooking spray and sauté potatoes until golden brown.
2. Add onions and peppers and cook a few minutes longer.
3. Break bacon into pieces and put on top of potatoes. Remove from heat.
4. Mix together eggs and milk.
5. Spray skillet with vegetable cooking spray and scramble eggs until almost set.
6. Place potato mixture in greased 9" × 13" baking dish. Sprinkle half the cheese over potatoes. Put scrambled eggs on cheese and sprinkle remaining cheese over eggs.
7. Bake at 350° until cheese melts.

❦ **Makes 8–10 servings**

Potluck Pointer

Use foil pans and lids to carry hot foods to potlucks. Use a thick layer of newspaper to wrap and insulate the pan, then seal it with tape. Your food will stay hot, and you won't accidentally leave behind a good pan.

Egg and Spinach Casserole

Topping a hot casserole with a cool, fragrant tomato mixture makes a delicious and hearty egg-and-vegetable breakfast casserole even better.

2 tablespoons butter

2 onions, finely chopped

3 cloves garlic, minced

2 red bell peppers, chopped

1 (16-ounce) package frozen cut leaf spinach, thawed

1 teaspoon dried basil leaves

18 eggs

1 cup sour cream

1 tablespoon flour

1 teaspoon salt

¼ teaspoon white pepper

2 cups grated pepper jack cheese

3 cups chopped grape tomatoes

1 cup sour cream

½ cup torn fresh basil leaves

½ cup grated Parmesan cheese

1. Spray a 5-quart slow cooker with nonstick cooking spray and set aside. In large skillet, melt butter over medium heat. Add onions and garlic; cook and stir until tender, about 6 minutes. Add red bell peppers; cook and stir for 3 minutes longer.

2. Drain spinach well and add to skillet; cook and stir until liquid evaporates. Stir in basil and remove mixture from heat; let stand for 20 minutes.

3. In large bowl, beat eggs with 1 cup sour cream, flour, salt, and pepper. Stir in pepper jack cheese; then stir in vegetable mixture. Pour into prepared slow cooker.

4. Cover and cook on low for 7–8 hours or until set. Meanwhile, in medium bowl combine tomatoes, 1 cup sour cream, basil leaves, and Parmesan cheese. Serve casserole with this sour cream and tomato topping.

❦ **Makes 12 servings**

Dad's Best Sausage Rolls

These sausage rolls are like meatballs, but shaped like sausages, and flavored for breakfast. They are slightly spicy and very pleasing.

1½ cups soft bread crumbs

2 eggs, beaten

¼ cup brown sugar

½ cup applesauce

1 teaspoon salt

⅛ teaspoon pepper

2 pounds mild bulk pork sausage

1 pound hot bulk pork sausage

2 tablespoons butter

1 tablespoon olive oil

½ cup maple syrup

½ cup chicken broth

1. In large bowl, combine crumbs, eggs, brown sugar, applesauce, salt, and pepper. Mix well. Stir in both mild and hot sausage.
2. Shape into 3" × 1" rolls. In large skillet, combine butter and olive oil over medium heat. Add sausage rolls, about 8 at a time, and cook until browned on all sides, about 5–6 minutes. As rolls cook, drain on paper towels, then place into 4-quart slow cooker.
3. In bowl, combine maple syrup and chicken broth and mix well. Pour over sausage rolls in slow cooker.
4. Cover slow cooker and cook on low for 8–9 hours or until sausage rolls are thoroughly cooked, to 165°F on a meat thermometer. Remove from slow cooker with slotted spoon to serve.

❀ **Makes 12**

Slow Cooker Scrambled Eggs

Scrambled eggs can be made at your leisure in the slow cooker. Keep them warm for only one hour after cooking time is done. If any are left over at that point (doubtful!), discard them.

¼ cup unsalted butter

18 eggs

1 (16-ounce) jar Alfredo sauce

½ cup heavy cream

1 teaspoon salt

⅛ teaspoon white pepper

2 cups shredded Swiss cheese

¼ cup grated Parmesan cheese

1. Using 1 tablespoon of the butter, grease a 4-quart slow cooker. Melt the rest of the butter and pour into slow cooker.
2. In large bowl, beat eggs with Alfredo sauce, cream, salt, and pepper. Stir in Swiss cheese and pour into slow cooker.
3. Sprinkle with Parmesan cheese, cover, and cook on high for about 2 to 2½ hours, stirring twice during cooking time, until eggs are creamy and reach a temperature of 145°F.

❦ **Makes 12 servings**

Bacon and Potato Strata

The potatoes have to be evenly and thinly sliced in order to cook thoroughly in this easy and hearty casserole recipe. And the bacon must be crisp!

1 pound bacon

2 onions, chopped

6 russet potatoes

3 (4-ounce) jars mushrooms, drained

2 cups shredded Cheddar cheese

1 cup shredded Havarti cheese

10 eggs

1 (16-ounce) jar four-cheese Alfredo sauce

¼ teaspoon pepper

1 teaspoon dried thyme leaves

1. In large skillet, cook bacon until crisp. Drain bacon on paper towels, crumble, and set aside. Drain all but 2 tablespoons drippings from skillet. Add onions; cook and stir until tender, about 6 minutes. Set aside.
2. Spray 4- to 5-quart slow cooker with nonstick cooking spray. Thinly sliced unpeeled potatoes (about ⅛" thick). Layer potatoes, crumbled bacon, onions, mushrooms, and cheeses in slow cooker.
3. In large bowl, combine remaining ingredients and beat well. Pour into slow cooker. Cover and cook on low for 8–9 hours or until casserole is set and temperature registers 145°F.

❦ **Makes 12 servings**

Bacon Sweet Potato Hash

Hash recipes usually use leftover russet potatoes, but this one is different. Sweet potatoes add great flavor and nutrition to the recipe, and the bacon and pecans are a wonderful touch.

8 slices bacon

1 onion, chopped

4 sweet potatoes, peeled

1/3 cup brown sugar

1/4 cup orange juice

1/3 cup applesauce

2 tablespoons butter, melted

1/2 teaspoon salt

1/8 teaspoon pepper

1/2 cup chopped pecans, if desired

1. In skillet, cook bacon until crisp; drain on paper towels, crumble, cover, and refrigerate. Drain all but 2 tablespoons drippings from skillet. Add onion; cook and stir for 5 minutes, until onion softens, stirring to loosen brown bits from skillet.
2. Cut sweet potatoes into 1" cubes. Combine potatoes and onions in 4-quart slow cooker; stir to mix.
3. In small bowl, combine all remaining ingredients except pecans and stir well. Pour into slow cooker. Cover and cook on low for 8–9 hours or until potatoes are tender.
4. Stir in reserved bacon and the pecans; cover and cook for 30 minutes longer. If desired, place a fried egg on top of each serving of hash.

❧ **Makes 8 servings**

Corn Bread Sausage Strata

A bit of corn bread and sausage in the morning is a great way to start the day. This rich strata is delicious served with a fresh fruit salad.

1 pound hot bulk Italian sausage

2 onions, chopped

2 (4-ounce) jars sliced mushrooms, drained

2 cups flour

1 cup yellow cornmeal

¼ cup sugar

3 teaspoons baking powder

1 teaspoon baking soda

1 teaspoon salt

2 eggs

1 cup whole milk

½ cup butter, melted

1½ cups shredded Colby cheese

1. In large skillet, cook sausage with onions over medium heat, stirring to break up sausage, until sausage is cooked. Drain well. Add mushrooms and remove from heat.
2. In large bowl, combine flour, cornmeal, sugar, baking powder, baking soda, and salt. In medium bowl, combine eggs, milk, and butter. Mix well.
3. Add egg mixture to dry ingredients, stirring just until combined.
4. Spray a 4-quart slow cooker with nonstick baking spray containing flour. Place half of the batter in the slow cooker; top with half of the sausage and half of the cheese. Repeat layers.
5. Cover and cook on high for 2½ to 3½ hours or until corn bread tests done when tested with a toothpick. Serve immediately by spooning out of the slow cooker as in spoon bread.

❀ **Makes 10–12 servings**

When these days were completed, the king gave for all the people present in the citadel of Susa, both great and small, a banquet lasting for seven days, in the court of the garden of the king's palace.

—Esther 1:5

Breakfast Casserole

The combination of textures, flavors, and colors in this rich and hearty casserole is just wonderful. Serve with some fresh fruit for a complete breakfast.

1½ pounds breakfast link sausage

10 slices cracked wheat bread, cubed

1 red bell pepper, chopped

1 cup shredded Swiss cheese

1 cup shredded Muenster cheese

8 eggs

1 cup whole milk

1 cup small-curd cottage cheese

2 tablespoons yellow mustard

½ teaspoon salt

⅛ teaspoon white pepper

⅓ cup shredded Romano cheese

1. Cook the link sausage until done in large skillet over medium heat. Drain on paper towels, then cut into 1" pieces. Spray a 5-quart slow cooker with nonstick cooking spray.
2. Layer sausage pieces, bread, bell pepper, and Swiss and Muenster cheeses in slow cooker.
3. In food processor or blender, combine eggs, milk, cottage cheese, mustard, salt, and white pepper. Process or blend until smooth. Pour into slow cooker. Let stand for 20 minutes.
4. Sprinkle with Romano cheese; cover. Cook on high for 2 hours, then reduce heat to low and cook for another 1–1½ hours or until casserole is set.

❧ **Makes 10–12 servings**

Breakfast Granola Bake

Apples, pears, and granola are a wonderful combination in this casserole. It's a little like hot cereal, but with more texture.

2 apples, peeled, cored, and chopped

3 pears, peeled, cored, and chopped

2 tablespoons lemon juice

4 cups granola

1 cup chopped pecans

⅓ cup maple syrup

1 (4-ounce) jar puréed pears

1 teaspoon cinnamon

⅛ teaspoon salt

3 tablespoons butter, melted

1. Place apples and pears in bottom of a 4-quart slow cooker. Sprinkle with lemon juice. Top with granola and pecans.
2. In medium bowl, combine remaining ingredients and mix well. Pour into slow cooker. Cover and cook on low for 7–9 hours or until apples and pears are tender. Serve with cold maple syrup and heavy cream, if desired.

❧ **Makes 8–10 servings**

Artichoke Tomato Strata

Make sure you purchase regular canned artichoke hearts, not marinated, unless you want a spicy breakfast! Be sure to read labels very carefully.

8 croissants, cut into cubes

1 (15-ounce) can artichoke hearts, drained

2 tablespoons butter

1 onion, chopped

3 cloves garlic, minced

½ teaspoon salt

1 teaspoon dried marjoram leaves

5 eggs

1 cup light cream

⅛ teaspoon white pepper

6 tomatoes, cubed

1 cup cubed mozzarella cheese

2 cups cubed Colby cheese

1 cup sour cream

1 cup chopped tomatoes

¼ cup chopped fresh chives

1. Preheat oven to 400°F. Place croissant cubes on large cookie sheet. Bake for 10 minutes, turning cubes once, until browned. Set aside. Cut artichoke hearts into small pieces. Spray a 6-quart slow cooker with nonstick cooking spray and set aside.
2. In large skillet, melt butter over medium heat. Add onion and garlic; cook and stir until tender, about 6 minutes. Add artichokes; cook and stir for 2 minutes longer. Set aside.
3. In medium bowl, combine salt, marjoram, eggs, cream, and pepper. Beat until blended.
4. In prepared slow cooker, layer croissant cubes with onion mixture, cubed tomatoes, and cheeses. Pour egg mixture over all; let stand for 15 minutes, pushing bread into the egg mixture as necessary.
5. Cover and cook on low for 4–5 hours or until set. Scoop out of the slow cooker to serve; top with sour cream, tomatoes, and chopped chives.

🥄 **Makes 8–10 servings**

He brought me to the banqueting house, and his intention toward me was love. Sustain me with raisins, refresh me with apples.

—*Song of Solomon 2:4*

Cinnamon Crunch Muffins

These muffins fill your home with such a good smell that you'll have a hard time waiting for them to come out of the oven. You'll have to make an extra batch or you won't have enough to take with you.

3 cups flour

1½ cups packed brown sugar

½ teaspoon salt

1 teaspoon cinnamon

1 teaspoon ginger

⅔ cup shortening

½ cup chopped walnuts or pecans

1 teaspoon cinnamon

2 teaspoons baking powder

½ teaspoon baking soda

2 eggs, beaten

1 cup buttermilk

1. In a large bowl, mix together flour, brown sugar, salt, 1 teaspoon cinnamon, and ginger. Add the shortening and mix with fork until crumbly. Remove ⅔ cup of the mixture to a small bowl.
2. Add the walnuts and 1 teaspoon cinnamon to the small bowl. Stir to mix and set aside for topping.
3. Add the baking powder and baking soda to the shortening mixture in the large bowl and stir until just blended. Add the eggs and buttermilk and stir until just combined.
4. Fill greased muffin cups ⅔ full. Sprinkle the reserved topping evenly over the muffins.
5. Bake at 375° for 17–22 minutes or until a wooden toothpick inserted in the center comes out clean. Cool in the pans for 3–5 minutes.
6. Remove to a wire rack to cool completely.

❧ **Makes 16**

And unleavened bread, and cakes unleavened tempered with oil, and wafers unleavened anointed with oil: of wheaten flour shalt thou make them.

—*Exodus 29:2*

French Breakfast Puffs

Didn't you just love the aroma of cinnamon wafting through the house when your mother baked? Put cinnamon sticks in water on top of your stove and simmer all day long—it brings back wonderful childhood memories, as do these puffs.

1/3 cup shortening

1/2 cup sugar

1 egg

1 1/2 cups flour

1 1/2 teaspoons baking powder

1/4 teaspoon nutmeg

1/2 teaspoon salt

1/2 cup milk

1/2 cup sugar

1 teaspoon cinnamon

1/2 cup melted butter

1. Preheat oven to 350°.
2. Mix together shortening, sugar, and egg. Stir in flour, baking powder, nutmeg, and salt.
3. Alternating this mixture with milk, fill greased muffin tins. Bake 20–25 minutes.
4. Mix 1/2 cup sugar and cinnamon.
5. When puffs are done, dip in melted butter, then in cinnamon sugar mixture.

❦ **Makes 6**

Banana-Oatmeal Muffins

Here's a great way to enjoy those bananas that you otherwise throw away. Surprise someone who needs a lift by taking these muffins to them and giving them a few minutes of your time. You can make someone's day a good one!

1 cup flour

1 1/4 cups oats

3 teaspoons baking powder

1/2 teaspoon salt

1/4 teaspoon cinnamon

1/3 cup oil

1/2 cup sugar

1/2 cup packed brown sugar

2 eggs

2 bananas mashed

1. In a bowl, combine flour, oats, baking powder, salt, and cinnamon, mixing well.
2. In another bowl, combine oil, sugars, eggs, and bananas, mixing well.
3. Combine mixtures and pour into greased muffin tins.
4. Bake at 400° for 20 minutes.

❦ **Makes 12**

Apple-Pumpkin Muffins

Do you know the muffin lady? She's the one who has so many muffin recipes to share. When the leaves are turning, it's time to make these—pumpkin just seems to go with autumn and the winter months ahead.

Muffins

2½ cups flour

1 cup sugar

1 teaspoon cinnamon

1 teaspoon nutmeg

½ teaspoon allspice

½ teaspoon salt

1 cup pumpkin

½ cup vegetable oil

2 eggs, beaten

1 teaspoon vanilla

½ cup chopped pecans

1¾ cups peeled and finely chopped apples

Streusel topping

½ cup packed dark brown sugar

2 teaspoons cinnamon

½ cup finely chopped pecans

2 tablespoons melted butter

To make the muffins:

1. In a bowl, combine flour, sugar, spices, and salt.
2. In another bowl, combine pumpkin, oil, eggs, vanilla, and ½ cup pecans and mix well.

3. Add pumpkin mixture to dry ingredients and stir until moistened. Fold in apples. Spoon into greased muffin tins.

To make the streusel topping:

1. Combine dark brown sugar, 2 teaspoons cinnamon, ½ cup pecans, and melted butter. Sprinkle topping over each muffin cup.
2. Bake at 350° for 35–40 minutes or until toothpick comes out clean.

🍎 **Makes 18**

Bran Muffins

These muffins are as moist as can be. This healthy combo of fruits and fiber never tasted so good. Just don't let the children know how good they are for you.

Muffins

½ cup oats

1 cup All-Bran cereal

1 (20-ounce) can crushed pineapple, drained, with ½ cup plus 1 tablespoon juice, reserved

1 egg, beaten

¾ cup sugar

1 teaspoon salt

¼ cup oil

1 cup buttermilk

1½ teaspoons baking soda

1½ cups flour

1 cup chopped walnuts

Glaze

½ cup powdered sugar

1 tablespoon pineapple juice

For the muffins:
1. In a bowl, combine oats and cereal.
2. In a small saucepan, place ½ cup of reserved pineapple juice and bring to boil. Pour over cereal mixture and allow to cool.
3. Stir in egg and, mixing well, add remaining ingredients except 1 tablespoon pineapple juice and the powdered sugar.

4. Grease muffin tins and fill ¾ full of batter. Bake at 400° for 15 minutes. Cool slightly and remove muffins.

For the glaze:
1. In a small bowl, combine 1 tablespoon pineapple juice with the powdered sugar. Stir until smooth.
2. Spoon glaze over baked muffins.

❦ **Makes 18–20**

Potluck Pointer

Orange juice can be used if you don't have enough reserved pineapple juice.

Banana Bread

Banana bread is a classic for breakfast. Made in the slow cooker, it is moist and tender. Let it cool completely on a wire rack before serving.

1¾ cups flour

1 teaspoon baking powder

½ teaspoon baking soda

¼ teaspoon salt

¼ cup butter, softened

¼ cup sugar

½ cup brown sugar

1 egg

⅓ cup buttermilk

1½ cups mashed bananas (about 3)

1 teaspoon vanilla

1 cup chopped pecans

1. Spray a baking insert or 2-pound coffee can with nonstick baking spray containing flour; set aside. In medium bowl, combine flour, baking powder, baking soda, and salt. Mix well.
2. In large bowl, beat butter with sugar and brown sugar until combined. Add egg, buttermilk, bananas, and vanilla. Add to flour mixture and beat until combined. Add pecans.
3. Pour into prepared pan or can. Place crumpled foil or a wire rack in bottom of 4-quart slow cooker. Place pan in slow cooker, cover, and cook on high for 4–5 hours or until toothpick inserted near center of bread comes out clean. Cool on wire rack for 15 minutes, then loosen edges of bread. Remove from insert and cool completely on wire rack.

❧ **Makes 8–10 servings**

Then the Lord said to Moses, "I am going to rain bread from heaven for you, and each day the people shall go out and gather enough for that day."

—Exodus 16:4

Maple-Apple Bread Pudding

Serve this dish along with some fresh fruit and scrambled eggs for the perfect brunch after Easter services.

6 apples, cored and chopped

½ cup apple juice

1 cup brown sugar

⅓ cup maple syrup

¼ cup butter, melted

6 eggs, beaten

1 cup whole milk

2 teaspoons vanilla

1 teaspoon cinnamon

10 slices raisin swirl bread

½ (16-ounce) container cream cheese frosting

6 large croissants, cubed

1 cup raisins

1. In saucepan, combine apples with apple juice. Bring to a simmer; simmer for 5 minutes, stirring frequently. Remove from heat and set aside for 10 minutes. Drain apples, reserving juice.
2. In small bowl, combine brown sugar, maple syrup, and butter; mix well and set aside. In large bowl, combine reserved apple juice, eggs, milk, vanilla, and cinnamon; beat well and set aside.
3. Spread one side of the bread slices with the frosting; cut into cubes. In 6-quart slow cooker, layer ⅓ of the bread cubes, croissant cubes, raisins, apples, and the brown sugar mixture. Repeat layers. Pour egg mixture over all.
4. Cover and cook on high for 3½–4½ hours, until pudding is set. Turn off slow cooker and let cool for 30 minutes, then serve.

❧ **Makes 8–10 servings**

Chocolate-Pumpkin Bread Pudding

Serve this wonderful bread casserole with warmed maple syrup, along with a side of crisp bacon and some cold orange juice.

8 cups cubed French bread

1½ cups semisweet chocolate chips

½ cup canned solid-pack pumpkin

½ cup heavy cream

1 cup milk

½ cup brown sugar

3 eggs

¼ cup butter, melted

½ teaspoon salt

1 teaspoon cinnamon

¼ teaspoon cardamom

2 teaspoons vanilla

1. Spray a 3½- to 4-quart slow cooker with nonstick baking spray containing flour. Place bread and chocolate chips in slow cooker; stir gently to mix.
2. In medium bowl, combine pumpkin and heavy cream; stir until combined. Add remaining ingredients and mix until smooth.
3. Pour mixture into slow cooker. Push bread down into the liquid if necessary. Let stand for 15 minutes. Cover and cook on high for about 2 hours or until pudding is set. Turn off slow cooker; remove cover. Loosely cover top of slow cooker with foil and let bread pudding stand for 15 minutes before serving.

❦ **Makes 8 servings**

Carrot Zucchini Bread

Can you imagine that this tasty, moist bread is healthy for you as well? It is a great combination of fruits and vegetables all rolled into one. Wrap it up, tie it with a bow, and surprise a friend with it.

1 cup unsweetened applesauce

¾ cup shredded carrots

¾ cup peeled and shredded zucchini

½ cup sugar

½ cup egg substitute

1½ teaspoons pumpkin pie spice

1 teaspoon ground cinnamon

½ teaspoon ground nutmeg

3 cups self-rising flour

¾ cup orange juice

1. In a bowl, combine the first 8 ingredients. Add flour alternately with orange juice to carrot mixture. Pour into 2 greased and floured 8" × 4" × 2" loaf pans.
2. Bake at 350° for 45 minutes or until bread tests indicate doneness. Cool for 10 minutes; remove from pans to a wire rack to cool.

❦ **Makes 2 loaves**

Carrot Bread

A moist carrot bread is a nice change from the usual breakfast quick breads. Serve this with a spread made with 8 ounces cream cheese, ½ cup brown sugar, ⅓ cup toasted chopped walnuts, and 1 teaspoon cinnamon.

1¼ cups flour

½ cup whole wheat flour

1½ teaspoons baking powder

½ teaspoon baking soda

¼ teaspoon salt

¼ cup sugar

⅓ cup brown sugar

1 egg

1 (8-ounce) can crushed pineapple in juice, drained

1 cup finely grated carrots

1 teaspoon vanilla

3 tablespoons butter, melted

1 cup chopped walnuts

1. Spray a baking insert or 2-pound coffee can with nonstick baking spray containing flour; set aside. In large bowl, combine flour, whole wheat flour, baking powder, baking soda, salt, sugar, and brown sugar; mix well.
2. In small bowl, combine egg, drained pineapple, carrots, vanilla, and melted butter. Add to flour mixture and beat until combined. Add walnuts.
3. Pour into prepared pan or can. Place crumpled foil or a wire rack in bottom of 4-quart slow cooker. Place pan in slow cooker, cover, and cook on high for 4–5 hours or until toothpick inserted near center of bread comes out clean. Remove insert from slow cooker and cool on wire rack for 15 minutes. Gently loosen sides of bread and invert onto wire rack; cool completely.

Makes 8–10 servings

Ho, everyone who thirsts, come to the waters, and you that have no money, come, buy and eat! Come, buy wine and milk without money and without price. Why do you spend your money for that which is not bread, and your labor for that which does not satisfy? Listen carefully to me, and eat what is good, and delight yourselves in rich food.

—Isaiah 55:1

Dill Cheese Bread

A non-sweet bread is a pleasant change for a breakfast or brunch buffet. This tender bread has a nice dill flavor and a tender texture.

3 tablespoons butter

1 onion, finely chopped

1 (3-ounce) package cream cheese

¼ cup buttermilk

½ cup small-curd cottage cheese

½ cup ricotta cheese

2 eggs

1½ cups flour

1 cup whole wheat flour

¼ cup sugar

2 teaspoons baking powder

1 teaspoon baking soda

½ teaspoon salt

2 teaspoons dill seed

1 tablespoon butter, melted

1. Spray a 3-quart slow cooker that has a removable liner with nonstick baking spray containing flour and set aside. In small saucepan, melt 3 tablespoons butter over medium heat. Add onion; cook and stir until tender, about 6 minutes.
2. Remove from heat and stir in cream cheese and buttermilk; stir until cream cheese is melted. Pour into medium bowl and add cottage cheese, ricotta cheese, and eggs; beat until combined.
3. In large bowl, combine flour, whole wheat flour, sugar, baking powder, baking soda, salt, and dill seed; mix well. Add cream cheese mixture and stir just until combined. Pour into prepared slow cooker.
4. Cover and cook on high for 1 hour. Put oven mitts on your hands and carefully turn the slow cooker liner ½ turn. Cover and cook for 1 hour to 1 hour 10 minutes longer until bread is golden brown and sounds hollow when gently tapped with fingers. Uncover and let stand for 20 minutes, then turn out onto wire rack and brush with 1 tablespoon melted butter. Let cool.

Makes 8 servings

Can that which is tasteless be eaten without salt, or is there any flavor in the juice of mallows?

—Job 6:6

Cherry Nut Bread

This is a super-easy bread recipe—no yeast required! This would be great with a topping of 2 tablespoons sugar, ¼ teaspoon cinnamon, and ½ cup slivered almonds. Be sure to add the topping before baking.

2 eggs
2 cups sugar
1 teaspoon salt
2 teaspoons baking soda
1 teaspoon almond extract
½ cup oil
2 cups flour
1 (20-ounce) can cherry pie filling
1 cup chopped nuts

1. Mix all ingredients together.
2. Pour into 2 greased and floured 9" × 5" × 3" loaf pans.
3. Bake at 350° for 1 hour.

❦ **Makes 2 loaves**

Cheesy Onion Bread

This is a good accompaniment for many meals. Take lasagna and a salad along with this, and you'll have a complete meal for any family.

1 tube frozen white bread, partially thawed
¼ cup melted butter or margarine
1 cup thinly sliced Vidalia onions
1 cup shredded Asiago blend cheese

1. Spray 9" × 13" baking dish with vegetable cooking spray.
2. Cut unbaked bread into 20 slices. Place 10 slices in pan and drizzle with butter. Place half of the sliced onions on the bread and top with half of the grated cheese. Repeat layers.
3. Let rise 1 hour in warm place before baking.
4. Bake at 375° for 25 minutes.

❦ **Makes 10–14 servings**

Liz's Spoon Bread

Here's another good southern recipe: creamy, smooth spoon bread–real comfort food.

4 eggs

4 cups milk

1 cup white cornmeal

1 tablespoon butter

½ teaspoon salt

1. Beat eggs with 1 cup of the milk.
2. Combine cornmeal, butter, salt, and the remaining 3 cups of milk.
3. Bring cornmeal mixture to a boil and stir. Slowly blend egg and milk mixture into meal mixture. Pour into a greased 2-quart casserole.
4. Place casserole in a pan of hot water. Bake at 400° for 45 minutes.
5. Serve with butter.

❦ **Makes 9 servings**

Poppy Seed Bread

This recipe used to call for coconut pudding, but it can be hard to find; so now I use vanilla pudding and add coconut flavoring. It's a good substitution when making this delicious bread.

1 (18.25-ounce) package white cake mix

4 eggs

¼ cup poppy seed

½ cup cooking oil

1 cup hot water

1 (3-ounce) package vanilla instant pudding

1 teaspoon coconut flavoring

1. In large bowl, combine all ingredients and beat for 4 minutes.
2. Bake at 350° for 30–40 minutes in 2 waxed-paper-lined 9" × 5" × 2" pans.

❦ **Makes 2 loaves**

My Mom's Nut Bread

Some great cooks never write down anything when they create a recipe, so you have to re-create recipes from memory with the help of other family members. This one is straight from the source.

4 cups flour

6 teaspoons baking powder

1 teaspoon salt

1 cup sugar

1 cup nuts

2 eggs, beaten

1 cup milk

1. In large bowl, mix together flour, baking powder, salt, sugar, and nuts. Add beaten eggs and milk.
2. Put into 2 greased and floured 9" × 5" × 3" loaf pans and let stand for 20 minutes.
3. Bake at 350° for about 50 minutes.

❦ **Makes 2 loaves**

Lemon Bread

The wonderful glaze on this bread gives it a terrific lemony flavor. This bread will melt in your mouth.

⅔ cup butter

2 cups sugar

4 eggs

3 cups flour

1 cup milk

1 tablespoon baking powder

2 teaspoons salt

1 cup pecan pieces

4 tablespoons lemon juice

⅔ cup sugar

1. Combine all ingredients except lemon juice and sugar. Blend well.
2. Put into 2 greased 9" × 5" × 3" loaf pans. Bake at 350° for 50 to 60 minutes.
3. While bread is still warm, combine lemon juice and sugar. Pour over bread.

❦ **Makes 2 loaves**

Butter and honey shall he eat, that he may know to refuse the evil, and choose the good.

—Isaiah 7:15

Frosty Pumpkin Bread

This is wonderfully good any time of the year, but it's especially good during the holiday season. The icing on this bread is a must.

Bread

3⅓ cups flour

1 teaspoon cinnamon

1 teaspoon nutmeg

1 teaspoon cloves

4 eggs

2 cups canned pumpkin

½ cup pecan pieces

2 teaspoons baking soda

1½ teaspoon salt

1 cup vegetable oil

⅔ cup water

3 cups sugar

Icing

1 teaspoon butter, softened

1 8-ounce package cream cheese, softened

1 16-ounce box of powdered sugar

1 cup of pecans

1 teaspoon vanilla

For the bread:

1. In large bowl, combine all ingredients. Mix well.
2. Pour mixture into three greased and floured 9" × 5" × 3" loaf pans.
3. Bake at 350° for 50 to 60 minutes.

For the icing:

1. With electric mixer, beat together butter and cream cheese. Add powdered sugar and beat until smooth. Stir in pecans and vanilla.
2. Frost pumpkin bread while still warm.

❧ **Makes 3 loaves**

And the house of Israel called the name thereof Manna: and it was like coriander seed, white; and the taste of it was like wafers made with honey.

—Exodus 16:31

Apple Pear Bread

This moist bread can be cooked in a bread and cake insert made to go in the slow cooker, or in a 2-pound coffee can that has been thoroughly cleaned.

⅓ cup butter, softened

⅓ cup sugar

3 tablespoons brown sugar

2 eggs

1¾ cups flour

½ teaspoon baking powder

½ teaspoon baking soda

½ teaspoon cinnamon

pinch cardamom

¼ teaspoon salt

½ cup pear purée

¼ cup applesauce

¼ cup cored, finely chopped apple

1 cup chopped walnuts

1. Spray an 8-cup bread and cake insert for the slow cooker with nonstick baking spray containing flour. Set aside. In large mixing bowl, combine butter, sugar, and brown sugar and beat until light. Add eggs and mix until fluffy.

2. Sift together flour, baking powder, baking soda, cinnamon, cardamom, and salt. Add half of flour mixture to butter mixture and beat. Mix pear purée into butter and flour mixture. Add remaining flour mixture to combined ingredients and beat well. Add applesauce and chopped apple; mix until combined.

3. Stir in walnuts and place batter into prepared insert. Place a rack, trivet, or crumpled foil in 3½- or 4-quart slow cooker. Place insert onto rack. Cover and cook on high for 2–3½ hours, testing after 2 hours, until bread springs back when lightly touched. Remove insert from slow cooker and place on wire rack; let cool for 10 minutes. Loosen sides of bread and carefully remove from pan; finish cooling on wire rack.

🍂 **Makes 8 servings**

I would feed you with the finest of the wheat, and with honey from the rock I would satisfy you.

—Psalms 81:16

Pineapple Nut Bread

This is an impressive and delicious bread that is wonderfully moist and nutty. Don't forget to add the cinnamon mixture as a finishing touch before you put it in the oven.

¾ cup brown sugar

¼ cup shortening

1 egg, beaten

2 cups flour

1 teaspoon baking soda

½ teaspoon salt

3 ounces frozen orange juice concentrate

1 cup crushed pineapple, undrained

½ cup chopped pecans

2 tablespoons sugar

½ teaspoon cinnamon

1. In medium bowl, cream brown sugar and shortening. Add egg. Add orange juice concentrate and crushed pineapple to creamed mixture.
2. Sift together flour, baking soda, and salt and add to creamed mixture, blending well.
3. Stir in pecans.
4. Pour into 2 greased and floured 9" × 5" × 3" loaf pans.
5. Combine sugar and cinnamon and sprinkle on top of loaves.
6. Bake at 350° for 50–60 minutes.

❦ **Makes 2 loaves**

Thou gavest also thy good spirit to instruct them, and withheldest not thy manna from their mouth, and gavest them water for their thirst.

—Nehemiah 9:20

Spiced Applesauce Loaf

This fast and easy bread will appeal to everyone who loves apples. The wonderful smell will beckon everyone into the kitchen. You may be tempted to keep it for yourself and your family rather than give it away.

1¼ cups applesauce

1 cup sugar

½ cup cooking oil

2 eggs

3 tablespoons milk

2 cups flour

1 teaspoon baking soda

½ teaspoon baking powder

½ teaspoon cinnamon

¼ teaspoon salt

¼ teaspoon nutmeg

¾ cup chopped pecans

¼ cup brown sugar

½ teaspoon cinnamon

1. Combine applesauce, sugar, oil, eggs, and milk. Mix well.
2. Sift together flour, baking soda, baking powder, cinnamon, salt, and nutmeg. Stir into applesauce mixture and mix well.
3. Fold in ½ cup of the pecans.
4. Place in 2 greased 9" × 5" × 3" loaf pans.
5. Combine the remaining pecans, brown sugar, and cinnamon. Sprinkle over batter. Bake at 350° for 1 hour.
6. Remove from pan and cool.

❧ **Makes 2 loaves**

Potluck Pointer

Save your fingers!
When transporting knives, slide them into a paper towel roll (a full one has the added advantage of being at-the-ready to pick up spills). or insert them into a thick piece of cardboard.

Banana Tea Bread

Don't throw away those ripe bananas. Instead, make them into bread. Enjoy it warm from the oven, or toasted and topped with jam later in the week.

2 cups sugar

1 cup butter, softened

6 ripe bananas, mashed

4 eggs

2½ cups flour

1 teaspoon salt

2 teaspoons baking soda

1. In a large bowl, cream sugar and butter until fluffy. Add bananas and eggs and blend.
2. Sift together the flour, salt, and soda 3 times. Carefully blend flour mixture into bananas. Do not overmix.
3. Pour into 2 greased 9" × 5" × 3" loaf pans. Bake at 350° for 50 to 55 minutes.
4. Cool for 10 minutes.

❧ **Makes 2 loaves**

Pineapple Zucchini Bread

Sometimes the only way to get your children to eat healthy foods is by including them in your recipes. This bread is so delicious that your children won't know they are eating something that's good for them.

3 eggs, beaten slightly

1 cup vegetable oil

2 teaspoons vanilla extract

2 cups sugar

2 cups grated zucchini

1 teaspoon baking soda

3 cups flour

1 teaspoon salt

1 teaspoon baking powder

1 cup chopped pecans

1 (20-ounce) can crushed pineapple, drained

2 tablespoons sugar

½ teaspoon cinnamon

1. In a large mixing bowl, mix together eggs, oil, vanilla, sugar, and zucchini.
2. Add baking soda, flour, salt, baking powder, pecans, and drained pineapple. Pour into 2 greased loaf pans.
3. Mix together sugar and cinnamon. Sprinkle over loaves. Bake at 350° for 50 to 60 minutes or until a toothpick inserted near center comes out clean.

❧ **Makes 2 loaves**

Cheese Biscuits

What can we say about cheese biscuits? They're *so* good. Make a batch of these, and they'll be gone before you know it. Best when served warm.

2 cups flour

3 teaspoons baking powder

1 teaspoon salt

1/4 cup shortening

1/3 cup shredded Cheddar cheese

1 teaspoon salt

3/4 cup milk

1. In a bowl, mix together flour, baking powder, and salt. Cut shortening into flour with pastry blender or fork until it looks like cornmeal. Stir in grated cheese. Add milk to mixture just enough to hold dough together.
2. Roll dough 1/2" thick.
3. Cut and bake on ungreased cookie sheet at 425° for 12–15 minutes.

❦ **Makes 16–20**

Garlic Cheese Biscuits

If you like the biscuits at Red Lobster, you'll love this recipe for these garlic cheese biscuits. They're as good as the ones served at the restaurant.

11 ounces cold milk

2 1/4 cups Bisquick

3 ounces shredded Cheddar cheese

1/2 cup melted butter

1 teaspoon garlic powder

1/8 teaspoon onion powder

1/8 teaspoon dried parsley flakes

1. To cold milk, add Bisquick and cheese and blend together.
2. Using a small scoop, place dough on greased cookie sheet.
3. Bake at 375° for 10–12 minutes or until golden brown.
4. Brush baked biscuits with garlic topping made with butter, garlic powder, onion powder, and parsley.

❦ **Makes 12**

Salads

❧

Navy Wife

Potlucks and carry-ins bring back many warm and funny memories. One of my first carry-in experiences was particularly memorable. It happened when my husband Larry was an admiral's aide back in the late '60s. His assignment was in Oakland, California, and we lived on the naval base, Treasure Island, located in the San Francisco Bay between San Francisco and Oakland. Every day we had a breathtaking view of San Francisco from our living room window.

Two weeks after we arrived, the admiral's wife asked me to attend a carry-in luncheon for new Navy wives in the area. Since we were not yet settled, I decided to make it easy on myself and bring a seven-layer salad. The morning of the luncheon, I woke up early and quickly put it together. I dropped off my son at the base nursery and arrived at the admiral's home 5 minutes late—fashionably late, as they used to say. I walked up the steps carefully with a tight grip on my salad. I'm very accident prone, so I was trying to be cautious.

As I rang the doorbell, I became a little jittery, wanting to make sure that I did and said the right thing. The admiral's wife greeted me with a warm smile and friendly manner. As I stepped into the house, her big black Lab came running up to me. I still don't know quite how it all happened, but the next thing I knew, the salad was all over the floor, all over the dog, and all over me. I could have died of humiliation! She couldn't have been more gracious. After everything was all cleaned up, including the dog and me, she joked with me about my "tossed" salad. I can't remember how many times I apologized. As you can see, I have never forgotten my first carry-in, and I will fondly remember the kindness and warm hospitality I received. 🍓

—Susie Siegfried

Macaroni Salad

What's a picnic without macaroni salad? This version uses sweetened condensed milk, and it is out of this world. Make it for your next summer picnic.

2 (16-ounce) packages macaroni

1 cup chopped green pepper

½ cup chopped onion

1 cup chopped celery

1 cup shredded carrots

1 cup chopped yellow pepper

1 (14-ounce) can sweetened condensed milk

1 cup vinegar

1 cup sugar

2 cups mayonnaise

¼ teaspoon salt

¼ teaspoon pepper

1. Prepare the macaroni according to package directions. Drain and let cool in a large bowl.
2. When cool, add all the vegetables to the macaroni.
3. In a small bowl, using a whisk, combine the condensed milk and remaining ingredients. Pour dressing over the macaroni and vegetables and toss together, coating mixture evenly.
4. Refrigerate a few hours before serving.

🦀 **Makes 14–16 servings**

My Favorite Seven-Layer Salad

Everyone seems to have his or her own version of this very popular salad. It's easy to prepare and great tasting–no wonder it is a staple at so many church dinners.

1 head lettuce, torn into pieces

1 cup spinach leaves

1 cup chopped onion

1 cup chopped yellow peppers

1 can sliced water chestnuts, drained

1 (10-ounce) package frozen asparagus spears, thawed

½ pound shredded deli ham

2 cups finely shredded Cheddar and Monterey jack cheeses

2 cups light mayonnaise

¼ cup sugar

1. Cover the bottom of a 9" × 13" dish with the lettuce and spinach.
2. Layer onion, peppers, water chestnuts, asparagus, ham, and cheese in that order.
3. In a small bowl, combine mayonnaise and sugar and stir until smooth. With a spatula, spread the mayonnaise and sugar mixture over salad.
4. Refrigerate until ready to serve.

🦀 **Makes 12 servings**

Chinese Chicken Salad

There are lots of versions of this recipe. As with many other favorite recipes, you probably first tasted this at a potluck supper.

Salad

 1 head Napa cabbage, shredded

½ cup shredded carrots

¾ cup sliced green onions

1 (8-ounce) can sliced water chestnuts, drained

12 ounces cooked chicken breasts, shredded

¾ cup slivered almonds, toasted

Dressing

1 cup vegetable oil

4 tablespoons rice vinegar

4 tablespoons soy sauce

2 teaspoons chicken bouillon

2 teaspoons sugar substitute

4 teaspoons toasted sesame seeds

For the salad:
> In large bowl, toss together the cabbage, carrots, green onions, and water chestnuts. Top with chicken and almonds and refrigerate.

For the dressing:
> In a small bowl, combine all ingredients for the dressing and refrigerate. When time to serve, pour on desired amount of dressing and toss.

❦ **Makes 6–8 servings**

Corned Beef Salad

This recipe was discovered at a PTO– Parent Teacher Organization. It's especially good to make it during the summer months. It's more than a salad since it has vegetables and beef in it.

1 (3-ounce) package lemon gelatin

1 cup boiling water

2 tablespoons vinegar

1 12-ounce can corned beef

2 cups chopped celery

½ cup chopped onion

3 hard-boiled eggs, chopped

1 (10-ounce) package frozen peas, cooked and drained

1¾ cups mayonnaise

¼ cup ketchup

1. Dissolve lemon gelatin in boiling water. Add vinegar, corned beef, celery, onion, hard-boiled eggs, peas, and 1 cup of mayonnaise. Put in greased 9" × 13" dish and refrigerate until set.
2. When set, spread with remaining ¾ cup mayonnaise mixed with the ketchup.

❦ **Makes 12 servings**

Hot Turkey Salad

Here's another great way to use your left-over turkey from Thanksgiving. It also tastes great with chicken or ham. The shredded Cheddar and Monterey jack cheese combination is only one of the many varieties you'll find available at your grocer's. Two of my other favorites are the four cheeses and the Italian cheeses.

4 cups chopped cooked turkey

2 cups finely chopped celery

2 cups mayonnaise

½ cup chopped almonds, toasted

½ cup chopped onion

2 cups cooked rice

1 cup shredded Cheddar and Monterey jack cheeses

1 cup crushed potato chips

1. Combine turkey, celery, mayonnaise, almonds, and onion in a large mixing bowl. Mix with rice.
2. Spoon into a greased 9" × 13" baking dish, cover, and bake at 350° for 15 minutes.
3. Sprinkle cheese and potato chips on top and return to oven for 5–10 minutes.

❦ **Makes 8–10 servings**

Pasta Salad

This salad is so easy to make it will be one of the first recipes that will come to your mind when you're asked to contribute to a potluck.

4 cups tricolor rotini, uncooked

Sugar substitute or sugar to taste

¾ cup Kraft Three-Cheese Italian dressing

1 (3-ounce) can sliced black olives, drained

1 (10-ounce) can chicken breast, drained

1. Cook rotini as directed on package. Drain.
2. Mix together dressing and sugar substitute. Toss rotini with dressing. Add olives and chicken, tossing together lightly.
3. Refrigerate until time to serve.

❦ **Makes 8–10 servings**

Strawberry Salad

Here's another family holiday favorite, but you can make this any time of the year. Frozen strawberries will have some juice; but if you use fresh strawberries, mash a few of them to make some juice and add it to your strawberries.

2 (3-ounce) packages strawberry gelatin

1½ cups boiling water

2 (10-ounce) packages frozen strawberries, partially thawed

1 (13-ounce) can crushed pineapple, undrained

1 (8-ounce) package cream cheese, softened

½ cup sour cream

1. Dissolve gelatin in boiling water. Stir in strawberries and add pineapple. Pour half of mixture into 9" × 13" baking dish. Refrigerate until set. Keep remaining mixture at room temperature.
2. Beat cream cheese until soft, add sour cream, and beat until smooth. Spread cream cheese mixture over gelatin in dish. Refrigerate for 10 minutes.
3. Add remaining gelatin mixture.

❦ **Makes 12–15 servings**

Sauerkraut Salad

This 75-year-old recipe was a favorite of folks who came over from Germany in the early 1900s. I always add a little bit more sugar to it.

1 (32-ounce) can sauerkraut, drained and rinsed

1 cup finely chopped green or red peppers

½ cup finely chopped celery

½ cup finely chopped onion

1 cup sugar

½ cup diced radishes

½ cup shredded carrots

1. Combine all ingredients in medium bowl.
2. Cover bowl and refrigerate overnight.

❦ **Makes 12–15 servings**

Potluck Pointer

Pasta salads come together quickly when you add several ice cubes to the noodles in the colander after draining them. Stir gently until the ice melts and the noodles are chilled and ready to use.

Tasty Slaw

It's a lot easier to make slaw now that you can buy the prepackaged cole slaw mix that is available in your local grocery store produce department. This is a classic dish with a special twist.

½ cup vinegar

2 tablespoons flour

¼ cup sugar

1 tablespoon prepared mustard

1 tablespoon celery seed

1 (16-ounce) package coleslaw

½ cup chopped Vidalia onions

½ cup chopped green peppers

1. In skillet, blend together vinegar, flour, sugar, mustard, and celery seed over medium heat. Add vegetables and stir until mixture is thickened. Remove from heat.
2. Serve warm or cold.

Makes 8–10 servings

Layered Potato Salad

This is a different take on the classic potato salad that we all love. It has been at many a church potluck. Try it for your next one.

First Layer

1 (12-ounce) can corned beef, chopped

¼ cup chili sauce

1 tablespoon finely chopped onion

2 teaspoons prepared mustard

1 teaspoon horseradish

1 envelope unflavored gelatin, divided in half

¼ cup water

½ cup mayonnaise

Second Layer

2½ cups cooked, diced potatoes

½ cup diced celery

2 tablespoons finely chopped onions

1 teaspoon salt

Dash pepper

2 tablespoons finely chopped green pepper

¼ cup water

½ cup mayonnaise

2 teaspoons vinegar

1. Combine corned beef, chili sauce, onion, mustard, and horseradish.
2. Soften half package of gelatin in ¼ cup hot water until dissolved; stir into ½ cup mayonnaise and add to the beef mixture. Spread and press into greased 9" × 13" dish and chill until firm.

(continued)

(Layered Potato Salad—continued)

3. In a large bowl, combine potatoes, celery, onions, salt, pepper, and green peppers.
4. Dissolve the other half package of gelatin in ¼ cup hot water. Blend in mayonnaise and vinegar. Mix well and pour over potato mixture.
5. Toss potato mixture until well coated and spoon on top of corned beef mixture. Chill until firm.

❦ **Makes 12–15 servings**

I went down into the garden of nuts to see the fruits of the valley, and to see whether the vine flourished and the pomegranates budded.

—*Song of Solomon 6:11*

Another Oriental Salad

With so many oriental salad recipes out there, it's hard to choose one. I've included three in this section. Try all three and pick your favorite.

1 head Napa cabbage, shredded

1 bunch sliced green onions

2 (3-ounce) packages ramen noodles

4 ounces slivered almonds

½ cup sesame seeds

1 cup oil

1 cup sugar

2 tablespoons soy sauce

½ cup vinegar

1. Combine cabbage and green onions in large bowl and set aside.
2. Crumble ramen noodles (this can be done while still in package).
3. Spray skillet with vegetable cooking spray. Sauté the almonds, sesame seeds, and Ramen noodles in the skillet.
4. In a small bowl, combine the oil, sugar, soy sauce, and vinegar. Mix well.
5. Combine all ingredients when serving.

❦ **Makes 6–8 servings**

Veggie Salad

This is bound to become a regular on your summer menu. You can use fresh vegetables instead of frozen during the summer. Try a combo of cauliflower, broccoli, zucchini, and yellow squash.

Salad
1 (16-ounce) package frozen mixed vegetables, cooked until crisp and drained
½ cup chopped onions
1 cup chopped celery
½ cup chopped green pepper
½ cup chopped yellow pepper
1 (15-ounce) can red beans, drained

Dressing
¾ cup sugar
½ cup vinegar
1 tablespoon mustard
2 tablespoons flour
¼ teaspoon salt

1. Place dressing ingredients in medium saucepan and cook until thick. Remove from heat and cool.
2. Stir into vegetables and refrigerate until time to serve.

☙ **Makes 6–8 servings**

Tuna Salad

This recipe is a very strange combination of soup, gelatin, and tuna fish. It's much better than it sounds—in fact, it's delicious. Fix it in the summer for get-togethers.

1 (3-ounce) package lemon gelatin
1 teaspoon unflavored gelatin
½ cup boiling water
1 (10.75-ounce) can chicken noodle soup
1 (6-ounce) can white tuna in water, drained
½ cup mayonnaise
½ cup frozen whipped topping, thawed
½ cup chopped celery
¼ cup onion

1. Mix gelatins and dissolve in boiling water. Add chicken noodle soup. Put into 8" × 8" baking dish. Chill, but do not set.
2. Mix together tuna, mayonnaise, topping, celery, and onion. Add to gelatin mixture. Refrigerate until set.

☙ **Makes 6–9 servings**

Spinach Salad

Summertime is the perfect time to prepare gelatin salads. Try this refreshing recipe sometime.

2 (3 ounce) packages lemon gelatin

2 cups boiling water

1 cup cold water

3 tablespoons vinegar

3 tablespoons mayonnaise

½ teaspoon salt

Dash pepper

2 cups cottage cheese

1 (16-ounce) package frozen spinach, thawed and drained well

1 cup chopped celery

4 tablespoons minced onion

1 cup frozen whipped topping, thawed

1. Dissolve gelatin in boiling water. When dissolved, add cold water. Chill for 20 minutes.
2. Add vinegar, mayonnaise, salt, and pepper to gelatin and beat with electric mixer until blended. Add cottage cheese, beat until fluffy; then add spinach, celery, and onion. Fold in whipped topping.
3. Pour into 9" × 13" dish and refrigerate for 3–4 hours.

❦ **Makes 12–15 servings**

Linda's Potato and Green Bean Salad

This salad is particularly tasty when made in the summer with freshly-picked beans and chives.

1 pound Yukon Gold or red potatoes, peeled and cut into ¾" cubes

2 cups fresh green beans, ends trimmed

Dressing

¼ cup olive oil

2 tablespoons whole-grain Dijon mustard or other grainy mustard

2 tablespoons cider vinegar

2 tablespoons chopped fresh chives

2 tablespoons crumbled gorgonzola cheese

1. Cook potatoes in a large pot of boiling water for about 5 minutes. Add the beans, cook until tender, and drain.
2. In a small bowl, whisk together olive oil, mustard, and vinegar. Pour over beans and potatoes. Chill.
3. Just before serving, add the chives and crumbled gorgonzola. Gently toss.

❦ **Makes 6–8 servings**

Applesauce Salad

If you like Red Hots, you'll love the flavor of this applesauce salad. It's especially popular with children, and it will become a frequently requested favorite at gatherings any time of the year.

1 (3-ounce) package cherry gelatin

1 cup boiling hot water

¼ cup Red Hots

1 (16-ounce) jar applesauce

1. Dissolve gelatin in hot water.
2. Add Red Hots and dissolve.
3. Add applesauce and stir well. Put in 8" × 8" square dish.
4. Refrigerate until set.

❧ **Makes 6–9 servings**

And all they of the land came to a wood; and there was honey upon the ground.

—1 Samuel 14:25 A

7-Up Salad

Whoever thought gelatin with 7-Up would taste so good? The marshmallows and whipped topping give this a dessert-type feel, but it can be used as an accompaniment to dinner as well.

2 (3-ounce) packages lemon gelatin

2 cups boiling water

2 cups 7-Up

1 (16-ounce) package mini marshmallows

1 (20-ounce) can crushed pineapple, drained

1 cup pineapple juice

2 tablespoons butter

2 tablespoons flour

1 egg

1 cup sugar

1 (8-ounce) container frozen whipped topping, thawed

1 cup shredded Cheddar cheese

1. Dissolve gelatin in boiling water. Add 7-Up, marshmallows, and pineapple. Pour into 9" × 13" dish and refrigerate until set.
2. In small saucepan, combine juice, butter, flour, egg, and sugar. Blend with wire whisk and cook until thickened like a pudding. Remove from heat, fold whipped topping into pudding mixture, and spread over gelatin. Refrigerate for 4 hours.
3. When time to serve, top with cheese.

❧ **Makes 12–15 servings**

French Beef Salad

This is a great "second day" meal. You can also use leftover roast beef instead of meat from the deli.

1 pound mushrooms, sliced

2 tablespoons lemon juice

Salt and pepper to taste

8 tablespoons olive oil

8 teaspoons red-wine vinegar

1 teaspoon minced jarred garlic

¼ teaspoon dry mustard

¼ teaspoon thyme

⅛ teaspoon basil

1 head romaine lettuce, torn into pieces

1 pound deli roast beef, chipped

8 ounces shredded Swiss cheese

1. Spray skillet with vegetable cooking spray and sauté mushrooms until tender. Remove from heat and toss with lemon juice, salt, and pepper. Set aside to cool.
2. In small bowl, combine olive oil, vinegar, garlic, mustard, thyme, and basil.

3. Line a large bowl with lettuce. Add mushrooms, beef, and cheese. Pour dressing over salad and toss well.

❦ **Makes 6–8 servings**

Potluck Pointer

Prevent limp, soggy salads by keeping the dressing separate until the last minute. Store your salad dressing in a screw-top container placed in the salad bowl. Toss with the greens or veggies just before serving.

Crunchy Chinese Chicken Salad

This recipe is from a former teacher. Try to keep in touch with a few of your childhood teachers—they really appreciate it and they'll be thrilled to hear from you!

4 cups cooked chicken, shredded

1 head iceberg lettuce, shredded

2 tablespoons toasted sesame seeds

Dash pepper

¼ cup sunflower oil

¼ cup sesame seed oil

6 tablespoons rice vinegar

2 tablespoons sugar

1 (3-ounce) package ramen noodles, crushed

½ cup roasted and salted cashew pieces

1. In large bowl, combine chicken, lettuce, and sesame seeds.
2. In bowl, mix together dressing of pepper, oils, vinegar, and sugar.
3. Toss chicken salad with dressing, adding ramen noodles and nuts at last minute.

❦ **Makes 6–8 servings**

Spinach Salad with Mushroom Dressing

The mushroom dressing makes this spinach salad an outstanding one. It takes just a few minutes to fix and is good all year round.

1 pound sliced fresh mushrooms

1½ teaspoons poppy seeds

¾ cup white or red vinegar

1½ cups oil

¾ cup sugar

1½ tablespoons chopped green onion

1½ teaspoons salt

¾ teaspoon dry mustard

1 pound bacon

1 (5-ounce) package spinach

1 head lettuce

2 (8-ounce) packages shredded Swiss cheese

1. In small bowl, combine first eight ingredients to make dressing. Refrigerate until ready to serve.
2. Fry bacon in skillet until crisp. Drain on paper towels to remove grease.
3. Combine spinach, lettuce, cheese, and bacon in large bowl. Toss with dressing.

❦ **Makes 6–8 servings**

Cole Slaw

This is a one-bowl dish that provides you with a crunchy sweet-sour taste. It's sure to become a regular on your summer menu. It's such a quick recipe to use and serves so many that you can have it for those times when you have little or no notice.

2 (16-ounce) packages cole slaw mix

1 cup chopped onion

1 cup and 2 tablespoons sugar

1 teaspoon dry mustard

1 teaspoon celery seed

1 teaspoon salt

1 cup vinegar

¾ cup vegetable oil

1. In large bowl, combine cole slaw mix and onions. Sprinkle 1 cup sugar over cole slaw mix and onion and toss.
2. Combine 2 tablespoons sugar, mustard, celery seed, salt, vinegar, and oil and heat to boiling. Pour over cabbage mixture and refrigerate overnight.
3. Stir before serving.

❦ **Makes 16 servings**

Pickled Noodles

This is a funny name for such a good dish. It's basically a pasta salad, and pasta is so popular these days. It's amazing how good the pasta is with the crunchy cucumbers.

1 pound rigatoni

2 cups sugar

1 teaspoon pepper

2 teaspoons prepared mustard

1 tablespoon salt

2½ cups cider vinegar

1 teaspoon garlic powder

1 finely chopped onion

1 finely chopped unpeeled cucumber

1 teaspoon jarred minced garlic

1. Cook pasta according to directions on package. Drain well and rinse with cold water. Drain again.
2. In saucepan, combine sugar, pepper, mustard, salt, vinegar, and garlic powder and heat until sugar dissolves.
3. Put pasta in large bowl. Add onion, cucumber, and garlic to pasta. Pour dressing over mixture and toss. Cover and refrigerate at least 24 hours.

❦ **Makes 8–10 servings**

Lois's Yummy Salad

Sometimes the old tried-and-true recipes are the best. This one's been around for a long time, and has graced many tables—both at church potlucks and family gatherings.

1 (3-ounce) box lime gelatin

1 (3-ounce) box lemon gelatin

2 cups boiling water

1½ cups cold water

¾ cup chopped pecans

1 (20-ounce) can crushed pineapple, drained

1 (3-ounce) package cream cheese, softened

4 ounces frozen whipped topping, thawed

1½ cups pineapple juice

1 cup sugar

3 tablespoons flour

1 tablespoon lemon juice

3 eggs, beaten well

1. Dissolve gelatins in boiling water. Add cold water. Add pecans and crushed pineapple. Put in 9" × 13" dish. Refrigerate until set.
2. Beat together cream cheese and whipped topping. Spread on set gelatin. Refrigerate for 20 minutes.
3. Combine pineapple juice, sugar, flour, lemon juice, and eggs and cook until thickened. Put on top of cream cheese mixture when cool.
4. Let set 24 hours.

❧ **Makes 12–15 servings**

Potluck Pointer

Try baking instead of boiling your potatoes for your famous potato salad. Baked potatoes are less crumbly and will slice more easily.

Vinegar-and-Oil Potato Salad

You won't have to worry about taking this salad for a picnic since it has no mayonnaise in it. It's made with a vinegar and oil dressing and will hold up during a hot summer day.

2 (15-ounce) cans green beans, drained

4 cups cooked potatoes, cubed

2 green onions, sliced

½ cup sliced red onion

¼ cup oil

2 tablespoons white wine vinegar

1 teaspoon jarred minced garlic

½ teaspoon oregano, or to taste

1 teaspoon salt

⅛ teaspoon pepper

1. Mix together green beans, potatoes, and onions in medium bowl.
2. Combine remaining ingredients in small bowl and pour over vegetables. Toss gently to mix well.
3. Cover and chill for a few hours.

☙ **Makes 4–6 servings**

Spinach Bacon Salad

In California, where fresh veggies abound, spinach salads of every sort are common fare. This one, with bacon and eggs, is good for breakfast, brunch, or a light supper.

French Dressing

3 tablespoons cider vinegar, wine vinegar, or lemon juice

9 tablespoons olive or salad oil

1 teaspoon salt

Freshly ground pepper

Dash Tabasco

6 cloves garlic, quartered

Salad

8 bacon slices

1 (16-ounce) package fresh spinach

3 hard cooked eggs

¾ cup French dressing

1. Two hours ahead, make dressing by combining vinegar, oil, salt, pepper, Tabasco, and garlic.
2. Fry bacon over low heat until crisp and drain on paper towel.
3. In salad bowl, tear spinach into pieces.
4. Chop eggs, crumble bacon, and sprinkle over spinach.
5. Remove garlic from French dressing, and then pour dressing over salad. Toss and serve.

☙ **Makes 6 servings**

Cranberry Chicken Salad

Make this to take to your next bridge party for lots of compliments. One taste and you'll know why everyone raves about it.

1 cup mayonnaise

1 (16-ounce) can jellied cranberry sauce

½ teaspoon celery seed

2 cups shell macaroni, cooked and drained

1 tablespoon minced green onion

2 cups diced cooked chicken

1 cup seedless grapes, halved

½ cup cashews

1. In small bowl, mix together mayonnaise, cranberry sauce, and celery seed.
2. In medium bowl, combine macaroni, onion, chicken, grapes, and cashews.
3. Toss macaroni chicken mixture with cranberry mixture. Refrigerate until time to serve.

❦ **Makes 4–6 servings**

Homemade Cucumber Salad

Don't forget to make a cup of love one of your special ingredients in this salad. It's a great recipe to share, as it makes a generous amount and it travels well.

7 cups unpeeled cucumbers

2 medium yellow onions, sliced

1 finely diced red pepper

1 tablespoon salt

1 cup white vinegar

2 cups sugar

1 tablespoon celery seed

1. Wash cucumbers and slice very thin.
2. In large bowl, gently toss cucumber, onions, and red pepper with salt. Refrigerate overnight.
3. Drain cucumber mixture and pat dry.
4. Mix vinegar, sugar, and celery seed in microwaveable dish for about 20–30 seconds or until sugar is completely dissolved.
5. Return to bowl and toss with dressing.

❦ **Makes 9 cups**

Soups

⚜

S oups have been nourishing people for generations. You can make soup out of practically anything, or almost nothing at all. And soups are really made for the slow cooker. Soup recipes are very tolerant; that is, you can change ingredients, add or subtract just about anything, and they'll still taste wonderful.

Think about using homemade stocks (use the slow cooker!) or boxed broths instead of canned in these recipes. It goes without saying that homemade stocks are richer and more flavorful than canned. Boxed broths are better than canned; they have a smoother and more blended taste. But you can use whatever you have on hand or is available in your local supermarket. Also, look for the lower-sodium varieties.

When you're serving a crowd, it's easy to organize a soup buffet. Make several different soups and set them up with lots of toppings, including shredded cheese, croutons, flavored popcorn, sour cream, and chopped vegetables, along with accompaniments such as crackers, toasted bread, buns, and breadsticks. For a complete and satisfying meal, all you really need with soup is something crunchy, and either a fruit or green salad.

Have lots of bowls and big spoons on hand, along with plenty of napkins. Some of these soups are fun to serve in mugs; then folks can just drink them, which is enjoyable and saves you time on cleanup.

—*Linda Larsen*

Ham and Split Pea Soup

This velvety and delicious soup is perfect for a cold fall night. Serve it after Advent services, along with a green salad and some homemade biscuits.

2 tablespoons butter

1 tablespoon olive oil

2 onions, chopped

3 cloves garlic, minced

4 carrots, sliced

1½ pounds dried split peas

1 ham hock

3 cups water

8 cups chicken broth

1 teaspoon salt

¼ teaspoon white pepper

1 teaspoon dried marjoram leaves

1 cup heavy cream

1. In large skillet, heat butter and olive oil over medium heat. Add onions and garlic; cook and stir until crisp-tender, about 4 minutes. Place in 5-quart slow cooker and add carrots.
2. Pick over the peas and remove any extraneous material. Rinse peas and drain. Add to slow cooker along with ham hock, water, chicken broth, salt, pepper, and marjoram leaves.
3. Cover and cook on low for 8–9 hours or until peas are tender. Remove ham hock and cut off meat. Return meat to slow cooker. Using a potato masher, mash some of the peas.
4. Stir in cream, cover, and cook on high for 20–30 minutes or until soup is blended. Serve immediately.

❦ **Makes 10 servings**

Broccoli Cheese Soup

The combination of cream cheese and American cheese makes a mild and creamy soup that everyone will love. The condensed soups add flavor and texture.

2 tablespoons butter

2 tablespoons olive oil

2 onions, chopped

6 cloves garlic, minced

¼ teaspoon pepper

1 teaspoon dried basil leaves

2 (16-ounce) packages frozen cut broccoli

1 (32-ounce) box chicken broth

1 (10-ounce) can condensed cream of broccoli soup

1 (10-ounce) can condensed cheddar cheese soup

2 cups milk

1 cup light cream

1 (8-ounce) package cream cheese, cubed

4 cups diced processed American cheese

1. Turn 6-quart slow cooker to high. Add butter and olive oil and heat until melted. Add onions and garlic. Cook, uncovered, for 30 minutes.

2. Stir onions and garlic. Add pepper, basil, broccoli, broth, and soups. Stir well, then cover and cook on low for 5–6 hours or until broccoli is tender.

3. Turn off slow cooker. Using an immersion blender or potato masher, purée the broccoli in the soup. Stir in remaining ingredients. Cover and cook on low for 1–2 hours or until cheese melts and soup is hot. Stir to combine, then serve.

❦ **Makes 10 12 servings**

Chicken, Cheese, and Broccoli Soup

From the South comes this hearty soup, perfect for lunch or brunch. Try it using just boneless chicken breasts—it's a little easier.

One fryer, 1½ to 2 pounds
Water to cover the chicken
1 cup chopped green peppers
1 cup chopped red peppers
½ cup chopped onion
½ cup chopped carrots
Salt and pepper
1 bay leaf
½ pound egg noodles
1 (16-ounce) package frozen broccoli, thawed
1 quart milk
½ to 1 quart chicken broth
1 pound Velveeta cheese, cubed

1. In a big pot, cover chicken with water; add all the vegetables except the broccoli along with the salt, pepper, and bay leaf.
2. Bring to a boil, then simmer about 40–50 minutes, until meat falls off the bones.
3. When chicken is done, lift it out to cool, deskin, cut into bite-size pieces, and debone.
4. While chicken is cooling, add enough water so you have about 8 cups of water and return to a boil. Add the noodles; boil for 2 minutes, then add the broccoli. Cook for 10–15 minutes
5. Add the milk and cheese and warm until cheese melts.
6. Adjust seasonings. Add the chicken. Bring back to serving temperature.

❧ **Makes 12 cups**

Then he said unto him, Come home with me, and eat bread.

—1 Kings 13:15

Ida's Savory Minestrone

Minestrone is a thick vegetable soup that contains pasta. It's hearty and delicious. You can make it vegetarian by using vegetable broth instead of chicken broth.

2 tablespoons olive oil

1 tablespoon butter

2 onions, chopped

6 cloves garlic, minced

6 carrots, sliced

6 cups chicken broth

2 cups tomato juice

2 (15-ounce) cans cannellini beans, drained

3 potatoes, peeled and cubed

1 teaspoon dried basil leaves

1 teaspoon dried oregano leaves

1 teaspoon salt

¼ teaspoon white pepper

2 (14-ounce) cans diced tomatoes, undrained

1 (6-ounce) can tomato paste

1 cup orzo pasta

½ cup grated Parmesan cheese

1. In large skillet, combine olive oil and butter over medium heat. When butter melts, add onions and garlic; cook and stir for 5 minutes.
2. Pour into 6- to 7-quart slow cooker. Add carrots, chicken broth, tomato juice, beans, potatoes, basil, oregano, salt, and pepper. Mix well. Cover and cook on low for 7–8 hours or until potatoes are tender.
3. In large bowl, combine diced tomatoes with tomato paste until paste dissolves. Stir into slow cooker along with orzo. Cover and cook on high for 30–40 minutes or until soup is hot and orzo is tender.
4. Top each serving with cheese.

❦ **Makes 8–10 servings**

Yet he commanded the skies above, and opened the doors of heaven; he rained down on them manna to eat, and gave them the grain of heaven. Mortals ate of the bread of angels; he sent them food in abundance.

—Psalms 78:23–25

Chicken Tortilla Soup

Versatile and easy, simmer it in a slow cooker while you chat with friends who've gathered. You can make it spicier with hot salsa instead of medium salsa.

1 (14.5-ounce) can chicken broth

2 (14.5-ounce) cans tomatoes with green chilies

1 (16-ounce) jar salsa, medium

1 (10.3-ounce) can Cheddar cheese soup

1 (10.3-ounce) can pepper jack cheese soup

1 (16-ounce) package Velveeta cheese, sliced

2 cups cooked chicken, shredded

1. Combine all ingredients except chicken in slow cooker. Cook several hours.
2. Shred chicken and add to slow cooker. Warm for 30 minutes.

❦ **Makes 14–16 cups**

Meatball Veggie Soup

There are many varieties of frozen meatballs available, from Italian flavored to wild rice. Use your favorites in this hearty stew.

2 tablespoons olive oil

1 tablespoon butter

2 onions, chopped

5 cloves garlic, minced

2 (8-ounce) jars sliced mushrooms, undrained

2 (14-ounce) cans diced tomatoes, undrained

2 (16-ounce) packages frozen small meatballs

3 cups frozen corn

1 (16-ounce) bag baby carrots

2 (32-ounce) boxes beef broth

2 cups water

1/4 teaspoon pepper

1 teaspoon dried oregano leaves

1 teaspoon dried thyme leaves

1 (12-ounce) package orzo pasta

1 cup grated Parmesan cheese

1. In large skillet, combine olive oil and butter over medium heat. Add onions and garlic; cook and stir until tender, about 5 minutes. Place in 6- to 7-quart slow cooker.
2. Add all remaining ingredients except pasta and cheese. Cover and cook on low for 7–8 hours or until meatballs are hot and vegetables are tender.
3. Stir in pasta. Cover and cook on high for 20–30 minutes or until pasta is tender, stirring twice during cooking time. Top with cheese and serve.

❦ **Makes 12–14 servings**

Black Bean Soup

This spicy soup is delicious when served with a cool tomato and sour cream mixture and crisp tortilla chips. It's a meal in itself!

1 tablespoon butter

1 tablespoon olive oil

1 onion, chopped

4 cloves garlic, minced

4 large carrots, sliced

1 (32-ounce) box vegetable stock

1 (16-ounce) jar chunky medium salsa

3 (15-ounce) cans black beans, drained

1 teaspoon cumin

¾ cup sour cream

3 tablespoons minced green onions, white and green parts

1 tablespoon minced chives

½ cup chopped tomatoes

2 tablespoons lime juice

2 cups crushed blue corn tortilla chips

1. In medium skillet, melt butter and olive oil over medium heat. Add onion and garlic; cook and stir until tender, about 5 minutes. Place in 5-quart slow cooker along with carrots, vegetable stock, salsa, black beans, and cumin.
2. Cover slow cooker and cook on low for 7–8 hours. Meanwhile, in serving bowl combine sour cream, green onion, chives, and tomatoes; refrigerate.
3. When soup is done, stir in lime juice. Serve with sour cream mixture and tortilla chips as topping.

❀ **Makes 8 servings**

Tomato Bean Soup

You must use canned beans in this recipe, because the acid in the tomato will slow down the softening of dried beans.

2 (10-ounce) cans condensed tomato soup

2 (14-ounce) cans diced tomatoes, undrained

3 (15-ounce) cans navy beans, drained

8 plum tomatoes, chopped

2 onions, chopped

4 cups tomato juice

2 cups water

1 tablespoon sugar

1 teaspoon dried basil leaves

¼ teaspoon pepper

Combine all ingredients in 6-quart slow cooker. Cover and cook on low for 8–9 hours or until soup is hot and blended. Stir and serve immediately.

❀ **Makes 12–14 servings**

Potluck Pointer

Slip a clean kitchen towel around the lid of your casserole dish before replacing the lid. This will prevent moisture from building up on the inside of the lid and dripping onto your food.

Rich Vegetable Soup

Buying a wedge of real Parmesan cheese may seem expensive, but for a special occasion the flavor just can't be beat. And the rind adds incredible flavor to this soup.

2 tablespoons butter

2 onions, chopped

4 cloves garlic, minced

1 cup water

1 (32-ounce) box vegetable broth

1 (4-inch) wedge of Parmesan cheese

3 (14-ounce) cans diced tomatoes, undrained

1 (16-ounce) package baby carrots

1 teaspoon dried basil leaves

1 teaspoon dried oregano leaves

½ teaspoon salt

⅛ teaspoon white pepper

2 (6-inch) yellow summer squash, sliced

½ cup grated Parmesan cheese

¼ cup minced fresh chives

2 tablespoons grated lemon zest

1. In large skillet, melt butter over medium heat. Add onions and garlic; cook and stir until onions start to brown, about 9–11 minutes. Carefully add water and broth to skillet; cook and stir until mixture boils.
2. Pour into 5-quart slow cooker. Grate cheese from the wedge, reserving cheese. Add cheese rind along with remaining ingredients except for squash, grated cheese, chives, and lemon zest to slow cooker. Cover and cook on low for 8–9 hours or until vegetables are tender.
3. Remove cheese rind from soup and discard. Add squash to soup and cook on high for 20–30 minutes or until squash is crisp-tender.
4. In medium bowl, combine grated cheese, chives, and lemon zest. Serve soup in bowls and top with chive mixture.

🌿 **Makes 8 servings**

So Laban gathered together all the people of the place, and made a feast.

—*Genesis 29:22*

Pepper's Tomato Soup

Nothing says comfort food like this classic tomato soup. Be sure to make grilled cheese sandwiches using thickly sliced bread to serve with this delicious soup.

1 quart milk

1 (28-ounce) can diced tomatoes

Dash salt

½ teaspoon baking soda

2 tablespoons butter

1. Heat milk to scalding in medium saucepan. Add tomatoes, dash salt, and baking soda and stir until smooth.
2. Stir in butter.

❦ **Makes 6 servings**

Butternut Soup

You can make this with fresh squash but you'll find the prepared squash in the freezer section at your grocery store, Use that—it tastes just as good.

1 tablespoon olive oil

3 (10-ounce) packages frozen squash, thawed

1 medium onion, chopped

1 teaspoon jarred minced garlic

½ teaspoon ground allspice

2 (14.5-ounce) cans chicken broth

½ cup sour cream

Saltine crackers

1. Heat oil in large saucepan on medium heat. Add squash, onion, and garlic; cook for 5 minutes, stirring occasionally. Add allspice; cook, stirring, for 1 minute. Add chicken broth and bring to boil. Cover and reduce heat to low.
2. Add sour cream. Simmer 15 minutes.
3. Serve with crackers.

❦ **Makes 8 servings**

Creamy Ginger-Pumpkin Soup

Pumpkin soup is creamy, velvety, hearty, and delicious. Choose garlic or plain croutons to top this wonder.

2 (15-ounce) cans solid-pack pumpkin

2 onions, chopped

5 cloves garlic, minced

2 tablespoons minced fresh gingerroot

1 (32-ounce) box chicken broth

2 cups water

1 teaspoon salt

1/4 teaspoon white pepper

1/2 teaspoon ground ginger

1 cup heavy cream

1/2 cup sour cream

2 tablespoons cornstarch

1 1/2 cups croutons

1. In 5-quart slow cooker, combine pumpkin with onions, garlic, and gingerroot; mash to combine. Gradually stir in chicken broth, stirring with wire whisk until blended.
2. Add water, salt, pepper, and ground ginger. Stir to combine. Cover and cook on low for 5–6 hours or until soup is hot and blended.
3. In medium bowl combine heavy cream, sour cream, and cornstarch; mix well. Stir into soup, cover, and cook on high for 30 minutes or until soup is hot. Top with croutons and serve.

❧ **Makes 8–10 servings**

Ham and Bean Soup

Ham hocks add incredible flavor to this easy soup. Serve it with toasted cheese bread and coleslaw.

1 1/2 pounds dried great Northern beans

2 onions, chopped

5 cloves garlic, minced

4 carrots, sliced

1/3 cup brown sugar

2 (32-ounce) boxes chicken broth

2 cups water

2 ham hocks

1 bay leaf

1/4 teaspoon white pepper

1/2 cup heavy cream

1. Sort and pick over beans to remove stones or extraneous material; rinse and drain. Place beans in a soup pot. Cover with water and bring to a boil over high heat. Boil for 2 minutes, then cover, remove from heat, and let stand for 2 hours.
2. Drain beans, then place in 6-quart slow cooker. Add onions, garlic, and carrots. In small bowl, dissolve brown sugar in 1 cup chicken broth. Add it and the rest of the chicken broth and 2 cups water to the slow cooker.

(continued)

Ham and Bean Soup—continued)

3. Add ham hocks, bay leaf, and pepper to the slow cooker. Cover and cook on low for 8–10 hours or until beans are tender.
4. Remove ham hocks from slow cooker and cut off meat. Meanwhile, mash some of the beans in slow cooker with a potato masher. Discard ham bones.
5. Return meat to slow cooker along with cream. Cover and cook on low for 30–40 minutes or until soup is hot. Remove bay leaf and serve.

❦ **Makes 10–12 servings**

Potato Soup au Gratin

You can spice up this soup even more by substituting a 16-ounce jar of hot salsa in place of the tomato and green chilies. Or use this recipe "as is"—it's just hot enough for families.

1 (4.9-ounce) package Betty Crocker au gratin potatoes

1 (10-ounce) package frozen corn, thawed

1 (14.5-ounce) can diced tomatoes with green chilies, undrained

1½ cups water

1 stick margarine

2 cups milk

2 cups cubed processed American cheese

1. In a saucepan, combine the package of au gratin potatoes and sauce mix with corn, tomatoes, green chilies, water, and margarine. Mix well. Bring to a boil.
2. Reduce heat; cover and simmer for 15–18 minutes or until potatoes are tender. Add milk and cheese.
3. Cook and stir until cheese melts. Serve with tortilla chips.

❦ **Makes 8–10 cups**

Sweet Potato–Bacon Soup

Two kinds of bacon make this creamy soup very rich and hearty. You can serve it as part of a soup course, or in smaller portions as an appetizer.

8 slices bacon

2 onions, chopped

3 pounds sweet potatoes

1 pound Yukon Gold potatoes

1 russet potato

1 (8-ounce) package sliced Canadian bacon, chopped

1 (32-ounce) box chicken broth

1 (32-ounce) box vegetable broth

2 teaspoons dried thyme leaves

1 teaspoon dried oregano leaves

1 teaspoon salt

¼ teaspoon white pepper

2 tablespoons cornstarch

½ cup apple juice

1. In large skillet, cook bacon until crisp. Drain on paper towels, crumble, and set aside in refrigerator. Add onions to drippings remaining in skillet and cook for 4 minutes.

2. Peel all the potatoes and cut into 1" cubes. Combine in 5- to 6-quart slow cooker with Canadian bacon, broths, thyme, oregano, salt, and pepper.

3. Cover and cook on low for 8–9 hours or until potatoes are tender. Turn off slow cooker. Using an immersion blender or potato masher, blend or mash potatoes, leaving some chunks.

4. In small bowl, combine cornstarch and apple juice and blend well. Stir into soup along with reserved crisp bacon. Cover and cook on high for 30 minutes. Stir well before serving.

🍲 **Makes 10–12 servings**

Chicken Corn Soup

This delicious soup is slightly creamy and perfect with the Havarti cheese melting into each spoonful. You can use the technique of topping hot soup with a cheese and vegetable mixture with many other recipes.

2 tablespoons butter

1 tablespoon olive oil

1 onion, chopped

3 cloves garlic, minced

8 boneless, skinless chicken breasts, cubed

1 (10.75-ounce) can cream of chicken soup

1 (32-ounce) box chicken broth

4 cups water

1 teaspoon dried basil leaves

1/4 teaspoon white pepper

1 teaspoon dried marjoram

3 cups frozen corn

2 (15-ounce) cans cream-style corn

1 cup chopped tomatoes

1/3 cup chopped fresh basil

1 cup diced Havarti cheese

1. In large skillet, melt butter and olive oil over medium heat. Add onion and garlic; cook and stir until crisp-tender, about 5 minutes. Place in 6- to 7-quart slow cooker.

2. Add remaining ingredients except tomatoes, basil, and cheese to slow cooker. Keep cheese refrigerated until ready to serve. Stir to blend. Cover and cook on low for 7–8 hours or until chicken is thoroughly cooked and soup is blended.

3. In small bowl, combine chopped tomatoes, basil, and cheese. Top each serving of soup with the tomato mixture.

❀ **Makes 10–12 servings**

Tomato Chicken Bisque

A bisque is a soup that has cream or milk added. Cream adds a wonderful richness and mouthfeel that you just can't get with anything else.

2 tablespoons butter

2 onions, chopped

4 cloves garlic, minced

1 (6-ounce) can tomato paste

2 (14-ounce) cans diced tomatoes, undrained

1 (28-ounce) can puréed tomatoes

2 pounds boneless, skinless chicken breasts, cubed

2 (14-ounce) cans chicken broth

1 teaspoon dried basil

½ teaspoon salt

⅛ teaspoon white pepper

⅓ cup butter

⅓ cup flour

2 cups heavy cream

1. In large skillet, melt 2 tablespoons butter over medium heat. Add onions and garlic; cook and stir for 8 minutes, until translucent and beginning to brown. Add tomato paste. Stir, then let cook for 4–5 minutes until tomato paste starts to brown in spots.

2. Add diced tomatoes; cook and stir until bubbly. Pour into 5- to 6-quart slow cooker. Add puréed tomatoes, cubed chicken breasts, chicken broth, basil, salt, and white pepper; stir well.

3. Cover and cook on low for 7–8 hours or until chicken is thoroughly cooked.

4. In medium saucepan, melt ⅓ cup butter over medium heat. Add flour; cook and stir until bubbly. Stir in heavy cream and cook until thickened. Stir this mixture into the slow cooker.

5. Cover and cook on high for 20–30 minutes or until soup is steaming. Serve immediately.

❀ **Makes 12 servings**

Curried Turkey and Squash Bisque

Apples and squash combine beautifully; they are both sweet and become very tender when cooked in the slow cooker. Add ground turkey and some curry for a hearty bisque.

1 (2-pound) butternut squash

1 (1-pound) acorn squash

1 (16-ounce) bag baby carrots

2 pounds ground turkey

2 onions, chopped

3 tart apples, cored, peeled and chopped

2 tablespoons curry powder

1 teaspoon salt

¼ teaspoon white pepper

2 (32-ounce) boxes chicken broth

3 tablespoons cornstarch

1 cup heavy whipping cream

1. Peel butternut squash and remove seeds and membranes. Cut into 1" pieces. Do the same with acorn squash. Place in 6- to 7-quart slow cooker along with baby carrots.

2. In large skillet, cook turkey until done, stirring to break up meat. Remove turkey to slow cooker. Add onions to skillet; cook and stir to loosen pan drippings. Add onions to slow cooker along with apples.

3. Sprinkle contents of slow cooker with curry powder, salt, and pepper. Pour chicken broth into slow cooker. Cover and cook on low for 8–9 hours or until squash is tender.

4. In small bowl, combine cornstarch with cream and mix well. Stir into slow cooker. Cover and cook on high for 20–30 minutes or until bisque is thickened. Serve immediately.

❁ **Makes 12–14 servings**

Curried Chicken Noodle Soup

Coconut milk and curry powder add great flavor and a touch of the exotic near East to this classic soup.

2 tablespoons butter

1 tablespoon olive oil

6 boneless, skinless chicken breasts

1½ teaspoons salt

¼ teaspoon pepper

1 tablespoon curry powder

2 onions, chopped

2 green bell peppers, chopped

1 (16-ounce) bag baby carrots

1 tablespoon curry powder

2 (32-ounce) boxes chicken broth

3 cups egg noodles

1 (13-ounce) can coconut milk

1. In large skillet, heat butter and olive oil over medium heat. Sprinkle chicken with salt, pepper, and 1 tablespoon curry powder. Add to skillet; cook, turning once, for 4–5 minutes or until chicken begins to brown.
2. Remove chicken from skillet. Add onions to skillet; cook and stir until crisp-tender, about 5 minutes; remove from heat.
3. Place bell peppers and baby carrots in 6-quart slow cooker. Add onions and chicken to slow cooker along with 1 tablespoon curry powder. Pour broth over all.
4. Cover and cook on low for 5–6 hours or until chicken and vegetables are tender. Remove chicken from slow cooker and shred. Return chicken to slow cooker; add noodles and coconut milk.
5. Turn heat to high and cook for 15–20 minutes or until noodles are tender. Serve in warmed bowls, topped with minced green onion if desired.

❧ **Makes 10–12 servings**

The sated appetite spurns honey, but to a ravenous appetite even the bitter is sweet.

—Proverbs 27:7

Mom's Mashed Potato Soup

You know how it is with some recipes—you just throw a little bit of this in, add some of that, etc., but you never can tell others the exact proportions. This soup thickens as it simmers, so you may want to add some more milk.

2½ pounds potatoes

¼ pound carrots

1½ sticks celery

1 whole onion, peeled

¾ stick margarine

3¼ cups milk

1. Peel and dice potatoes. Place in 5-quart pan and cover with water. Add carrots, celery, and onion. Cook over medium heat until potatoes are tender.
2. Drain potatoes and remove carrots, celery, and onion. Put potatoes back into pan and mash by hand. Add ¼ stick margarine and ¼ cup of milk and beat with electric mixer.
3. After making mashed potatoes, gradually add 3 cups milk and ½ stick of margarine to potatoes.
4. Serve warm with butter. Soup will thicken as it sets, so when reheating, add milk as needed.

❧ **Makes 9 cups**

Albondigas

This classic Mexican soup is filling and hearty. You can increase the spice level by adding some jalapeño peppers, or using more chili powder.

2 tablespoons butter

1 onion, chopped

4 cloves garlic, minced

1 (32-ounce) box beef broth

2 cups chicken broth

2 cups water

1 teaspoon salt

¼ teaspoon pepper

1 tablespoon chili powder

½ teaspoon cumin

1 (16-ounce) bag baby carrots

1 (16-ounce) jar medium salsa

3 cups frozen green beans

1 (16-ounce) package small frozen precooked meatballs

½ cup chopped cilantro

1 cup sour cream

1. In large skillet, melt butter over medium heat. Add onions and garlic; cook and stir until tender, about 6–7 minutes. Place in 6-quart slow cooker along with all remaining ingredients except cilantro and sour cream.
2. Cover and cook on low for 8–9 hours or until vegetables are tender and meatballs are hot. Combine cilantro and sour cream in small bowl and serve with soup.

❧ **Makes 8–10 servings**

Chicken Dumpling Soup

Just the smell of this palate-pleasing soup will bring back memories. You must have certain nostalgic recipes. Great feeling, isn't it!

8 cups chicken broth

2 (16-ounce) bags frozen stew vegetables

½ teaspoon onion powder

½ teaspoon garlic powder

2 beaten eggs

2 cups flour

¼ teaspoon salt

3 (5-ounce) cans chicken breast

1. Heat chicken broth large pot until it comes to a boil. Add frozen vegetables and seasonings. Simmer for 10 minutes.
2. Put flour in medium bowl. Dip fork into flour and add eggs to flour. Mix eggs and flour together until the mixture forms little dumplings.
3. Add chicken to soup, bringing soup back to boiling.
4. Take tiny spoonfuls of dumplings and add to boiling broth. Boil soup for 3 minutes. Turn down heat and simmer for 5 more minutes.

❧ **Makes 12 cups**

And the manna ceased on the morrow after they had eaten of the old corn of the land; neither had the children of Israel manna any more; but they did eat of the fruit of the land of Canaan that year.

—Joshua 5:12

Chicken–Wild Rice Soup

Wild rice and chicken cook together beautifully in this excellent soup recipe. The slow cooker is the perfect appliance for cooking wild rice.

2 tablespoons butter

1 tablespoon olive oil

2 onions, chopped

5 cloves garlic, minced

1½ cups wild rice

1 (16-ounce) bag baby carrots

3 cups frozen corn

5 boneless, skinless chicken breasts, cubed

2 (32-ounce) boxes chicken broth

1½ teaspoons seasoned salt

¼ teaspoon pepper

1 teaspoon dried thyme leaves

1 bay leaf

2 cups water

1. In large skillet, heat butter and olive oil over medium heat. Add onions and garlic; cook and stir until crisp-tender, about 5 minutes.
2. Place wild rice in bottom of 6- or 7-quart slow cooker and top with carrots, corn, and onion mixture. Add chicken breasts; do not stir.
3. Pour one box of the chicken broth into slow cooker. Sprinkle food with seasoned salt, pepper, thyme, and add bay leaf. Pour second box of broth and water into slow cooker over seasonings.
4. Cover and cook on low for 5 hours; then remove bay leaf, and stir soup. Cover and cook on low for 1–2 hours longer or until wild rice is tender and chicken is thoroughly cooked at 165°F.

❀ **Makes 12–14 servings**

Black-Eyed Pea Soup

In the South, eating black-eyed peas on New Year's Day is a guarantee of good luck in the New Year. It's delicious anytime.

1 (16-ounce) bag black-eyed peas

1 ham hock

2 onions, chopped

6 cloves garlic, minced

1 (32-ounce) box chicken stock

6 cups water

1 teaspoon salt

½ teaspoon pepper

1 teaspoon dried tarragon leaves

2 (14-ounce) cans diced tomatoes, undrained

½ cup instant brown rice

1. Sort and rinse black-eyed peas to remove any extraneous material. Place in large saucepan and cover with water. Bring to a boil; boil hard for 2 minutes. Cover pan, remove from heat, and let stand for 2 hours.
2. Drain peas and place in 6-quart slow cooker with ham hock, onions, and garlic. Pour stock and water over; sprinkle with salt, pepper, and tarragon.
3. Cover and cook on low for 8–9 hours until peas are tender. Remove ham hock from slow cooker; cut off meat, dice, and return to slow cooker. Discard ham bone.
4. Stir in tomatoes and instant rice. Cover and cook on high for 20–30 minutes or until rice is tender.

❦ **Makes 12 servings**

Lentil Soup

Lentils cook better when the broth is low in salt and acid. Acidic ingredients include tomatoes, lemon juice, and vinegar. Be sure to follow the directions for this recipe closely; the tomato purée and vinegar called for are not to be added until the cooking is nearly complete. This hearty soup is inexpensive and filling.

2 onions, chopped

5 cloves garlic, minced

5 carrots, cut into chunks

2 cups lentils, rinsed

1 (32-ounce) box vegetable broth

4 cups water

1 teaspoon dried oregano leaves

2 bay leaves

1 teaspoon salt

¼ teaspoon pepper

1 (15-ounce) can tomato purée

3 tablespoons balsamic vinegar

1. Combine all ingredients except tomato purée and vinegar in 6-quart slow cooker. Cover and cook on low for 8–9 hours or until lentils and vegetables are tender.
2. Stir in tomato purée and vinegar. Cover and cook on high for 20–30 minutes longer or until soup is hot. Stir and serve immediately.

❦ **Makes 12 servings**

Carrot Potato Bisque

This rich and elegant soup is inexpensive to make, and it serves a crowd. Pair it with a simple green salad and some crisp bread-sticks.

2 onions, chopped

4 cloves garlic, minced

6 carrots, sliced

6 russet potatoes, peeled and cubed

3 (32-ounce) boxes vegetable broth

1/4 teaspoon white pepper

2 teaspoons dried marjoram

1 teaspoon dried oregano

1/4 cup cornstarch

1 cup heavy cream

1 cup light cream

1. Combine all ingredients except cornstarch and both kinds of cream in 6 quart slow cooker. Cover and cook on low for 7–8 hours or until vegetables are very tender.
2. Turn off slow cooker. Using a potato masher or immersion blender, mash or purée the vegetables right in the slow cooker.
3. In large bowl, combine cornstarch with both kinds of cream; mix well with wire whisk. Stir into slow cooker, cover, and cook on high for 20–30 minutes or until soup is slightly thickened and creamy.

❧ **Makes 18 servings**

Chicken Bisque

This super-rich and creamy soup is filling and satisfying on a cold winter day. Serve it with crisp breadsticks and a baby spinach salad with tomatoes and celery.

6 boneless, skinless chicken breasts, chopped

2 (32-ounce) boxes chicken broth

2 cups water

2 onions, chopped

1 cup chopped celery with leaves

1/2 cup butter

1/2 cup flour

1 teaspoon salt

1/4 teaspoon white pepper

2 teaspoons dried thyme leaves

1 cup light cream

2 cups heavy cream

1. In 6-quart slow cooker, combine chicken, broth, water, onions, and celery. Cover and cook on low for 6–7 hours or until chicken is cooked and vegetables are tender.
2. At this point, melt butter in a medium saucepan over medium heat. Add flour, salt, pepper, and thyme; cook and stir until bubbly, about 5 minutes. Stir in both kinds of cream and bring to a simmer.
3. Stir this mixture into the slow cooker. Cover and cook on high for 20–30 minutes or until soup is hot and blended.

❧ **Makes 12–14 servings**

Creamy Onion Soup

This rich soup is usually made with beef broth, but chicken broth makes a lighter taste. You can serve this one in mugs for people to sip slowly as they mingle.

3 tablespoons butter

6 onions, chopped

6 cloves garlic, minced

1 teaspoon salt

1 tablespoon sugar

¼ cup flour

2 (32-ounce) boxes chicken broth

1 teaspoon dried marjoram leaves

1 teaspoon dried thyme leaves

1½ cups heavy cream

2 cups shredded Gruyère cheese

1. Place butter in 5-quart slow cooker and turn to high. When butter melts, add onions and garlic. Sprinkle with salt and sugar. Cover and cook on low for 6–7 hours, stirring twice during cooking time, until onions are golden brown.
2. Turn off slow cooker. Using a potato masher or immersion blender, purée the onions. Add flour. Cover and cook on high for 30 minutes.
3. Gradually stir in 2 cups of the chicken broth. Add remaining broth along with marjoram and thyme. Cover and cook on low for 2–3 hours.
4. Stir in heavy cream and shredded cheese; cook and stir on high until cheese melts and soup is creamy, about 10–15 minutes. Serve immediately.

Makes 12–14 servings

Stews, Chowders, and Chilies

❦

W hat's the difference between stews, chilies, and chowders? It's really just semantics; although traditionally stews are heavy on the vegetables, chilies have lots of meat and beans, and chowders have some kind of dairy product such as milk or cream added. They're all thick and delicious.

Stews, chilies, and chowders are more than just thick soups. Each is a meal in itself, and can be used in other ways. Chili can be served as part of a Mexican salad or served over spaghetti for Tex-Mex pasta, while chowder can be the sauce for filled crêpes.

Stews are among the most tolerant of all recipes. You can change the vegetables, the meat, the seasonings, and the liquid you use—it will still be delicious. Remember, the slow cooker doesn't evaporate liquid as it cooks, and the ingredients will release water as they cook, so don't add too much liquid at first. Keep an eye on the stew, and add more liquid if needed after about half of the cooking time has passed.

Slow cooker stews are thickened with flour or cornstarch, or sometimes with mashed vegetables. One method is to dredge the meat in flour, then sauté until brown to add flavor and color and help thicken the mixture. Another is to stir a cornstarch slurry into the stew at the end of the cooking time.

—Linda Larsen

Sausage and Potato Stew

Boxes of chicken stock are not only easier to store, but they taste better than canned broths. You don't have to decant leftovers into another container; just close the box and pop it in the fridge.

4 slices bacon

1 pound Polish sausage

1 onion, chopped

3 cloves garlic, minced

4 potatoes, peeled and cubed

1 (32-ounce) box chicken broth

2 cups water

2 cups frozen corn

1 red bell pepper, chopped

1 (13-ounce) can evaporated milk

2 tablespoons cornstarch

1 (15-ounce) can creamed corn

¼ cup chopped chives

1. In large skillet, cook bacon until crisp. Drain on paper towels, crumble, and refrigerate. Cut sausage into 1" links and cook for 2–3 minutes in bacon drippings. Remove and place in 4-quart slow cooker.
2. Add onion and garlic to skillet; cook and stir for 4 minutes. Pour all ingredients from skillet into slow cooker. Add potatoes, chicken broth, water, and frozen corn.
3. Cover and cook on low for 8 hours. Add red bell pepper and evaporated milk to slow cooker. In small bowl, combine cornstarch and creamed corn; mix well. Add to slow cooker along with reserved bacon.
4. Cover and cook on high for 30 minutes, or until soup is thickened. Sprinkle with chives. Serve.

❧ **Makes 8 servings**

Turkey–Wild Rice Chowder

Buy the mushrooms already sliced to save time when preparing soups and chowders.

¼ cup butter

2 onions, chopped

6 cloves garlic, minced

⅓ cup flour

1 teaspoon salt

¼ teaspoon pepper

1 tablespoon fresh thyme leaves or 1 teaspoon dried thyme leaves

1 tablespoon chopped fresh rosemary

2 (1-pound) turkey tenderloins, cubed

2 cups water

1½ cups wild rice, rinsed

4 carrots, sliced

1 (8-ounce) packages sliced mushrooms

3 cups frozen corn

2 (32-ounce) boxes chicken broth

1 cup heavy whipping cream

1. In large skillet, melt butter over medium heat, then add onions and garlic; cook and stir for 4 minutes. Remove onions and garlic with slotted spoon to 5-quart slow cooker.
2. On shallow plate, combine flour, salt, pepper, thyme, and fresh rosemary. Toss cubed turkey in this mixture. Brown turkey in remaining drippings in skillet, stirring frequently, about 4–5 minutes total. Add water to skillet and bring to a boil, stirring to loosen drippings.
3. Place wild rice, carrots, and mushrooms in slow cooker. Add mixture from skillet along with frozen corn and chicken broth. Stir to combine.
4. Cover and cook on low for 8 hours or until turkey is cooked and rice and vegetables are tender. Stir in cream; cover and cook for 20 minutes longer until hot. Serve topped with croutons, if desired.

❦ **Makes 10–12 servings**

Curried Chicken Stew

Dark meat chicken cooks beautifully in the slow cooker for longer periods of time. This exotic stew is a real treat.

1½ teaspoons salt

¼ teaspoon pepper

2 tablespoons curry powder

⅓ cup flour

8 chicken thighs, cubed

¼ cup butter

1 tablespoon olive oil

2 cups apple juice

4 sweet potatoes, peeled and cubed

1 cup golden raisins

1 (16-ounce) bag baby carrots

2 onions, chopped

2 (32-ounce) boxes chicken broth

1 (10-ounce) can coconut milk

1 (16-ounce) bottle mango chutney

1. On plate, combine salt, pepper, curry powder, and flour. Dredge cubed chicken in this mixture.
2. Heat butter and olive oil in large skillet over medium heat. Add chicken; cook and stir until browned, about 4–5 minutes. Remove chicken from skillet to a 6-quart slow cooker using a slotted spoon.
3. If there is any flour mixture left, add it to the skillet; cook and stir for 2 minutes. Add apple juice; cook and stir to loosen pan drippings. Bring to a boil.
4. Combine mixture in skillet and all other ingredients except coconut milk and chutney in 6-quart slow cooker. Cover and cook on low for 8–9 hours or until chicken is thoroughly cooked and vegetables are tender.
5. Stir in coconut milk and chutney. Cover and cook on low for another 20–30 minutes or until stew is hot and blended.

❦ **Makes 8–10 servings**

Potluck Pointer

If you want to add a little fun to your potluck, ask everyone to bring a dish beginning with a certain letter of the alphabet. For an "A" party, you might request artichokes, antipasti, asparagus, aïoli pasta, arugula salad, apple strudel . . . or allow your guests to make an "A" dish from the various food categories.

Beef Burgundy Stew

This stew comes from the Burgundy region of France. If you choose to use the wine, be aware that not all of the alcohol will cook out.

2 pounds beef sirloin steak

¼ cup flour

1 teaspoon salt

⅛ teaspoon pepper

1 tablespoon oil

2 tablespoons butter

2 onions, chopped

½ pound portobello mushrooms, chopped

½ pound button mushrooms, sliced

1 (16-ounce) bag baby carrots

1 (32-ounce) box beef broth

1 (14-ounce) can diced tomatoes, undrained

1 (10-ounce) can condensed tomato soup

1 cup Burgundy wine, or apple juice

1 teaspoon dried marjoram

2 tablespoons balsamic vinegar

2 tablespoons cornstarch

⅓ cup water

1. Trim excess fat from steak and cut into 1½" cubes. On shallow plate, combine flour, salt, and pepper. Dredge beef in this mixture.

2. Combine oil and butter in large skillet over medium heat. Add beef; cook and stir until browned, about 4 minutes. As beef browns, remove to 4- to 5-quart slow cooker with a slotted spoon.

3. Add onions to skillet and cook and stir until tender, about 5 minutes. Add to slow cooker along with mushrooms and carrots; stir gently.

4. Add broth, tomatoes, soup, wine or apple juice, and marjoram. Cover and cook on low for 8–9 hours or until beef and vegetables are very tender.

5. In small bowl, combine vinegar, cornstarch, and water. Mix well. Stir into slow cooker. Cover and cook on high for 15–20 minutes or until stew thickens. Serve immediately.

❦ **Makes 10–12 servings**

Just before daybreak, Paul urged all of them to take some food, saying, "Today is the fourteenth day that you have been in suspense and remaining without food, having eaten nothing. Therefore I urge you to take some food, for it will help you survive; for none of you will lose a hair from your heads."

—Acts 27:33

French Chicken Stew

Thyme and tarragon give this stew a French flair. Serve with breadsticks and a fruit salad.

4 slices bacon

2 tablespoons butter

2 onions, chopped

6 cloves garlic, minced

6 boneless, skinless chicken breasts, sliced

1 teaspoon salt

½ teaspoon pepper

2 teaspoons dried thyme leaves

1 teaspoon dried tarragon leaves

1 (28-ounce) can stewed tomatoes, chopped

1 cup dry white wine or apple juice

1 (32-ounce) box chicken broth

2 cups water

5 carrots, cut into chunks

18 tiny whole new red potatoes

¼ cup cornstarch

1 cup heavy cream

1. In large skillet, cook bacon until crisp. Drain on paper towels, crumble, and set aside in refrigerator. Drain all but 2 tablespoons drippings from skillet. Add butter. When butter melts, add onions and garlic; cook and stir over medium heat until crisp-tender, about 5 minutes.

2. In 6-quart slow cooker, combine onion mixture with chicken breasts, salt, pepper, thyme, tarragon, tomatoes, wine or apple juice, chicken broth, water, carrots, and potatoes.

3. Cover and cook on low for 7 hours or until vegetables are tender. In bowl combine cornstarch with cream; mix well. Stir into slow cooker along with reserved bacon. Cover and cook on high for 30 minutes or until stew is thickened. Serve.

❧ **Makes 10–12 servings**

Chicken Waldorf Stew

This thick stew is a nice twist on the classic Waldorf salad, with the same flavors and textures. It's rich and creamy, perfect for a cold fall day.

6 boneless, skinless chicken breasts, cubed

2 onions, chopped

4 tart apples, cored, peeled and chopped

2 tablespoons lemon juice

6 stalks celery, sliced

1 teaspoon celery seed

1 teaspoon salt

¼ teaspoon pepper

1 (32-ounce) box chicken broth

3 cups apple juice

1 cup white grape juice

3 tablespoons cornstarch

1 cup heavy cream

2 cups purchased croutons

1 cup chopped walnuts, toasted

1. In 6-quart slow cooker, combine all ingredients except cornstarch, cream, croutons, and walnuts. Cover and cook on low for 5–7 hours or until chicken is thoroughly cooked and apples are tender.
2. In small bowl, combine cornstarch and cream and mix well. Stir into slow cooker. Cover and cook on high for 20–25 minutes or until stew is thickened.
3. Serve topped with croutons and toasted walnuts.

Makes 8–10 servings

Veggie Chili with Beef

This is a really fast chili you can have ready to go in less than an hour. Double or triple the recipe when you take it for a crowd.

1 (28-ounce) can tomato sauce

1 pound ground beef, browned and drained

1 (15-ounce) can mixed vegetables, with liquid

1 (16-ounce) can kidney beans, drained and rinsed

1 (14.5-ounce) can diced whole tomatoes

2 teaspoons chili powder

Shredded Cheddar cheese

¾ cup diced green onions

Corn chips

1. In 3-quart saucepan, combine all ingredients except cheese, onions, and corn chips.
2. Bring to a boil. Reduce heat, cover, and simmer for 20–30 minutes, stirring occasionally.
3. Serve hot with shredded cheese, diced green onions, and corn chips as toppers.

Makes 8 servings

Four-Bean Chili

Serve this hearty chili with sour cream, chopped avocados, chopped tomatoes, and more salsa.

1 pound spicy bulk pork sausage

1 pound lean ground beef

2 onions, chopped

5 cloves garlic, minced

1 (6-ounce) can tomato paste

2 cups tomato juice

1 (16-ounce) jar mild or medium salsa

1 green bell pepper, chopped

2 (32-ounce) boxes beef broth

2 tablespoons chili powder

1 teaspoon cumin

1/4 teaspoon pepper

1/8 teaspoon cayenne pepper

1 (15-ounce) can black beans, drained

1 (15-ounce) can kidney beans, drained

1 (15-ounce) can pinto beans, drained

1 (15-ounce) can lima beans, drained

1 (4-ounce) can chopped green chiles, drained

1. In large skillet, brown pork sausage and ground beef until done, stirring to break up meat. Drain well and place in 6- to 7-quart slow cooker. Add onions and garlic; cook and stir until tender.

2. Add tomato paste to skillet; cook and stir over medium heat until paste begins to brown in spots. Add tomato juice to skillet; cook and stir to loosen pan drippings. Pour into slow cooker.

3. Add all remaining ingredients. Cover and cook on low for 7–9 hours or until chili is blended and thick.

❧ **Makes 18–20 servings**

Is there anyone among you who, if your child asks for a fish, will give a snake instead? Or if the child asks for an egg, will give a scorpion? If you then, who are evil, know how to give good gifts to your children, know much more will the heavenly Father give the Holy Spirit to those who ask Him!

—Luke 11:11–13

Sweet Chili

If you like your barbecue sauce on the sweet side, you may like this sweet yet spicy chili.

1 pound ground beef

1 tablespoon chili powder

1 teaspoon ketchup

1 (16-ounce) can kidney beans

1 (16-ounce) can chili beans

½ cup brown sugar

1 (6-ounce) can tomato paste

1 (10.75-ounce) can tomato soup

1. Brown hamburger with a pinch of chili powder and ketchup.
2. Mix all ingredients in slow cooker and let simmer for a minimum of 2 hours.

❀ **Makes 6–8 servings**

Tortilla Chili

Don't add the tortilla chips when you take this to a carry-in. Instead, crush some tortilla chips and take them in a bowl along with bowls of Cheddar cheese and sour cream. Then everyone can put in their own chips, cheese, and sour cream if they wish. Works out well.

2 pounds boneless, skinless chicken breast, cut into bite-size pieces

2 (1.25-ounce) packages chili seasoning mix

2 (14.5-ounce) cans diced tomatoes

1 (15-ounce) can pinto beans, juice and all

2 (15.25-ounce) cans Mexican-style corn, drained

2 cups water

2 cups broken tortilla chips

1. Heat a lightly oiled large skillet over medium high heat. Add chicken. Cook and stir for about 5 minutes, until lightly browned. Stir in remaining ingredients except tortilla chips and bring to a boil. Reduce heat to low.
2. Cover and simmer for 15 minutes, stirring occasionally. Mix in tortilla chips.
3. Serve with shredded Cheddar cheese and sour cream, if desired.

❀ **Makes 10 servings**

Cincinnati Chili in a Dish

Even outside this city, people know about Cincinnati's famous chili. There are a couple of restaurants in Ohio that offer it on their hot dogs and spaghetti, with your choice of onion, beans, and cheese—any combination you want. This casserole is close to the original Cincinnati chili.

1 pound ground beef

1 chopped onion

1 (16-ounce) can tomatoes

1 (16-ounce) can kidney beans

1 teaspoon garlic powder

1 or 2 dashes pepper

1½ teaspoons ground cloves

¼ teaspoon salt

Few drops Tabasco sauce

1 teaspoon cinnamon

8 ounces cooked angel hair pasta, drained

2 cups shredded Cheddar cheese

1 cup chopped onions

1. Brown beef with onions. Drain well. Put in large pan and add remaining ingredients except for last three; simmer for 45–60 minutes.
2. Stir chili frequently adjusting seasoning to taste.
3. Place pasta in greased 9" × 13" baking dish. Top with chili. Sprinkle cheese on top of chili and add onions on top of cheese.
4. Cover with foil and keep warm in 250° oven until served.

🌀 **Makes 6–8 servings**

Tortilla Chili Casserole

Give everyone's taste buds a spicy treat for a change. I like to make this using 1 pound hot sausage and 1 pound ground beef instead of the 2 pounds ground beef.

2 pounds lean ground beef

1 (14.5-ounce) can chili beans

1 (11-ounce) bag corn chips or tortilla chips

1 pint sour cream

½ head lettuce, shredded or thinly sliced

¾ pound shredded Mexican cheese

3 cups chopped tomatoes

1 bunch small green onions

1 (4.5-ounce) can sliced black olives

1. Brown ground beef in skillet. Drain if necessary. Add canned chili mix and heat until bubbling.
2. Reduce heat, keep warm, and allow to simmer gently a few minutes.
3. In greased 9" × 13" dish, place layer of corn chips topped with chili. Spread with sour cream. Add lettuce, shredded cheese, tomatoes, green onions, and black olives. Serve immediately.

🌀 **Makes 8–10 servings**

Ribollita

Ribollita means "re-boiled" in Italian. It's usually made with the leftovers of a vegetable soup, layered with bread and baked in the oven. This version is easier, and it's sublime.

6 slices bacon

3 tablespoons olive oil

2 onions, chopped

6 cloves garlic, minced

1 (6-ounce) can tomato paste

2 cups water

1½ teaspoons dried Italian seasoning

½ teaspoon pepper

4 carrots, sliced

4 russet potatoes, peeled and cubed

2 (15-ounce) cans cannellini beans, drained

2 (14-ounce) cans diced tomatoes, undrained

2 (32-ounce) boxes beef broth

8 (1-inch) thick slices Italian bread

¼ cup olive oil

1½ cups grated Parmesan cheese, divided

1 (16-ounce) bag frozen cut leaf spinach, thawed

1. In large skillet cook bacon until crisp. Remove bacon from skillet, drain on paper towels, crumble, and refrigerate. Remove all but 2 tablespoons drippings from skillet. Add olive oil.

2. Cook onions and garlic in drippings and olive oil until crisp-tender, about 5 minutes. Add tomato paste, stir, and then let cook until tomato paste begins to brown in spots. Add 2 cups water, Italian seasoning, and pepper; cook and stir to loosen drippings from pan.

3. In 7-quart slow cooker, layer carrots, potatoes, and beans. Add mixture from skillet along with canned tomatoes and beef broth. Cover and cook on low for 8–9 hours or until potatoes and carrots are tender.

4. Preheat oven to 400°F. Cut bread into 1" cubes and place on cookie sheet. Drizzle with ¼ cup olive oil and ½ cup cheese; toss to coat. Toast bread in the oven until golden brown, about 10–15 minutes.

5. Stir spinach and bread cubes into soup. Cover and cook on high for 25–35 minutes or until bread dissolves into the soup. Serve with remaining cheese.

❧ **Makes 14–16 servings**

Wild Rice–Cheese Chowder

Bacon flavors this delicious and thick stew, which features tender wild rice. It's a meal all in one pot.

6 slices bacon

2 tablespoons butter

2 onions, chopped

6 cloves garlic, minced

3 tablespoons flour

1 teaspoon salt

¼ teaspoon pepper

1 teaspoon dried tarragon leaves

4 cups water

2 cups wild rice

1 (16-ounce) bag baby carrots

1 (32-ounce) box beef broth

2 cups frozen corn

2 cups apple juice

3 cups shredded Swiss cheese

2 tablespoons cornstarch

1½ cups light cream

⅓ cup chopped flat-leaf parsley

1. In large skillet, cook bacon until crisp. Drain bacon on paper towels, crumble, and set aside in refrigerator. Add butter to skillet; cook onion and garlic until crisp-tender, about 5–6 minutes.
2. Add flour, salt, pepper, and tarragon to skillet; cook and stir until bubbly. Add water and bring to a simmer, stirring frequently.
3. Place wild rice in 6-quart slow cooker. Top with baby carrots and onion mixture. Pour in beef broth, corn, and apple juice.
4. Cover and cook on low for 7–8 hours or until rice is tender. In large bowl, toss cheese with cornstarch. Stir into slow cooker along with cream and reserved bacon.
5. Cover and cook on high for 20–30 minutes or until cheese is melted and chowder is thick. Sprinkle with parsley and serve.

🍲 **Makes 12–14 servings**

Yet he commanded the skies above, and opened the doors of heaven; he rained down on them manna to eat, and gave them the grain of heaven. Mortals ate of the bread of angels; he sent them food in abundance.

—Psalms 78:23–25

Classic Beef Barley Stew

Barley is a wonderful grain; it's chewy and nutty tasting. In this hearty stew, with beef and vegetables, it's filling and warming.

2 pounds beef stew meat, cubed

¼ cup flour

2 teaspoons paprika

1 teaspoon salt

¼ teaspoon pepper

2 tablespoons olive oil

1 tablespoon butter

2 onions, chopped

4 cloves garlic, minced

1 (16-ounce) bag baby carrots

1 (8-ounce) package sliced fresh mushrooms

1 cup medium pearl barley

1 (32-ounce) box beef broth

4 cups water

2 bay leaves

1. Trim excess fat from stew meat. On large plate, combine flour, paprika, salt, and pepper; mix well. Toss beef in this mixture to coat.
2. Heat olive oil and butter in large skillet. Add beef cubes; brown, stirring, on all sides, about 5–6 minutes.
3. Remove beef from skillet and place in 6-quart slow cooker. Add onions and garlic to skillet; cook and stir until crisp-tender, about 5 minutes, stirring to loosen pan drippings.
4. Add onions and garlic to slow cooker. Add all remaining ingredients. Cover and cook on low for 7–9 hours or until barley and vegetables are tender. Remove bay leaves and serve.

❧ **Makes 10–12 servings**

And when the dew fell upon the camp in the night, the manna fell upon it.

—Numbers 11:9

Mexican Stew

The heat in jalapeños is contained in the seeds and membranes. If you remove those, the stew will be milder. Top with guacamole and sour cream for a cooling contrast.

1 pound ground beef

1 pound spicy bulk pork sausage

2 cups chopped chorizo sausage

2 onions, chopped

6 cloves garlic, minced

2 or 3 jalapeño peppers, minced

1 (15-ounce) can tomato sauce

3 cups tomato juice

3 cups beef broth

3 (14-ounce) cans diced tomatoes

2 tablespoons chili powder

1 teaspoon cumin

1 teaspoon salt

1/4 teaspoon pepper

1/8 teaspoon cayenne pepper

2 (15-ounce) can chili beans, undrained

1. In skillet, cook ground beef and pork sausage until done, stirring to break up meat. Drain well.
2. Meanwhile, combine chorizo, onions, garlic, and jalapeño peppers in 6- or 7-quart slow cooker. Add meat mixture from skillet; then add remaining ingredients.
3. Cover and cook on low for 7–9 hours or until soup is blended and thick. Serve with guacamole and sour cream for toppings.

🍲 **Makes 18–20**

Mystery Stew

You'll enjoy this stew, although it's a mystery to me why it's named mystery stew. It's a superb choice for a big family dinner or a potluck.

2 pounds ground turkey

2 cups diced celery

1 cup chopped onion

4 cups tomato juice

1 (1.25-ounce) package chili seasoning mix

2 (16-ounce) cans French-cut green beans

1 (14.5-ounce) can diced carrots, drained

1 (10-ounce) package frozen corn, thawed

1. Brown celery and onion with the ground turkey.
2. Drain and add turkey mixture to tomato juice in large pan.
3. Add seasoning mix and enough water to make slightly soupy.
4. Bring to a boil and simmer about 15 minutes.
5. Add green beans, carrots, and corn.
6. Simmer for 15 minutes more.

🍲 **Makes 6–8 cups**

Oyster Stew

Oyster stew is traditional for Christmas Eve in the eastern United States. This version is rich and creamy, and so easily made in the slow cooker. The combination of smoked and canned oysters adds a great depth of flavor.

½ cup butter

2 onions, chopped

6 cloves garlic, minced

4 (8-ounce) cans whole oysters

6 stalks celery, sliced

3 potatoes, peeled and cubed

1 teaspoon salt

¼ teaspoon white pepper

1 (32-ounce) box chicken stock

2 cups water

3 (12-ounce) cans evaporated milk

3 (3-ounce) packages smoked oysters

¼ cup cornstarch

1 cup heavy cream

1 (8-ounce) package cream cheese, cubed

⅓ cup minced chives

1. In large skillet melt butter over medium heat. Add onions and garlic; cook and stir until crisp-tender, about 5 minutes.
2. Meanwhile, drain oysters, reserving juice. Cover oysters and refrigerate. Pour juice into skillet; cook and stir until mixture bubbles.
3. Place celery and potatoes in a 6- to 7-quart slow cooker. Top with salt, pepper, onion mixture, chicken stock, water, and evaporated milk.
4. Cover and cook on low for 7–9 hours or until potatoes are tender. Stir in both types of oysters. In medium bowl, combine cornstarch and cream and mix well. Stir into slow cooker along with cubed cream cheese.
5. Cover and cook on high for 20–30 minutes or until stew is thickened and oysters are hot. Stir to blend. Serve with chives and oyster crackers.

❦ **Makes 10–14 servings**

On the fourth day they got up early in the morning, and he prepared to go, but the girl's father said to his son-in-law, "Fortify yourself with a bit of food, and after that you may go."

—*Judges 19:5*

Shrimp and Corn Chowder

This thick and creamy chowder should be served in small portions. It's delicious as the meal starter for a more formal dinner.

6 slices bacon

2 tablespoons butter

2 onions, chopped

6 cloves garlic, minced

2 leeks, sliced

4 potatoes, peeled and cubed

1½ teaspoons seasoned salt

¼ teaspoon white pepper

1 teaspoon Old Bay Seasoning

1 (32-ounce) box chicken broth

3 cups water

1 (16-ounce) package frozen corn

¼ cup cornstarch

1 cup heavy cream

2 pounds frozen cooked shrimp, thawed

⅓ cup chopped flat-leaf parsley

1. In large skillet, cook bacon until crisp. Drain bacon on paper towels, crumble, and set aside in refrigerator.
2. Add butter to skillet; cook onions, garlic, and leeks for 4–5 minutes to loosen pan drippings. Place in 5- or 6-quart slow cooker along with potatoes.
3. Add salt, pepper, Old Bay, chicken broth, water, and corn. Stir gently, then cover and cook on low for 7–9 hours or until potatoes are tender.
4. In bowl, combine cornstarch with cream; mix well. Stir into slow cooker along with shrimp. Cover and cook on high for 20–30 minutes or until stew is thick and shrimp is hot and tender. Sprinkle with reserved bacon and parsley and serve.

🍲 **Makes 10–12 servings**

Spicy Black Bean Chili

Chipotles are smoked jalapeño peppers canned in adobo sauce. Serve with chopped tomatoes, sour cream, Cheddar cheese, and corn chips.

1½ pounds spicy bulk pork sausage

2 onions, chopped

6 cloves garlic, minced

2 jalapeño peppers, minced

1 tablespoon chopped chipotle peppers

1 (4-ounce) can chopped green chiles, undrained

4 (15-ounce) cans black beans

2 (14-ounce) cans diced tomatoes

2 cups frozen corn

2 (32-ounce) boxes beef broth

2 tablespoons chili powder

1 teaspoon cumin

1 teaspoon salt

¼ teaspoon pepper

¼ teaspoon cayenne pepper

3 tablespoons cornstarch

1 cup apple juice

1. Cook sausage until done, stirring to break up meat. Place in 6- or 7-quart slow cooker along with onions, garlic, jalapeño peppers, chipotle peppers, and green chiles.

2. Drain two cans of the beans and add to slow cooker. Add the other two cans of beans, including liquid. Stir in tomatoes, corn, beef broth, and seasonings.

3. Cover and cook on low for 8 hours or until chili is blended. In bowl, combine cornstarch and apple juice and stir well. Stir into slow cooker.

4. Cover and cook on high for 20–30 minutes. Stir well and serve with toppings.

❀ **Makes 12–14 servings**

Split Pea Chowder

This soup is puréed right in the slow cooker. Be sure to use an immersion blender approved for use with stoneware. If you can't find one, just mash the ingredients before stirring in the cream and Canadian bacon.

2 onions, chopped

6 cloves garlic, minced

1 pound green split peas, rinsed

4 potatoes, peeled and cubed

1 ham hock

1 teaspoon salt

¼ teaspoon pepper

1 teaspoon dried tarragon leaves

4 cups water

1 (32-ounce) box chicken broth

1½ cups heavy cream

¼ cup cornstarch

2 cups cubed Canadian bacon

1. Combine onions, garlic, split peas, potatoes, and ham hock in 6- or 7-quart slow cooker. Sprinkle with salt, pepper, and tarragon. Pour water and chicken broth over all.

2. Cover and cook on low for 7–9 hours or until potatoes and peas are tender. Remove ham hock and cut off meat; reserve. Discard ham bone.

3. Turn off slow cooker. Using an immersion blender or potato masher, mash the ingredients in the slow cooker until desired consistency.

4. In small bowl, combine cream with cornstarch; stir into slow cooker along with Canadian bacon and meat from ham hock. Cover and cook on high for 20–30 minutes longer or until chowder is thick and meat is hot.

❧ **Makes 12–14 servings**

Lamb–Sweet Potato Stew

Fresh rosemary is really essential to this stew. Dried rosemary tends to be very spiky and hard, with a more subtle flavor; don't substitute it for fresh in this recipe.

3 pounds boneless lamb stew meat, cubed

1½ teaspoons seasoned salt

½ teaspoon pepper

⅓ cup flour

2 tablespoons butter

2 tablespoons olive oil

3 cups water

4 sweet potatoes, peeled and cubed

2 (16-ounce) packages baby carrots

2 onions, sliced

1 (32-ounce) box beef broth

2 fresh rosemary sprigs

2 fresh thyme sprigs

¼ cup cornstarch

1 cup apple cider

3 cups frozen cut green beans, thawed

1. Trim excess fat from lamb. On shallow plate, combine salt, pepper, and flour; mix well. Dredge lamb cubes in this mixture to coat.
2. In large skillet, heat butter and olive oil over medium heat. Add lamb; cook and stir until browned, about 5–6 minutes. Remove lamb to 7-quart slow cooker.
3. Add water to skillet; cook and stir to loosen pan drippings. Pour over lamb. Add sweet potatoes, carrots, and onions to slow cooker. Pour in broth and bury rosemary and thyme sprigs in broth.
4. Cover and cook on low for 8–9 hours or until potatoes are tender and lamb registers 160°F. In small bowl combine cornstarch and cider; stir into stew along with green beans. Cover and cook on high for 20–30 minutes or until stew is thickened and hot. Remove rosemary and thyme stems, stir, and serve immediately.

☙ **Makes 12–14 servings**

Then Abigail hurried and took two hundred loaves, two skins of wine, five sheep ready dressed, five measures of parched grain, one hundred clusters of raisins, and two hundred cakes of figs.

—1 Samuel 25:18

Pork and Cabbage Stew

Cabbage adds great flavor and nutrition to this hearty stew, which is full of vegetables. Using red and green cabbage also adds color!

2 pounds bulk pork sausage

3 cups water

3 onions, chopped

5 carrots, sliced

4 potatoes, sliced

2 cups chopped green cabbage

2 cups chopped red cabbage

1 (32-ounce) box chicken broth

3 tablespoons apple cider vinegar

3 tablespoons brown sugar

1 teaspoon salt

¼ teaspoon pepper

1 teaspoon dried marjoram leaves

1 teaspoon dried basil leaves

2 (14-ounce) cans diced tomatoes, undrained

½ cup potato flakes

1. In large skillet, cook pork sausage until done, stirring to break up meat. Drain pork well and place in 7-quart slow cooker. Do not wipe out skillet.

2. Add water to skillet and bring to a boil, stirring to loosen pan drippings. Remove from heat.

3. Layer onions, carrots, potatoes, and both kinds of cabbage in slow cooker. Pour skillet mixture over vegetables, along with chicken broth and all remaining ingredients except potato flakes.

4. Cover and cook on low for 7–9 hours or until potatoes and cabbage are tender. Stir in potato flakes; cover and cook on high for 30 minutes longer until mixture is thickened. Serve immediately.

❧ **Makes 12–14 servings**

Salmon Chowder

Salmon packaged in a pouch already has the skin and bones removed, saving you a lot of work. This creamy chowder is a great way to showcase this fish.

6 slices bacon

2 onions, chopped

4 cloves garlic, minced

4 potatoes, peeled and cubed

4 cups frozen corn

1 (32-ounce) box chicken broth

2 cups water

1 teaspoon dried thyme leaves

½ teaspoon dried dill weed

1 teaspoon salt

¼ teaspoon white pepper

1½ cups heavy cream

½ cup whole milk

⅓ cup potato flakes

4 (7.1-ounce) pouches salmon, drained

1. In large skillet, cook bacon until crisp. Drain bacon on paper towel, crumble, and refrigerate. Add onions and garlic to skillet; cook and stir for 5 minutes to loosen pan drippings.
2. Place potatoes and corn in 6- or 7-quart slow cooker. Add onion mixture to slow cooker along with broth, water, thyme, dill weed, salt, and pepper. Cover and cook on low for 7–9 hours or until potatoes are tender.

3. Stir in cream, milk, potato flakes, salmon, and reserved bacon. Cover and cook on high for 20–30 minutes or until chowder is thick and hot. Serve immediately.

❧ **Makes 12–14 servings**

But the father said to his slaves, "Quickly, bring out a robe—the best one—and put it on him; put a ring on his finger and sandals on his feet. And get the fatted calf and kill it, and let us eat and celebrate; for this son of mine was dead and is alive again; he was lost and is found!" And they began to celebrate.

—Luke 15:22–24

Cheddar Chowder

Kids may call this "cheese soup," and it may become one of their favorites. It's one of the few ways you can get them to eat vegetables, so double the carrots and the celery given in this recipe.

2 cups boiling water

2 cups chopped potatoes

½ cup chopped carrots

½ cup chopped celery

¼ cup chopped onion

1 cup ham, cut into cubes

¼ cup margarine

2 cups milk

¼ cup flour

2 cups shredded Cheddar cheese

1. In large pan, combine water, vegetables, and ham. Cover and simmer 10 to 20 minutes or until vegetables are tender.
2. In saucepan, melt margarine and add flour; stir until bubbly. Gradually add milk with wire whisk and stir until thickened. Add cheese and stir until melted. Pour into vegetable and ham mixture.
3. Heat for 10 minutes.

 Makes 6–8 cups

Creamy Corn Chowder

Red peppers seem to taste sweeter when they simmer in this "soup pot." This is even more American than apple pie.

1 cup chopped onions

½ cup chopped red bell pepper

½ teaspoon of minced jarred garlic

1 tablespoon butter or margarine

2 medium peeled potatoes, cut into ½" cubes

2 (14.5-ounce) cans chicken broth

1 (15-ounce) can cream-style corn

¼ teaspoon pepper

½ cup half-and-half

1 tablespoon chopped parsley

1. Combine onion, bell pepper, garlic, and butter in skillet and cook until tender. Add potatoes, chicken broth, corn, and pepper to mixture.
2. Cook, stirring occasionally, on medium heat for 30–40 minutes or until potatoes are tender. Stir in half-and-half until heated through. Sprinkle with parsley and serve.

 Makes 6–8 servings

Cowboy Chili

True Texas chili doesn't contain tomatoes, onions, or beans—but some people don't think it's chili without them. Serve with sour cream and shredded cheese for toppings.

3 pounds beef chuck steak

2 teaspoons salt

¼ teaspoon pepper

⅓ cup flour

1 teaspoon dried oregano leaves

3 tablespoons olive oil

3 cups water

2 onions, chopped

4 cloves garlic, minced

2 tablespoons chili powder

1 (32-ounce) box beef broth

1 (15-ounce) can chili beans, undrained

2 (15-ounce) cans kidney beans, drained

1. Trim excess fat from steak and cut into 2" cubes. On shallow plate, combine salt, pepper, flour, and oregano; mix well. Toss steak cubes in flour mixture.

2. In skillet, heat olive oil over medium heat. Brown steak cubes in oil for 5–6 minutes, stirring occasionally. Place meat in 5- or 6-quart slow cooker.

3. Add water to skillet; cook and stir until mixture boils, stirring to loosen pan drippings. Pour into slow cooker.

4. Add all remaining ingredients. Cover and cook on low for 8–9 hours or until steak is very tender.

✿ **Makes 12–14 servings**

I am the living bread which came down from heaven: if any man eat of this bread, he shall live forever: and the bread that I will give is my flesh, which I will give for the life of the world.

—John 6:51

Chicken and Turkey Entrées

⚜

Chicken is inexpensive, satisfying, and adapts to any cuisine. My mother makes the best fried chicken, but she never used the slow cooker. I use the slow cooker all the time for moist and tender chicken, flavored in umpteen ways. Any of the following recipes could be easily changed to suit local flavors or produce.

Some of these recipes call for chicken that has already been cooked. The slow cooker is the ideal way to cook plain chicken. For boneless, skinless chicken breasts, follow instructions for Poached Chicken Breasts and Broth (page 413). For bone-in, skin-on chicken breasts, place in slow cooker and add a cup of chicken broth or water. Cover and cook on low for 7–9 hours until internal temperature reaches 170°F. Boneless chicken thighs and legs should cook for 7–9 hours; bone-in thighs and legs for 8–9 hours.

Remove the cooked chicken from the slow cooker and let cool for 10–15 minutes until cool enough to handle. Then pull or cut meat from bones and shred by hand or chop with a knife. Refrigerate or freeze promptly.

Always use a food thermometer to make sure you cook chicken thoroughly, to the proper temperature. Chicken breasts should be cooked to 165°F, dark meat chicken to 170°F, and whole chickens to 180°F. Also be careful handling raw chicken. Be sure to wash your hands, countertops, and utensils thoroughly with hot soapy water after contact with raw poultry.

Everyone has his or her own favorite family holiday recipes for turkey and stuffing. You can make them together in the slow cooker for real ease. If you want to roast a turkey or two in the oven for a Christmas or Thanksgiving banquet, think about making some slow cooker dressings from page 284 (Side Dishes), not only for food safety, but because that will allow you to offer a selection of dressings to suit everyone's tastes!

—Linda Larsen

Honey Mustard Chicken

This chicken dish is always a hit with the adults as well as the kids. Make plenty—it'll disappear quickly. It is good served at room temperature.

¼ cup light mayonnaise

¼ cup Dijonnaise

2 tablespoons honey

¼ teaspoon salt

2 pounds chicken tenders

2 cups corn flakes or crushed crackers

1. Preheat oven to 350°.
2. In medium bowl, combine mayonnaise, Dijonnaise, honey, and salt.
3. Coat chicken with above mixture and roll in crumbs.
4. Spray 9" × 13" baking dish with vegetable cooking spray. Place coated chicken in baking dish. Bake at 350° for 1 hour, and test for doneness.

Makes 8–10 servings

Honey Mustard Turkey Roast

A turkey roast is a nice entrée to serve after a Bible study gathering on Sunday afternoon. Round out this meal with cooked carrots, a green salad, and crisp breadsticks.

1 (3-pound) turkey roast, thawed if frozen

3 onions, sliced

4 cloves garlic, minced

¼ cup honey

3 tablespoons Dijon mustard

1 teaspoon dried thyme leaves

½ teaspoon salt

¼ teaspoon pepper

1 cup chicken broth

½ cup apple cider

2 tablespoons cornstarch

1. Cut the turkey in half lengthwise to make two equal pieces. Place onions in bottom of 4- or 5-quart slow cooker and top with turkey.
2. In a bowl, combine garlic, honey, mustard, thyme, salt, and pepper. Rub over turkey. Pour chicken broth into slow cooker, cover, and cook on low for 6 hours or until meat thermometer registers 170°F.
3. Remove turkey and onions from slow cooker. In small bowl, combine cider and cornstarch; mix well. Add to liquid remaining in slow cooker; cook on high for 15 minutes or until thickened.

(continued)

(Honey Mustard Turkey Roast—continued)

4. Meanwhile, slice the turkey. Return turkey and onions to slow cooker; cook for 10–15 minutes longer until hot. Serve immediately.

❧ **Makes 12 servings**

Potluck Pointer

Think beyond parsley when garnishing your foods. Other herb sprigs or flowers make a lovely addition to your meat, pasta, fruit, and sandwich platters for a gathering. Some, like nasturtium and violets, are not only colorful, but edible! Try sage, delicate tarragon, leafy oregano, darkly bright rosemary . . . use your imagination.

Chicken and Potato Hot Dish

The easiest way to thaw the potatoes is to let the package stand in the refrigerator overnight. Then drain and mix with the other ingredients.

12 boneless, skinless chicken thighs, cubed

2 onions, chopped

3 cloves garlic, minced

2 (4-ounce) jars sliced mushrooms, undrained

2 green bell peppers, chopped

2 cups frozen corn kernels

1 (32 ounce) package frozen hash brown potatoes, thawed

2 (10.75-ounce) cans cream of chicken soup

1 cup chicken broth

1 cup barbecue sauce

½ cup grated Parmesan cheese

1. In 6-quart slow cooker, combine chicken, onions, garlic, mushrooms, bell peppers, corn, and potatoes; mix well.
2. In medium bowl, combine remaining ingredients except cheese; mix well. Pour into slow cooker. Cover and cook on low for 9–10 hours or until chicken is thoroughly cooked. Stir once during cooking time. Add cheese, stir again, and serve immediately.

❧ **Makes 8–10 servings**

Slow Cooker Chicken and Cheese Soufflé

This recipe is like a cross between a soufflé and a strata. It's hearty and comforting and mildly flavored.

8 cups cubed French bread

2 cups shredded Cheddar cheese

1 cup cubed Havarti cheese

3 cups cubed cooked chicken

1 tablespoon olive oil

1 onion, chopped

1 red bell pepper, chopped

1 (3-ounce) package cream cheese

1 (13-ounce) can evaporated milk

½ cup whole milk

½ teaspoon dried thyme leaves

½ teaspoon salt

⅛ teaspoon white pepper

6 eggs, beaten

2 tablespoons grated Parmesan cheese

½ teaspoon paprika

1. In 5-quart slow cooker, combine bread with Cheddar, Havarti, and cubed cooked chicken; set aside.

2. In medium saucepan, heat olive oil over medium heat. Add onion; cook and stir for 3 minutes. Add red bell pepper; cook and stir for 2 minutes longer. Add to slow cooker and toss gently to combine with bread mixture.

3. Mix cream cheese and evaporated milk in saucepan; cook and stir over low heat until cheese melts. Remove from heat and beat in whole milk, thyme, salt, and pepper. Beat in eggs until smooth.

4. Pour into slow cooker and let stand for 15 minutes. Sprinkle with Parmesan cheese and paprika. Cover and cook on low for 3½–4½ hours or until soufflé is set. Serve immediately.

🍂 **Makes 8 servings**

Scalloped Chicken

This hearty casserole is a combination of stuffing, gravy, and chicken, all in one! Serve with a fruit salad for a complete meal for a Ladies Aid meeting.

3 tablespoons butter

1 onion, chopped

1 cup chopped, cored apple

3 cups soft bread crumbs

½ cup coarsely chopped pecans

½ cup raisins

¼ cup butter

¼ cup flour

1 teaspoon salt

⅛ teaspoon pepper

3 cups chicken stock

1 cup light cream

4 cups chopped cooked chicken

1. Spray a 4 quart slow cooker with nonstick cooking spray and set aside. In large skillet, melt 3 tablespoons butter over medium heat. Add onion; cook and stir until tender, about 5 minutes. Add apple; cook and stir for 2 minutes longer.
2. Add bread crumbs to skillet, and toss to coat. Stir in pecans and raisins; set aside.
3. In large saucepan, melt ¼ cup butter over medium heat. Add flour, salt, and pepper. Cook and stir until flour begins to brown, about 8–10 minutes. Stir in chicken stock and cream; cook and stir until sauce bubbles and thickens.
4. Layer half of bread crumb mixture, half of cooked chicken, and half of sauce in prepared slow cooker. Repeat layers.
5. Cover and cook on low for 7–9 hours or until casserole is set and bubbling. Serve immediately.

❧ **Makes 8 servings**

Escalloped Chicken

Nostalgic recipes can instantly bring you back to your younger days. This is one such recipe. It was offered at the cafeteria in the union at Purdue University where escalloped chicken was one of their best dishes. The days of the cafeteria are over, but memories linger on.

1 rotisserie chicken purchased from store

4 tablespoons flour

4 tablespoons butter

1 quart chicken broth

¼ teaspoon pepper

1 teaspoon salt

1½ quarts dry bread crumbs

2 beaten eggs

1 stalk celery, chopped

2 tablespoons onion, chopped

4 tablespoons butter or margarine, melted

1. Remove skin from chicken. Remove meat and cut into bite size pieces.
2. Place chicken in buttered 9" × 13" baking dish.
3. Melt butter over medium heat in skillet.
4. Add flour and stir until bubbly, gradually blending in broth with wire whisk.
5. Add pepper and salt and remove gravy from heat.
6. In medium bowl, combine bread crumbs, eggs, celery, onion, and butter.
7. Spoon bread crumb mixture over chicken.
8. Pour gravy over bread mixture.
9. Bake at 350° for 30–40 minutes.

❦ **Makes 8–10 servings**

Pam's Escalloped Chicken

Here's another escalloped chicken recipe. It's very easy, especially when you use the rotisserie chicken from your local grocery store.

1 large rotisserie chicken purchased from store

2½ cups croutons

Salt and pepper

1 pint whipping cream

1½ cups chicken broth

1. Remove chicken from bone. Place chicken in greased 9" × 13" baking dish. Scatter croutons over chicken. Add salt and pepper to taste.
2. Pour 1 pint whipping cream over chicken then pour chicken broth over whipping cream.
3. Bake at 325° for 40–50 minutes, then at 350° for 10 more minutes or until lightly browned.

❧ **Makes 8–10 servings**

Slow Cooker Chicken à la King

Chicken à la King is a classic recipe that's comforting and easy to make. And everybody loves it!

3 pounds chicken tenders, cut in half

1 (16-ounce) package baby carrots

2 red bell peppers, chopped

2 onions, chopped

3 cloves garlic, minced

1 (8-ounce) package cream cheese, cut into cubes

2 (16-ounce) jars four-cheese Alfredo sauce

1 cup milk

1 (10-ounce) can cream of chicken soup

1 teaspoon dried basil leaves

⅛ teaspoon pepper

Hot cooked noodles, mashed potatoes, biscuits, or baked puff pastry shells

1. Place chicken tenders in 5–6-quart slow cooker. Add carrots, bell peppers, onions, and garlic; mix gently.
2. In food processor or blender, combine cream cheese with Alfredo sauce and milk; process or blend until combined. Pour into large bowl and add cream of chicken soup, basil, and pepper. Mix well.
3. Pour sauce into slow cooker. Cover and cook on low for 7–9 hours or until chicken and vegetables are tender. Serve over hot cooked noodles, mashed potatoes, biscuits, or baked puff pastry shells.

❧ **Makes 8–10 servings**

Slow Cooker Chicken Divan

Mushrooms and bell pepper add color, texture, and flavor to this easy recipe. It's a delicious casserole that will please adults and kids alike.

4 cups fresh broccoli florets

2 tablespoons lemon juice

2 onions, chopped

1 (8-ounce) package sliced mushrooms

2 red bell peppers, chopped

5 cups chopped cooked chicken

2 (10-ounce) cans cream of broccoli soup

1 cup light cream

2 cups shredded Swiss cheese

1. Toss broccoli with lemon juice. Place in bottom of 6-quart slow cooker. Top with onions, mushrooms, bell peppers, and chicken.
2. In medium bowl, combine soup with cream and cheese; mix until blended. Pour into slow cooker.
3. Cover and cook on low for 5–6 hours or until thoroughly heated. Stir well, then serve.

❦ **Makes 8 servings**

Chicken Asparagus Supreme

This is especially great with fresh asparagus. If you use fresh, be sure to precook it for about 5 to 10 minutes before putting it in the baking dish. It's also good with white asparagus.

2 (8-ounce) packages frozen asparagus spears, drained and cooked

5 cups cooked cut-up chicken

2 (10.75-ounce) cans cream of chicken soup

1 cup mayonnaise

1 teaspoon lemon juice

8 ounces shredded Cheddar cheese

1 cup corn flake crumbs

Butter

1. Cover bottom of greased 9" × 13" casserole dish with asparagus spears, then cover asparagus with cut-up chicken.
2. Mix soup with mayonnaise and lemon juice. Pour mixture over chicken and sprinkle with grated cheese.
3. Top with corn flake crumbs and dot generously with butter. Bake at 350° for 30 minutes or until golden brown and bubbly.

❦ **Makes 8–10 servings**

Chicken Artichoke Casserole

This recipe was taken from a local Friends of the Library collection. Its blend of flavors is sure to please.

4 whole chicken breasts, skinless and cut into bite-size pieces
1 teaspoon paprika
½ cup butter
1 cup chopped onion
15 large mushrooms, sliced
2 (16-ounce) cans artichoke hearts in marinade
1 teaspoon tarragon
1½ tablespoons butter
1½ tablespoons flour
2 cups chicken broth
¼ cup sherry

1. Season chicken with paprika.
2. In large skillet, sauté onion in butter and add mushrooms. Add chicken to skillet and sauté for about 5–10 minutes. Add artichoke hearts and tarragon.
3. Make roux with butter and flour.
4. In saucepan, bring chicken broth to boil. Add boiling chicken broth and sherry to roux, stirring with wire whisk to blend smoothly. Pour over the chicken mixture. Bake in a greased 9" × 13" casserole at 350° for 45 minutes.

Makes 6–8 servings

Chicken Broccoli Casserole

Chicken and broccoli—do any ingredients say "potluck" more than these do? Prepare this "makes 12 servings" recipe for your next gathering, or cook it for Sunday supper and enjoy the leftovers throughout the week.

16 ounces cream cheese

2 cups milk

1½ teaspoons garlic powder

½ teaspoon salt

5 chicken breasts

3 (16-ounce) packages frozen chopped broccoli, thawed

1 cup Parmesan

1. Simmer cream cheese, milk, garlic powder, and salt on low heat until smooth.
2. Boil chicken until done, about 20–30 minutes.
3. Chop chicken into 1" pieces.
4. Cook broccoli for 3 to 5 minutes then drain.
5. Combine chicken and broccoli. Add ½ cup Parmesan cheese and sauce. Put mixture into 9" × 13" baking dish and top with ½ cup Parmesan. Bake covered at 350° for 25–30 minutes.

☙ **Makes 12 servings**

Bride's Never-Fail Company Chicken

This incredible good old southern recipe is rich, smooth, and hearty. Sometimes just plain *good* food tastes best.

8–10 pieces chicken, either cut-up pieces or chicken breasts

8–10 slices Swiss cheese

1 (10.75-ounce) can cream of chicken soup

¼ cup cooking white wine

½ package or more Pepperidge Farm Original Stuffing Mix

¼ cup melted margarine

1. Grease a baking dish that will accommodate the pieces lying flat and place chicken in dish. Lay a slice of cheese over the top of each piece of chicken.
2. Mix soup and wine and spoon over chicken and cheese. Spread the stuffing over the top of the chicken.
3. Drizzle the melted margarine over the stuffing.
4. Bake at 360° for 30–40 minutes for boneless pieces, 45–55 minutes for chicken with bones.

☙ **Makes 8–10 servings**

Chicken à la Ritz

The Ritz crackers on this chicken dish give it just the right crunch. Surprise one of your busy friends with this dish for dinner. You'll make her day!

10 chicken breasts

2 (10.75-ounce) cans cream of chicken soup

1 cup sour cream

32 Ritz crackers, crushed

2 teaspoons poppy seeds

6 tablespoons melted butter

1. Cut chicken into bite-size pieces and place in greased 9" × 13" baking dish.
2. Mix together soup and sour cream and pour over chicken. Sprinkle crackers on top and then poppy seeds on top of crackers. Drizzle butter over crackers.
3. Bake at 350° uncovered for 30–40 minutes, until bubbly around the sides.
4. Serve over rice if desired.

☙ **Makes 8–10 servings**

Glazed Chicken with Blueberry Chutney

Make the chutney at the same time you're making the chicken if you wish to serve it as a warm sauce, or make it ahead of time and refrigerate for the contrast of a cold sauce.

2 onions, chopped

4 cloves garlic, minced

8 boneless, skinless chicken breasts

1 (6-ounce) container frozen lemonade concentrate, thawed

½ cup honey

1 teaspoon salt

⅛ teaspoon pepper

1 teaspoon ground ginger

2 cups Blueberry Raisin Chutney (page 11)

1. Place onions and garlic in bottom of a 5–6-quart slow cooker. Top with chicken breasts.
2. In small bowl combine lemonade concentrate, honey, salt, pepper, and ginger; mix well. Pour into slow cooker.
3. Cover and cook on low for 5–7 hours or until chicken is thoroughly cooked. Drain chicken, slice, and serve with Blueberry-Raisin Chutney.

☙ **Makes 8 servings**

Corn Bread and Cranberry–Stuffed Turkey Breast

Corn bread and cranberries make an all-American stuffing for a moist turkey breast in this twist on a classic recipe.

3 cups cubed corn bread

3 shallots, minced

1 leek, rinsed and chopped

¾ cup chopped fresh cranberries

½ cup dried cranberries

2 pears, peeled, cored, and chopped

⅓ cup butter, melted

½ cup mayonnaise

1 teaspoon dried thyme leaves

1 teaspoon salt

¼ teaspoon white pepper

1 (4-pound) boneless turkey breast, thawed

¼ cup fresh sage leaves

2 tablespoons butter, melted

1. Preheat oven to 350°F. Place cubed corn bread on a baking sheet in a single layer. Bake for 15–25 minutes or until crisp. Place in large bowl.
2. Add shallots, leek, fresh and dried cranberries, and pears; mix gently. Add ⅓ cup melted butter, mayonnaise, thyme, salt, and pepper. Mix to coat.
3. Place stuffing in a 6- to 7-quart slow cooker. Loosen skin from turkey breast. Place sage leaves in a decorative pattern on the turkey flesh; smooth skin back into place. Brush with 2 tablespoons melted butter. Place turkey on stuffing.
4. Cover slow cooker and cook on low for 8–10 hours or until turkey registers 170°F on a meat thermometer. Turn off slow cooker and let stand for 10 minutes; then slice turkey to serve. Serve with stuffing.

🍂 **Makes 8 servings**

Updated Chicken Cordon Bleu

Instead of being stuffed with ham and cheese, this tender chicken is wrapped in ham and served with a flavorful cheese sauce. Yum.

8 boneless, skinless chicken breasts

1 teaspoon salt

1/8 teaspoon white pepper

1 teaspoon dried thyme leaves

8 thin slices boiled ham

2 onions, chopped

4 cloves garlic, minced

1 (16-ounce) bag baby carrots

1 (16-ounce) jar Alfredo sauce

1 (10-ounce) can condensed chicken soup

2 cups shredded Swiss cheese

1. Sprinkle chicken breasts with salt, pepper, and thyme. Wrap a slice of ham around each breast and secure with toothpicks.
2. Place onion, garlic, and carrots in a 5- to 6-quart slow cooker. Top with wrapped chicken breasts.
3. In medium bowl, combine remaining ingredients. Pour into slow cooker. Cover and cook on low for 6–8 hours or until chicken is thoroughly cooked. Serve chicken and carrots with sauce.

❧ **Makes 8 servings**

Thai Chicken Drumsticks

For crisp skin, you have to brown these drumsticks after they are cooked. But that's easy to do under the broiler, and that step adds wonderful caramelized flavor to the finished dish.

4 pounds chicken drumsticks

2 onions, chopped

6 cloves garlic, minced

1/2 cup peanut butter

1 (14-ounce) can diced tomatoes, undrained

1 (6-ounce) can tomato paste

1/3 cup low-sodium soy sauce

1 cup chunky mild or medium salsa

2 tablespoons minced gingerroot

1/4 teaspoon pepper

1/2 teaspoon hot pepper sauce

2 cups chopped peanuts

1. Place drumsticks in a 6- to 7-quart slow cooker. Add onions and garlic. In medium bowl, stir together remaining ingredients except peanuts. Pour into slow cooker.
2. Cover and cook for 6–8 hours on low, or until internal temperature reaches 170°F. Remove chicken from slow cooker and roll each piece in the chopped peanuts. Arrange on broiler pan. Preheat broiler.
3. Broil chicken 6" from heat source, turning frequently, until browned, about 6–8 minutes. Serve immediately.

❧ **Makes 12 servings**

Chicken Oriental

French-fried onion rings, water chestnuts, and almonds give this dish a nice, crunchy taste. You can substitute chow mein noodles to give it more of an oriental twist, if you like.

¾ cup mayonnaise

2 teaspoons soy sauce

2 tablespoons lemon juice

1 cup diced onion

1½ cups thinly sliced celery

6 thinly sliced mushrooms

4 cups cooked chicken, diced

1 (8-ounce) can water chestnuts, drained

¼ cup slivered almonds

1 (3-ounce) can French-fried onion rings

1. Preheat oven to 350°.
2. Combine mayonnaise, soy sauce, and lemon juice in a large bowl. Mix well.
3. Spray skillet with cooking spray. Add onions, celery, and mushrooms, and sauté until tender for about 10 minutes. Stir in chicken, water chestnuts, and almonds.
4. Transfer to mayonnaise mixture and mix well.
5. Place in greased 8" × 8" baking dish. Bake for 30 minutes.
6. Sprinkle with onion rings. Bake 5–10 minutes more.

❦ **Makes 6 servings**

Turkey Tenderloin Curry

Turkey tenderloin is delicious when cooked with curry and chutney. Serve over lots of hot cooked rice.

2½ pounds turkey tenderloins

2 onions, chopped

1 (16-ounce) bag baby carrots

1 (16-ounce) can crushed pineapple, undrained

5 cloves garlic, minced

4 cups chicken broth

2 tablespoons curry powder

1 tablespoon grated gingerroot

½ teaspoon turmeric

1 teaspoon salt

¼ teaspoon pepper

1 (12-ounce) jar mango chutney

3 tablespoons cornstarch

½ cup apple juice

1. Cut turkey into 2" pieces. Place onions, carrots, pineapple, and garlic in a 5-quart slow cooker. Top with turkey pieces.
2. In medium bowl, combine chicken broth, curry powder, gingerroot, turmeric, salt, and pepper; mix well. Pour into slow cooker.

(continued)

(Turkey Tenderloin Curry—
continued)

3. Cover and cook on low for 6–8 hours or until vegetables are tender and turkey is thoroughly cooked. In bowl, combine chutney, cornstarch, and apple juice; mix well. Stir into slow cooker.
4. Cover and cook on high for 20–30 minutes. Stir thoroughly, then serve over hot cooked rice.

❦ **Makes 8–10 servings**

Potluck Pointer

Limp vegetables, dry cake, or soggy salads won't appeal to anyone. Make sure you use only the freshest ingredients for your recipe, and don't make the food too far ahead. Some frozen dishes will tolerate a few days' storage in your freezer, but other items are best when presented at their peak flavor and color.

Turkey Fettuccine

Most of the recipes in this book are easy and quick to prepare. This one can be prepared with chicken or ham or both. If you have a vegetarian in the family, try fixing it with mushrooms and artichoke hearts instead of meat.

1 pound turkey

½ cup chopped onion

½ cup chopped green pepper

1 (8-ounce) package cream cheese, cubed

1 (10.75-ounce) can cream of celery soup

½ cup water

½ cup milk

¼ teaspoon garlic salt

2 cups cooked fettuccine

½ cup Parmesan cheese

1. Preheat oven to 350°.
2. Brown turkey, onion, and green pepper in a large skillet until turkey is done. Drain any grease.
3. Stir in cream cheese, soup, water, milk, and garlic salt. Add noodles, and simmer over medium heat for about 10 minutes.
4. Put mixture into greased 9" × 13" baking dish. Sprinkle with Parmesan cheese. Bake for 20–30 minutes.

❦ **Makes 8–10 servings**

Chicken on Chipped Beef

A new twist on the traditional creamed chipped beef served over toast, this recipe blends the salted and smoked dried beef with bacon and chicken for a hearty, tasty meal.

1 (2.25-ounce) jar dried beef

8 boneless, skinless chicken breasts

8 strips bacon

1 (16-ounce) container sour cream

1 (10.75-ounce) can cream of mushroom soup

1. Line the bottom of a 9" × 13" pan with chipped dried beef.
2. Wrap boneless chicken breasts with strips of raw bacon.
3. In a bowl, mix sour cream and mushroom soup and pour over chicken.
4. Bake at 275° for 3 hours. Cover with foil for the first hour and a half; remove foil for remaining 1½ hours.

❧ **Makes 8–10 servings**

Alpine Chicken

Almonds add a healthy crunch to a family-favorite chicken dish. Add more if you care to.

4 cups cooked chicken, cut up

2 cups celery

2 cups bread crumbs

½ cup milk or broth

1 (8-ounce) package shredded Swiss cheese

1 cup Miracle Whip

¼ cup chopped onion

1 teaspoon salt

1 teaspoon pepper

¼ cup slivered almonds

1. Mix together all ingredients except almonds. Sprinkle almonds on top.
2. Pour into greased 9" × 13" baking dish.
3. Bake 40 minutes at 350°.

❧ **Makes 8–10 servings**

Stuffed Chicken

No longer do you have to flatten the chicken in this recipe. Thin chicken breasts are available in your local grocery store. If you can't find them and you want to save some time, ask your meat cutter at your grocer's to do the work for you while you do your shopping.

10 boneless chicken breast halves

10 slices deli ham

10 slices provolone cheese

½ cup flour

½ cup grated Parmesan cheese

1 teaspoon rubbed sage

¼ teaspoon paprika

Dash pepper

¼ cup vegetable oil

1 (10.75-ounce) can cream of celery soup

1 (10.75-ounce) can cream of chicken soup

1 cup chicken broth

1. Flatten chicken to ⅛" thickness. Place 1 slice of the ham and 1 slice of the cheese on each breast. Roll up and tuck in ends and secure with a toothpick.
2. Mix together the flour, Parmesan cheese, sage, paprika, and pepper. Dredge chicken in mixture. Cover and refrigerate for 1 hour.
3. In a large skillet, brown chicken in oil over medium-high heat. Place in 9" × 13" baking dish when done.
4. Combine soups and broth and pour over chicken. Bake in 9" × 13" baking dish at 325° for 30–45 minutes.

🍂 **Makes 10 servings**

Chicken–Spinach Roll-Ups

This is one of those quick recipes to fix when you're having a hectic day. It doesn't take long to prepare, and you can take a few minutes to unwind while it's baking in the oven.

2 (10.75-ounce) cans cream of chicken soup

2 cups sour cream

4 tablespoons Dijonnaise

1 cup minute rice

2 cups small curd cottage cheese

2 eggs

½ cup chopped onion

½ cup flour

1 (10-ounce) package chopped spinach, thawed and drained

20 slices deli chicken breast

½ cup breadcrumbs

1. Preheat oven to 350°.
2. In small bowl, combine soup, sour cream, and Dijonnaise.
3. In a medium-size bowl, mix half of the soup mixture with the rice, cottage cheese, eggs, onion, flour, and spinach.
4. Place 2 tablespoons of the mixture on each slice of chicken breast. Spread mixture with spoon and roll up.
5. Spray 11" × 17" baking dish with vegetable cooking spray. Placing seam side down, put chicken rolls in dish.
6. Top with remaining soup mixture and bread crumbs.
7. Bake for 30–35 minutes.

❦ **Makes 10**

And Solomon gave Hiram twenty thousand measures of wheat for food to his household, and twenty measures of pure oil: thus gave Solomon to Hiram year by year.

—1 Kings 5:11

Apple-Stuffed Chicken Rolls

Tender chicken stuffed with an apple-and-raisin mixture will be incredibly popular at your next potluck.

4 slices oatmeal bread

¾ cup finely chopped, cored, peeled apple

½ cup raisins

1 tablespoon lemon juice

2 tablespoons butter, melted

2 tablespoons sugar

½ teaspoon salt

8 boneless, skinless chicken breasts

2 onions, chopped

⅓ cup apple juice

½ teaspoon cinnamon

1. Toast bread until golden brown, then cut into cubes. In medium bowl, combine apple, raisins, lemon juice, melted butter, sugar, and salt; mix well. Stir in bread cubes.
2. Arrange chicken breasts on work surface. Pound gently with a meat mallet or rolling pin until ⅓" thick. Divide bread mixture among chicken breasts. Roll up chicken and secure with a toothpick.
3. Place onions in bottom of 6-quart slow cooker. Top with filled chicken rolls. In bowl, combine apple juice and cinnamon; spoon over chicken.
4. Cover and cook on low for 5–6 hours, or until chicken registers 165°F on food thermometer. Remove toothpicks and serve chicken with the cooked onions.

❧ **Makes 8**

Chicken and Wild Rice Salad

This easy recipe cooks the chicken and wild rice together, so all you have to do is add a dressing and a few more ingredients and then chill the salad.

2 cups wild rice

2 onions, chopped

8 boneless, skinless chicken breasts, cubed

4 cups chicken broth

2 cups apple juice

1 teaspoon salt

¼ teaspoon pepper

2 teaspoons dried thyme leaves

2 cups mayonnaise

1 cup yogurt

½ cup apple juice

2 cups small pecans

3 cups seedless red grapes

6 stalks celery, chopped

1. In 5-quart slow cooker, combine wild rice and onion. Place chicken on top. Sprinkle with salt, pepper, and thyme, then pour chicken broth and apple juice over all. Cover and cook on low for 6 hours or until wild rice is tender and chicken is cooked.

2. In large bowl, combine mayonnaise, yogurt, and apple juice. Remove chicken mixture from slow cooker using large slotted spoon or sieve and stir into mayonnaise mixture along with remaining ingredients. Cover and chill for 3–4 hours until cold. Stir gently before serving.

❦ **Makes 12 servings**

Chicken Tacos

Tacos are always fun, and when made with chicken they are delightfully different. Use your community's favorite toppings in this easy recipe.

2 onions, chopped

4 cloves garlic, minced

1 jalapeño pepper, minced

8 boneless, skinless chicken breasts

2 tablespoons chili powder

1 teaspoon cumin

1 teaspoon salt

¼ teaspoon cayenne pepper

1 cup chunky medium or hot salsa

1 (8-ounce) can tomato sauce

10–12 taco shells

2 cups grated Cheddar cheese

2 cups shredded lettuce

1 cup sour cream

1 cup chopped avocados

2 cups chopped tomatoes

1. In 5-quart slow cooker, combine onions, garlic, and jalapeño pepper. Sprinkle chicken with chili powder, cumin, salt, and cayenne pepper; place on top of onions.
2. Pour salsa and tomato sauce over all. Cover and cook on low for 6–7 hours or until chicken is thoroughly cooked.
3. Using two forks, shred chicken. Stir mixture in slow cooker.
4. Heat taco shells as directed on package. Serve chicken filling with the taco shells and remaining ingredients; let everyone make their own tacos.

❧ **Makes 8–10 servings**

Chicken Quiche

Enjoy this "anytime" recipe for breakfast, lunch, or dinner!

1/8 teaspoon white pepper

1 pound boneless, skinless chicken breasts, cut into bite-size pieces

1/4 cup vegetable oil

1 large peeled onion, thinly sliced and separated into rings

1 large tomato, peeled, seeded, cubed, and drained

3 eggs

3/4 cup milk

3/4 cup half-and-half

3/4 cup Gruyère cheese

1/4 cup Parmesan cheese

1 (10") partially baked pastry shell

1 teaspoon butter

1. Preheat oven to 375°. Sprinkle pepper over chicken, and sauté chicken in oil for 5–6 minutes. Remove from pan and set aside.
2. Add onion rings to skillet and cook over medium low heat until tender. Add tomato. Cook until tender.
3. Beat eggs and add milk, half-and-half, and cheeses. Arrange onion, tomato, and chicken in pie shell and pour egg mixture over all. Dot with butter. Bake at 375° for 35–40 minutes in the upper part of the oven.

Makes 8–10 servings

Tex-Mex Chicken

If you would like this dish a little spicier, add some jalapeños to it and it will be sure to clean out your sinuses.

1 (14-ounce) can fat-free chicken broth

1 (4-ounce) can drained chopped green chilies

1 cup chopped onion

1 cup fat-free sour cream

3/4 teaspoon salt

1/2 teaspoon cumin

1/2 teaspoon freshly ground black pepper

2 (10.5-ounce) cans condensed 98% fat-free cream of chicken soup

1 clove minced garlic

20–24 (6") corn tortillas

4 cups shredded cooked chicken breast

2 cups finely shredded Mexican blend cheese

1. Heat oven to 350°.
2. Coat a 9" × 13" baking dish with cooking spray.
3. In a large pan, combine broth, chilies, onion, sour cream, salt, cumin, pepper, soup, and garlic and mix well. Bring to boil, stirring constantly. Remove from heat. Spread 1 cup mixture in dish.

(continued)

4. Arrange 6 tortillas over soup mixture, breaking to fit dish. Top with 1 cup chicken and ½ cup cheese. Repeat layers, ending with the cheese. Spread remaining soup mixture over cheese. Bake 30 minutes or until bubbly.

🐾 **Makes 6–8 servings**

Chicken Jewel

If you need a recipe that comes together in just a few minutes and passes the family taste test, here's a jewel of a chicken casserole.

2 (10-ounce) cans of chicken breast, drained

½ cup chopped onion

1½ cups shredded Cheddar cheese

2 cups crushed Nacho Cheese Doritos

1 (10.75-ounce) can cream of mushroom soup

1 (10.75-ounce) can cream of chicken soup

1 (14.5-ounce) can Rotel tomatoes and green chilies

1 can water

1. Place shredded chicken on the bottom of a greased 9" × 13" pan. Put onions on top of chicken. Sprinkle ½ cup of the cheese on top of onion, and top with crushed Doritos.
2. On the stove, over medium heat, mix together and cook soups, tomatoes, and water. Pour on top of Doritos.
3. Sprinkle remaining 1 cup of cheese on the casserole.
8. Bake in the oven at 350° for 30–45 minutes until bubbly and crust forms on top.

🐾 **Makes 8–10 servings**

Georgia's Fried Chicken

Talk about fried chicken! This is by far the best fried chicken ever.

Pure canola oil
15 chicken legs
3 cups flour
Black pepper
Salt

1. Heat griddle to 400°. Add ½" canola oil.
2. Rinse and drain chicken legs. Put flour into large paper sack and shake chicken legs in flour.
3. Place one piece of chicken at a time onto the griddle. Season with a little salt and pepper. When the first side is lightly browned, approximately 10 minutes, turn the chicken over and sprinkle this side with salt and pepper.
4. Fry to a golden tan for about 45 minutes, turning chicken over about every 10 minutes to keep from burning. Drain on paper towels.

🍂 **Makes 15**

Chicken with White Barbecue Sauce

White barbecue sauce—who ever heard of such a thing? For you mayonaise lovers, it's sure to move to the top of your list. It's a good ol' Southern standard you'll enjoy no matter where you live.

1 cup mayonnaise
2 tablespoons Worcestershire sauce
2 tablespoons vinegar
2 teaspoons ground black pepper
Vegetable cooking spray
8 to 10 chicken breasts

1. Combine all ingredients except chicken breasts in medium or large mixing bowl. Blend well.
2. Spray 9" × 13" baking dish with vegetable cooking spray. Place chicken in dish and pour marinade over it. Marinate for 1 hour in refrigerator.
3. Preheat oven to 350° and bake chicken for 35–45 minutes.

🍂 **Makes 8–10 servings**

Dill Rice Chicken

New moms and dads always appreciate a donated meal. They're tired and hungry and a home-cooked casserole they can pop in the oven and enjoy is one of the best gifts you can offer. Take it to friends who have a newborn—they'll be thrilled.

1 cup sour cream

1 (10.75-ounce) can cream of chicken soup

1 (10.75-ounce) can cream of mushroom soup

1 (16-ounce) bag frozen vegetables, thawed

3 cups cooked chicken

3 cups cooked rice

1 teaspoon poppy seed

1¼ teaspoons dill weed

¼ teaspoon onion salt

¼ teaspoon garlic salt

1 cup shredded Cheddar cheese

1. In a large bowl, mix together all ingredients.
2. Spray 9" × 14" baking dish with vegetable cooking spray. Place chicken mixture in dish and bake at 350° for 30 minutes.
3. If desired, add crushed crackers on top in the last 10 minutes.

❦ **Makes 8–10 servings**

Laura's Chicken Risotto

Brown rice not only has more fiber and nutrients than white rice, but it cooks well in the slow cooker. Purists may look askance at this recipe, but it's delicious!

2 cups brown rice

2 onions, chopped

6 boneless, skinless chicken breasts, cubed

1 teaspoon salt

¼ teaspoon pepper

1 teaspoon dried thyme leaves

3 cups chicken broth

1 (10-ounce) can cream of chicken soup

3 cups frozen baby peas

3 tablespoons butter

1 cup grated Parmesan cheese

1. Combine brown rice and onions in 5-quart slow cooker. Top with chicken breasts. In large bowl, combine salt, pepper, thyme, chicken broth, and canned soup; mix with wire whisk until blended. Pour into slow cooker.
2. Cover and cook on low for 8–10 hours or until rice is tender and chicken is thoroughly cooked, stirring after 4 hours.
3. Stir in peas, butter, and cheese. Cover and cook on high for 20–30 minutes or until peas are hot and butter and cheese are melted. Stir gently and serve.

❦ **Makes 8–10 servings**

Fix-Ahead Chicken Casserole

Make this recipe the night before serving. You can use fettuccine noodles in place of the elbow macaroni.

2 cups uncooked elbow macaroni

4 cups cooked diced chicken

1 (10.75-ounce) can cream of mushroom soup

1 (10.75-ounce) can cream of chicken soup

2 tablespoons onions

1 tablespoon chopped green pepper

8 ounces shredded American cheese, reserving part for top

1. Mix together all ingredients and place in a greased 9" × 13" baking dish. Cover and refrigerate overnight.
2. Bake at 350° for 1 hour 30 minutes or until hot and bubbly. During the last half hour of baking, sprinkle with reserved shredded cheese.

🌿 **Makes 8–10 servings**

Chicken Dinner

Now this is a meal in one dish! You could add any root vegetable you'd like to this easy recipe; turnips and rutabagas would be two good choices.

6 potatoes, cut into chunks

2 sweet potatoes, peeled and cut into chunks

6 carrots, cut into chunks

2 onions, chopped

¼ cup olive oil

2 tablespoons butter

4 cloves garlic, minced

1 teaspoon dried thyme

1 teaspoon dried basil

1½ teaspoons seasoned salt

¼ teaspoon pepper

2 (3-pound) cut-up chickens, skinned

1. In 6- to 7-quart slow cooker, combine potatoes, sweet potatoes, carrots, and onions. In small saucepan, heat olive oil and butter until butter melts; add garlic. Cook and stir for 2–3 minutes until garlic is tender.
2. Remove saucepan from heat and stir in thyme, basil, salt, and pepper. Brush some of this mixture over chicken. Pour remaining mixture into slow cooker over vegetables.
3. Place chicken in slow cooker. Cover and cook on low for 8–9 hours or until chicken is thoroughly cooked and vegetables are tender.

🌿 **Makes 8–10 servings**

Chicken à la Pineapple

Fruit and chicken just seem to go together. This version has a fruity teriyaki taste but isn't too sweet. You can purchase bottled teriyaki sauce and just add some sugar and pineapple to make this recipe even easier.

½ cup sugar

½ cup water

½ cup soy sauce

2 tablespoons oil

1 20-ounce can crushed pineapple

1 teaspoon ginger

½ teaspoon garlic powder

3 pounds boneless chicken

1. Combine ingredients, blending well.
2. Place chicken in greased 9" × 13" baking dish. Cover and refrigerate for 4 hours, stirring occasionally. Bake at 350° for 40 minutes.

Makes 8–10 servings

Turkey with Cranberries

Looking for another way to use your left-over turkey from your holiday meals? Just eliminate the first four steps of this recipe and place the turkey over the cranberry sauce and heat for 10–15 minutes instead of 30.

¾ cup flour

¼ teaspoon pepper

8 boneless skinless turkey breast halves

¼ cup butter or margarine

1 cup fresh or frozen cranberries

1 cup water

½ cup packed brown sugar

1 tablespoon red wine vinegar

Dash ground nutmeg

1. In shallow bowl, combine flour and pepper. Dredge the turkey in flour mixture.
2. In a large skillet, cook turkey in butter until browned on both sides. Remove turkey and place in greased 9" × 13" baking dish.
3. In the same skillet, combine the cranberries, water, brown sugar, vinegar, and nutmeg. Cover, simmer for 5 minutes, and pour sauce over turkey. Bake at 350° for 30 minutes.

Makes 8–10 servings

Thanksgiving

Last Thanksgiving I decided to prepare the big bird, a 22-pound turkey, on the grill instead of roasting it in the oven. My sister-in-law, Gayle, had mentioned that a couple of her friends always put it on the grill and the result was moist and tender. It sounded like a great idea to me. Doing so would also make it easier to prepare the other dishes, since the oven would be available for all the other food we would be baking.

We looked up instructions online on grilling a turkey. We wrapped the turkey per instructions, started the grill—and how easy it was! We checked the turkey a time or two, then got busy fixing a ham, preparing our traditional oyster stuffing, making gravy, and greeting everyone as they began gathering for our holiday dinner.

Then my husband Larry walked into the kitchen and casually said, "You know the glass on the grill is cracked, don't you?" Gayle and I looked at each other and ran out to check the grill and our turkey. The glass wasn't just cracked—it had exploded! The glass was all over the deck and all over the foil as well. What a mess. We couldn't tell whether the glass had gotten into the turkey. We looked it over once and decided that the turkey and the grill both had to go. I was glad that I had a ham baking in the oven. Needless to say, we still had a wonderful time in spite of our turkey mishap.

I went out and bought a new grill to try it again next year, but this time my grill will be minus one item—the glass! It's given us a laugh or two now, but it wasn't so funny then; and luckily none of us was out there when it happened. •

—Susie Siegfried

Turkey and Stuffing Casserole

Classic turkey and stuffing cook beautifully in the slow cooker. The pattern the herbs make under the turkey skin is very beautiful too.

2 tablespoons butter, melted

2 onions, chopped

2 red bell peppers, chopped

1 (8-ounce) package sliced mushrooms

8 cups seasoned stuffing mix

2½ cups chicken broth

¼ teaspoon pepper

½ teaspoon dried sage leaves

1 teaspoon dried thyme leaves

1 (4–5 pound) boneless turkey breast

½ teaspoon salt

⅛ teaspoon pepper

¼ cup fresh sage leaves

2 tablespoons fresh rosemary leaves

3 tablespoons olive oil

1. In large bowl, combine melted butter, onions, bell peppers, and mushrooms; stir to coat. Add stuffing mix; toss to coat. Gradually add chicken broth, tossing to coat, until stuffing is just barely moist. Season with pepper, sage, and thyme.
2. Spray a 6- to 7-quart slow cooker with nonstick cooking spray. Place stuffing mixture in slow cooker.
3. Loosen skin from turkey breast and sprinkle flesh with salt and pepper. Arrange sage leaves and rosemary leaves in a pattern on the flesh. Carefully smooth skin back over the flesh, keeping the herbs in place.
4. Heat olive oil in large skillet. Add turkey, skin side down, and brown, moving turkey around as necessary, for 6–8 minutes.
5. Place turkey on top of stuffing, pressing down gently. Cover and cook on low for 8–10 hours or until turkey registers 165°F. Slice turkey and serve with stuffing.

❧ **Makes 8–10 servings**

Chicken Dijon

Dijon mustard adds a wonderful kick of spice and piquancy to this simple chicken dish. Serve it with mashed potatoes, noodles, or rice to soak up the flavorful sauce.

8 boneless, skinless chicken breasts

1 teaspoon salt

1/8 teaspoon white pepper

1 teaspoon dried tarragon leaves

1 onion, chopped

1 (16-ounce) bag baby carrots

1 (10-ounce) container refrigerated Alfredo sauce

1/4 cup Dijon mustard

1/2 cup apple juice

1/2 cup chicken broth

2 tablespoons cornstarch

1/4 cup water

1. In 5-quart slow cooker, combine all ingredients except cornstarch and water. Cover and cook on low for 6–7 hours or until chicken registers 165°F with a meat thermometer.
2. In small bowl, combine cornstarch and water; mix well. Add to slow cooker. Cover and cook on high for 20–30 minutes or until sauce is thickened. Serve over hot cooked noodles, rice, or mashed potatoes.

❦ **Makes 8 servings**

Turkey and Bean Cassoulet

Cassoulet is French for "casserole." It's traditionally made with duck breasts and sausage, but this simplified version has just as much flavor, with less fat!

2 tablespoons olive oil

1 tablespoon butter

2 pounds turkey sausage links

2 onions, chopped

4 cloves garlic, minced

1 (16-ounce) bag baby carrots

2 (15-ounce) can navy beans, drained

2 (15-ounce) cans black beans, drained

1 (28-ounce) can tomato purée

1/2 cup red wine or chicken broth

1 teaspoon dried marjoram

1/4 teaspoon pepper

1 bay leaf

1. Heat olive oil and butter in large saucepan over medium heat. Add turkey sausage; cook and stir until browned, but not cooked through. Remove sausage to plate and cut into 1" pieces.
2. Add onions and garlic to saucepan; cook and stir to loosen drippings. Place onions and garlic in 6- to 7-quart slow cooker along with sausage and remaining ingredients. Stir well to combine.
3. Cover and cook on low for 8–9 hours or until sausage is cooked and vegetables are tender. Remove bay leaf and serve.

❦ **Makes 10–12 servings**

Creamy Turkey and Biscuits

This shortcut recipe gives comfort and says love to those who are the recipients of this old-fashioned cooking. These biscuits may not be quite as good as mom and grandma used to make, but all you have to do is open the can and place them on the top of this casserole.

1/3 cup chopped green pepper

1/3 cup chopped onion

3 tablespoons butter

1 (10.75-ounce) can cream of mushroom soup

1 soup can milk

1 cup cooked turkey, cubed

1 (10-ounce) package mixed vegetables, thawed

2 (7.5-ounce) tubes refrigerated buttermilk biscuits

3/4 cup shredded Cheddar cheese

1. In a large saucepan, sauté green pepper and onion in butter until tender. Gradually add cream of mushroom soup and milk. Stir until mixed well, then bring to a boil. Cook and stir for 2 minutes.
2. Stir in turkey and mixed vegetables. Transfer to a greased 9" × 13" baking dish.
3. Separate biscuits and arrange over the top. Sprinkle with the cheese. Bake, uncovered, at 425° for 17–20 minutes or until golden brown.

❦ **Makes 8–10 servings**

Homemade Chicken Pot Pie

If you love old-fashioned cooking but don't think you have the time to fix it, try this recipe. This pot pie comes close to the old version, but will take little time to prepare.

1²/₃ cups frozen mixed vegetables, thawed

1 cup cooked chicken, cut into bite-size pieces

1 (10.75-ounce) can cream of chicken soup

1 cup Bisquick original baking mix

1/2 cup milk

1 egg

1. Preheat oven to 400°.
2. Mix together vegetables, chicken, and soup in an ungreased 9" pie plate.
3. Stir remaining ingredients with fork until blended. Pour over chicken mixture.
4. Bake at 400° for 30 minutes or until golden brown.

❦ **Makes 6 servings**

Classic Chicken and Dumplings

Pizza dough, when cut into small pieces, cooks into fluffy dumplings in this comforting and classic recipe. You may need the larger slow cooker depending on the size of the chicken breasts.

8 boneless, skinless chicken breasts

1 teaspoon salt

1/8 teaspoon pepper

1 teaspoon paprika

1/2 teaspoon poultry seasoning

4 stalks celery, sliced

1/2 cup chopped celery leaves

4 carrots, sliced

1 onion, chopped

6 cloves garlic, minced

1 (16-ounce) jar four-cheese Alfredo sauce

1 (16-ounce) jar Cheddar cheese pasta sauce

1 (10-ounce) can condensed cream of celery soup

1 cup heavy cream

1 (13.8-ounce) tube refrigerated pizza dough

1. Cut chicken breasts into cubes. Sprinkle with salt, pepper, paprika, and poultry seasoning; toss to coat.
2. Combine celery, celery leaves, carrots, onions, and garlic in 6- to 7-quart slow cooker; mix well. Add chicken breasts and stir.
3. In medium bowl, combine Alfredo sauce, pasta sauce, soup, and heavy cream; mix well. Pour into slow cooker. Cover and cook on low for 6–7 hours or until chicken and vegetables are tender.
4. On lightly floured surface, roll out the pizza dough to 1/2" thickness and cut into 1" pieces. Stir into slow cooker, making sure the dough is evenly distributed. Cover and cook on high for 1–1½ hours or until dumplings are cooked through. Serve immediately.

❀ **Makes 10–12 servings**

Chicken Lasagna

Lasagna in the slow cooker is a great time-saver and is so easy. You don't have to boil the noodles separately!

5 boneless, skinless chicken breasts

1 teaspoon salt

1/8 teaspoon pepper

1/2 teaspoon paprika

2 tablespoons butter

2 tablespoons olive oil

1 onion, chopped

4 cloves garlic, minced

1 red bell pepper, chopped

1 (26-ounce) jar spaghetti sauce

1/2 cup water

1 teaspoon dried Italian seasoning

1 (8-ounce) package cream cheese, softened

2 eggs

1 (16-ounce) container ricotta cheese

2 cups frozen cut-leaf spinach, thawed and drained

1/2 cup grated Parmesan cheese

6–9 lasagna noodles

1 cup shredded mozzarella cheese

1/2 cup shredded Romano cheese

1. Cut chicken breasts into 1" cubes. Sprinkle with salt, pepper, and paprika; toss to coat.
2. Heat butter with olive oil in large saucepan over medium heat. Add chicken; cook and stir until chicken is thoroughly cooked, about 9 minutes. Remove chicken from pan with slotted spoon.
3. In drippings remaining in skillet, cook onion and garlic until tender. Stir in red bell peppers, spaghetti sauce, water, and Italian seasoning; bring to a simmer.
4. Meanwhile, in bowl combine cream cheese, eggs, and ricotta cheese; beat until smooth. Stir in drained spinach and Parmesan cheese.
5. Break lasagna noodles in half. Place about 1 cup of the chicken mixture in bottom of 6-quart slow cooker. Top with a layer of lasagna noodles, more chicken mixture, some cream cheese mixture, and mozzarella cheese. Repeat layers, ending with cheese.
6. Sprinkle with Romano cheese, cover, and cook on low for 6–7 hours or until noodles are tender. To serve, scoop down deeply into the slow cooker to get all the layers.

❦ Makes 10–12 servings

On that day there shall be inscribed on the bells of the horses, "Holy to the Lord." And the cooking pots in the house of the Lord shall be as holy as the bowls in front of the altar.

—Zechariah 14:20

Spanish Chicken and Rice

If you like it really spicy, add a minced jalapeño pepper or substitute cayenne pepper for the black pepper.

3 pounds boneless, skinless chicken breasts

1 teaspoon paprika

¼ teaspoon pepper

1 teaspoon salt

2 tablespoons olive oil

2 onions, chopped

4 cloves garlic, minced

1½ cups long grain brown rice

2 green bell peppers, chopped

1 cup barbecue sauce

2 (14-ounce) cans diced tomatoes, undrained

1 (8-ounce) can tomato sauce

1 cup chicken broth

1 teaspoon cumin

1 tablespoon honey

2 tablespoons apple cider vinegar

¼ cup chopped parsley

¼ cup chopped cilantro

1. Cut chicken breasts into 1" cubes. Sprinkle with paprika, pepper, and salt; mix well. Heat olive oil in large skillet over medium heat. Add chicken; cook and stir until chicken starts to brown, about 4–5 minutes.

2. Remove chicken from skillet and place in 6-quart slow cooker. Add onions and garlic to skillet; cook until onion is tender, stirring to remove pan drippings, about 5 minutes.

3. Add rice to skillet; cook and stir for 3–4 minutes until coated. Add rice mixture to slow cooker.

4. Stir in remaining ingredients except parsley and cilantro. Cover and cook on low for 6–7 hours or until chicken is thoroughly cooked and rice is tender. Stir in parsley and cilantro and serve.

❧ **Makes 8–10 servings**

And thou shalt rejoice in thy feast, thou, and thy son, and thy daughter, and thy manservant, and thy maidservant, and the Levite, the stranger, and the fatherless, and the widow, that are within thy gates.

—Deuteronomy 16:14

Country Captain Chicken Casserole

The almonds and currants are a great addition to this recipe. Be sure to bring along a side of rice when you take this for a special occasion.

1 4-pound chicken cut in serving pieces, or 12 chicken breasts and thighs
Seasoned flour
½ cup shortening or oil
2 to 3 onions, finely chopped
1 to 2 green peppers, coarsely chopped
1 to 2 cloves garlic, minced
¼ to 4 teaspoons curry powder, to taste
1½ teaspoons salt
Dash pepper
1 teaspoon thyme
2 (20-ounce) cans tomatoes
½ teaspoon to 1 tablespoon parsley, chopped
Hot cooked rice
¼ to 1 pound almonds, toasted
½ to ⅔ cup currants (optional)
Parsley sprigs

1. Skin chicken, dredge in flour, and fry in oil until brown. Remove and keep warm.
2. Cook onions, green peppers, garlic in remaining oil until tender. Stir in curry powder, salt, pepper, thyme, tomatoes, and parsley.
3. Place chicken in large casserole or roaster pan and pour sauce over chicken. Bake at 350° for 45 minutes or until tender. Remove from oven and garnish chicken with almonds, currants, and parsley sprigs.
4. Serve in a ring of rice or rice on the side.

❦ **Makes 8–10 servings**

Be not forgetful to entertain strangers: for thereby some have entertained angels unawares.

—Hebrews 13:2

Lake Laura Spaghetti

This recipe was "thrown together" by someone in search of something for dinner for her three visiting sons. They were at their summer home in Lake Laura, Wisconsin, hence the name.

1 pound spaghetti
1 pound ground turkey
1 pound bacon, cut into thirds
1 pound longhorn cheese, sliced or grated
Black pepper
1 (14.50-ounce) can tomatoes
2 (10.75-ounce) cans tomato soup
1 (12-ounce) can tomato paste
1 onion

1. Cook spaghetti according to directions on package. Drain well.
2. Cook ground turkey and bacon separately.
3. Mix everything together well in a large bowl. Pour mixture into 9" × 13" baking dish and bake at 350° for 40 minutes. Serve with Parmesan cheese.

❦ **Makes 6–8 servings**

Apple Chicken with Pecans

Chicken, apples, and pecans are classic ingredients in chicken salad. When combined together in a hot casserole, the flavors and textures blend beautifully. Serve this dish over hot cooked rice.

8 boneless, skinless chicken breasts
1 teaspoon dried thyme leaves
1/4 teaspoon pepper
1 teaspoon salt
2 onions, sliced
4 Granny Smith apples, cored, peeled, and sliced
1/2 cup chicken broth
1/2 cup apple cider
1/2 cup brown sugar
3 tablespoons butter, melted
2 cups small whole pecans, toasted

1. Sprinkle chicken with thyme, pepper, and salt. Place onions in bottom of a 5-quart slow cooker. Top with chicken and apples.
2. In small bowl, combine remaining ingredients except pecans and mix well. Pour into slow cooker.
3. Cover and cook on low for 6–7 hours or until chicken is thoroughly cooked and apples are tender. Stir in pecans and serve over hot cooked rice.

❦ **Makes 8 servings**

Cranberry Chicken

This combination of cranberry sauce and Catalina dressing, along with the onion soup mix, seems pretty strange. But those of you who are familiar with the recipe using Russian dressing and onion soup mix will also like this one.

10 boneless skinless chicken breasts
1 (16-ounce) can whole-berry cranberry sauce
1 (16-ounce) bottle Catalina dressing
1 (2-ounce) package dry onion soup mix
Rice

1. Place chicken breasts in a greased 9" × 13" baking dish.
2. Mix together cranberry sauce, dressing, and onion soup mix. Pour mixture over chicken breasts. Cover with foil and bake at 350° for 50–60 minutes. Uncover and bake 15 minutes more.
3. Serve with rice.

❦ **Makes 10 servings**

Brunswick Stew

A number of years ago, a couple were at a football game in Williamsburg, Virginia. They went into a restaurant and ordered the Brunswick Stew. They went home and re-created the recipe–they were able to tell what ingredients were in it just from eating it.

3 medium potatoes, pared and cut in ½" pieces
1 (10-ounce) package frozen baby lima beans
1 (10-ounce) package frozen okra
1 (10-ounce) package frozen corn
3 cups cooked chicken, diced
1 tablespoon sugar
1 teaspoon salt
½ teaspoon rosemary
Dash pepper
⅛ teaspoon cloves
1 bay leaf
4 cups chicken broth
1 (16-ounce) can tomatoes

1. Place potatoes and frozen vegetables in a Crock-Pot. Add chicken, sugar, salt, rosemary, pepper, cloves, and bay leaf. Pour chicken broth and undrained tomatoes over mixture.
2. Cover and cook on low heat setting for 8–10 hours.
3. Remove bay leaf and stir well before serving.

❦ **Makes 10 servings**

Beef Entrées

✣

Beef is one of the most popular meats today, and with good reason. It's tender, filling, and hearty. And you can prepare it in so many ways! My paternal grandmother made the best pot roast in the world, and no one ever got her recipe. There's a good idea for a fundraiser: Collect heirloom recipes and make a cookbook.

One of the best things about the slow cooker is that it lets you use less expensive cuts of beef; in fact, those cuts are preferred for this type of cooking. The long, slow cooking in moist heat tenderizes tough cuts of beef so they literally fall apart on your fork.

When you're cooking ground beef in the slow cooker, you must first brown the beef in a skillet for best results, cooking it thoroughly and draining off any fat before it goes into the slow cooker. The beef will not overcook in the appliance; it will be tender and moist.

Many other cuts of beef are browned before cooking because this step adds flavor and improves the appearance of the final dish. If the beef is first dredged in seasoned flour, that can help thicken the final dish.

Beef roasts and steaks should be cooked to an internal temperature of 145°F; this is considered rare. Ground beef must be cooked to 165°F. Use your imagination when thinking about beef; consider ethnic cuisines and the preferences of the crowd you're serving.

—Linda Larsen

Sweet-and-Sour Meatball Casserole

This is a great hot dish for an evening Bible study. There are many varieties and types of frozen fully cooked meatballs. A favorite, especially in this recipe, are ground beef meatballs made with wild rice.

1 onion, chopped

3 cloves garlic, minced

1 cup wild rice, rinsed

1 (14-ounce) can ready-to-serve beef broth

1½ cups water

3 tablespoons sugar

¼ cup apple cider vinegar

1 (8-ounce) can pineapple tidbits in juice, undrained

1 (1-pound) package frozen meatballs

1 red bell pepper, chopped

1 green bell pepper, chopped

2 tablespoons cornstarch

5 tablespoons ketchup

2 tablespoons water

1. In 4- or 5-quart slow cooker, combine onions, garlic, and rice. Pour broth and water over all. Add sugar, cider vinegar, and pineapple tidbits; stir to combine. Then add meatballs. Cover and cook on low for 7–8 hours.
2. Add red and green bell peppers; stir. Cover and cook on low for 45 minutes.

3. Turn heat to high. In small bowl, combine cornstarch, ketchup, and water; mix well. Add to slow cooker and stir. Cook on high for 15–20 minutes or until liquid is thickened and bell peppers are tender. Serve immediately.

❧ **Makes 8 servings**

Solomon's provision for one day was ten fat oxen, twenty pasture-fed oxen, a hundred sheep besides deer, gazelles, roebucks, and fattened fowl.

—1 Kings 4:22–23

Spaghetti Sauce

Spaghetti sauce that cooks slowly in a slow cooker has the best flavor. Enjoy this one with some buttery toasted garlic bread.

2 pounds 90% lean ground beef

2 onions, chopped

3 cloves garlic, minced

1 (8-ounce) package sliced mushrooms

2 (14-ounce) cans diced tomatoes, undrained

1 (6-ounce) can tomato paste

1 (8-ounce) can tomato sauce

1 (10-ounce) can condensed tomato soup

1 cup tomato juice

1 tablespoon sugar

1 teaspoon salt

1½ teaspoons dried basil

1½ teaspoons dried oregano

¼ teaspoon pepper

2 (12-ounce) packages spaghetti pasta, cooked and drained

1 cup grated Parmesan or Romano cheese

1. In large skillet, cook ground beef until done; drain well and place in 5-quart slow cooker. Add remaining ingredients except pasta and cheese, stirring to mix.
2. Cover and cook on low for 8–9 hours, until sauce is blended and vegetables are tender. Serve over cooked spaghetti and top with grated Parmesan or Romano cheese.

❦ **Makes 10–12 servings**

Tender Pot Roast

There's nothing better than the aroma of pot roast in the kitchen on a cold winter's day.

4-pound beef chuck roast

1 teaspoon salt

¼ teaspoon pepper

2 teaspoons paprika

2 tablespoons olive oil

2 onions, chopped

3 carrots, chopped

3 cloves garlic, minced

1 (14-ounce) can ready-to-serve beef broth

1 (6-ounce) can tomato paste

2 tablespoons balsamic vinegar

1 tablespoon sugar

1. Sprinkle roast with salt, pepper, and paprika. In large skillet, heat olive oil over medium heat. Add roast; brown on all sides, turning frequently, about 10 minutes total. Remove from heat.
2. In 6- to 7-quart slow cooker, combine onions, carrots, and garlic. Top with roast. Add broth, tomato paste, vinegar, and sugar to skillet; mix until paste dissolves. Pour over roast.
3. Cover and cook on low for 8–10 hours or until beef is tender and registers at least 155°F. Remove beef from slow cooker and cover to keep warm. Turn off slow cooker; using an immersion blender, purée the mixture in the slow cooker. Serve sauce along with the roast.

❦ **Makes 12–14 servings**

Baked Beef Stew

This stew may take 3 hours to bake, but it only takes 5 minutes of your time to prepare.

3 pounds lean stew beef
1 (2-ounce) package onion soup mix
2 (10.75-ounce) cans golden-mushroom soup
½ cup Sauterne wine

1. Combine all ingredients and place in 9" × 13" greased baking dish. Cover with foil.
2. Bake at 300° for 3 hours.

Makes 8–10 servings

Take thou also unto thee wheat, and barley, and beans, and lentiles, and millet, and fitches, and put them in one vessel, and make thee bread thereof, according to the number of the days that thou shalt lie upon thy side, three hundred and ninety days shalt thou eat thereof.

—*Ezekiel 4:9*

Beefy Baked Beans

Canned beans are an inexpensive and nutritious way to feed a crowd. Serve this over hot cooked rice for a hearty and filling dinner.

2 pounds 90% lean ground beef
3 onions, chopped
6 cloves garlic, minced
3 (16-ounce) cans baked beans, drained
2 (15-ounce) can black beans, drained
2 (15-ounce) cans lima beans, drained
½ cup brown sugar
¼ cup apple cider vinegar
1 cup ketchup
1 cup barbecue sauce

1. In large skillet, brown ground beef, stirring to break up meat. Drain well and place in 5- to 6-quart slow cooker.
2. Add all remaining ingredients and stir gently. Cover and cook on low for 8–9 hours. If sauce needs thickening, remove cover and cook on high for 20–30 minutes.

Makes 12 servings

Picadillo

Picadillo can be served as a stew, over rice, as a taco or burrito filling, or as part of a taco salad. This versatile dish is bursting with flavor.

1 tablespoon olive oil

1 tablespoon butter

3 potatoes, peeled and chopped

1½ pounds ground beef

2 onions, chopped

4 cloves garlic, minced

½ teaspoon salt

¼ teaspoon pepper

¼ teaspoon ground cloves

1 teaspoon cumin

1 cup sliced green pimento-stuffed olives

1 cup raisins

2 (14-ounce) cans diced tomatoes, undrained

1 (6-ounce) can tomato paste

2 tablespoons apple cider vinegar

4 tomatoes, chopped

1. In large skillet, heat olive oil and butter together. Add chopped potatoes; cook and stir for 5 minutes. Place potatoes in 5-quart slow cooker and set aside.
2. In same skillet, cook ground beef with onions and garlic until beef is browned, stirring to break up meat. Drain well, then add salt, pepper, cloves, and cumin to meat.
3. Place olives and raisins in slow cooker over potatoes. Add tomatoes, tomato paste, and vinegar to beef mixture; bring to a simmer. Simmer for 10 minutes, stirring frequently.
4. Layer beef mixture with chopped tomatoes in slow cooker. Cover and cook on low for 8–9 hours or until potatoes are tender. Stir and serve immediately.

☙ **Makes 8 servings**

He asked for water and she gave him milk; in a magnificent bowl she brought him curds.

—Judges 5:25

Reuben Casserole

Who doesn't like a good Reuben sandwich? Be sure to buy your corned beef for this dish from the deli, as it really makes a difference. Also, rinse the sauerkraut a couple of times with cold water so it won't be quite so salty.

2 cups sauerkraut, drained
1 cup sour cream
1 pound deli chipped corned beef
3 cups shredded Swiss cheese
8 slices rye bread
½ cup butter
Thousand Island dressing

1. Mix together sauerkraut and sour cream and spread in bottom of 9" × 13" greased baking dish. Spread corned beef over sauerkraut mixture. Sprinkle cheese on top of corned beef.
2. Break bread into pieces and scatter on top of cheese. Pour melted butter on top and bake at 350° for 30 minutes.
3. Serve with Thousand Island dressing.

🐾 **Makes 8–10 servings**

Open-Faced Reuben

Stuffed Reuben loaves are so good, but take a lot of time to prepare. Make this one instead, as it is simpler and a bit less time-consuming.

1 loaf Italian or French bread
4 tablespoons butter
½ cup Thousand Island dressing
1½ pounds thinly sliced corned beef
1 (16-ounce) can sauerkraut, drained
2 cups shredded Swiss cheese
Thousand Island dressing

1. Preheat oven to 375°.
2. Slice bread lengthwise and butter both pieces. Spread dressing on both pieces; then top each piece with layers of corned beef, sauerkraut, and cheese. Bake for 7–10 minutes until cheese melts. Wrap in foil.
3. Cut in pieces when ready to serve and offer extra Thousand Island dressing.

🐾 **Makes 16 pieces**

Reuben Roll-Ups

When you're making these, be sure to take along a bottle or a container of Thousand Island dressing. I like to drizzle just a little over my roll-up. Another easy recipe.

1 (8-ounce) package refrigerator crescent rolls
8 thin slices of deli corned beef
1 (8-ounce) can sauerkraut, drained
2 tablespoons Thousand Island dressing
2 slices Swiss cheese, cut in ½" strips

1. Preheat oven to 350°.
2. Unroll crescent rolls and separate into triangles. Place a slice of corned beef across wide end of each triangle.
3. Combine sauerkraut with salad dressing. Spread 2 tablespoons of mixture on corned beef and top with 2 strips of cheese. Roll up, beginning at wide end of triangle, and place on an ungreased baking sheet.
4. Bake for 10–15 minutes or until golden brown. Remove from oven and slice each into thirds. Serve warm or cold.

🐞 **Makes 8 servings**

Italian Roast Beef

Italian seasonings add great flavor to a simple rump roast in this easy recipe. Leftovers (if there are any!) are great in sandwiches.

1 (4-pound) boneless beef rump roast
1 teaspoon salt
¼ teaspoon pepper
¼ cup flour
2 tablespoons butter
1 tablespoon olive oil
2 onions, chopped
1 (8-ounce) package sliced mushrooms
½ teaspoon dried oregano
1 teaspoon dried basil
1 teaspoon dried Italian seasoning
2 cups spaghetti sauce

1. Trim excess fat from roast and sprinkle with salt, pepper, and flour. In large skillet, combine butter and olive oil over medium heat. When butter melts, brown beef on all sides, about 10 minutes total. Place beef in 6- to 7-quart slow cooker.
2. Add onions and mushrooms to skillet. Cook and stir until tender, about 6–7 minutes. Add to beef in slow cooker.
3. Add oregano, basil, Italian seasoning, and spaghetti sauce to skillet and stir. Pour into slow cooker. Cover and cook on low for 8–9 hours or until beef is tender.

🐞 **Makes 12–14 servings**

Tangy Apricot Cube Steaks

Sweet fruit and tangy onions are always a good combination. Add that to tender cube steaks and you have a feast!

2½ pounds cube steak

1 teaspoon salt

¼ teaspoon pepper

⅓ cup flour

1 teaspoon paprika

2 tablespoons oil

1 tablespoon butter

1½ cups beef broth

1 (16-ounce) jar apricot preserves

2 (1-ounce) envelopes dry onion soup mix

1 cup chopped dried apricots

1. Cut steak into serving-sized pieces. On shallow plate, combine salt, pepper, flour, and paprika; stir to blend. Dredge steaks in this mixture.
2. In large skillet, combine oil and butter over medium heat. Brown steaks on both sides, turning once, about 3–4 minutes.
3. As steaks brown, place in 4-quart slow cooker. When all the steaks are cooked, add beef broth to skillet. Cook and stir over medium heat to loosen drippings. Remove from heat and add remaining ingredients to skillet.
4. Pour contents of skillet into slow cooker. Cover and cook on low for 7–8 hours or until meat is very tender. Serve meat with sauce.

❧ **Makes 8–10 servings**

Taco Salad

When you need something in a hurry, make this salad, and take along a bag of tortilla chips to add when it's time to serve. You can mix the dressing in a small container and take it along as well. It's the perfect "take-out" salad.

1 pound ground beef

1 head lettuce

1 cup chopped onions

2 cups diced tomatoes

1 cup grated Cheddar cheese

5 ounces (½ 10-ounce package) tortilla chips

1 cup French dressing

¼ cup mayonnaise

¼–½ cup salsa

1. Brown ground beef in skillet. Drain on paper towels to remove grease.
2. Tear lettuce apart and put into large bowl.
3. Place meat, onions, tomatoes, cheese, and chips on top of lettuce.
4. Mix together French dressing, mayonnaise, and salsa and pour over salad when ready to serve. Toss well.

❧ **Makes 6–8 servings**

Tostada Pie

Tex-Mex food lovers are everywhere—not just in the Southwest. This take-along pie, made easy by using packaged crescent rolls, appeal to almost everyone. If you know the crowd likes food with a "kick," try substituting hot salsa.

1 (8-ounce) tube crescent rolls

1½ pounds ground beef

¾ cup mild salsa

¾ cup medium salsa

1 cup sour cream

1 (16-ounce) can refried beans

1 cup Mexican blend shredded cheese

½ cup sliced black olives

½ cup chopped tomatoes

¼ cup sliced green onions

1. Preheat oven to 375°.
2. Spray 9" pie plate with vegetable cooking spray. Press crescent rolls into pie plate to form crust.
3. Brown meat and drain well.
4. In bowl, combine ground beef, salsas, and sour cream.
5. Spread refried beans onto crescent rolls. Put ground beef mixture on top of refried beans, and top with cheese, olives, tomatoes, and onions. Bake for 15 minutes or until cheese is melted.

🍃 **Makes 6–8 servings**

Crustless Pizza Pie

If you're hungry for pizza and you're in a hurry, try this pizza recipe. You could also use chopped pepperoni and green peppers on top of the ground beef to make a supreme pizza.

1½ pounds ground beef

¾ teaspoon pepper

1½ cups well-drained canned tomatoes

3 tablespoons chopped parsley

⅜ teaspoon dried basil

1½ teaspoons garlic powder

3 tablespoons finely chopped onion

¼ teaspoon oregano

¾ cup shredded Mozzarella cheese

1. Mix ground beef with salt and pepper. Pat out in a 9" pie plate. Spread drained tomatoes over ground beef and sprinkle with remaining ingredients.
2. Bake at 375° for 15–20 minutes. Cut in wedges and serve.

🍃 **Makes 6 servings**

Tex-Mex Steak and Potato Salad

Cooking sirloin tip and potatoes together until tender is a wonderful way to make a lot of salad with ease. This is a good choice for a summer picnic.

3 pounds sirloin tip

2 tablespoons chili powder

1½ teaspoons salt

½ teaspoon pepper

6–8 potatoes, peeled and cubed

2 onions, chopped

5 cloves garlic, minced

2 jalapeño peppers, minced

1 (16-ounce) jar mild or medium salsa

1½ cups mayonnaise

1½ cups plain yogurt

1 (16-ounce) jar mild or medium salsa

2 green bell peppers, chopped

2 red bell peppers, chopped

2 cups cubed pepper jack cheese

⅓ cup chopped fresh cilantro

1. Cut sirloin into 1" pieces. Sprinkle with chili powder, salt, and pepper. Place potatoes, onions, garlic, and jalapeños in bottom of 6-quart slow cooker. Top with beef. Pour one jar salsa over all.
2. Cover and cook on low for 8–9 hours or until beef and potatoes are tender.
3. In large bowl, combine mayonnaise, yogurt, second jar of salsa, green and red bell peppers, and cheese; mix well. Remove hot beef mixture from slow cooker with large slotted spoon or sieve and add to mixture in bowl. Discard liquid left in slow cooker. Stir gently to coat.
4. Cover and refrigerate for 4–5 hours until cold. Stir gently before serving, and top with cilantro.

❦ **Makes 12–14 servings**

Spend the money for whatever you wish— oxen, sheep, wine, strong drink, or whatever you desire. And you shall eat here in the presence of the Lord your God, you and your household rejoicing together.

—Genesis 14:26

Estofado

Share this exotic-sounding and wonderfully different recipe with your dinner club friends. Isn't that the way it is? Good recipes get passed around and around. Thank heavens.

3 pounds lean beef, cut in 1" cubes

1 tablespoon cooking oil

1 cup dry red wine

1 (8-ounce) can tomatoes

1 large onion, sliced ¼" thick

1 green pepper, cut in strips

¼ cup raisins

¼ cup dried apricots, halved

½ teaspoon jarred minced garlic

1½ teaspoons salt

⅛ teaspoon pepper

1 recipe bouquet garni (see below)

½ cup sliced fresh mushrooms

¼ cup sliced ripe olives

1 tablespoon flour

1 cup cold water

Hot cooked rice

1. In large skillet, brown meat in hot oil.
2. Add wine, tomatoes, onion, green pepper, raisins, apricots, garlic, salt, and pepper.
3. Make bouquet garni by tying together in cheesecloth 1 teaspoon dried basil, 1 teaspoon dried thyme, 1 teaspoon dried tarragon, and 1 bay leaf.
4. Simmer, covered, for 1 hour.
5. Add mushrooms and olives.
6. Simmer for 30 minutes.
7. Discard bouquet garni.
8. Combine flour and cold water and stir into stew.
9. Cook, stirring constantly, until mixture thickens and bubbles.
10. Serve over rice.

Makes 12 servings

Lasagna

Everyone has a special lasagna recipe. Some are passed down through generations of Italian mothers and aunts. Others, like this one, were enjoyed and recreated through the generosity of friends sharing their cooking secrets.

1½ (8-ounce) boxes lasagna noodles

2 tablespoons vegetable oil

1½ pounds lean ground beef

¼ teaspoon pepper

2 cups spaghetti sauce (I use 1 package French's mix—using the tomato paste alternative, it makes exactly 2 cups)

1 (16-ounce) container small curd cottage cheese

¼ cup sour cream

2 (8-ounce) packages mozzarella cheese slices

Vegetable oil

1. Cook noodles as package directs; drain. Toss with 2 tablespoons vegetable oil until well coated.
2. In skillet, brown ground beef and drain very well. Add pepper and spaghetti sauce and stir well.
3. Combine cottage cheese with sour cream.
4. Arrange half of noodles in 9" × 13" greased baking dish. Cover with half of meat sauce mixture. Add layer of cheese slices (using ½ total cheese). Add all cottage cheese–sour cream mixture and top with remaining noodles.
5. Cut mozzarella cheese into ½" strips, and weave it, lattice fashion, across the top. Spoon remaining meat-sauce mixture into lattice spaces. Cover tightly and refrigerate until ready to bake.
6. Heat oven to 350°.
7. Brush surface of cheese strips with vegetable oil. Bake 30 minutes or until cheese melts and is golden.

❦ **Makes 8–10 servings**

My meat also which I gave thee, fine flour, and oil, and honey, wherewith I fed thee, thou hast even set it before them for a sweet savour: and thus it was, saith the Lord God.

—Ezekiel 16:19

Spanish Rice

There are a few Spanish rice recipes that just stand out—and this is one of them.

1 pound ground beef

1 pound sausage

1 tablespoon vegetable oil

1½ cups chopped onions

1½ cups chopped green pepper

2 cups rice

2 cups hot water

2 8-ounce cans diced tomatoes

2 (10.75-ounce) cans tomato soup

2 tablespoons paprika

1. Cook ground beef and sausage until brown. Drain well on paper towels.
2. In same skillet, heat oil and cook onions and green pepper for 2–3 minutes. Add ground beef and sausage to onions and peppers.
3. In large saucepan, mix together remaining ingredients. Add beef mixture. Cook on medium heat until sauce thickens and rice is tender, usually 20–30 minutes.
4. Top with sour cream, shredded cheese, or other favorite condiments.

☙ **Makes 10–12 servings**

Meatloaf

Cracker crumbs, bread crumbs, potatoes . . . every meatloaf has its filler. Saltines add substance and flavor to this quickly assembled family staple. Enjoy one with your family and freeze the second one.

Meatloaf

2 pounds ground beef

1 pound ground pork

1 tablespoon Worcestershire sauce

1 teaspoon garlic

¼ cup minced onion

2 sleeves Saltines, crushed

2 eggs

¾ cup ketchup

Sauce

¾ cup brown sugar

2 tablespoons Worcestershire sauce

¾ to 1 cup ketchup

1. Mix together meatloaf ingredients. Divide in half and put in 2 greased 9" × 5" × 3" loaf pans. Bake at 350° for 35–45 minutes.
2. In small bowl, combine sauce ingredients.
3. Remove meatloaves from oven, poke holes on top with fork, and cover with sauce. Return to oven for 10–20 minutes until sauce is bubbly.

☙ **Makes 2 loaves**

Mom's Meatloaf

Potatoes add moisture and flavor to this comforting, hearty meatloaf recipe. Everyone will ask how you did it, and then ask for seconds.

2 tablespoons olive oil

1 onion, chopped

3 cloves garlic, minced

1 cup chopped mushrooms

½ cup refrigerated mashed potatoes from package

1 egg

¼ cup heavy cream

¼ cup yellow mustard

¼ cup ketchup

¼ cup beef broth

1 tablespoon Worcestershire sauce

¼ teaspoon pepper

1½ pounds lean ground beef

1 pound lean ground pork

2 tablespoons honey

2 tablespoons mustard

½ teaspoon paprika

1. In large skillet, heat olive oil over medium heat. Add onion, garlic, and mushrooms. Cook and stir until mushrooms give up their liquid and that liquid evaporates, about 10 minutes.
2. Remove skillet from heat and transfer onion mixture to a large bowl. Add potatoes, egg, and cream; mix well. Stir in mustard, ketchup, beef broth, Worcestershire sauce, and pepper; mix well.
3. Stir in beef and pork, and mix gently with your hands. Form into an 8" ball. Tear off two 24" sheets of heavy-duty foil and fold into thirds lengthwise. Place crosswise in bottom of 5-quart slow cooker. Place meatloaf on top.
4. In small bowl, combine honey, mustard, and paprika. Spread over meatloaf. Cover slow cooker. Cook on low for 7–8 hours or until meat thermometer registers 165°F.
5. Using the foil, carefully lift the meatloaf out of the slow cooker. Drain on paper towels for 5 minutes, then slice to serve.

❧ **Makes 8 servings**

In those days when there was again a great crowd without anything to eat, Jesus called his disciples and said to them, "I have compassion for the crowd, because they have been with me now for three days and have nothing to eat. If I send them away hungry to their homes, they will faint on the way—and some of them have come from a great distance."

—*Mark 8:1–3*

Ranchero Beef Roast

There's nothing better than Tex-Mex seasonings with beef. The spices blend together in the long cooking time to turn mild and savory.

1 (4-pound) boneless beef rump roast

1 teaspoon salt

¼ teaspoon pepper

1 tablespoon chili powder

¼ cup flour

2 tablespoons butter

1 tablespoon olive oil

2 onions, chopped

5 cloves garlic, minced

2 jalapeño peppers, chopped

1 teaspoon cumin

1 teaspoon dried oregano leaves

1 (16-ounce) jar chunky mild or medium salsa

1. Trim excess fat from roast. In small bowl combine salt, pepper, chili powder, and flour. Sprinkle over roast. In large skillet, combine butter and olive oil over medium heat. When butter melts, brown beef on all sides, about 10 minutes total. Place beef in 6- to 7-quart slow cooker.
2. Add onions, garlic, and jalapeños to skillet. Cook and stir until tender, about 6–7 minutes. Add to beef in slow cooker.
3. In bowl, combine cumin, oregano, and salsa and mix well. Pour into slow cooker. Cover and cook on low for 8–9 hours or until beef is tender.

❧ **Makes 12–14 servings**

Shepherd's Pie

This flavorful pie full of beef and vegetables is topped with creamy and cheesy mashed potatoes.

1½ pounds ground beef

2 onions, chopped

1 leek, chopped

5 cloves garlic, minced

1 teaspoon salt

¼ teaspoon pepper

1 teaspoon dried thyme leaves

4 carrots, sliced

1 (8-ounce) package sliced mushrooms

1 (14-ounce) can diced tomatoes, undrained

1 (6-ounce) can tomato paste

½ cup ketchup

¼ cup yellow or Dijon mustard

2 tablespoons Worcestershire sauce

1 (24-ounce) package refrigerated mashed potatoes

½ cup sour cream

½ cup grated Parmesan cheese

1. In large skillet, brown ground beef with onions, leek, and garlic, stirring to break up meat. When beef is thoroughly cooked, drain well.
2. Add salt, pepper, and thyme; mix well. Pour mixture into 5 quart slow cooker. Stir in carrots, mushrooms, tomatoes, tomato paste, ketchup, mustard, and Worcestershire sauce. Mix well.

(continued)

(Shepherd's Pie—continued)

3. Prepare mashed potatoes as directed on package. Stir in sour cream and Parmesan cheese. Spoon on top of meat mixture in slow cooker.
4. Cover and cook on low for 6–7 hours or until mixture is hot and bubbling.

🐾 **Makes 8 servings**

Shortcut Shepherd's Pie

This meat pie is a classic dish that can be made with instant mashed potatoes if you're in a hurry. It won't be quite as good, but it will take less of your time.

2 chopped onions

1 pound ground beef

2 tablespoons ketchup

¼ teaspoon Worcestershire sauce

1 (16-ounce) bag frozen mixed vegetables, thawed

4 to 6 cups mashed potatoes

¼ cup milk

3 tablespoons butter

Dash salt

1. Brown onions and ground beef together in large skillet. Drain well. Add ketchup, Worcestershire sauce, and vegetables. Pour into greased 8" × 8" square baking dish.
2. Beat together potatoes, milk, butter, and salt. Spread over filling, sealing to edge. Bake at 425° for 35 minutes.

🐾 **Makes 6–8 servings**

Beef and Bean Pot Pie

This mild pie is comforting and rich. The corn bread topping stays moist and tender when cooked in the slow cooker. This recipe could also be made with ground turkey or pork.

1½ pounds ground beef

2 onions, chopped

6 cloves garlic, minced

½ teaspoon salt

⅛ teaspoon pepper

1 teaspoon dried marjoram

2 (15-ounce) cans kidney beans

2 (4-ounce) jars sliced mushrooms, drained

4 carrots, sliced

1 (10-ounce) can condensed tomato soup

1 (8-ounce) can tomato sauce

1 (8-ounce) package corn muffin mix

1 egg

½ cup sour cream

2 tablespoons oil

⅓ cup grated Parmesan cheese

1. In large skillet, cook ground beef with onions and garlic until ground beef is done, stirring to break up meat. Drain well. Add salt, pepper, and marjoram; stir.
2. Stir in kidney beans and mushrooms with their liquid, carrots, soup, and tomato sauce; bring to a simmer.
3. Spray a 5-quart slow cooker with nonstick cooking spray. Pour beef mixture into slow cooker.
4. In medium bowl, combine remaining ingredients and stir just until combined. Spoon by tablespoons over beef mixture in slow cooker.
5. Cover and cook on low for 6–8 hours or until corn bread is set and toothpick inserted in center of topping comes out clean.

🍃 **Makes 8 servings**

But when you give a banquet, invite the poor, the crippled, the lame, and the blind. And you will be blessed, because they cannot repay you, for you will be repaid at the resurrection of the righteous.

—Luke 14:13–14

Open-Faced Stroganoff Loaf

You can make this loaf ahead of time and freeze it for when you need to take something unexpectedly. It is perfect to take to a family in time of need, as they can use it immediately or freeze it for later use.

1½ pounds ground beef

½ cup chopped onion

1 cup water

½ cup sour cream

1 (1.5-ounce) envelope stroganoff seasoning
  mix

1 loaf Vienna bread, unsliced

Butter

1 green pepper, sliced in rings

Cherry tomatoes, halved

1 (4.5-ounce) can sliced mushrooms, drained

1. Brown meat and onion. Drain well.
   Stir in water, sour cream, and
   seasoning mix. Cover and simmer
   10 minutes.
2. Cut bread in half lengthwise. Butter
   bread and top with meat mixture.
   Arrange green peppers and tomatoes
   alternately, then place mushrooms on
   top. Bake at 375° for 7–10 minutes.
3. Wrap in foil to keep warm.

❧ **Makes 10–12 servings**

Pesto Beef Strata

Pesto is a paste or sauce made of basil leaves, Parmesan cheese, garlic, pine nuts, and olive oil. It's flavorful and delicious used in this easy recipe.

2 pounds lean ground beef

2 onions, chopped

4 cloves garlic, minced

1 (14-ounce) can diced tomatoes, undrained

1 (10-ounce) can condensed tomato soup

1 teaspoon dried basil

½ teaspoon salt

⅛ teaspoon pepper

6 potatoes, peeled and sliced

1 (16-ounce) jar Alfredo sauce

2 (7-ounce) containers refrigerated pesto

½ cup grated Parmesan cheese

1. In large skillet, cook ground beef with
   onions and garlic, stirring to break up
   beef, until beef is thoroughly cooked.
   Drain well. Add tomatoes, tomato
   soup, basil, salt, and pepper. Bring to a
   simmer.
2. Slice potatoes ⅛" thick. In medium
   bowl, combine Alfredo sauce, pesto,
   and cheese. Layer ¼ of beef mixture,
   ¼ of potatoes, and ¼ of pesto mixture
   in 5-quart slow cooker. Continue until
   all ingredients are used.
3. Cover and cook on low for 7–9 hours
   or until potatoes are tender.

❧ **Makes 8–10 servings**

Stroganoff Steak Sandwich

Sandwiches can be boring–not so with this beef, piled high with savory toppings. It may take a little more time than most, but it's well worth it.

²/₃ cup beer

¹/₃ cup cooking oil

1 teaspoon salt

¼ teaspoon garlic powder

¼ teaspoon pepper

2 pounds flank steak, 1" thick

2 tablespoons margarine or butter

½ teaspoon paprika

Dash salt

4 cups sliced onion

12 slices French bread, toasted

1 cup sour cream, warmed

½ teaspoon prepared horseradish

Paprika

1. In shallow dish, combine first 5 ingredients to make a marinade. Place flank steak in marinade; cover. Marinate overnight in refrigerator or several hours at room temperature. Drain.
2. Broil flank steak 3" from heat for 5–7 minutes for medium-rare.
3. In saucepan, melt margarine and blend in paprika and dash salt. Add onion. Cook till tender but not brown.
4. Thinly slice meat on the diagonal across grain. For each serving, arrange meat slices over 2 slices French bread. Top with onions.
5. Combine sour cream and horseradish and spoon onto each sandwich. Sprinkle with paprika if desired.

❦ **Makes 6 servings**

And Boaz said unto her, At mealtime come thou hither, and eat of the bread, and dip thy morsel in the vinegar. And she sat beside the reapers: and he reached her parched corn, and she did eat, and was sufficed, and left.

—Ruth 2:14

Spicy Steak Bake

Serve this delicious mixture over hot cooked pasta or hot mashed potatoes for a homey meal.

2 pounds beef sirloin tip steak

1/3 cup flour

1 teaspoon seasoned salt

1/8 teaspoon pepper

1/8 teaspoon cayenne pepper

2 tablespoons olive oil

2 onions, chopped

4 cloves garlic, minced

2 green bell peppers, chopped

2 tablespoons Worcestershire sauce

1/4 cup honey

2 (14-ounce) cans diced tomatoes, undrained

1 (6-ounce) can tomato paste

1 cup beef broth

2 tablespoons yellow mustard

1. Trim excess fat from steak and cut into 1½" cubes. On shallow plate, combine flour, seasoned salt, pepper, and cayenne pepper; mix well. Toss steak in this mixture to coat.
2. Heat olive oil in large skillet over medium heat. Add steak; cook and stir until browned, about 4–5 minutes. Remove meat to 4-quart slow cooker.
3. Add onions and garlic to skillet; cook and stir for 4–5 minutes, scraping pan to remove drippings. Pour into slow cooker along with bell peppers.
4. Add Worcestershire sauce, honey, undrained tomatoes, tomato paste, beef broth, and mustard to skillet. Bring to a simmer, then pour into slow cooker.
5. Cover and cook on low for 8–9 hours or until beef is very tender. Serve mixture over hot cooked pasta or rice.

❈ **Makes 8 servings**

Orange Beef with Broccoli

Orange marmalade, juice, and zest add fresh flavor to this dish, which is usually made as a stir-fry.

3½ pounds round steak

⅓ cup flour

1 teaspoon salt

1 teaspoon paprika

¼ teaspoon pepper

2 tablespoons butter

2 tablespoons olive oil

2 cups beef broth

4 shallots, peeled and chopped

6 cloves garlic, minced

1 cup orange marmalade

1 teaspoon dried thyme leaves

1 tablespoon grated orange zest

¼ cup soy sauce

3 tablespoons cornstarch

½ cup orange juice

2 (16-ounce) packages frozen broccoli florets, thawed

6 cups hot cooked rice

1. Trim excess fat from steak and cut into 1½" cubes. On shallow plate, combine flour, salt, paprika, and pepper; mix well. Toss steak in flour mixture to coat.

2. In large saucepan, melt butter and olive oil over medium heat. Add steak; cook and stir until browned, about 5–7 minutes total. Remove beef from skillet with slotted spoon and place in 5- to 6-quart slow cooker.

3. Add beef broth to saucepan and cook until mixture bubbles, stirring to remove drippings. Pour into slow cooker. Add remaining ingredients except for cornstarch, orange juice, broccoli, and rice. Cover and cook for 7–8 hours or until beef is very tender.

4. In small bowl, combine cornstarch and orange juice and mix well. Stir into slow cooker along with thawed and drained broccoli. Turn slow cooker to high and cook for 20–30 minutes until sauce is thickened and broccoli is hot and tender. Serve over hot cooked rice.

❦ **Makes 10–12 servings**

When the Lord your God enlarges your territory, as he has promised you, and you say, "I am going to eat some meat," because you wish to eat meat, you may eat meat whenever you have the desire.

—Genesis 12:20

Beef with Root Vegetables

You can thicken the sauce with a slurry of 2 tablespoons cornstarch and ¼ cup water at the end of cooking time; cook on high for 20 minutes longer after adding this mixture.

2½ pounds bottom round steak

⅓ cup flour

1 teaspoon salt

1 teaspoon dried Italian seasoning

⅛ teaspoon pepper

2 tablespoons butter

2 tablespoons olive oil

1 cup water

2 onions, chopped

5 cloves garlic, minced

4 carrots, sliced

3 russet potatoes, peeled

2 sweet potatoes, peeled

2 cups cubed rutabaga

2 cups beef broth

1. Trim excess fat from steak and cut into 2" cubes. On shallow plate, combine flour, salt, Italian seasoning, and pepper; sprinkle over beef. In large skillet, combine butter and olive oil over medium heat.
2. Add beef to skillet; cook and stir until browned, about 6–7 minutes. Remove beef cubes from skillet and set aside. Add water to skillet; cook and stir until mixture comes to a boil, stirring to release drippings.
3. In 6-quart slow cooker, combine onions, garlic, carrots, both kinds of potatoes, and rutabaga. Place browned beef on top.
4. Add beef broth to skillet. Pour into slow cooker. Cover and cook on low for 9–10 hours or until vegetables are tender.

❀ **Makes 10 servings**

Barbecue Cups (Fu Manchu on Sundays)

Kids can be finicky about what they eat. If you're not sure whether yours will eat these barbecue cups, serve "Fu Manchu on Sundays." The silliness of the name may intrigue them enough to try it. Once they taste it, they'll be hooked.

1 pound ground beef
½ cup chopped onion
Salt and pepper to taste
1 tablespoon brown sugar
¼ cup bottled barbecue sauce
1 (7.5-ounce) tube refrigerated biscuits

1. Brown ground beef and onion; pour off excess fat. Add seasoning, sugar, and barbecue sauce. Simmer for 5 minutes.
2. Separate biscuits. Press into bottom and sides of a greased muffin tin. Fill with meat mixture and top with cheese.
3. Bake at 400° for 10–15 minutes.

🌿 **Makes 8 servings**

Classic Swiss Steak

What's a church dinner without Swiss steak? This classic is updated with lots of vegetables and made easily in the slow cooker.

2½ pounds beef round steak
5 tablespoons flour
1 teaspoon salt
½ teaspoon garlic salt
1 teaspoon paprika
½ teaspoon pepper
2 teaspoons steak seasoning
2 tablespoons butter
3 tablespoons olive oil
4 carrots, cut into chunks
2 onions, sliced
1 (8-ounce) package sliced mushrooms
6 cloves garlic, minced
4 stalks celery, sliced
2 cups beef broth
1 (14-ounce) can diced tomatoes, undrained
1 cup chili sauce
1 (6-ounce) can tomato paste

1. Cut steak into 8 portions and trim off excess fat. On shallow plate, combine flour, salt, garlic salt, paprika, pepper, and steak seasoning; mix well. Dredge steaks in this mixture. Place steaks between two sheets of waxed paper, and pound to tenderize.

(continued)

(Classic Swiss Steak—continued)

2. In large skillet, heat butter and olive oil over medium heat. Add steaks; brown on both sides, turning once, about 4–5 minutes total. Remove from heat.
3. Combine carrots, onions, mushrooms, garlic, and celery in 6-quart slow cooker. Top with steaks.
4. Add beef broth, tomatoes, chili sauce, and tomato paste to skillet; cook and stir over high heat until mixture simmers. Pour into slow cooker.
5. Cover and cook on low for 7–8 hours or until beef and vegetables are very tender. Serve steak with vegetables and sauce over mashed potatoes or cooked pasta.

🍲 **Makes 8 servings**

Bring me game, and prepare for me savory food to eat, that I may bless you before the Lord before I die.

—Genesis 27:7

Braised Chuck Rosemary

Just a little rosemary goes a long way. This tasty herb adds a special touch to an ordinary chuck roast.

4–5 pounds beef rump roast
1 cup sliced onion rings
1 teaspoon minced jarred garlic
½ cup ketchup
½ teaspoon rosemary
½ cup water
¼ cup red wine vinegar
2 tablespoons Worcestershire sauce
1 teaspoon dry mustard
3 pounds peeled white potatoes

1. Brown meat well on both sides in a heavy pan sprayed with vegetable cooking spray. Add onion and garlic, and cook until onions are tender.
2. Combine remaining ingredients except potatoes. Pour over meat. Cover and cook slowly over medium heat until meat is fork tender, about 2½ hours.
3. Drop potatoes around roast and cook for 25 minutes. Cover and cook till potatoes are done.

🍲 **Makes 12–15 servings**

Beef à la King

Chicken à la King may be a lunchroom staple, but using beef instead elevates this dish to a new level. You could add sliced carrots if you'd like.

3 pounds sirloin tip

⅓ cup flour

2 teaspoons steak seasoning

½ teaspoon salt

⅛ teaspoon pepper

2 tablespoons butter

2 tablespoons olive oil

2 onions, chopped

4 cloves garlic, minced

2 (8-ounce) packages sliced mushrooms

1 (32-ounce) box beef broth

1 cup heavy cream

3 tablespoons cornstarch

3 cups frozen baby peas

14 frozen puff pastry shells

1. Trim excess fat from beef and cut into 1" cubes. On shallow plate, combine flour, steak seasoning, salt, and pepper; mix well. Dredge beef in flour mixture to coat.
2. In large skillet, heat butter with olive oil over medium heat. Add steak; brown cubes, stirring frequently, for about 6 minutes. Place in 6-quart slow cooker.
3. Add onions and garlic to skillet. Cook and stir to loosen pan drippings; cook for 4 minutes. Add to slow cooker along with mushrooms and beef broth.
4. Cover and cook on low for 7–8 hours or until beef and vegetables are tender. In small bowl, combine cream and cornstarch; stir into slow cooker along with peas. Turn to high; cook for 20–25 minutes until sauce thickens.
5. Prepare puff pastry shells as directed on package. Serve beef mixture over the hot baked shells.

Makes 14 servings

Judee's Sloppy Joes

These sloppy joes are much quicker to prepare than the ones you make on the top of your stove. You do have to remember to stir them about every 20 or 30 minutes. But it beats standing over a hot stove browning your ground beef when you could be doing something else.

2 pounds ground beef

1 cup chopped onion

½ cup chopped green pepper

1 (10.75-ounce) can mushroom soup

½ (10.75-ounce) can tomato soup

¾ cup ketchup

½ teaspoon prepared mustard

Dash Worcestershire sauce

1. Mix all ingredients together. Put in greased 9" × 13" baking dish. Bake at 350° for 1½ hours, stirring occasionally.
2. Pour off any grease on top.

❧ **Makes 8–10 servings**

Beef Barbecue

This recipe can be fixed in a slow cooker, shortening the time you need to fix it and making it very easy to take to any event. The sauce has been handed down through the years by many a good cook.

3 pounds beef stew meat

¼ cup broth from cooking beef

½ cup Montgomery Inn barbecue sauce

1 cup ketchup

½ teaspoon Worcestershire sauce

2 tablespoons brown sugar

1. Put beef in pan and cover with water. Cook on top of stove for 2–3 hours or until tender. Drain liquid, reserving ¼ cup for sauce.
2. Shred beef with fork or a potato masher. Add broth and remaining ingredients.
3. Heat and serve on buns.

❧ **Makes 12–15 servings**

Cajun Beef

You can find Cajun seasoning and steak seasoning in the spice aisle of any supermarket. They add a sweet heat to this wonderful recipe.

3 pounds bottom round steak

⅓ cup flour

2 tablespoons Cajun seasoning

2 teaspoons steak seasoning

¼ teaspoon pepper

2 tablespoons butter

2 tablespoons olive oil

2 onions, chopped

8 cloves garlic, minced

2 poblano peppers, chopped

1 yellow bell pepper, chopped

1 orange bell pepper, chopped

1 red bell pepper, chopped

1 (14-ounce) can diced tomatoes, undrained

1 (6-ounce) can tomato paste

1 (8-ounce) can tomato sauce

3 cups beef broth

1½ cups instant brown rice

1. Trim excess fat from beef. Cut into 2" cubes. On shallow plate, combine flour, Cajun seasoning, steak seasoning, and pepper; mix well. Dredge beef cubes in this mixture.
2. In large skillet, heat butter and olive oil over medium heat. Brown beef, stirring occasionally, about 5–6 minutes total.
3. Remove beef from skillet and place in 6- to 7-quart slow cooker. Add onions and garlic to skillet; cook and stir to release drippings. Add to slow cooker along with remaining ingredients except rice; stir.
4. Cover and cook on low for 8–9 hours or until beef is cooked and vegetables are tender.
5. Turn heat to high. Stir in brown rice, making sure rice is submerged in liquid. Cover and cook for 25 minutes. Stir and serve.

🍃 **Makes 12–14 servings**

They shall eat the lamb that same night; they shall eat it roasted over the fire with unleavened bread and bitter herbs.

—Exodus 12:8

Beef Curry

Balsamic vinegar adds a nice tang to this dish. You could stir in frozen peas at the end of cooking time (just long enough to warm through) to stretch the dish and add color.

3 pounds beef stew meat

⅓ cup flour

2 tablespoons curry powder

1 teaspoon salt

½ teaspoon pepper

¼ cup butter

3 onions, chopped

6 cloves garlic, minced

3 green bell peppers, chopped

3 tablespoons minced fresh gingerroot

1 (28-ounce) can tomato purée

1 (6-ounce) can tomato paste

1 cup beef broth

3 tablespoons balsamic vinegar

Cooked rice, mashed potatoes, or cooked noodles

1. Trim excess fat from beef and cut into 2" cubes. On shallow plate, combine flour, curry powder, salt, and pepper. Dredge meat in flour mixture.
2. Melt butter in large skillet over medium heat. Brown beef in batches, stirring occasionally, until browned, about 5–6 minutes per batch. Place beef in 6-quart slow cooker.
3. Add onions and garlic to skillet; cook and stir to loosen pan drippings. Cook for 4 minutes until crisp-tender. Add to slow cooker along with bell peppers and gingerroot.
4. Add tomato purée, tomato paste, and beef broth to skillet; cook and stir until mixture bubbles. Pour into slow cooker. Cover and cook on low for 7 hours or until beef is tender. Stir in balsamic vinegar and serve over rice, mashed potatoes, or noodles.

❧ **Makes 12–14 servings**

5-Hour Barbecue

If barbecue tempts your taste buds, you'll want to add this quick-to-fix but slow-to-cook recipe to your list of favorites.

2 tablespoons vinegar
2 tablespoons Worcestershire sauce
1 tablespoon salt
¼ teaspoon red pepper
½ teaspoon black pepper
1 teaspoon paprika
1 teaspoon chili powder
1 (8-ounce) bottle ketchup
2 cups water
2 medium onions, chopped
1 (5-ounce) can tomato sauce
3 pounds chuck or rump roast

1. Mix together all ingredients but the last. Pour over meat, and bake covered at 325° for 5 hours.
2. Drain off any grease from sauce.
3. Shred with 2 forks, and serve on fresh buns with cole slaw.

☙ **Makes 12 sandwiches**

Cabbage Roll Casserole

Cabbage rolls are a little time-consuming to make, but doesn't everyone love them? This casserole is a snap to make.

1 small head of cabbage
1 pound ground beef or turkey
Salt and pepper
½ tablespoon minced garlic
1 small onion, diced
⅓ cup rice, uncooked
1 (16-ounce) can sauerkraut
1 (8-ounce) can tomato sauce
1½ cups water

1. Chop cabbage into bite-size pieces and place in greased 9" × 13" pan.
2. Brown meat, drain, and add salt, pepper, garlic, and onion.
3. Scatter rice over cabbage. Pour meat mixture over cabbage and rice then cover with sauerkraut, tomato sauce, and water. Bake uncovered at 350° for 20 minutes.
4. Cover and continue baking for another hour or until rice is tender.

☙ **Makes 8–10 servings**

Slow Cooker Stuffed Cabbage

This easy layered casserole tastes like stuffed cabbage, but with much less work. The gingersnaps add a layer of flavor to the sauce.

1 cup pearl barley

2 cups beef broth

2½ pounds ground beef

2 onions, chopped

6 cloves garlic, minced

1 (14-ounce) can diced tomatoes, undrained

2 (8-ounce) cans tomato sauce

1 (6-ounce) can tomato paste

1 teaspoon salt

¼ teaspoon pepper

¼ cup brown sugar

¼ cup red wine vinegar

6 gingersnaps, crumbled

9 cups shredded red cabbage

1 (8-ounce) can tomato sauce

1. In large saucepan, combine barley and broth and bring to a boil. Reduce heat to low, cover, and simmer for 30–35 minutes or until barley is almost tender. Drain well, if necessary; set aside.

2. In large skillet, brown ground beef with onions and garlic, stirring to break up beef. When beef is almost cooked, drain well. Add tomatoes, 2 cans tomato sauce, tomato paste, salt, pepper, brown sugar, vinegar, and gingersnaps. Simmer until gingersnaps dissolve.

3. Stir barley into beef mixture. In 7-quart slow cooker, place a layer of ⅓ (3 cups) of the cabbage, then top with half of the beef mixture. Repeat layers, ending with cabbage. Pour 1 can tomato sauce over all.

4. Cover and cook on low for 8–9 hours or until cabbage is tender.

❧ **Makes 12–14 servings**

Tropical Breeze Pot Roast

This flavorful roast offers a taste of the islands! Beef with fruit is a wonderful combination, and some ginger and spice will really wake up your taste buds.

4 pound beef chuck roast

⅓ cup flour

1 teaspoon salt

1 teaspoon cumin

½ teaspoon cinnamon

¼ teaspoon cayenne pepper

3 tablespoons olive oil

3 onions, chopped

4 cloves garlic, minced

½ cup beef broth

2 jalapeño peppers, minced

3 tablespoons minced fresh gingerroot

1 (20-ounce) can pineapple tidbits in juice, undrained

1 (8-ounce) can crushed pineapple in juice, undrained

1 (20-ounce) can tropical fruit salad in juice, drained

½ cup orange juice

3 tablespoons cornstarch

8 cups hot cooked rice

1. Trim excess fat from roast. On shallow plate, combine flour, salt, cumin, cinnamon, and cayenne pepper. Dredge meat in this mixture.
2. In large skillet, heat olive oil over medium heat. Brown roast on both sides, turning once, for about 7–8 minutes. Transfer to 6- to 7-quart slow cooker.
3. Add onions and garlic to skillet; cook and stir about 4–5 minutes, stirring to loosen pan drippings. Add beef broth and bring to a simmer. Pour into slow cooker.
4. Add jalapeño peppers, gingerroot, pineapple tidbits, and crushed pineapple to slow cooker. Cover and cook on low for 8–9 hours or until beef is very tender.
5. Remove beef from slow cooker and cover to keep warm. Add tropical fruit salad to slow cooker. In small bowl, combine orange juice with cornstarch and stir into slow cooker. Cover and cook on high for 20 minutes until thickened.
6. Slice beef and serve with fruit sauce over the hot cooked rice.

❧ **Makes 12–14** servings

Pork and Ham Entrées

✣

My maternal grandmother really loved pork, and so does my mother. We ate tender, juicy chops and roasts quite often when I was growing up. And my husband loves pork too, especially smoked pork, because he grew up in Germany where it's practically the national meat.

Pork includes roasts, chops, ham, bacon, and ribs. These foods cook well in the slow cooker (except bacon) and can be transformed into hearty one-pot meals or elegant entrées. A pork loin roast is an inexpensive way to serve a crowd. And you can combine pork with everything from curry to chili powder!

Bacon is delicious used as a flavoring in many main dish recipes. Just cook it crisply in a skillet and use the drippings to sauté meat or vegetables. When using bacon in a slow cooker, it's best to refrigerate the cooked bacon and add it toward the end of cooking time so it retains its texture.

We no longer have to cook pork to well-done. Today's pork is bred to be leaner, and it's safe to cook pork until there's just a tinge of pink in the center. Using a food thermometer is always a good idea. Cook pork to 155°F. For roasts, let the pork stand, covered, for about 10 minutes after cooking before slicing to let the juices redistribute.

—*Linda Larsen*

Orange and Apricot Pork Chops

This sweet and tangy sauce complements the tender pork beautifully. Serve with a wild rice pilaf and a fruit salad for the perfect Lenten meal.

10 boneless loin pork chops

1 teaspoon seasoned salt

1/4 teaspoon white pepper

1 teaspoon paprika

1/4 cup butter

2 onions, chopped

1 cup orange marmalade

1 cup apricot preserves

1 cup golden raisins

1/2 cup honey

1/4 cup mustard

1 teaspoon grated orange peel

1. Sprinkle pork chops with seasoned salt, pepper, and paprika. In large skillet, melt butter over medium heat. Add pork chops; brown on both sides, about 4–5 minutes total.
2. Remove pork chops to a 6- to 7-quart slow cooker. Add onions to drippings remaining in pan; cook and stir for 4 minutes to loosen pan drippings, until onions are crisp-tender. Add to slow cooker.
3. In medium bowl, combine all remaining ingredients and mix well. Stir into slow cooker.
4. Cover and cook on low for 7–9 hours or until pork registers 155°F and is tender. Serve with hot cooked rice or mashed potatoes.

❧ **Makes 10 servings**

Creamy Mustard Pork Chops

Mustard was made for pork. The spicy, sweet-and-sour taste blends with the sweet and nutty flavor of pork chops. Serve this dish with mashed potatoes.

8 boneless pork loin chops

½ teaspoon salt

⅛ teaspoon white pepper

2 tablespoons olive oil

2 onions, sliced

¼ cup Dijon mustard

1½ cups chicken broth

1 tablespoon prepared horseradish

2 tablespoons cornstarch

1 cup sour cream

2 tablespoons Dijon mustard

1. Sprinkle pork chops with salt and pepper. In large skillet, heat olive oil over medium heat. Add chops; brown, turning once, for about 4–6 minutes.
2. Place onions in the bottom of a 5- to 6-quart slow cooker. Add a layer of pork chops, then spread some of the mustard over. Repeat, using the rest of the pork chops and the mustard.
3. Add chicken broth to slow cooker. Cover and cook on low for 7–8 hours or until chops are tender and register 155°F.
4. Remove chops from slow cooker and cover to keep warm. In small bowl, combine horseradish, cornstarch, sour cream, and Dijon mustard; mix well. Pour into slow cooker and stir well.
5. Return chops to slow cooker, cover, and cook on high for 30 minutes until sauce is thickened. Serve immediately.

❦ **Makes 8 servings**

Smoked Pork Chop Casserole

This will satisfy all those meat and potato lovers at your next gathering. You can fix this the day before or in the early morning and then just pop it in the oven when you're ready to serve. You won't have to worry about rushing or cleaning up the kitchen.

3 tablespoons margarine or butter

3 tablespoons flour

1 (14.5-ounce) can chicken broth

8 to 10 smoked pork chops

2 tablespoons oil

Salt and pepper

8 cups sliced potatoes

1 medium onion, sliced

1. In saucepan, melt margarine or butter. Stir in flour, salt, and pepper. Add chicken broth. Cook and stir until mixture boils; boil for 2 more minutes. Remove from heat and set aside.
2. In skillet, brown chops in oil with dash salt and pepper. Drain on paper towels.
3. Place potatoes in greased 9" × 13" baking dish and top with onions. Pour broth mixture over potatoes and onions.
4. Place pork chops on top and cover with aluminum foil. Bake at 350° for 50–60 minutes. Uncover and bake 20–30 minutes more.

Makes 8–10 servings

He causeth the grass to grow for the cattle, and herb for the service of man: that he may bring forth food out of the earth.

—Psalms 104:14

Hot German Potato Salad

Hot potato salad is a classic German side dish. Adding sausages elevates it to a hearty main dish.

4 slices bacon

2 tablespoons butter

1 onion, chopped

4 cloves garlic, minced

1½ pounds Polish sausage

9 potatoes, cut into chunks

½ cup sugar

½ cup chicken broth

½ teaspoon celery seed

⅛ teaspoon pepper

¼ cup flour

½ cup apple cider vinegar

1 cup sour cream

1. In large skillet, cook bacon until crisp. Drain bacon on paper towels, crumble, and set aside in refrigerator. Drain all but 1 tablespoon drippings from skillet. Add butter to skillet.
2. Add onion and garlic to skillet; cook and stir for 5 minutes. Remove from heat. Cut sausage into 1" chunks.
3. Combine potatoes and sausage in 5- to 6-quart slow cooker. Add sugar, chicken broth, celery seed, and pepper to skillet with onions and mix well. Pour into slow cooker.
4. Cover and cook on low for 8–10 hours or until potatoes are tender. In small bowl, combine flour, vinegar, and sour cream and mix well. Stir into slow cooker. Cover and cook on high for 20–30 minutes or until hot and blended. Sprinkle with reserved bacon before serving.

❀ **Makes 10–12 servings**

Then he looked up at his disciples and said: "Blessed are you who are poor, for yours is the kingdom of God. Blessed are you who are hungry now, for you will be filled.

—Luke 6:20–21

Pork Chops and Rice

This recipe is so easy that your kids can put it together for you on a busy day. Kids can have it ready for you when you came home after a busy day.

1 (10.75-ounce) can cream of celery soup

1 (10.75-ounce) can cream of mushroom soup

2 cups rice, uncooked

1 cup milk

1 cup sour cream

8 pork chops

1. Mix together soups, rice, milk, and sour cream and pour into a greased 9" × 13" baking dish.
2. Place pork chops on top.
3. Cover and bake at 350° for 45–60 minutes until done.

❧ **Makes 8 servings**

But Jesus said unto her, Let the children first be filled: for it is not meet to take the children's bread, and to cast it unto the dogs.

—Mark 7:27

Ham and Cheese Potatoes

Kids will love this recipe. It's hot, creamy, and comforting, made easy by starting with frozen potatoes.

1 (32-ounce) package frozen straight cut French fry potatoes

2 onions, chopped

4 cloves garlic, minced

3 cups cubed ham

2 cups shredded Havarti cheese

2 (10-ounce) cans cream of potato soup

1 cup ricotta cheese

1/8 teaspoon pepper

1 teaspoon dried marjoram

2 cups frozen baby peas, thawed

1/2 cup grated Romano cheese

1. In 5- to 6-quart slow cooker, combine potatoes, onions, garlic, ham, and Havarti cheese; mix well. In medium bowl, combine soup, cheese, pepper, and marjoram. Pour over potato mixture.
2. Cover and cook on low for 8–9 hours or until potatoes are tender. Stir in peas and Romano cheese. Cover and cook on high for 30–40 minutes or until peas are hot. Serve immediately.

❧ **Makes 8–10 servings**

Ham and Cheesy Mashed Potatoes

It's wonderful that so many good cooks are willing to share their recipes and their cooking tips. Food has a way of bringing people together.

8 cups mashed potatoes
1½ teaspoons garlic powder
3 cups diced fully cooked ham
3 cups shredded Cheddar cheese
1 cup whipping cream

1. In a large bowl, combine the mashed potatoes and garlic powder. Pat the potatoes into a greased 9" × 13" baking dish. Distribute ham evenly over the potatoes.
2. Combine the cheese and the whipping cream then pour mixture over the ham.
3. Bake uncovered at 450° for 15 minutes or until golden.

❦ **Makes 12–15 servings**

Hash Brown Casserole

The French-fried onions give this recipe a nice crunchy taste. You may even want to double the amount of onions that are recommended.

1 (8-ounce) package cream cheese, softened
2 (10.75-ounce) cans cream of celery soup
1 (32-ounce) package frozen hash browns, thawed
1½ cups diced green peppers
2 cups cooked ham, cut into cubes
1 cup shredded Cheddar cheese
1 can French-fried onions

1. Cook cream cheese and soup in saucepan until blended, stirring with wire whisk.
2. Place hash browns in bowl and toss with soup mixture, peppers, and ham. Put mixture in greased 9" × 13" baking dish and bake at 350° for 30–45 minutes.
3. Top with Cheddar cheese and French-fried onions and bake for 10–15 minutes more.

❦ **Makes 8–10 servings**

Spicy Ham and Corn Bake

Corn muffin mix is the secret ingredient in this hearty casserole. You can substitute Canadian bacon for the ham.

2 tablespoons butter

1 onion, chopped

3 cloves garlic, minced

1–2 jalapeño peppers, minced

2 (8-ounce) boxes corn muffin mix

3 eggs

1 cup mascarpone cheese

3 cups chopped ham

2 cups frozen corn

1½ cups shredded Cheddar cheese

1 cup salsa

¼ cup chopped green onions, white and green parts

¼ cup sliced black olives

1. In large skillet, melt butter over medium heat. Add onion and garlic; cook and stir for 5 minutes. Add jalapeño peppers and remove from heat.
2. In large bowl, combine both boxes muffin mix with onion mixture, eggs, and mascarpone cheese; mix well.
3. Spray a 4-quart slow cooker with nonstick cooking spray. Place half of the muffin mixture in bottom of slow cooker. Top with half of the ham, corn, and cheese. Repeat layers, ending with cheese.
4. Cover and cook on high for 2½–3½ hours or until toothpick inserted in center comes out clean.
5. Meanwhile, in small bowl combine salsa, green onions, and olives; mix well. To serve, scoop casserole out of slow cooker onto serving plates. Offer salsa mixture as a topping.

❦ **Makes 8 servings**

Indian Chicken Drummies ● page 7

Sweet-and-Sour
Nut Mix
page 20

Spicy Meatballs
page 17

Bob's Won Tons ● page 12

Chocolate-Pumpkin Bread Pudding ● page 53

Bacon Sweet
Potato Hash
page 43

Breakfast Granola Bake
page 45

Raspberry–Cream Cheese Coffeecake ● page 32

Macaroni Salad
page 68

Linda's Potato and
Green Bean Salad
page 75

Chicken Bacon Pizza ● page 230

Updated Chicken
Cordon Bleu
page 147

Tropical Breeze Pot Roast
page 204

Mexican Lasagna • page 230

Deviled Spare Ribs • page 223

Fruity Sweet
Potatoes
page 301

Grandmother's Best
Chicken Salad
Sandwiches
page 322

Caramel Turtle
Brownies
page 351

Toffee Peach Crisp
page 394

Easy Éclairs ● page 373

Banana–Graham Cracker Icebox Dessert ● page 386

Split Pie • page 400

Sausage-Sweet Potato Supper

Sweet potatoes, apples, and pork really complement each other. Add curry powder and some onions and garlic, and you have a fabulous one-dish meal.

2 pounds sweet Italian sausage links

2 tablespoons butter

2 onions, chopped

4 cloves garlic, minced

¼ cup flour

1 teaspoon salt

⅛ teaspoon pepper

1 tablespoon curry powder

⅓ cup brown sugar

½ cup chicken broth

1 cup apple cider

6 sweet potatoes, peeled

3 apples, peeled and sliced

2 tablespoons brown sugar

1. In large skillet, cook sausage until almost done; remove from skillet. Add butter to drippings remaining in skillet. Add onions and garlic; cook and stir until tender, about 6 minutes.
2. Add flour, salt, pepper, and curry powder; cook and stir until bubbly. Add ⅓ cup brown sugar, then stir in chicken broth and cider. Cook and stir until thickened.
3. Slice sweet potatoes into ⅛" thick rounds. Slice the sausage into 1" chunks. Layer sweet potatoes, apples, sausage pieces, and onion mixture in 5- to 6-quart slow cooker. Top with 2 tablespoons brown sugar.
4. Cover and cook on low for 9–10 hours or until sweet potatoes are tender. Serve immediately.

❦ **Makes 10 servings**

While they were eating, he took a loaf of bread, and after blessing it he broke it, gave it to them, and said, "Take, this is my body." Then he took a cup, and after giving thanks he gave it to them, and all of them drank from it. He said to them, "This is my blood of the covenant, which is poured out for many."

—Mark 14:22

Biscuits and Gravy

This is comfort food at its best. You may not want to count the calories in this, but the flavor is wonderful. Savor every delicious bite.

1 pound sausage
1 (10.75-ounce) can cream of chicken soup
1 cup half-and-half
½ teaspoon dry mustard
¼ teaspoon seasoned salt
¼ teaspoon pepper
1 cup sour cream
1 (7.5-ounce) tube biscuits

1. In a heavy skillet, crumble sausage and cook over medium heat until browned. Drain and remove sausage from skillet.
2. In the same skillet, mix soup and half-and-half. Add mustard, salt, and pepper, and bring to a boil.
3. Reduce heat and stir in sausage and sour cream. Simmer until heated through but do not boil.
4. Split biscuits in half and place in greased 9" × 13" baking dish and pour gravy over biscuits. Cover with foil to keep warm.

Makes 10 servings

Escalloped Cabbage

Ham and cabbage go hand in hand with each other. Many a memory of stuffed cabbage dinners will come back to you when you serve this dish.

1 medium head cabbage, shredded
2 cups milk
2 tablespoons butter
3 tablespoons flour
2 cups cooked diced ham
1 cup bread crumbs
1 cup shredded cheese

1. Cook cabbage in boiling salted water for 3 to 5 minutes. Drain well.
2. In medium bowl, whisk together milk, butter, and flour. Stir cabbage into saucem then add ham.
3. Place in greased 9" × 13" baking dish and cover with bread crumbs and cheese. Bake at 350° for 30–35 minutes or until golden brown on top.

Makes 10–12 servings

Stuffed Ham Rolls

Get deli ham sliced fairly thin. It tastes better than with the prepackaged ham. These would be good made with other deli meats such as turkey or chicken breast.

1 cup chopped fresh spinach
1 cup cooked rice
2 green onions, sliced
¼ teaspoon pepper
1 pound deli ham slices
1 cup mayonnaise
2 tablespoons mustard

1. Spray 9" × 13" baking dish with nonstick cooking spray.
2. Wash and drain spinach. Pat dry with paper towel.
3. Combine rice, green onions, spinach, and pepper in a medium bowl.
4. Place 2 tablespoons rice mixture in the center of each ham slice. Roll up and secure with toothpicks. Lay the rolls in the bottom of the prepared pan. Bake, covered, at 350° for 20–25 minutes until heated through.
5. Meanwhile, blend mayonnaise and mustard and warm in saucepan. Top the ham rolls with the sauce and bake for 5 more minutes.

🌰 **Makes 15–18 rolls**

Ham with Wild Rice

Wild rice cooks perfectly in the slow cooker, unlike white rice.

2 onions, chopped
6 cloves garlic, minced
2 (4-ounce) jars sliced mushrooms
2 cups wild rice
1 (16-ounce) bag baby carrots
4 cups cubed cooked ham
1 (10-ounce) container refrigerated Alfredo sauce
1 (10-ounce) can condensed cream of mushroom soup
5 cups chicken stock
1 teaspoon dried tarragon leaves
⅛ teaspoon white pepper
½ cup grated Parmesan cheese

1. In 5-quart slow cooker, combine onions, garlic, mushrooms with their liquid, wild rice, carrots, and ham; stir gently.
2. In large bowl, combine Alfredo sauce, soup, chicken stock, tarragon, and pepper; mix well. Pour into slow cooker.
3. Cover and cook on high for 1 hour, then stir. Cover again and cook on low for 6 hours or until wild rice and carrots are tender. Stir in cheese and serve.

🌰 **Makes 12 servings**

Breaking Bread

All of us have many stories about our cooking experiences. Most of them we can look back on and recall with laughter and fond memories; other stories are still bittersweet; and some we don't want to recall at all.

I remember when I was engaged and was going to dinner at my future in-laws' house for the third time or so. Larry's mother, Gladys, was busy cooking in the kitchen. Wanting to make a good impression, I asked if I could be of any help. She had me help set the table and fix the drinks, but then she asked me to put a brown paper bag over her loaf of bread baking in the oven to help prevent it from burning.

Well, she had a gas stove. You can probably guess the rest. I removed the bread from the oven, placed it in the sack, and started to put it back in the oven. Somehow—to this day, I don't know how—I managed to catch the bag on fire. It must have been too close to one of the burners. She was in the other room and, of course, she walked in while I was attempting to put out the fire. I got so nervous, I took the whole bag and put it in the sink and sprayed it with water. Her homemade bread was ruined, and I was the one who ruined it! What a way to start out with your future mother-in-law. I appreciated her graciousness in taking it so well and making me feel welcomed to the family. Now that I am a new mother-in-law with a very sweet daughter-in-law, I will do my best to make her feel just as welcome in our family.

—*Susie Siegfried*

Tex-Mex Pork and Corn Bake

Two kinds of corn add flavor and texture to this spicy dish. Serve it with some chopped fresh tomatoes and tortilla chips.

8 boneless pork loin chops

1 teaspoon salt

1/8 teaspoon pepper

1 tablespoon olive oil

1 tablespoon butter

2 onions, chopped

4 cloves garlic, minced

1 tablespoon chili powder

1 (4-ounce) can chopped green chiles

1 (16-ounce) can cream-style corn

2 cups frozen corn

2 green bell peppers, chopped

1 jalapeño pepper, chopped

2 cups grated Swiss or pepper jack cheese

1. Sprinkle chops with salt and pepper. In large skillet, heat olive oil and butter over medium heat. Add chops; brown on both sides, turning once, about 5 minutes total. Remove chops from pan.
2. Add onions and garlic to pan; cook and stir until tender, about 5 minutes. Add chili powder, green chiles with liquid, cream-style corn, and frozen corn. Cook and stir for 4 minutes.
3. In 5- to 6-quart slow cooker, layer corn mixture with pork chops and green bell peppers. Sprinkle top with jalapeño pepper. Cover and cook on low for 7–8 hours or until chops are tender.
4. Uncover and stir in cheese. Cover and cook on high for 20 minutes longer or until cheese melts. Serve immediately.

❧ **Makes 8 servings**

Blessed are those who hunger and thirst for righteousness, for they will be filled.

–Matthew 5:6

Spicy Fruited Pork Chops

Dried fruit really complements the flavor of pork. You could use any combination you'd like; dried currants and peaches would be nice additions.

8 boneless pork loin chops

1 teaspoon salt

1/8 teaspoon white pepper

2 tablespoons butter

1 tablespoon olive oil

1/3 cup brown sugar

1/3 cup white wine vinegar

1 1/2 teaspoons cinnamon

1/2 teaspoon allspice

2 cups chicken broth

10 dried apricots, chopped

1 cup golden raisins

10 dried prunes, chopped

2 tablespoons cornstarch

1/4 cup water

1. Sprinkle chops with salt and pepper. In skillet, heat butter and olive oil over medium heat. When butter melts, brown chops on both sides, about 5 minutes total. Place in 5-quart slow cooker.
2. Add brown sugar, vinegar, cinnamon, allspice, and chicken broth to skillet; bring to a simmer. Stir in apricots, raisins, and prunes. Pour over chops in slow cooker.
3. Cover and cook on low for 7 hours or until chops and fruit are tender. In bowl, combine cornstarch and water. Add to slow cooker; cover and cook on high for 20 minutes or until sauce thickens.

❧ **Makes 8 servings**

Keep falsehood and lies far from me; give me neither poverty nor riches, but give me only my daily bread.

—Proverbs 30:8

Ham and Potato Salad

Cooking ham and potatoes together in the slow cooker makes a wonderful base for a ham salad. Add dressing and it's waiting for you in the fridge!

4 potatoes, peeled and cubed

4 sweet potatoes, peeled and cubed

2 onions, chopped

4 cloves garlic, minced

1 cup chicken broth

3 cups cubed ham

1½ cups mayonnaise

1½ cups plain yogurt

⅓ cup milk

½ cup yellow mustard

1 teaspoon salt

¼ teaspoon pepper

2 teaspoons dried basil leaves

2 green bell peppers, chopped

4 stalks celery, chopped

2 pints grape tomatoes

1. In 5- to 6-quart slow cooker, combine potatoes, sweet potatoes, onions, garlic, chicken broth, and cubed ham. Cover and cook on low for 8–9 hours or until potatoes are tender when pierced with fork. Drain if necessary.

2. In large bowl, combine mayonnaise, yogurt, milk, mustard, salt, pepper, and dried basil; mix well. Remove hot potato mixture from slow cooker with large slotted spoon or sieve. Stir into dressing in bowl, then add remaining ingredients and stir gently to coat.

3. Cover and refrigerate for 3–4 hours or until salad is cold. Stir gently before serving.

❦ **Makes 10–12 servings**

Curried Pork

Curry and chutney are Indian condiments that are sweet and spicy at the same time. Cooked with lots of fruit and pork and served over rice or mashed potatoes, this makes a delicious and easy dinner.

2 onions, chopped

4 cloves garlic, minced

3 tart apples, peeled, cored, and chopped

1 cup golden raisins

1 cup dark raisins

2½ pounds lean pork, cubed

1–2 tablespoons curry powder

1 teaspoon salt

¼ teaspoon white pepper

1 cup apple juice

1 cup chicken broth

2 tablespoons lemon juice

1 (16-ounce) jar mango chutney

2 tablespoons cornstarch

⅓ cup mango nectar

1. In 5- to 6-quart slow cooker, combine all ingredients except chutney, cornstarch, and mango nectar. Cover and cook on low for 8–9 hours or until pork is tender.
2. In medium bowl, combine chutney, cornstarch, and mango nectar. Stir into slow cooker. Cover and cook on high for 20–30 minutes or until sauce is thickened. Serve over hot cooked rice or mashed potatoes.

❀ **Makes 8–10 servings**

The Best Spareribs

Spareribs are delicious for a summer picnic. Serve with Potato Salad (page 310) and a nice fruit salad.

4 pounds country-style pork spareribs

1 tablespoon olive oil

1 onion, chopped

3 cloves garlic, minced

1 cup chili sauce

½ cup barbecue sauce

¼ cup Dijon mustard

¼ cup honey

1 teaspoon salt

¼ teaspoon pepper

1. Cut spareribs into serving-sized pieces and place, meat side up, on broiler rack. Broil for 3–4 minutes or until spareribs brown; set aside.
2. In large saucepan, heat olive oil over medium heat. Add onion and garlic; cook and stir until tender, about 5 minutes. Add remaining ingredients and bring to a simmer.
3. Place ribs in 5- to 6-quart slow cooker and pour sauce over. Cover and cook on low for 7–8 hours or until ribs are cooked and tender. Uncover and cook on high for 30 minutes to help thicken sauce, if necessary.

❀ **Makes 8–10 servings**

Deviled Spareribs

A little bit of spice is the perfect finish for super-tender ribs. Serve these spareribs with lots of water or soft drinks and lots of paper napkins!

4–5 pounds spareribs

2 tablespoons butter

2 onions, chopped

3 cloves garlic, minced

1 (16-ounce) bottle barbecue sauce

¼ cup honey

¼ teaspoon cayenne pepper

1 cup chili sauce

½ teaspoon salt

⅛ teaspoon white pepper

1. Preheat broiler. Place spareribs on broiler rack and broil 6" from heat source for 4–5 minutes or until browned. Turn and broil for 4–5 minutes longer. Cut into serving-sized pieces, if necessary, and place in 7-quart slow cooker.
2. In large saucepan, melt butter over medium heat. Add onions and garlic; cook and stir until tender, about 5 minutes. Add remaining ingredients; cook and stir for 4 minutes.
3. Pour sauce over ribs in slow cooker. Cover and cook on low for 8–10 hours, until ribs are tender. Serve immediately.

❧ **Makes 12–15 servings**

Barbecued Pulled Pork

Here's a slow cooker barbecue recipe that can cook all day and be ready at dinnertime with no hassles. Serve it on buns, with coleslaw either on the side or on your sandwich, my preference.

1 cup water

3 pounds boneless pork tenderloin, cut up

1 (42-ounce) bottle barbecue sauce

Buns

Cole slaw

1. Put water and cut-up pork tenderloin in slow cooker and cook for 8–10 hours or overnight, until it falls apart. Drain and pull apart.
2. Add barbecue sauce and cook an additional hour in slow cooker.

❧ **Makes 12–14 servings**

Pulled Pork Burritos

A dry rub helps season the meat in these excellent burritos. You also can use this pork filling for wrap sandwiches; spread corn tortillas with some refried beans, and then add the pork.

4-pound boneless pork loin roast

¼ cup brown sugar

1 teaspoon dry mustard powder

1 tablespoon chili powder

1 teaspoon salt

¼ teaspoon cayenne pepper

2 onions, chopped

6 cloves garlic, minced

1 cup vinegar

2 cups chicken stock

16 (10-inch) flour tortillas

2 (16-ounce) cans refried beans

2 cups shredded Muenster cheese

2 cups shredded sharp Cheddar cheese

1. Cut roast into 3 pieces. In small bowl, combine brown sugar, mustard powder, chili powder, salt, and cayenne pepper; mix well. Sprinkle over roast and rub into surface.

2. Cover and marinate pork in refrigerator overnight. In the morning, place onions and garlic in bottom of 5- or 6-quart slow cooker. Place pork on top. Pour vinegar and chicken stock over all. Cover and cook on low for 8–9 hours or until pork is very tender.

3. Remove pork from slow cooker along with onions. Shred pork, using two forks. Add vegetables and enough of the cooking liquid to moisten meat. At this point you can use the meat for wrap sandwiches or other purposes if you wish. If making burritos, continue with next steps.

4. Preheat oven to 375°F. Spread tortillas with refried beans. Top each with some of the shredded pork and the cheeses; then roll up. Place, seam side down, in two greased 13" × 9" casserole dishes.

5. Cover with foil and bake for 20–30 minutes or until cheese is melted and burritos are hot.

❀ **Makes 16 servings**

Pork Flautas

Military personnel have some of the best recipes! This one comes from the air force, where it was a hit at a neighborhood cook-out on the base.

12 corn tortillas

10 ounces pork sausage

2 tablespoons chopped onion

$1/3$ cup shredded Cheddar cheese

2 ounces cream cheese, softened

$1/4$ teaspoon marjoram

$1/3$ cup sour cream

1. Soften tortillas by frying in a skillet sprayed with vegetable cooking spray.
2. Combine sausage, onion, cheese, cream cheese, and marjoram.
3. Place 2 tablespoons of filling in center of tortilla. Roll up and bake at 375° for 35 minutes in a greased 9" × 13" baking dish.
4. Warm sour cream in microwave for 20 seconds and spoon over flautas.

❀ **Makes 12**

Pork Loin with Apple Chutney

This is a delicious way to serve the Apple Chutney, which you can make in large quantities. The pork can be served on its own, too; the sauce can be thickened with cornstarch and water.

1 onion, chopped

3 cloves garlic, minced

1 (4-pound) boneless pork loin roast

$1/2$ teaspoon salt

$1/4$ teaspoon pepper

1 teaspoon dried thyme leaves

1 cup chicken broth

$1/2$ cup apple cider

2 cups Apple Chutney (page 412)

1. Place onion and garlic in bottom of 5- to 6-quart slow cooker. Sprinkle pork with salt, pepper, and thyme. Place in slow cooker.
2. In medium bowl combine chicken broth and $1/2$ cup apple cider; mix well. Pour over pork. Cover and cook on low for 8 hours until pork registers 155°F.
3. Slice pork and serve with chutney, either warm or cold.

❀ **Makes 12 servings**

Stuffed Pork Casserole

Years ago, you'd have to start this recipe with pork chops and cut them off the bone before cooking. The boneless pork tenderloin makes this recipe a lot easier to prepare.

1 (3-pound) pork tenderloin, cut into ½" thick slices

2 (10.75-ounce) cans cream of chicken soup

1 (14.5-ounce) can chicken broth

¾ cup Miracle Whip

1 (8-ounce) canister of chicken-flavored Stove Top stuffing

1. Place pork in the bottom of a greased 9" × 13" baking dish.
2. Mix soup, broth, and Miracle Whip and heat in saucepan until warm. Pour over pork.
3. Prepare stuffing mix by package directions. Spoon stuffing evenly over chicken and soup mixture. Bake at 350° for 45 minutes.

❧ **Makes 8–10 servings**

Spicy Pork Tenderloin

Mustard, honey, and tender pork combine beautifully in this simple recipe. Serve it with Herbed Brown Rice Pilaf (page 294) or mashed potatoes to soak up the sauce.

2 (2-pound) pork tenderloins

10 cloves garlic, peeled and sliced

1½ teaspoons salt

¼ teaspoon white pepper

1 teaspoon cumin

¼ cup Dijon mustard

⅓ cup honey

1½ cups chicken broth

2 tablespoons cornstarch

½ cup water

1. Poke 20 holes into each of the tenderloins with a knife. Cut each clove of garlic into four slices. Insert a slice of garlic into each hole. In small bowl, combine salt, pepper, cumin, mustard, and honey; mix well. Spread over tenderloins.
2. Place pork in 4- to 5-quart slow cooker. Pour chicken broth into slow cooker.
3. Cover and cook on low for 5–6 hours or until meat thermometer registers 155°F. Remove pork from slow cooker, cover, and let stand for 15 minutes.
4. Meanwhile, combine cornstarch and water in a small bowl. Stir into the liquid remaining in slow cooker. Cook on high for 15–20 minutes or until sauce thickens. Slice pork and serve with sauce.

❧ **Makes 8–10 servings**

Pork Tenderloin and Potato Bake

Treat your family or friends to this dish when you want wonderful comfort food. Potatoes served with pork make for a hearty meal.

1 (3-pound) pork tenderloin, cut into ½" slices

1 (10.75-ounce) can cream of mushroom soup

½ cup milk

⅔ cup sour cream

2 cups shredded mild Cheddar cheese

½ teaspoon seasoned salt

1 (32-ounce) bag frozen plain hash brown potatoes, thawed

2 cans French-fried onions

1. Lightly brown each slice of tenderloin in 4 to 5 tablespoons oil. Remove tenderloins onto platter.
2. Combine soup, milk, sour cream, 1 cup shredded cheese, and ½ teaspoon seasoned salt.
3. Pat thawed potatoes with paper towel to remove any water. Stir soup mixture into thawed potatoes. Spoon half of the potato mixture into greased 9" × 13" baking dish. Arrange tenderloin pieces on top of potato mixture. Spoon remaining potato mixture over tenderloin pieces.
4. Bake covered with foil for 30 minutes. Sprinkle remaining shredded cheese over potatoes and top with onions. Bake uncovered about 3–5 minutes longer or until cheese melts and onions are lightly browned.

❧ **Makes 8–10 servings**

Man did eat angels' food:
he sent them meat to the full.

—Psalms 78:25

Pork and Bean Tacos

Make a pot of this filling, along with the other taco fillings in the book, and set up a taco bar. Olé!

2 tablespoons chili powder

1 teaspoon cumin

1 teaspoon salt

¼ teaspoon pepper

¼ cup flour

1 (4-pound) boneless pork loin roast

2 tablespoons butter

2 tablespoons oil

2 onions, chopped

6 cloves garlic, minced

1 (15-ounce) can refried beans

2 (15-ounce) cans kidney beans

1 (16-ounce) jar mild or medium salsa

12–14 taco shells

2 cups shredded lettuce

2 cups shredded Muenster cheese

2 cups chopped tomatoes

1. On shallow plate, combine chili powder, cumin, salt, pepper, and flour; mix well. Dredge pork in this mixture until completely coated.
2. In skillet, melt butter with oil over medium heat. Add pork; sear on all sides until browned, about 6 minutes. Place pork in 5- to 6-quart slow cooker.
3. Add onions and garlic to skillet; cook and stir until tender, stirring to scrape up drippings. Add refried beans and heat for 4 minutes, stirring well. Add kidney beans and salsa; pour over pork.
4. Cover and cook on low for 7–9 hours or until pork is very tender. Using two forks, shred pork. Stir to mix with rest of filling.
5. Heat taco shells as directed on package. Make tacos with filling, lettuce, cheese, and tomatoes.

❧ **Makes 12 servings**

"Did not your father eat and drink and do justice and righteousness? Then it was well with him. He judged the cause of the poor and needy; then it was well. Is not this to know me?" says the Lord.

—Jeremiah 22:15–16

Slow Cooker Tex-Mex Lasagna

Using corn tortillas instead of pasta works well in the slow cooker, which can overcook pasta. You can vary the spice level to suit your taste. Serve this spicy casserole with more sour cream, guacamole, and chopped chives.

2 pounds spicy bulk pork sausage

2 onions, chopped

4 cloves garlic, minced

1 (16-ounce) jar mild or medium salsa

1 (16-ounce) can refried beans

1 (6-ounce) can tomato paste

1 tablespoon chili powder

½ teaspoon salt

⅛ teaspoon cayenne pepper

1 (8-ounce) package cream cheese, softened

1 cup sour cream

2 tablespoons flour

2 cups frozen corn

1 (4-ounce) can chopped green chiles, drained

12 corn tortillas

2 cups shredded pepper jack cheese

1 cup shredded Cheddar cheese

1. In skillet, cook pork sausage with onions and garlic until sausage is cooked, stirring to break up meat. Drain well. Add salsa, refried beans, tomato paste, chili powder, salt, and cayenne pepper; stir until combined. Remove from heat.

2. In large bowl beat cream cheese until soft. Gradually add sour cream; beat well. Mix in flour. Add corn and drained chiles.

3. Place a layer of the pork mixture in the bottom of a 5- to 6-quart slow cooker. Top with some of four corn tortillas, overlapping slightly. Top with corn mixture, then some of the cheeses. Repeat layers, ending with cheese.

4. Cover and cook on low for 7–9 hours or until casserole is hot and bubbling. Serve with guacamole, more sour cream, and chopped chives if desired.

❦ **Makes 8–10 servings**

Mexican Lasagna

This is a different spin on lasagna that is quite a treat. You can make it spicier by adding some jalapeños to the cottage cheese mixture.

1 pound ground pork

½ cup chopped onion

½ cup chopped green pepper

2 cups diced tomato

1 (1.25-ounce) envelope taco seasoning

2 cups cottage cheese

2 eggs

6 flour tortillas

6 ounces shredded Cheddar cheese

Toppings

½ cup diced tomatoes

¼ cup sliced olives

¼ cup sliced green onions

1. Brown ground pork with onion and pepper. Add tomatoes and taco seasoning.
2. In a bowl, mix cottage cheese, Cheddar cheese, and eggs.
3. Grease a 9" × 13" baking dish and place 3 tortillas on bottom. Spread tortillas with half of meat mixture and half of cottage cheese mixture.
4. Layer with 3 tortillas and then remaining meat and cottage cheese mixture. Bake uncovered at 350° for 40 minutes. Remove from oven and add toppings.

❦ **Makes 8–10 servings**

Chicken-Bacon Pizza

Easy to fix, easy to serve, easy to enjoy. Whip this up before a get-together and enjoy with your friends and loved ones.

4 ounces cream cheese, softened

½ cup sour cream

1 8-ounce tube crescent rolls

½ cup bacon bits

1 (10-ounce) can chicken breast, drained

⅓ cup yellow peppers

⅓ cup green peppers

½ cup diced onions

½ cup sliced mushrooms

½ cup diced tomatoes

1. Preheat oven to 375°.
2. In a bowl, combine cream cheese and sour cream. Mix well.
3. Spray 9" pie plate with vegetable cooking spray. Press crescent rolls into pie plate to form crust. Spread cream cheese mixture evenly over crescent rolls. Top cream cheese with bacon bits, chicken, and chopped vegetables.
3. Bake for 10–15 minutes. Cut into wedges and serve.

❦ **Makes 12 servings**

Broccoli and Ham Pasta

This is another good ham and cheese recipe. You can vary it by substituting another type of cheese and another type of pasta.

1 cup mayonnaise

2 (10-ounce) packages frozen broccoli florets, thawed and drained

2 cups shredded Swiss cheese

3 cups cooked ham, diced

2 cups rotini, cooked and drained

¾ cup chopped yellow pepper

½ cup milk

1 cup croutons

1. Combine mayonnaise, broccoli, 1½ cups cheese, ham, rotini, yellow pepper, and milk. Put mixture into greased 9" × 13" baking dish. Top with remaining cheese and croutons.
2. Bake at 350° for 30 minutes.

🍎 **Makes 12 servings**

April's Macaroni

This is an old recipe passed down through the generations. Obviously a keeper.

1 pound bacon

1 large onion

2 heels bread, crumbled

1 (46-ounce) can tomato juice

1 (16-ounce) box elbow macaroni

1. Freeze bacon for an hour to make it easier to cut then cut into small pieces; dice onion.
2. Sauté bacon and onion in skillet until almost done. Add bread and finish cooking until crisp and brown. Drain.
3. Cook macaroni as directed and drain.
4. Combine all ingredients including tomato juice and put in a 9" × 13" baking dish. Bake at 350° for 30 minutes. Serve with bread and butter.

🍎 **Makes 10–12 servings**

Stuffed Zucchini

This recipe takes a little more time to make than most of the other recipes in this book, but it's worth it. It's a good way to use the zucchini that all your neighbors bring you in the summer from their gardens.

8 zucchinis, scrubbed, not peeled

3 tablespoons olive oil

1 cup finely chopped onions

½ teaspoon chopped jarred garlic

1 pound ground beef or Italian sausage or pork

2 eggs slightly beaten

1 cup Italian bread crumbs

1 cup Parmesan cheese

1 teaspoon oregano

1 teaspoon salt

½ teaspoon pepper

3 cups tomato sauce

1. Cut zucchini in half lengthwise and spoon out most of pulp, leaving boat-like shells. Set aside.
2. Chop pulp coarsely.
3. Heat 3 tablespoons of olive oil, add onions, and cook until soft and lightly colored. Add pulp and garlic and cook 5 minutes longer. Transfer pulp mixture to bowl and set aside.
4. Brown meat in skillet, stirring constantly. When done, drain and add to pulp mixture in bowl.
5. In another bowl, combine zucchini mixture and meat. Beat eggs, bread crumbs, ½ cup of cheese, oregano, salt, and pepper into mixture. Spoon into shells.
6. Pour tomato sauce in greased 9" × 13" baking dish. Arrange zucchini on sauce. Sprinkle with remaining cheese and cover with foil. Bake at 350° for 20–30 minutes; remove foil and bake 10 minutes longer.

❦ **Makes 16 servings**

And they will salute thee, and give thee two loaves of bread; which thou shalt receive of their hands.

—1 Samuel 10:4

Sausage and Bean Casserole

This sweet and spicy casserole is fun to make and serve. Just drain the beans; don't rinse them. The sweet sauce they are packed in adds flavor and texture to the dish.

2 pounds sweet bulk Italian sausage

2 onions, chopped

2 (15-ounce) cans lima beans, drained

1 (15-ounce) can chili beans, undrained

1 (15-ounce) can black beans, drained

4 carrots, sliced

1 (6-ounce) can tomato paste

½ cup chili sauce

½ cup honey

⅓ cup brown sugar

¼ cup Dijon mustard

1 teaspoon fennel seed

1. In large skillet, cook sausage with onions until sausage is browned, stirring to break up meat. Drain thoroughly.
2. Place sausage and onions in 5-quart slow cooker. Add carrots, all of the beans, and mix well.
3. In skillet combine remaining ingredients and stir over low heat until blended. Pour into slow cooker.
4. Cover and cook on low for 7–8 hours or until vegetables are tender and casserole is hot and bubbly. Serve immediately.

❦ **Makes 10–12 servings**

Amy's Root Beer Pork Roast

Root beer helps tenderize the pork as it cooks. You can slice and serve this by itself, or shred the pork, return it to the sauce, and serve in tortillas or on toasted buns.

2 (2-pound) pork tenderloins

1 teaspoon garlic salt

⅛ teaspoon pepper

2 onions, sliced

1 (12-ounce) can root beer

½ cup ketchup

¼ cup chili sauce

1 tablespoon lemon juice

2 tablespoons Worcestershire sauce

2 tablespoons honey

1. Sprinkle tenderloins with garlic salt and pepper. Place onions in bottom of 5-quart slow cooker. Top with pork.
2. In medium bowl, combine remaining ingredients and stir with wire whisk until blended. Pour into slow cooker.
3. Cover and cook on low for 8–9 hours or until pork is tender. Shred pork and return to sauce. Turn slow cooker to high and cook uncovered for 30–40 minutes to thicken, or remove pork from sauce, slice, and serve with the sauce.

❦ **Makes 8–10 servings**

Aunt Peg's Pork Roast

The combination of apricots and spicy onions is really delicious with tender and juicy pork loin. This will become a favorite!

2 onions, chopped
3 cloves garlic, minced
1 (4-pound) boneless pork loin roast
½ teaspoon salt
¼ teaspoon pepper
1 (12-ounce) jar apricot preserves
1 envelope dry onion soup mix
½ cup apricot nectar
½ cup chicken broth
2 tablespoons Dijon mustard
2 tablespoons cornstarch
¼ cup cold water

1. Place onion and garlic in bottom of 5- to 6-quart slow cooker. Sprinkle pork with salt and pepper and place in slow cooker.
2. In medium bowl, combine preserves, onion soup mix, nectar, chicken broth, and mustard; mix well. Pour over pork. Cover and cook on low for 7–9 hours until pork registers 155°F.
3. Remove pork from slow cooker and cover to keep it warm. In small bowl, combine cornstarch and water; blend well. Pour into slow cooker and stir with wire whisk. Return pork to slow cooker.
4. Cover and cook on high for 25 minutes or until sauce thickens. Slice pork and serve with sauce.

❦ **Makes 12 servings**

Honey-Glazed Ham

You could have several slow cookers going with this ham for feeding a crowd at the holidays.

3 onions, sliced
4-pound fully cooked ham
½ cup brown sugar
¼ cup honey
¼ cup Dijon mustard
½ teaspoon dry mustard powder
2 tablespoons apple cider
⅛ teaspoon pepper

1. Place onions in bottom of 5- to 6-quart slow cooker. Place ham in slow cooker on top of onions.
2. In medium bowl, combine remaining ingredients and mix well. Spread over the ham.
3. Cover slow cooker and cook on high for 1 hour. Then turn heat to low and cook for 8–9 hours longer or until ham registers 140°F using a meat thermometer.

❦ **Makes 16 servings**

Fish and Seafood Entrées

❧

I've always loved seafood. In fact, when I was small and we ate out in restaurants (which didn't happen very often), my parents would let us order whatever we wanted; then they would order the most inexpensive thing on the menu in order to balance the budget. I, of course, always ordered shrimp. I love it to this day; it's sweet and tender and tastes of the sea. The best shrimp I ever had was in a restaurant in Florida. I ordered a shrimp cocktail to start. The shrimp was caught that day, and it came to the table still warm inside. Instead of ordering a main course, I got another shrimp cocktail! The chef peered around the door of the kitchen to see who was doing such a strange thing.

Seafood and the slow cooker don't automatically mix. Since fish fillets, shrimp, and other seafood cooks in such a short time, the long, slow cooking time usually results in overcooked, rubbery fish. But there are some tricks you can use.

Use the slow cooker to make a side dish: anything from potatoes to rice to vegetables. Then add the seafood during the last 30 to 60 minutes of cooking time. Voilà! Perfectly cooked seafood with very little work.

—*Linda Larsen*

Mom's Tuna Casserole

What's better than tuna casserole, especially Mom's version? Yes, you can cook pasta in the slow cooker; it just needs to be added at the very end of the cooking time.

2 onions, chopped

2 cloves garlic, minced

1 (8-ounce) package sliced mushrooms

2 (12-ounce) cans chunk white tuna, drained

1 (16-ounce) jar Alfredo sauce

½ cup milk

½ cup sour cream

2 cups shredded Colby cheese

1 pound green beans, trimmed

1 (12-ounce) package egg noodles

1 cup crushed sour cream and onion potato chips

1. In 5-quart slow cooker, combine onion, garlic, mushrooms, and tuna. Pour Alfredo sauce into slow cooker. Pour milk into the Alfredo sauce jar, close tightly, and shake. Pour this mixture into the slow cooker along with sour cream. Cover and cook on low for 7 hours.
2. Cut green beans in half and add to slow cooker along with the cheese. Cook on low for 1 hour. Then add the noodles and stir well. Cover and cook on low for 45 minutes to 1 hour or until noodles are tender. Top each serving of the casserole with a sprinkling of crushed potato chips.

❦ **Makes 8 servings**

Crunchy Tuna

Everybody has their own favorite tuna recipes, and this is one of mine. I usually prefer to use the albacore tuna rather than the regular tuna, but it tastes good with either one.

½ cup chicken broth

1 (10.75-ounce) can cream of mushroom soup

1 (10.75-ounce) can cream of celery soup

3 cups diced cooked chicken

1 (7-ounce) can tuna, flaked

¼ cup minced onions

1 cup sliced celery

1 (8-ounce) can water chestnuts, thinly sliced

1 (3-ounce) can chow mein noodles

⅓ cup sliced almonds

1. Blend broth into soups in casserole dish. Mix in remaining ingredients except almonds.
2. Bake at 325° for 45–50 minutes. Sprinkle with almonds before serving.

❦ **Makes 4 servings**

Tuna Dumpling Casserole

This meal-in-one is comforting and rich. You could use cooked chicken or ham instead of the tuna.

1 (16-ounce) bag baby carrots

2 onions, chopped

4 stalks celery, chopped

2 sweet potatoes, peeled and cubed

1 (32-ounce) box chicken broth

1 (10-ounce) can cream of celery soup

1 teaspoon dried oregano

1 teaspoon dried marjoram

1 teaspoon salt

¼ teaspoon pepper

2 (12-ounce) cans chunk tuna, drained

3 tablespoons cornstarch

⅓ cup apple juice

2 cups biscuit mix

½ cup grated Parmesan cheese

1 teaspoon dried marjoram

⅓ cup milk

⅓ cup light cream

2 tablespoons butter, melted

1. In 5-quart slow cooker, combine carrots, onions, celery, sweet potatoes, chicken broth, soup, oregano, 1 teaspoon marjoram, salt, and pepper. Cover and cook on low for 7–8 hours or until vegetables are tender.

2. Stir in drained tuna. In small bowl, combine cornstarch with apple juice and mix well; stir into slow cooker. Turn heat to high.

3. In medium bowl combine biscuit mix, cheese, and 1 teaspoon marjoram; mix well. Stir in milk, light cream, and melted butter just until blended.

4. Drop biscuit mixture by spoonfuls into slow cooker. Cover and cook on high for 30 minutes or until dumplings are cooked through. Serve.

❧ **Makes 12–14 servings**

Curried Tuna and Potato Casserole

Tuna and potatoes are a nice comforting combination. Add some curry powder and suddenly you have a gourmet dish!

8 potatoes, peeled

3 tablespoons butter

2 onions, chopped

4 cloves garlic, minced

5 tablespoons flour

1 tablespoon curry powder

1 teaspoon salt

⅛ teaspoon pepper

1½ cups heavy cream

½ cup milk

1 (16-ounce) jar Alfredo sauce

2 (12-ounce) cans chunk tuna, drained

1 (6-ounce) can chunk tuna, drained

1. Slice potatoes ⅛" thick and place in cold water. In large skillet, melt butter over medium heat. Add onions and garlic; cook and stir for 5 minutes. Add flour, curry powder, salt, and pepper; cook until bubbly.
2. Add heavy cream, milk, and Alfredo sauce and bring to a simmer. Drain potatoes thoroughly. Layer potatoes and both cans of tuna in 5-quart slow cooker. Pour cream mixture over all.
3. Cover and cook on low for 7–9 hours, or until potatoes are tender and casserole is bubbling.

❦ **Makes 8–10 servings**

Tuna and Pasta

Here's an economical dish that the whole family can enjoy. You can substitute broccoli or spinach for the frozen asparagus for a change. Also, try the tuna that now comes in a package instead of a can. You'll find it with the rest of the tuna in your grocery store.

1 cup chopped onion

1½ cups cooked small shell pasta

1 (10.75-ounce) can cream of celery soup

1 (6-ounce) can tuna, drained and flaked into pieces

½ cup sour cream

½ teaspoon dill weed

¼ cup milk

1 (8-ounce) package frozen asparagus spears, thawed

1. Preheat oven to 400°.
2. Coat skillet with vegetable cooking spray and sauté onion until tender. Stir in pasta, soup, tuna, sour cream, dill, and milk. Mix well. Cook 3 minutes or until hot.
3. Put asparagus into greased 2 quart baking dish. Pour mixture over asparagus and bake for 15 minutes.

❦ **Makes 6 servings**

Clam Linguine

This is an easy method for cooking lots of linguine in clam sauce. You could add more vegetables to the original mixture, to stretch the clams and add nutrition.

2 onions, chopped

1 leek, chopped

1 (8-ounce) package sliced fresh mushrooms

6 cloves garlic, minced

1 teaspoon salt

½ teaspoon pepper

2 (14-ounce) cans diced tomatoes with herbs, undrained

1 (28-ounce) can tomato purée

2 cups water

4 (6-ounce) cans clams, undrained

2 tablespoons lemon juice

2 (12-ounce) packages linguine pasta

¼ cup butter

½ cup chopped fresh flat leaf parsley

1 cup grated Parmesan cheese

1. In 5-quart slow cooker, combine onions, leek, mushrooms, garlic, salt, pepper, diced tomatoes, tomato purée, and water.
2. Cover and cook on low for 7–8 hours or until vegetables are tender. Stir in clams with their juice and lemon juice. Cover and cook on low for 20–30 minutes longer or until clams are hot.
3. 30 minutes before clam mixture is done, heat two large pots of salted water to boiling. Add linguine; cook according to package directions until almost tender. Drain and toss with butter.
4. Transfer linguine to three serving bowls. Ladle ⅓ of clam mixture into each bowl, and then top each with ⅓ of parsley and cheese. Serve.

❧ **Makes 12 servings**

Tuna Cashew Casserole

Cashews and chow mein noodles give this tuna casserole an extra crunch. It's a great meatless meal and may become a staple in your home, or a much-requested potluck contribution during Lent.

2 (10.75-ounce) cans cream of mushroom soup

½ cup water

2 (6-ounce) cans tuna

1 cup cashew pieces

2 cups diced celery

½ cup finely diced green peppers

½ cup shredded Cheddar cheese

4 chopped pimientos

1 cup chow mein noodles

1. Combine all ingredients except noodles and put in buttered 9" × 13" pan. Top with noodles.
2. Bake at 325° for 40 minutes.

❦ **Makes 12 servings**

Seafood Tetrazzini

This recipe will delight everyone, no matter where they dwell. It originated in Chicago, but is enjoyed by people everywhere.

2 tablespoons chopped onion

1 tablespoon butter

1 (10.75-ounce) can cream of mushroom soup

1 cup half-and-half

2 tablespoons dry sherry

8 ounces thin spaghetti, cooked

3 cups cooked shrimp

¼ cup chopped green peppers

¾ pound mushrooms

2 tablespoons chopped pimiento

½ cup grated Parmesan cheese

1. Cook onion in butter until tender.
2. Blend in soup, half-and-half, and sherry with onion. Do not boil.
3. Add spaghetti, shrimp, peppers, mushrooms, and pimiento to soup mixture.
4. Pour into a greased 2-quart casserole and sprinkle with Parmesan cheese.
5. Bake covered at 375° for 30 minutes.
6. If dry, add more half-and-half or sherry.

❦ **Makes 4–6 servings**

Pasta with Crab and Feta Cheese

The feta cheese gives this pasta recipe a really creamy flavor. You may substitute any other kind of cheese you like for the feta.

2 teaspoons jarred minced garlic

4 tablespoons olive oil, divided

1 (16-ounce) package artificial crab flakes

1 (12-ounce) jar roasted red peppers, drained and finly chopped

16 ounces farfalle bow-tie pasta

4 (4-ounce) packages feta cheese with basil and tomato

1 tablespoon parsley

1. Cook and stir garlic in 2 tablespoons of the olive oil on medium heat for 3 minutes.
2. Add crab meat, red peppers, and remaining 2 tablespoons olive oil.
3. Cook 2 minutes or until thoroughly heated.
4. Cook pasta as directed on package. Drain.
5. Toss crab mixture with hot pasta and feta cheese.
6. Sprinkle with parsley.
7. When carrying this to an event, put in 9" × 13" buttered baking dish and cover with foil to keep warm.

❧ **Makes 8–10 servings**

Hurry Curry

If someone in your family is allergic to shrimp, substitute cream of chicken soup and cooked chicken instead of the shrimp ingredients. Serve it with Major Grey's chutney. If you can't find this chutney in your grocery store, be sure to ask them if they carry it. It's not always with the condiments and can be hard to find.

½ teaspoon curry powder

½ cup chopped onion

1 tablespoon butter

1 (10.75-ounce) can cream of shrimp soup

1 cup sour cream

1 cup cooked shrimp

2 cups cooked rice

Chutney

1. Sauté curry powder and onion, in butter. Add soup to mixture.
2. Add sour cream and shrimp to soup mixture. Pour into greased 8" × 8" square baking dish.
3. Bake at 350° for 10 minutes.
4. Serve over rice.
5. Serve with chutney. Raisins, currants, scallions, and peanuts are some other tasty offerings to serve with curry.

❧ **Makes 4–6 servings**

Tortellini and Garlic-Cream Sauce

For those of you who are not fond of shrimp, this recipe would taste just as good with chicken. You can also substitute half-and-half for the heavy cream in this recipe to cut down on the calories.

1 (19-ounce) package frozen tortellini

1 tablespoon olive oil

6 tablespoons butter

2 teaspoons minced jarred garlic

2 pounds frozen cooked shrimp, thawed

½ cup heavy cream

1 teaspoon salt and pepper to taste

2 teaspoons Italian seasoning blend

2 tablespoons parsley

1. Prepare tortellini according to package directions. Cook same time as sauce. When finished, toss with olive oil and set aside.
2. In medium skillet, melt butter and sauté garlic on medium heat for 3–5 minutes. Add shrimp and sauté for 3–5 more minutes. Add cream, salt, pepper, and Italian seasoning blend, and bring to a simmer.
3. Toss sauce, pasta, and parsley in large bowl. Cover with foil to keep warm.

❧ **Makes 10 servings**

Crab Casserole

Equally good for brunches or for dinner, everyone seems to love this casserole at any time of day.

½ cup chopped celery

½ cup chopped onion

1 cup diced green pepper

12 slices white bread

1 (16-ounce) package artificial crab flakes

½ cup salad dressing

4 eggs

3 cups milk

1 (10.75-ounce) can cream of mushroom soup

1 cup shredded Asiago cheese

1. In skillet sprayed with vegetable cooking spray, sauté celery, onion, and pepper for 3–5 minutes until barely tender.
2. Break bread into pieces and put in greased 9" × 13" baking dish.
3. Combine crab, sautéed vegetables, and salad dressing and spoon over bread crumbs.
4. Combine eggs and milk and pour over all. Bake at 350° for 15 minutes.
5. Spoon soup over top and scatter cheese over soup. Bake at 325° for 45–60 minutes. Let stand for a few minutes before serving.

❧ **Makes 8–10 servings**

Orange-Ginger Fish and Sweet Potatoes

Sweet potatoes and onions form the base to cook tender and moist fish fillets in this wonderful recipe. It's a meal in one dish!

6 sweet potatoes, peeled

2 onions, chopped

3 cloves garlic, minced

1 tablespoon minced gingerroot

½ cup brown sugar

½ cup orange juice

3 tablespoons butter

½ teaspoon salt

⅛ teaspoon pepper

2 pounds fish fillets

1 cup sour cream

¼ cup orange marmalade

2 tablespoons orange juice concentrate, thawed

¼ teaspoon ground ginger

1. Cut sweet potatoes into 1" cubes and combine in oval 5-quart slow cooker with onions, garlic, and gingerroot. In small bowl, combine brown sugar, orange juice, butter, salt, and pepper; mix well. Spoon over potatoes.
2. Cover and cook on low for 7–8 hours or until potatoes are tender when pierced with fork.
3. Place fish fillets on top of potatoes. Cover and cook on low for 1 to 1½ hours, or until fish flakes when tested with fork.
4. Meanwhile, in small bowl combine sour cream, marmalade, thawed concentrate, and ground ginger; mix well. Serve along with fish and potatoes.

❦ **Makes 8 servings**

Red Snapper and Succotash

Succotash is a combination of lima beans and corn. Ginger and sour cream add fabulous flavor. The fish cooks perfectly in the moist heat of the slow cooker.

2 onions, chopped

3 (10-ounce) packages frozen lima beans

6 stalks celery, chopped

4 cups frozen corn kernels

1 teaspoon salt

1 teaspoon ground ginger

¼ teaspoon pepper

½ cup apple cider vinegar

½ cup sugar

2 tablespoons butter

½ cup sour cream

8–10 (6-ounce) red snapper fillets

Salt and pepper to taste

1 teaspoon paprika

1. In 6-quart oval slow cooker, combine onions, lima beans, celery, corn, salt, ginger, and pepper; mix gently. In small bowl, combine vinegar and sugar; blend well. Pour into slow cooker.
2. Cover and cook on low for 7–8 hours or until succotash is blended and hot. Stir in butter and sour cream.
3. Sprinkle fillets with salt and pepper to taste, along with paprika. Spoon some of the succotash out of the slow cooker. Layer fish and succotash in slow cooker, making sure no fillets are touching.
4. Cover and cook on low for 1–1½ hours or until fish flakes when tested with fork. Serve immediately.

❧ **Makes 8–10 servings**

And thou shalt have goats' milk enough for thy food, for the food of thy household, and for the maintenance for thy maidens.

—*Proverbs 27:27*

Crustless Quiche

A welcoming dish after church on Sunday, try this quiche with crab meat or chicken.

1 stick butter or margarine

½ cup flour

6 large eggs

1 cup milk

16 ounces Monterey jack cheese, cubed

1 (3-ounce) package cream cheese, softened

2 cups cottage cheese

½ teaspoon salt

1 teaspoon sugar

1 teaspoon baking powder

1 pound frozen cooked shrimp, thawed

1. Melt butter and stir in flour with whisk.
2. Beat eggs and milk and add to flour mixture. Add in cheeses and mix with wire whisk. Add salt, sugar, baking powder, and shrimp.
3. Pour into greased 9" × 13" baking dish, and bake at 350° for 45 minutes.

🐛 **Makes 8–10 servings**

Crab-Mushroom Quiche

Gruyère cheese gives this quiche a wonderful creamy flavor. Look for this cheese in the deli section with the special cheeses. You can also substitute one of your favorite cheeses for the Gruyère. There are so many selections available in shredded cheeses and no dicing or cutting is required–nice!

1 (4-ounce) can sliced mushrooms

1 teaspoon butter

1 (10") pastry shell, partially baked

1 (16-ounce) package artificial crab meat flakes

1⅓ cups finely diced Gruyère cheese

¾ cup sour cream

¼ cup mayonnaise

½ teaspoon salt

1 teaspoon flour

Light cream

3 eggs, slightly beaten

½ teaspoon hot pepper sauce

1. Bake pie crust at 450° for 5 minutes.
2. Drain mushrooms, reserving liquid.
3. Sauté mushrooms in butter for 2 minutes, and scatter mushrooms in partially baked pie shell. Place crab meat over mushrooms.
4. In a bowl, mix Gruyère cheese, sour cream, and mayonnaise with reserved mushroom liquid, salt, and flour. Add enough light cream to mixture to make 2 cups. Blend in eggs and hot pepper sauce and pour into shell. Bake at 350° for 55 minutes or until set. Let stand 15 minutes before cutting.

🐛 **Makes 6–8 servings**

Shrimp Quiche

Nutmeg and sherry add a delicate flavor to this version of the classic quiche. It's terrific.

1 (10") partially baked pie crust

¼ cup finely chopped celery

1 small onion, thinly sliced

1 pound small frozen shrimp, thawed

1 cup shredded Swiss cheese

4 eggs, lightly beaten

2 cups cream

2 tablespoons parsley flakes

2 tablespoons sherry

¼ teaspoon nutmeg

½ teaspoon salt

¼ teaspoon pepper

1. Bake pie crust at 450° for 5 minutes.
2. Spray skillet with vegetable cooking spray and sauté celery and onion until just tender.
3. In large bowl, mix together remaining ingredients; add celery and onion and pour into baked pie shell. Bake at 450° for 10 minutes. Reduce heat to 350° and bake for another 10–15 minutes or until toothpick inserted comes out clean.

❦ **Makes 8 servings**

Shrimp and Potato Tacos

Potatoes add a wonderful texture and flavor and stretch shrimp to serve many people. This can be made spicier with more chili powder and cayenne pepper.

6 potatoes, peeled and cubed

3 onions, chopped

5 cloves garlic, minced

3 tablespoons butter, melted

1 teaspoon salt

1 tablespoon chili powder

1 teaspoon cumin

1 teaspoon dried oregano leaves

¼ teaspoon cayenne pepper

1½ pounds frozen cooked medium shrimp, thawed

10–12 taco shells

2 cups chopped tomatoes

2 avocados, peeled and diced

1 tablespoon lemon juice

2 cups shredded pepper jack cheese

1. In 4-quart slow cooker, combine potatoes, onions, garlic, butter, salt, chili powder, cumin, oregano, and cayenne pepper; mix well. Cover and cook on low for 8–9 hours or until potatoes are very tender.
2. Stir in shrimp, increase heat to high, and cook for 20–30 minutes or until shrimp are hot, pink, and curled.

(continued)

(Shrimp and Potato Tacos—continued)

3. Heat taco shells according to package directions. In medium bowl combine chopped tomatoes, avocados, and lemon juice; mix well. Serve the shrimp mixture with tomato mixture and cheese, and let everyone make their own tacos.

☙ **Makes 8–10 servings**

Shrimp Casserole

Shared recipes can evoke tears and laughter as you remember to special person who gave them to you. This one's been passed through many hands.

3 cups cooked shrimp

2 hard-cooked eggs, chopped

1 (4-ounce) can sliced mushrooms

½ cup slivered almonds

¾ cup diced celery

1 tablespoon chopped onion

1 (10.75-ounce) can cream of chicken soup

¾ cup mayonnaise

1 (5-ounce) can chow mein noodles

1. Combine all ingredients except noodles in greased 2-quart casserole.
2. Sprinkle noodles on top.
3. Bake at 350° for 30 minutes.

☙ **Makes 4–6 servings**

Jambalaya

Jambalaya traditionally contains chicken, sausage, and seafood. This one leaves out the sausage to cut down on the fat. It's delicious, hearty, and flavorful.

2 onions, chopped

1 green bell pepper, chopped

1 red bell pepper, chopped

4 stalks celery, chopped

3 cloves garlic, minced

2 (14.5-ounce) cans diced tomatoes, undrained

4 boneless, skinless chicken breasts, cubed

1 teaspoon salt

¼ teaspoon pepper

1 teaspoon dried oregano leaves

1 teaspoon dried basil leaves

3 cups chicken broth

5 tablespoons cornstarch

¾ cup apple juice

1½ pounds frozen cooked shrimp, thawed

4–5 cups cooked rice

1. In 5-quart slow cooker, combine onions, green and red bell peppers, celery, garlic, and tomatoes; mix well. Sprinkle chicken with salt and pepper and place on top of vegetables in slow cooker.

2. Sprinkle contents of slow cooker with oregano and basil; pour chicken broth over all. Cover and cook on low for 7–8 hours or until chicken is thoroughly cooked.

3. In small bowl, combine cornstarch and apple juice; mix well. Stir into slow cooker along with shrimp. Cook on high for 20–30 minutes or until sauce is thickened and shrimp is hot.

4. Stir in rice and cook for 10 minutes longer. Serve immediately.

❀ **Makes 8–10 servings**

Slow Cooker Shrimp Gumbo

Gumbo is a recipe for a celebration! Serve this in large bowls with big spoons and lots of napkins and lemonade.

½ cup olive oil

½ cup flour

2 cups water

3 cups chicken broth

2 onions, chopped

5 stalks celery, chopped

2 green bell peppers, chopped

6 cloves garlic, minced

2 teaspoons Cajun seasoning

1 teaspoon smoked paprika

1 teaspoon dried oregano leaves

1 teaspoon salt

¼ teaspoon cayenne pepper

2 (14 ounce) cans diced tomatoes, undrained

2 pounds frozen cooked shrimp, thawed

1½ cups instant white rice

1. In heavy saucepan, combine oil and flour over medium heat. Cook and stir for 12–15 minutes until mixture turns golden brown. Carefully add water and chicken broth; cook and stir with wire whisk until flour mixture (called *roux,* pronounced roo) dissolves.

2. Pour contents of skillet into 6-quart slow cooker. Add all remaining ingredients except for shrimp and rice. Cover and cook on low for 7–8 hours or until vegetables are tender.

3. Turn slow cooker to high; stir in shrimp and rice. Cover and cook for another 15–20 minutes or until shrimp is hot and rice is tender. Serve immediately.

❀ **Makes 10–12 servings**

Sweet-and-Sour Shrimp

You have to serve this fresh-tasting, well-seasoned recipe over lots of hot cooked rice or pasta. Serve it with a green salad and some homemade rolls.

2 onions, chopped

4 cloves garlic, minced

2 tablespoons minced fresh gingerroot

1 (20-ounce) can pineapple tidbits in juice, undrained

5 carrots, sliced

2 cups water

1 (32-ounce) box chicken broth

⅓ cup sugar

¼ cup low-sodium soy sauce

¼ teaspoon white pepper

2 green bell peppers, chopped

¼ cup cornstarch

½ cup apple cider vinegar

2 pounds frozen cooked shrimp, thawed

1. Combine onions, garlic, gingerroot, undrained pineapple, carrots, water, chicken broth, sugar, soy sauce, and pepper in 5-quart slow cooker. Cover and cook on low for 7–8 hours or until vegetables are tender.
2. Stir green bell peppers into slow cooker. In small bowl, combine cornstarch and vinegar and mix well. Stir into slow cooker along with shrimp. Cover and cook on high for 20–30 minutes or until sauce is thickened and shrimp is hot. Serve over hot cooked rice.

❧ **Makes 12 servings**

Shrimp with Apricot Rice

To toast almonds, place them in a dry skillet over medium heat and toss until fragrant and golden brown. They add wonderful crunch and flavor to this special dish.

1 onion, chopped

1 leek, chopped

3 carrots, sliced

2½ cups long-grain brown rice

2 cups chicken broth

2 cups apricot nectar

1 cup water

1 teaspoon salt

¼ teaspoon white pepper

1 teaspoon dried thyme leaves

1 cup finely chopped dried apricots

1 (16-ounce) jar apricot preserves

2 pounds frozen cooked shrimp, thawed

⅓ cup sliced almonds, toasted

1. In 6-quart slow cooker, combine onion, leek, carrots, and brown rice. Add chicken broth, nectar, water, salt, pepper, thyme, and apricots. Stir well, then cover and cook on low for 6–8 hours or until rice and vegetables are tender.
2. Stir in apricot preserves and shrimp. Cover and cook on low for 1 hour or until casserole is hot and shrimp is hot and tender. Stir again, top with almonds, and serve immediately.

❧ **Makes 8 servings**

Shrimp Divan

You'll be making this recipe more often when the grocers offer shrimp on sale. The cooked and ready-to-eat shrimp makes it much easier to prepare seafood dishes. This would also be delicious with imitation crabmeat which I use often as it is less expensive to use and tastes great.

4 tablespoons butter

4 tablespoons flour

2/3 cup hot water

4 teaspoons chicken bouillon

1/2 cup whipping cream

4 tablespoons sherry

1/4 teaspoon nutmeg

1/2 cup shredded asiago cheese

20 ounces frozen broccoli spears, thawed

2 pounds cooked and ready-to-eat shrimp

4 tablespoons grated Parmesan cheese

Paprika

1. In medium saucepan, over medium heat, melt butter. Blend in flour with wire whisk. Stir in water, bouillon, cream, sherry, and nutmeg. Cook until thickened, stirring often. Stir in asiago cheese. Set aside.

2. Place broccoli in greased 9" × 13" baking dish. Arrange shrimp on top. Pour cream sauce over the broccoli. Sprinkle with Parmesan and paprika.

3. Bake at 350° for 15–25 minutes.

🦌 **Makes 8–10 servings**

Provideth her meat in the summer, and gathereth her food in the harvest.

—Proverbs 6:8

Chicken-Shrimp Rice Casserole

The combination of chicken and shrimp in this dish will satisfy both the chicken lover and the seafood lover.

1 cup half-and-half
2 (3-ounce) containers cream cheese with chives, softened
2 tablespoons cornstarch
2½ cups chicken broth
4 cups cooked rice
4 cups cooked chicken breast
1 pound cooked ready-to-eat shrimp
¼ teaspoon paprika

1. Blend half-and-half gradually into cream cheese with electric beater and beat until smooth.
2. In saucepan, blend cornstarch and chicken broth and add cheese and half-and-half mixture. Cook over medium heat until thick, stirring constantly.
3. Spread half the rice in the bottom of a greased 9" × 13" baking dish. Place half the chicken and half the shrimp over the rice and pour half the sauce over this layer. Repeat layers and sprinkle with paprika.
4. Bake at 350° for 30 minutes or until bubbly.

❦ **Makes 8–10 servings**

Shrimp–Crabmeat Seafood Casserole

Artificial crabmeat is full of protein and good for you as well, and it works great in seafood casseroles Both shrimp and crab-meat are low in calories and provide you with great taste.

1 (6-ounce) box long-grain and wild rice blend
2½ cups chicken broth
2 pounds artificial crabmeat
2 pounds cooked shrimp
1 (14-ounce) can artichokes, drained
1 (10.75-ounce) can cream of celery soup
½ cup mayonnaise
3 tablespoons onions, chopped
1 (8-ounce) can water chestnuts, drained and sliced
2 cups breadcrumbs

1. Cook the rice in the chicken broth according to the directions on the package.
2. Combine all ingredients and put them in a greased 9" × 13" baking dish. Cover with foil. Bake at 350° for 45 minutes or until hot and bubbly.
3. Remove foil and brown.

❦ **Makes 8–10 servings**

Casserole for Seafood Lovers

Do you love seafood? If so, here's a great and easy way to serve it for an entrée. Fix it for those seafood lovers that you know. You can substitute angel hair pasta for the macaroni, but any pasta that you like will work. You can break it up into pieces before adding it to the rest of the ingredients.

2 cups artificial crab flakes

2 cups cooked salad shrimp

1 cup evaporated milk or regular milk

3 cups chicken broth

1 cup uncooked pasta

¼ cup minced onion

2 cups shredded Swiss cheese

1 (4-ounce) can mushrooms drained

¼ teaspoon pepper

1 cup chopped celery

½ cup Parmesan cheese

1. Mix together all ingredients except Parmesan cheese and put in greased 9" × 13" baking dish.
2. Put Parmesan cheese on top.
3. Bake at 375° for 60–80 minutes.

🦐 **Makes 8–10 servings**

Shrimp-and-Mushroom Dumplings

For a satisfying supper dish, fix these dumplings along with salad and French bread, and you've got a great meal. The convenience items we can buy to make our cooking easier and our time spent cooking shorter are so plentiful and so available—take advantage of them.

1 (8-ounce) can refrigerated crescent rolls

2 cups diced cooked shrimp

1 cup shredded three-cheese blend

1 (8-ounce) can mushroom stems and pieces, drained

1 (10.75-ounce) can cream of shrimp soup

½ cup milk

1. Coat 8" square baking dish with vegetable cooking spray.
2. Separate rolls.
3. Mix together shrimp, cheese, and mushrooms. Fill each roll with shrimp mixture. Roll up starting at wide end.
4. Combine soup and milk and pour over rolls. Bake at 400° for 20–25 minutes.

🦐 **Makes 8 dumplings**

Scallop–Wild Rice Casserole

This rich and comforting casserole is a slight twist on the traditional, using cream of mushroom soup, wild rice, and creamy scallops.

3 cups wild rice

1 (32-ounce) box chicken broth

3 cups water

1 (10-ounce) can cream of mushroom soup

2 onions, chopped

1 (8-ounce) package sliced fresh mushrooms

1 teaspoon salt

¼ teaspoon pepper

1½ teaspoons dried tarragon leaves

3 pounds bay scallops

1 (12-ounce) package frozen cut green beans, thawed

1 cup sliced almonds, toasted

1. Put wild rice into 6-quart slow cooker. Pour chicken broth and 2 cups of the water over the rice.
2. In medium bowl, combine soup and remaining 1 cup water; mix well with wire whisk until smooth. Add to slow cooker along with onions, mushrooms, salt, pepper, and tarragon.
3. Cover and cook on low for 7–8 hours or until wild rice and vegetables are tender. Stir in scallops and green beans.
4. Cover and cook on high for 30–40 minutes or until scallops are opaque and green beans are hot and tender. To toast almonds, place in dry pan over medium heat; toast, shaking pan frequently, until nuts are fragrant. Stir food in slow cooker, sprinkle with almonds, and serve.

🍃 **Makes 12 servings**

When you beat your olive trees, do not strip what is left; it shall be for the alien, the orphan, and the widow. When you gather the grapes of your vineyard, do not glean what is left; it shall be for the alien, the orphan, and the widow.

—Deuteronomy 24:21

Fisherman's Chowder

A chowder is a soup that has been thickened with cornstarch or flour and made richer with some cream. This version is hearty and simple.

2 onions, chopped

4 cloves garlic, minced

4 carrots, cut into chunks

4 potatoes, peeled and cubed

1 sweet potato, peeled and cubed

6 cups water

2 cups clam juice

1½ teaspoons salt

¼ teaspoon white pepper

2 teaspoons dried thyme leaves

1 teaspoon dried basil leaves

1 cup heavy cream

3 tablespoons cornstarch

2 pounds halibut or haddock fillets, cubed

1 pound frozen cooked shrimp, thawed

2 cups shredded Swiss cheese

⅓ cup chopped fresh flat-leaf parsley

1. In 7-quart slow cooker, combine onions, garlic, carrots, potatoes, sweet potato, water, clam juice, salt, pepper, thyme, and basil; mix well.

2. Cover and cook on low for 7–8 hours or until vegetables are tender. In medium bowl, combine cream with cornstarch and mix with wire whisk. Stir into slow cooker along with cubed fish fillets. Cover and cook on high for 15 minutes or until fish is almost opaque.

3. Stir in shrimp and cheese. Cover and cook on high for 8–10 minutes longer or until chowder is thickened and fish is done. Sprinkle with parsley and serve immediately.

❦ **Makes 12–14 servings**

Seafood Enchiladas

Here the slow cooker is just used to heat the mixture through, so everything has to be cooked beforehand.

3 tablespoons butter

2 onions, chopped

6 cloves garlic, minced

2 green bell peppers, chopped

1 teaspoon salt

¼ teaspoon white pepper

1 tablespoon chili powder

2 (16-ounce) jars four-cheese Alfredo sauce

1 cup heavy cream

1 cup sour cream

2 tablespoons cornstarch

1 pound imitation crab, flaked

1 (16-ounce) bag frozen cooked shrimp, thawed

12 (6-inch) corn tortillas, cut into 4 wedges each

4 cups shredded pepper jack cheese

½ cup grated Parmesan cheese

1 teaspoon paprika

1. In large saucepan, melt butter over medium heat. Add onions and garlic; cook and stir until crisp-tender, about 5 minutes. Add green bell peppers; cook and stir for another 4 minutes. Sprinkle with salt, pepper, and chili powder; set aside.

2. In large bowl, combine Alfredo sauce, cream, sour cream, and cornstarch; mix well. Stir in imitation crab, shrimp, and the vegetable mixture.

3. Spray a 6-quart slow cooker with nonstick cooking spray. Place a couple of spoonfuls of the seafood sauce in the bottom. Layer tortillas over that, and then sprinkle on some cheese. Repeat layers, ending with seafood mixture. Sprinkle top with Parmesan cheese and paprika. Cover and cook on low for 4 hours or until casserole is hot. Serve.

Makes 12–14 servings

Salmon with Rice Pilaf

Rice pilaf cooks to perfection, and then salmon fillets coated with a dill sauce are placed on top to steam until flaky. Yum!

3 tablespoons butter

2 onions, chopped

4 cloves garlic, minced

1½ cups long grain brown rice

4 carrots, sliced

1 (8-ounce) package sliced mushrooms

4 cups chicken broth

1 teaspoon dried dill weed

2 pounds salmon fillets

1 teaspoon salt

⅛ teaspoon pepper

1 cup sour cream

2 tablespoons mustard

½ teaspoon dried dill weed

1. In large skillet, melt butter over medium heat. Add onion and garlic; cook and stir until tender, about 5 minutes.
2. Add rice; cook and stir until coated, about 3–4 minutes longer. Transfer to 4-quart slow cooker. Add carrots, mushrooms, chicken broth, and dill weed.
3. Cover and cook on low for 5 hours or until rice is almost tender. Sprinkle salmon with salt and pepper.
4. In small bowl, combine sour cream, mustard, and dill weed. Spread over salmon fillets. Place salmon in slow cooker on top of rice.
5. Cover slow cooker and cook on low for 1 to 1½ hours or until salmon flakes when tested with a fork. Serve fish with the rice pilaf.

❧ **Makes 8 servings**

I was hungry and you gave me food, I was thirsty and you gave me drink, I was a stranger and you welcomed me.

—Matthew 25:35

Sweet-and-Sour Cabbage and Salmon

The cabbage will cook down as it simmers. The combination of colors, textures, and flavors in this dish is wonderful.

14 cups chopped red cabbage

2 large red onions, chopped

6 cloves garlic, minced

1/3 cup brown sugar

1/3 cup apple cider vinegar

1 cup chicken broth

2 teaspoons dried thyme leaves

1 teaspoon salt

1/4 teaspoon white pepper

3 pounds salmon fillets

1/2 teaspoon salt

1/8 teaspoon cayenne pepper

2 tablespoons lemon juice

1. In 6-quart oval slow cooker, combine cabbage, red onions, and garlic; mix well. In medium bowl, combine brown sugar, vinegar, broth, thyme, 1 teaspoon salt, and white pepper; mix well. Pour into slow cooker. Cover and cook on low for 7–8 hours or until cabbage is tender.
2. Drain cabbage mixture. Sprinkle salmon with 1/2 teaspoon salt, cayenne pepper, and lemon juice. Arrange salmon on the cabbage mixture in slow cooker.
3. Cover and cook on low for 1–1 1/2 hours or until salmon flakes when tested with fork. Serve salmon with cabbage mixture.

❧ **Makes 10–12 servings**

June's Salmon Loaf

Here's a delicious salmon recipe shared by a sprightly 80-year-old woman. She's amazing.

1 cup cooked instant rice

3/4 cup cracker crumbs

2 eggs

1/2 teaspoon salt

1 tablespoon chopped onion

2 cans flaked canned salmon

2 teaspoons lemon juice

1. Combine all ingredients in medium bowl.
2. Place in a buttered 9" × 5" × 3" loaf pan.
3. Bake at 350° for 30–40 minutes.

❧ **Makes 6–8 servings**

Aunt Bessie's Salmon Loaf

The foil method lets you remove these loaves from the slow cookers with ease. Serve this classic with peas and carrots.

2 tablespoons butter

1 onion, finely chopped

4 cloves garlic, minced

1 green bell pepper, finely chopped

4 eggs

¾ cup heavy cream

¾ cup clam juice

2 cups crushed saltine crackers

½ cup dry bread crumbs

¼ teaspoon pepper

1 teaspoon dried thyme leaves

1 teaspoon dried basil leaves

3 (14-ounce) cans salmon, drained

1½ cups shredded Havarti cheese

½ cup grated Parmesan cheese

1. In large skillet, melt butter over medium heat. Add onions and garlic; cook and stir until crisp-tender, about 5 minutes. Add green bell pepper; cook and stir for another 3–4 minutes. Remove from heat.
2. In large bowl, combine eggs, cream, clam juice, crushed crackers, bread crumbs, pepper, thyme, and basil; mix well. Stir in onion mixture; then add all of the salmon and the Havarti cheese.
3. Spray two 4-quart slow cookers with nonstick cooking spray. Tear off four 24" sheets of heavy-duty foil. Fold each in thirds lengthwise; then place two in each slow cooker, forming an X.
4. Divide the salmon mixture in half. Place half in each slow cooker; form into a loaf shape as much as you can. Sprinkle each with half of the Parmesan cheese.
5. Cover and cook on high for 1 hour, then turn slow cookers to low and cook for 3–4 hours longer or until meat thermometer registers 160°F.
6. Turn off slow cookers and let stand, uncovered, for 15 minutes. Gently loosen loaves, using an offset spatula, and then lift the foil and loaves out of the slow cooker. Slice to serve.

❤ **Makes 10–12 servings**

Fish Dumplings in Spicy Broth

This unusual recipe has the flavors of the Orient. To serve, the tender dumplings are placed in bowls, and the broth with carrots and celery is spooned on top.

2 (32-ounce) boxes chicken broth

1 cup dry white wine or white grape juice

¼ teaspoon cayenne pepper

½ teaspoon crushed red pepper flakes

6 cloves garlic, minced

4 carrots, sliced

4 stalks celery, sliced

1½ pounds red snapper fillets, cubed

3 tablespoons flour

1 onion, finely chopped

1 teaspoon salt

⅛ teaspoon white pepper

1 teaspoon paprika

3 eggs

1 cup dried bread crumbs

2 tablespoons lemon juice

1. In 5-quart slow cooker, combine chicken broth, wine or grape juice, cayenne pepper, red pepper flakes, garlic, carrots, and celery. Cover and cook on low for 5–6 hours or until vegetables are tender.
2. Meanwhile, place fish and flour in food processor. Process, using the pulse feature, until fish is ground. Remove fish from food processor and place in large bowl.
3. Add onion, salt, pepper, paprika, eggs, bread crumbs, and lemon juice to fish; mix well. Using a small ice cream scoop, shape mixture into thirty-six 1½" dumplings and place on waxed paper. Cover and refrigerate.
4. When vegetables in broth are tender, bring a large pot of salted water to a boil. Cook the dumplings in salted water, about 8 at a time, until cooked through, to an internal temperature of 160°F.
5. Turn slow cooker to warm. As dumplings finish cooking, drop them into the slow cooker. To serve, place 3 or 4 dumplings in a serving bowl and top with some of the broth and vegetables.

🍲 **Makes 8 servings**

You shall eat in plenty and be satisfied, and praise the name of the Lord your God, who has dealt wondrously with you. And my people shall never again be put to shame.

—*Joel 2:26*

Clam Chowder

This rich and thick chowder is perfect for a gathering after singing Christmas carols. Serve it with tiny oyster crackers and a wilted spinach salad.

8 slices bacon

2 tablespoons butter

2 onions, chopped

4 cloves garlic, minced

4 (6-ounce) cans minced clams

4 carrots, sliced

5 stalks celery, chopped

¼ cup chopped celery leaves

5 potatoes, peeled and cubed

1½ teaspoons salt

¼ teaspoon white pepper

2 cups clam juice

2 cups chicken broth

4 cups water

¼ cup cornstarch

2 cups light cream

1 cup heavy cream

1. In large saucepan, cook bacon until crisp. Drain bacon on paper towels, crumble, and refrigerate. Drain all but 2 tablespoons drippings from saucepan and add butter. When butter melts, add onion and garlic; cook and stir until crisp-tender, about 5 minutes.

2. Drain clams, reserving liquid. Place clams in a bowl, cover, and refrigerate. Combine onion mixture, carrots, celery, celery leaves, potatoes, salt, pepper, clam juice, chicken broth, water, and reserved clam liquid in 7-quart slow cooker.

3. Cover and cook on low for 7–8 hours or until vegetables are tender. In medium bowl combine cornstarch with light cream; stir with wire whisk until smooth. Stir into slow cooker along with heavy cream; cover and cook on high for 15 minutes.

4. Stir in reserved bacon and clams. Cover and cook on high for 15–20 minutes or until soup is thoroughly heated. Serve immediately.

❦ **Makes 12–14 servings**

Potato Seafood Salad

You could add even more seafood to this recipe if you'd like, stirring in drained canned crab or salmon with the potato mixture.

5 pounds russet potatoes

2 onions, chopped

4 cloves garlic, minced

1½ teaspoons salt

¼ teaspoon white pepper

2 cups water

2 pounds red snapper fish fillets

1 pound frozen small cooked shrimp, thawed

3 cups frozen peas, thawed and drained

1½ cups mayonnaise

1 cup whipped salad dressing

½ cup plain yogurt

½ cup seafood cocktail sauce

⅓ cup whole milk

1. Peel potatoes and cut into cubes. Combine in 6- to 7-quart slow cooker with onions and garlic. Sprinkle with salt and pepper, then pour water over all. Cover and cook on low for 8–9 hours or until potatoes are tender.
2. Turn heat to high. Place red snapper fillets on potato mixture. Cover and cook on high for 30 minutes or until fish flakes easily with fork.

3. In large bowl, combine remaining ingredients and mix well. Remove fish and potato mixture from slow cooker with large slotted spoon or sieve and add to mixture in bowl. Stir gently to coat. Cover and chill for 4–5 hours until cold. Stir gently before serving.

❧ **Makes 10–12 servings**

And the crowds asked him, "What then should we do?" In reply Jesus said to them, "Whoever has two coats must share with anyone who has none; and whoever has food must do likewise."

—Luke 3:10–11

Vegetarian Entrées

⚓

I've tried to become a vegetarian, I really have, but I just can't do it. I really admire those who are vegetarian. Not only are they eating lower on the food chain, but they usually eat more fruits and vegetables than do non-vegetarians.

At any rate, it's important to offer vegetarian foods in any large gathering. In fact, more people than you think will choose the vegetarian entrée, because it is automatically lower in fat and usually contains more vegetables and fiber.

Vegetarian food doesn't have to be beans and tofu, although that can be delicious too! Inventive recipes that use vegetables, potatoes, and cheese in new ways will satisfy any appetite, and no one will miss the meat.

Vegetarians and vegans must be concerned about protein intake. Legumes (beans) and grains do not provide complete proteins by themselves, so they must be combined in a recipe or a meal. The combination of beans and grains, or beans and corn, will supply you with all the needed amino acids. Soy, buckwheat, quinoa, and amaranth do contain complete proteins. Ovo-lacto vegetarians who eat dairy products don't need to worry about this.

There are quite a few vegetarian substitutes and fake-outs on the market. Meatless soy crumbles look and taste just like ground beef, and there's a version that mimics pork sausage. You can even find "fake" chicken and chicken chunks! If you do use these products, be sure to label the finished dish so vegetarians won't think they're accidentally eating meat!

—*Linda Larsen*

Mexican Torte

Frozen meatless soy crumbles taste almost like ground beef, and have the exact same texture. They're delicious in this hearty casserole.

2 tablespoons olive oil

2 onions, chopped

4 cloves garlic, minced

2 (16-ounce) packages frozen meatless soy crumbles

2 (4-ounce) cans chopped green chiles, undrained

1 tablespoon chili powder

2 teaspoons dried oregano leaves

1 teaspoon salt

¼ teaspoon cayenne pepper

1 (14-ounce) can diced tomatoes, undrained

2 cups salsa

1 (16-ounce) can refried beans

12 (6-inch) corn tortillas

2 cups shredded Colby cheese

2 cups shredded pepper jack cheese

1 cup sour cream

1 cup chopped tomatoes

½ cup chopped green onions

1. In large skillet, heat olive oil over medium heat. Add onions and garlic; cook and stir until tender, about 6 minutes. Add crumbles, green chiles, chili powder, oregano, salt, pepper, and tomatoes; bring to a simmer.

2. In large bowl, combine salsa and refried beans and mix well. In 6-quart slow cooker, layer ¼ of the crumbles mixture, ¼ of the tortillas, ¼ of the salsa mixture, and ¼ of each of the cheeses.

3. Cover and cook on low for 6–7 hours or until hot and bubbly. Serve with sour cream, chopped tomatoes, and green onions.

❦ **Makes 8–10 servings**

He who supplies seed to the sower and bread for food will supply and multiply your seed for sowing and increase the harvest of your righteousness. You will be enriched in every way for your great generosity, which will produce thanksgiving to God through us.

2 Corinthians 9:10–11

Potato Gratin

This fabulously rich and creamy vegetarian main dish will be a hit with all ages. You could also serve it as a side dish, but if you do, scoop out small portions.

2 tablespoons butter

1 tablespoon olive oil

2 onions, chopped

6 cloves garlic, minced

2 tablespoons flour

1 teaspoon salt

1/4 teaspoon pepper

1/8 teaspoon nutmeg

1 cup milk

1 cup heavy cream

1 (8-ounce) package cream cheese, cubed

1 cup mascarpone cheese

3 pounds russet potatoes, peeled, sliced 1/8" thick

2 (8-ounce) jars mushrooms, drained

2 cups diced Swiss or Havarti cheese

1/2 cup grated Romano cheese

1. In large saucepan, melt butter with olive oil over medium heat. Add onions and garlic; cook and stir until tender, about 6 minutes.

2. Add flour, salt, pepper, and nutmeg to onion mixture; cook and stir until bubbly. Add milk and cream all at once, stirring with wire whisk; then stir in cream cheese and mascarpone cheese. Cook and stir until cheese melts and mixture is smooth.

3. Spray a 6-quart slow cooker with nonstick cooking spray. Layer 1/3 of potatoes, mushrooms, and Swiss cheese in slow cooker. Pour 1/3 of onion mixture over. Repeat layers, ending with onion mixture. Sprinkle with Romano cheese.

4. Cover and cook on low for 8–9 hours or until potatoes are tender.

❀ **Makes 12–14 servings**

Potato Omelet

Topping a moist and hearty potato omelet with an herb-and-tomato mixture really perks up the flavor and wakes up your taste buds.

1 (32-ounce) package frozen hash brown potatoes

2 onions, diced

4 cloves garlic, minced

1 cup shredded Cheddar cheese

1 cup shredded Muenster cheese

12 eggs

½ cup heavy cream

½ cup sour cream

1 teaspoon salt

¼ teaspoon pepper

2 cups chopped tomatoes

¼ cup chopped green onions, white and green parts

1 tablespoon fresh thyme leaves

1. Spray a 5-quart slow cooker with nonstick cooking spray. Layer potatoes, onions, garlic, and cheeses in slow cooker.
2. In large bowl, combine eggs with cream and sour cream and beat until blended. Stir in salt and pepper and mix well. Pour into slow cooker.
3. Cover and cook on high for 4–5 hours or until eggs are set. In medium bowl, combine tomatoes, green onion, and thyme; mix gently. Serve tomato topping with omelet.

❦ **Makes 10 servings**

Vegetarian Chili

Serve this hearty and filling dish with sour cream, shredded cheese, chopped jalapeños, guacamole, and tortilla chips for a satisfying meal in a bowl.

2 onions, chopped

5 cloves garlic, minced

2 jalapeño peppers, minced

2 (10-ounce) packages frozen meatless soy crumbles

2 green bell peppers, chopped

2 red bell peppers, chopped

3 (14-ounce) cans diced tomatoes, undrained

2 cups frozen corn

2 tablespoons chili powder

1 teaspoon cumin

1 teaspoon salt

1 teaspoon dried oregano

¼ teaspoon cayenne pepper

2 (15-ounce) cans kidney beans, drained

2 (15-ounce) cans black beans, drained

3 tablespoons cornstarch

⅓ cup water

1. In 6-quart slow cooker, combine all ingredients except cornstarch and water; mix gently. Cover and cook on low for 8–9 hours or until chili is blended.
2. In small bowl, combine cornstarch and water and mix well. Stir into slow cooker, cover, and cook on high for 20–30 minutes until thickened.

❦ **Makes 8–10 servings**

Vegetarian Gumbo

Increase the chipotle chiles and adobo sauce to add a spicy, smoky richness to this thick meatless stew.

2 tablespoons butter

¼ cup olive oil

6 tablespoons flour

1 teaspoon seasoned salt

¼ teaspoon pepper

2 onions, chopped

4 stalks celery, chopped

8 cloves garlic, minced

4 chipotle peppers in adobo sauce, chopped

3 tablespoons adobo sauce from chipotle chilies

2 (15-ounce) cans black beans, drained

1 (14-ounce) can diced tomatoes, undrained

2 cups vegetable broth

6 plum tomatoes, chopped

4 cups frozen corn

2 tablespoons Cajun seasoning

1 teaspoon dried thyme leaves

5 cups hot cooked rice

1. In heavy saucepan over low heat, combine butter and olive oil. When butter melts, add flour. Cook and stir over low heat until the flour turns brown. Watch it carefully so it doesn't burn.

2. Place in 6-quart slow cooker. Add salt, pepper, and remaining ingredients except for rice. Cover and cook on low for 7–8 hours or until vegetables are tender.

3. If the stew needs thickening, remove cover and cook on high for about 1 hour until thickened. Serve over hot cooked rice.

❦ **Makes 10–12 servings**

Potluck Pointer

Have you ever arrived at your potluck destination and discovered that your beautifully arranged plate of food lost half its contents? For no-worry transport of foods like stuffed peppers, place them in a bundt pan.

Tex-Mex Egg Casserole

Three kinds of cheese make this spicy casserole rich and creamy. Top each hot serving with cold salsa to create a delicious contrast.

1 tablespoon butter

1 tablespoon olive oil

2 onions, chopped

4 cloves garlic, minced

1 red bell pepper, chopped

1 jalapeño pepper, minced

1/4 cup flour

1 cup heavy cream

12 eggs, beaten

1 cup cottage cheese

1/2 teaspoon hot pepper sauce

1 teaspoon dried oregano

1 teaspoon salt

1/4 teaspoon pepper

1/8 teaspoon cayenne pepper

2 cups shredded pepper jack cheese

1 cup shredded Cheddar cheese

2 cups salsa

1. Spray a 4-quart slow cooker with nonstick cooking spray and set aside. In large skillet, melt butter and olive oil over medium heat. Add onions and garlic; cook and stir until tender, about 6 minutes. Add red bell pepper and jalapeño pepper; cook and stir for 3 minutes longer.

2. Sprinkle flour into skillet; cook and stir until bubbly, about 3–4 minutes. Stir in heavy cream and cook until thickened. Remove from heat; let stand for 20 minutes.

3. In large bowl, beat eggs with cottage cheese, hot pepper sauce, oregano, salt, pepper, and cayenne pepper. Stir in pepper jack and Cheddar cheeses; then stir in vegetable mixture. Pour into prepared slow cooker.

4. Cover and cook on low for 7–8 hours or until set. Serve with cold salsa.

Makes 8 servings

Let them gather all the food of these good years that are coming, and lay up grain under the authority of Pharaoh for food in the cities, and let them keep it.

—Genesis 41:33

Vegetarian Curry

Chickpeas and wild rice, a legume and a grain, combine to make a complete protein in this wonderful and delicious one-dish meal.

2 tablespoons olive oil

2 onions, chopped

5 cloves garlic, minced

2 tablespoons minced gingerroot

2 tablespoons curry powder

2 cups wild rice

2 pears, peeled, cored, and chopped

2 apples, peeled, cored, and chopped

1 cup golden raisins

½ cup dark raisins

½ cup dried currants

1 teaspoon salt

¼ teaspoon white pepper

3 (15-ounce) cans chickpeas, drained

2 (14-ounce) cans vegetable broth

2 cups water

1 (10-ounce) jar mango chutney

1. In large skillet, heat olive oil over medium heat. Add onions, garlic, gingerroot, and curry powder; cook and stir for 5 minutes.
2. Place wild rice in bottom of 6-quart slow cooker. Layer pears, apples, raisins, and currants on top.
3. Add salt, pepper, chickpeas, broth, water, and chutney to vegetables in skillet; bring to a simmer. Pour mixture into slow cooker.
4. Cover and cook on low for 8–9 hours or until wild rice is tender. Stir gently to mix.

❦ **Makes 12 servings**

Shepherd's Pie

Eggplant and mushrooms add a meaty flavor to this hearty and filling meatless main dish. You could flavor the potatoes that top it with everything from Cheddar cheese to green onions.

2 tablespoons olive oil

2 tablespoons butter

2 eggplants, peeled and cubed

2 onions, chopped

2 (8-ounce) packages sliced fresh mushrooms

5 cloves garlic, minced

1 teaspoon salt

¼ teaspoon pepper

1 teaspoon dried thyme leaves

4 carrots, sliced

1 (14-ounce) can diced tomatoes, undrained

1 (6-ounce) can tomato paste

¾ cup chili sauce

2 tablespoons Worcestershire sauce

1 (24-ounce) package refrigerated mashed potatoes

½ cup sour cream

½ cup grated Parmesan cheese

1. In large skillet, heat olive oil and butter over medium heat. When butter melts, add eggplant; cook and stir until almost tender. Remove with slotted spoon; set aside.

2. Add onions, mushrooms, and garlic to skillet; cook and stir for 5–6 minutes until crisp-tender. Stir in salt, pepper, thyme, carrots, tomatoes, tomato paste, chili sauce, and Worcestershire sauce, along with the eggplant; bring to a simmer.

3. Prepare mashed potatoes as directed on package. Stir in sour cream and Parmesan cheese.

4. Pour vegetable mixture into 6-quart slow cooker. Top with potato mixture. Cover and cook on low for 7–8 hours or until mixture is hot and bubbling.

❦ **Makes 8 servings**

Black Bean Tortilla Torte

Black beans are delicious; hearty and meaty-tasting. In this well-seasoned casserole, they blend beautifully with salsa, cheese, and tortillas.

2 tablespoons olive oil

3 onions, chopped

6 cloves garlic, minced

3 (15-ounce) cans black beans, drained

2 (16-ounce) jars mild or medium salsa

2 envelopes taco seasoning mix

1 (6-ounce) can tomato paste

1½ cups sour cream

2 cups shredded CoJack cheese

1 cup shredded pepper jack cheese

2 green bell peppers, chopped

12 (6-inch) corn tortillas

⅓ cup grated Cotija cheese

2 cups chopped tomatoes

1 (4-ounce) can green chiles, drained

½ cup chopped fresh cilantro leaves

1. In large skillet, heat olive oil over medium heat. Add onions and garlic; cook and stir until crisp-tender, about 5 minutes. Stir in black beans, salsa, taco seasoning mix, and tomato paste. Bring to a simmer; simmer uncovered for 5 minutes.
2. In medium bowl, combine sour cream, CoJack cheese, pepper jack cheese, and green peppers. Mix well.
3. Spray a 6-quart slow cooker with nonstick cooking spray. Place a spoonful of the black bean mixture in bottom. Layer some tortillas on top and add a layer of the sour cream mixture. Repeat layers, ending with sour cream mixture.
4. Sprinkle top with Cotija cheese. Cover and cook on low for 7–8 hours until casserole is bubbly. In small bowl, combine tomatoes, green chiles, and cilantro. Serve casserole with tomato mixture.

❦ **Makes 10–12 servings**

Beans and "Sausage"

Meatless soy vegetarian crumbles flavored to taste like sausage really do—taste like sausage, that is. This hearty casserole is tasty and filling.

2 tablespoons butter

2 onions, chopped

2 (12-ounce) packages sausage-style meatless soy vegetarian crumbles

2 (15-ounce) cans black beans, drained

2 (15-ounce) cans kidney beans, drained

1 (15-ounce) can navy beans, drained

1 (16-ounce) bag frozen lima beans, thawed

1 cup chili sauce

½ cup barbecue sauce

½ cup brown sugar

⅓ cup yellow mustard

1. In large skillet, melt butter over medium heat. Add onions; cook and stir until tender.
2. Combine onions with all remaining ingredients in a 6-quart slow cooker. Cover and cook on low for 7–8 hours or until everything is blended and crumbles are tender. Stir and serve immediately.

❀ **Makes 16–18 servings**

Gourmet Mac and Cheese

Five kinds of cheese make this dish rich and creamy. Use an oval slow cooker, and fill it just over half full.

2 tablespoons butter

2 onions, chopped

2 (13-ounce) cans evaporated milk

½ cup whole milk

¾ cup sour cream

⅓ cup Dijon mustard

½ teaspoon salt

¼ teaspoon white pepper

2 cups shredded sharp Cheddar cheese

3 cups shredded American cheese

2 cups shredded provolone cheese

1 (8-ounce) package cream cheese, cubed

1 (16-ounce) package elbow macaroni

½ cup grated Parmesan cheese

1 teaspoon paprika

1. In large skillet, melt butter over medium heat. Add onions; cook and stir until tender, about 6 minutes.
2. Add evaporated milk, whole milk, sour cream, mustard, salt, and pepper; heat until steaming. Remove from heat and stir in Cheddar, American, provolone, and cream cheeses.
3. Stir in macaroni and pour into 6-quart slow cooker. Sprinkle top with Parmesan cheese and paprika. Cover and cook on high for 2–3 hours or until macaroni is tender. Stir well and serve.

❀ **Makes 12–14 servings**

Greek Stew over Couscous

The flavors of Greece mingle in this delicious stew. You can find feta in several flavors: plain; with garlic and herbs; or with tomatoes and herbs.

1 acorn squash, peeled and cubed

1 butternut squash, peeled and cubed

2 onions, chopped

6 cloves garlic, minced

4 carrots, sliced

4 cups vegetable broth

4 cups water

1 teaspoon salt

1 teaspoon dried oregano

1 teaspoon dried thyme

¼ teaspoon white pepper

2 (15-ounce) cans chickpeas, drained

1 cup golden raisins

4 cups couscous

6 cups vegetable broth

1 cup crumbled feta cheese

1. Combine all ingredients except couscous, broth, and feta in a 6-quart slow cooker. Cover and cook on low for 9–10 hours or until vegetables are very tender.

2. Place broth in saucepan and bring to a boil over high heat. Stir in couscous, cover, and remove from heat. Let stand for 5 minutes, then fluff with fork. Place couscous in large serving bowl.

3. Stir mixture in slow cooker and spoon over couscous. Sprinkle with feta cheese and serve.

🍲 **Makes 14–16 servings**

If you offer your food to the hungry and satisfy the needs of the afflicted, then your light shall rise in the darkness and your bloom be like the noonday. The Lord will guide you continually, and satisfy your needs in parched places, and make your bones strong; and you shall be like a watered garden, like a spring of water, whose waters never fail.

—Isaiah 58:10–11

Meatless Lasagna

The squash and mushrooms add great texture and meaty flavor to this filling dish. If you vary the cheese (use Gruyère or Colby), you can create a new recipe.

3 tablespoons butter

2 tablespoons olive oil

1 zucchini, peeled and cubed

1 eggplant, peeled and cubed

1 yellow summer squash, peeled and cubed

1 (8-ounce) package sliced mushrooms

2 cups sliced portobello mushrooms

1 onion, chopped

4 cloves garlic, minced

3 (14-ounce) cans diced tomatoes, undrained

2 cups vegetable broth

1 (6-ounce) can tomato paste

1 teaspoon dried basil leaves

1 teaspoon dried oregano leaves

1½ teaspoons salt

¼ teaspoon white pepper

1 (15-ounce) container part-skim ricotta cheese

2 eggs

1 (12-ounce) tub soft cream cheese

2 cups shredded mozzarella cheese

½ cup grated Parmesan cheese, divided

12 lasagna noodles

1. In skillet, heat butter and olive oil over medium heat. Add zucchini and eggplant; cook and stir until crisp-tender, about 5 minutes. Remove vegetables to a large bowl with slotted spoon.
2. Add squash and both kinds of mushrooms to skillet; cook and stir until crisp-tender, about 5 minutes. Remove to same bowl with slotted spoon.
3. Add onions and garlic to skillet; cook and stir until crisp-tender, about 5 minutes. Stir in tomatoes, vegetable broth, tomato paste, basil, oregano, salt, and pepper; bring to a simmer.
4. In another large bowl combine ricotta cheese, eggs, and cream cheese; beat until blended. Stir in mozzarella cheese and ¼ cup Parmesan cheese.
5. Spray a 6- to 7-quart oval slow cooker with nonstick cooking spray. Add a spoonful of the tomato sauce to the bottom. Top with 4 lasagna noodles, then a layer of the squash mixture. Top with ricotta mixture. Repeat layers, ending with ricotta mixture.
6. Sprinkle top with remaining ¼ cup Parmesan cheese. Cover and cook on high for 4–5 hours or until lasagna noodles are tender. Turn off heat, remove cover, and let stand for 15 minutes before serving.

❦ **Makes 12–14 servings**

Cheesy Polenta Casserole

You use two slow cookers to make this casserole—one for the topping and one for the polenta—but the time saving is huge!

2½ cups yellow cornmeal

6½ cups vegetable broth

2 cups water

3 tablespoons butter

1½ teaspoons salt

¼ teaspoon white pepper

2 cups shredded extra-sharp Cheddar cheese

1 (8-ounce) package cream cheese, cubed

2 tablespoons butter

1 onion, chopped

2 green bell peppers, chopped

1 (14-ounce) can diced tomatoes, drained

1 (8-ounce) can tomato sauce

2 (15-ounce) cans chickpeas, drained

1 teaspoon dried oregano

⅛ teaspoon pepper

½ cup grated Parmesan cheese

1. Place cornmeal in a 4-quart slow cooker. In large saucepan, combine broth, water, 3 tablespoons butter, salt, and pepper; bring to a boil. Stir into cornmeal.
2. Cover and cook on high for 2 hours, or until liquid is absorbed. Stir polenta thoroughly, add Cheddar and cream cheese, stir gently, and turn off heat.
3. In large skillet, melt 2 tablespoons butter over medium heat. Add onion; cook and stir until tender, about 6 minutes. Add bell peppers, tomatoes, tomato sauce, chickpeas, oregano, and pepper; bring to a simmer. Remove from heat.
4. Place polenta in bottom of 7-quart slow cooker. Top with chickpea mixture, then sprinkle with Parmesan cheese. Cover and cook on low for 5–6 hours or until casserole is thoroughly heated.

❁ **Makes 12–14 servings**

Black-Eyed Pea and Rice Salad

The peas and rice combine to provide complete protein in this excellent and colorful main dish salad.

1 (16-ounce) bag dried black-eyed peas

1 cup wild rice

2 onions, chopped

4 jalapeño peppers, minced

1 (16-ounce) bag baby carrots

2 (32-ounce) boxes vegetable broth

2 cups water

2 tablespoons olive oil

1 teaspoon salt

1 cup mayonnaise

½ cup olive oil

⅓ cup Dijon mustard

¼ cup apple cider vinegar

1 teaspoon salt

1 teaspoon dried thyme leaves

¼ teaspoon pepper

2 red bell peppers, chopped

1. Sort and rinse peas. Place in large saucepan and cover with water. Bring to a boil; boil hard for two minutes. Remove saucepan from heat, cover, and let stand for 2 hours.

2. Drain peas and place in 6-quart slow cooker with wild rice, onions, jalapeño peppers, baby carrots, vegetable broth, water, 2 tablespoons olive oil, and 1 teaspoon salt. Cover and cook on low for 8 hours or until peas and rice are tender. Drain.

3. In large bowl, combine mayonnaise, ½ cup olive oil, mustard, vinegar, salt, thyme, and pepper; mix well. Stir in drained peas and rice mixture along with red bell peppers.

4. Cover and chill for 4–5 hours. Stir gently before serving.

❦ **Makes 18–20 servings**

Vegetarian Spaghetti

Carrots help keep the sauce from becoming watery, and add nutrition and flavor. The sauce can be served over any pasta; linguine or penne would be good.

3 onions, chopped

6 cloves garlic, minced

2 cups shredded carrots

2 (8-ounce) packages sliced fresh mushrooms

2 tablespoons olive oil

1 (6-ounce) can tomato paste

1 (15-ounce) can tomato sauce

2 (14-ounce) cans diced tomatoes, undrained

2 cups water

2 teaspoons dried Italian seasoning

1 bay leaf

1 teaspoon salt

¼ teaspoon pepper

2 (16-ounce) packages pasta

1 cup grated Parmesan cheese

1. Combine all ingredients except pasta and cheese in a 5-quart slow cooker. Cover and cook on low for 8–9 hours, stirring once during cooking time, until sauce is blended and thickened.
2. When sauce is ready, bring two pots of salted water to a boil. Add one package pasta to each pot; cook according to package directions until al dente. Drain pasta and place on two warmed serving dishes. Remove and discard bay leaf. Stir sauce and spoon over pasta. Sprinkle with cheese and serve.

❧ **Makes 10–12 servings**

Barley-and-Potato Salad

Barley adds a great chewy texture and nutty flavor to potato salad. You can find vegan mayonnaise, mustard, and milk if you're serving strict vegans.

1 cup pearl barley

4 pounds russet potatoes

2 onions, chopped

6 cloves garlic, minced

1½ teaspoons salt

¼ teaspoon white pepper

1 teaspoon dried tarragon

3 cups water

1½ cups mayonnaise

1 cup sour cream

½ cup plain yogurt

⅓ cup mustard

3 tablespoons Dijon mustard

⅓ cup whole milk

1 red bell pepper, chopped

1 green bell pepper, chopped

1 yellow bell pepper, chopped

2 pints grape tomatoes

1. Place barley in the bottom of 6-quart slow cooker. Peel potatoes and cut into cubes. Place on top of barley along with onions and garlic. Sprinkle with salt, pepper, and tarragon, then pour the water over all.

(continued)

(Barley-and-Potato Salad—
continued)

2. Make sure barley is covered with liquid.
   Cover and cook on low for 8–9 hours or
   until potatoes and barley are tender.
3. In bowl, combine mayonnaise, sour
   cream, yogurt, mustard, Dijon mustard,
   and milk; mix with wire whisk. Stir in
   remaining ingredients and mix well.
4. Remove hot potato mixture from slow
   cooker with large slotted spoon or
   sieve. Add to bowl and stir gently to
   coat. Cover and chill for 4–5 hours
   until cold. Stir gently before serving.

❦ **Makes 10–12 servings**

*And whoever gives even a cup
of water to one of these little
ones— none of these will lose
their reward.*

—Matthew 10:42

Grandma's Tomatoes and Pierogies

Pierogies are large ravioli-like pasta, stuffed
with a mixture of potatoes and cheese or
onions. They are found in the frozen entrées
section of the supermarket.

2 onions, chopped

6 cloves garlic, minced

6 tomatoes, chopped

6 plum tomatoes, chopped

2 (15-ounce) cans tomato paste

2 cups vegetable broth

1 teaspoon salt

1 teaspoon dried marjoram leaves

3 (12-count) packages frozen pierogies,
   thawed

2 cups shredded pizza blend cheese

1. Combine all ingredients except
   pierogies and cheese in a 6-quart slow
   cooker. Cover and cook on low for 6–7
   hours or until sauce is blended.
2. Separate the pierogies and add them to
   the slow cooker, distributing them
   evenly. Make sure all of the pierogies
   are covered with sauce.
3. Cover and cook on high for 1–2 hours
   longer, or until pierogies are hot in the
   center. Sprinkle with cheese and serve.

❦ **Makes 10–12 servings**

Ratatouille

The vegetables will cook down quite a bit in this recipe, so don't be alarmed if the slow cooker is really full right at the beginning.

1½ teaspoons salt

¼ teaspoon pepper

¼ teaspoon white pepper

1 teaspoon dried oregano leaves

1 teaspoon dried basil leaves

1 teaspoon dried Italian seasoning

1 tablespoon sugar

3 tablespoons olive oil

1 eggplant, sliced ½" thick

3 onions, chopped

6 cloves garlic, minced

3 yellow summer squash, sliced

2 zucchini, sliced

3 tomatoes, sliced

2 (8-ounce) packages sliced mushrooms

1 red bell pepper, sliced

2 green bell peppers, sliced

1 yellow bell pepper, sliced

¼ cup extra-virgin olive oil

1 (26-ounce) jar spaghetti sauce

1 (6-ounce) can tomato paste

3 tablespoons balsamic vinegar

1 cup diced feta cheese, if desired

1. In bowl combine salt, pepper, white pepper, oregano, basil, Italian seasoning, and sugar. Mix well and set aside. In large skillet, heat 3 tablespoons olive oil over medium heat. Add eggplant; sauté for 2–3 minutes on each side and then remove eggplant to a separate bowl. Add onions and garlic to skillet; cook and stir for 5 minutes.

2. Spray a 7-quart slow cooker with nonstick cooking spray. Layer all of the vegetables in the slow cooker, sprinkling each layer with some of the salt mixture and drizzling with some of the extra-virgin olive oil.

3. In food processor, combine half of the spaghetti sauce with the tomato paste; blend until smooth. Stir in remaining spaghetti sauce along with the vinegar. Pour into slow cooker.

4. Cover and cook on low for 7–9 hours or until vegetables are very tender. Sprinkle with cheese, if desired, and serve.

❦ **Makes 10 servings**

And all the people went their way to eat and drink and to send portions and to make great rejoicing, because they had understood the words that were declared for them.

—Nehemiah 8:12

Spicy Risotto

To seed tomatoes, cut in half and gently squeeze out the seeds and jelly. Then chop the tomatoes coarsely and set aside in a dish until it's time to add them to the recipe.

¼ cup olive oil

2 onions, chopped

4 cloves garlic, minced

1 or 2 jalapeño peppers, minced

2½ cups Arborio rice

1 (8-ounce) package sliced fresh mushrooms

1 teaspoon salt

¼ teaspoon white pepper

1 teaspoon cumin seeds

½ teaspoon crushed red pepper flakes

7 cups vegetable broth

1 cup tomato juice

6 tomatoes, seeded and chopped

1 cup heavy cream

1 cup grated Parmesan cheese

1. Heat oil in large skillet. Add onions, garlic, and jalapeño pepper; cook and stir for 4–5 minutes. Then stir in rice; cook and stir for 3–4 minutes longer.
2. Place onion mixture in 5-quart slow cooker. Add mushrooms, salt, pepper, cumin seeds, red pepper flakes, broth, and tomato juice.
3. Cover and cook on high for 2 hours, stirring twice during cooking time. Stir in chopped tomatoes, then continue cooking on high for another 1–2 hours, stirring every half hour, until rice is al dente (slightly firm in the center).
4. Stir in cream and cheese. Uncover and cook for 15–25 minutes longer or until risotto is creamy and hot. Serve immediately.

🐝 **Makes 10–12 servings**

Side Dishes

✤

I still remember lunches at the parochial grade school I attended. At almost every meal, the lunch ladies served the most marvelous mashed potatoes (made from scratch, of course), topped with melted butter. A lady would scoop mashed potatoes onto your plate, then make an indentation with the back of a tiny ladle, and pour some butter in. The combination was, and is, sublime.

A church can't function without its supporting cast: volunteers, secretaries, and deacons. So, too, no meal is complete without a side dish. And no matter what you choose for a main dish, side dishes cook perfectly in the slow cooker. Using a slow cooker for your side dishes means you can free up the stovetop and oven to make the entrée, desserts, and breads.

For a Thanksgiving service, or a Christmas buffet when you want to serve turkey and dressing, make extra dressing and let it slowly cook in the slow cooker. No turkey has enough stuffing to satisfy a large gathering, so you'll be able to easily feed a crowd using this technique.

When cooking side dishes in the slow cooker, be aware that many root vegetables and dried beans need to cook for a longer time than meats. These foods should be placed on the bottom of the slow cooker, where they can be surrounded by heat. Salt and acidic ingredients, including tomatoes and citrus juices, can prevent these foods from tenderizing, so add them toward the end of cooking time.

—Linda Larsen

Gingered Baked Beans

Adding ginger to baked beans wakes them up a bit. The onion and ginger become tender and mild during the long cooking time, forming the perfect complement to the beans.

2 tablespoons butter

1 onion, chopped

2 tablespoons minced fresh gingerroot

⅓ cup maple syrup

⅓ cup brown sugar

⅓ cup ketchup

2 tablespoons yellow mustard

2 (16-ounce) cans baked beans, undrained

1 (15-ounce) can black beans, drained

1 (15-ounce) can navy beans, drained

1. In medium skillet, melt butter over medium heat. Add onion; cook and stir until tender, about 6 minutes. Place in 4-quart slow cooker along with gingerroot, maple syrup, brown sugar, ketchup, and mustard; mix well.
2. Add undrained baked beans, drained black beans, and drained navy beans; mix well. Cover and cook on low for 7–9 hours.

🌿 **Makes 10–12 servings**

Calico Baked Beans

Remember how long it used to take your mom to make homemade baked beans? These "homemade" beans have an extra added appeal–sausage. You can use the hotter version if you want to really spice things up.

1 (16-ounce) package sausage

1 (15.25-ounce) can lima beans

1 (15-ounce) can kidney beans

1 (28-ounce) can baked beans

1 (5-ounce) can tomato sauce

½ cup chopped onion

½ cup brown sugar

1. Brown sausage in skillet until cooked and drain well.
2. Mix all ingredients together in large bowl. Put in greased 9" × 13" baking dish and bake at 350° for 1 hour.

🌿 **Makes 8–10 servings**

He has brought down the powerful from their thrones, and lifted up the lowly; he has filled the hungry with good things, and sent the rich away empty.

—Luke 1:52

Pepper's Beans

Pepper's beans are an essential ingredient for any picnic. What's a picnic without hot dogs, hamburgers, and baked beans? Take these to your next picnic.

¼ cup chopped green pepper

½ stick butter

2½ cups northern beans, cooked

1 (14.5-ounce) can diced tomatoes, drained

1 medium onion, thinly sliced

½ teaspoon dry mustard

½ cup sugar

1 tablespoon vinegar

½ teaspoon salt

1. Sauté green pepper in butter in large skillet. Add remaining ingredients.
2. Put into a greased 9" × 13" baking dish, and bake at 350° for 45–60 minutes.

❧ **Makes 8–10 servings**

Sweet-and-Spicy Beans

The addition of corn to this bean salad recipe adds a bright spot of color. In fact, you could use a can of Mexican-style corn in place of the regular corn.

1 (15.5-ounce) can red kidney beans, rinsed and drained

1 (15.25-ounce) can whole kernel corn, rinsed and drained

1 (15-ounce) can black beans, rinsed and drained

1 (15-ounce) can black-eyed peas, rinsed and drained

1 (2-ounce) jar diced pimientos, drained

4 green onions, sliced, approximately ½ cup

⅓ cup sugar

⅓ cup red wine vinegar

⅓ cup salad oil

½ teaspoon ground red pepper

½ teaspoon salt

1. In a large bowl, combine kidney beans, corn, black beans, black-eyed peas, pimientos, and green onions.
2. Whisk together sugar, red wine vinegar, oil, red pepper, and salt. Pour vinegar mixture over bean mixture and toss to coat. Cover, and chill for at least 2 hours or up to 24 hours. Serve with a slotted spoon.

❧ **Makes 8–10 servings**

Traditional Black Beans and Rice

More and more people choose a vegetarian meal at least one day a week. Black beans and rice are staples in the vegetarian's kitchen. Try this for your friends or family who prefer meatless meals.

1 tablespoon olive oil

¾ cup finely chopped onion

½ cup finely chopped green pepper

1 cup diced tomatoes

1 (15-ounce) can black beans, drained and with juice reserved

½ teaspoon thyme

1 teaspoon garlic salt

3 tablespoons cider vinegar

½ teaspoon hot pepper sauce

2 cups cooked rice

1. In a large skillet, heat olive oil. Cook onion and green pepper until tender. Stir in tomatoes, beans, thyme, and garlic salt. Cook 3 minutes. Add vinegar, pepper sauce, and reserved juice. Continue to cook for 5 minutes.
2. Serve over rice.

❧ **Makes 6–8 servings**

Anne's Cheesy Carrots

Even picky eaters will love this recipe. A creamy, cheesy sauce surrounds tender baby carrots. It's the perfect side dish for any entrée.

3 (16-ounce) packages baby carrots

2 cups water

2 tablespoons butter

1 (8-ounce) package processed American cheese, cubed

1 (8-ounce) package cream cheese, cubed

1 teaspoon dried thyme leaves

⅓ cup milk

1. In 4-quart slow cooker, combine carrots, water, and butter. Cover and cook on low for 5–6 hours or until carrots are tender.
2. Drain carrots and return to slow cooker. Stir in American cheese, cream cheese, thyme, and milk; mix gently. Cover and cook on low for 2 hours, stirring once during cooking time, until smooth sauce forms. Serve immediately.

❧ **Makes 10–12 servings**

But he said to them, "You give them something to eat."

—Luke 9:13

Creamy Potatoes

This creamy, cheesy recipe will be a hit at any gathering. Kids, especially, love this concoction, so it's perfect for a church potluck.

2 (32-ounce) packages frozen hash brown potatoes

2 onions, chopped

4 cloves garlic, minced

2 (10-ounce) cans condensed cream of potato soup

1 (8-ounce) package cream cheese, cubed

1 cup sour cream

2 cups grated Havarti or Swiss cheese

1. In 4- to 5-quart slow cooker, combine potatoes, onions, and garlic. In medium bowl, combine remaining ingredients; mix. Pour into slow cooker.
2. Cover and cook on low for 4 hours; then stir to mix. Cover and continue cooking on low for 3–4 hours longer, until potatoes and onions are tender.

❧ **Makes 10–12 servings**

Easy Homemade Mac 'n' Cheese

Homemade macaroni and cheese—real comfort food. This beats the packaged variety any day.

1 (16-ounce) box of elbow macaroni

½ stick butter

2 eggs

1 (8-ounce) package shredded Colby cheese

1 cup milk

1. Boil macaroni until done. Drain. Add butter, milk, and eggs to macaroni. Mix well. Add half package of cheese. Stir until cheese melts.
2. Pour into 8" square baking dish and put rest of cheese on top. Bake at 400° until cheese is melted and slightly brown.

❧ **Makes 6 servings**

Spicy Corn Spoon Bread

Baking bread in the slow cooker makes a moist and tender loaf, more like a spoon bread, which is a cross between a soufflé and bread. Make this a mild casserole by omitting the chili powder and green chiles.

2 (8-ounce) packages corn muffin mix

1 tablespoon chili powder, divided

2 eggs, beaten

1/3 cup milk

1/3 cup sour cream

1½ cups frozen corn

1 red bell pepper, chopped

1 (4-ounce) can chopped green chiles, drained

1 cup shredded Colby cheese

1/3 cup mild or medium salsa

1. In large bowl, combine both packages muffin mix and 2 teaspoons chili powder; mix to combine. In medium bowl, combine eggs, milk, and sour cream; mix well. Add to muffin mix and stir just until combined. Stir in corn and bell pepper.
2. In small bowl, combine drained chiles, cheese, and salsa. Spray a 3½- quart slow cooker with nonstick baking spray containing flour. Spoon half of the muffin mix batter into the slow cooker. Top with the green chile mixture, then add remaining batter. Smooth top and sprinkle with remaining 1 teaspoon chili powder.
3. Cover slow cooker and cook on high for 2–3 hours, or until top springs back when lightly touched. Uncover, then top with foil, leaving a corner vented, and cool for 20 minutes. Serve by scooping out hot bread with a large spoon.

❦ **Makes 8–10 servings**

What good is it, my brothers and sisters, if you say you have faith but do not have works? Can faith save you? If a brother or sister is naked and lacks daily food, and one of you says to them, "Go in peace, keep warm and eat your fill," and yet you do not supply their bodily needs, what is the good of that?

—James 2:14–17

Spinach Soufflé

Try this spinach recipe when you're in the mood for something a little different. The Tabasco sauce gives this dish a bit of a bite, but it's quite good.

2 (10-ounce) packages frozen chopped spinach
½ cup butter
¾ cup cracker crumbs
¼ cup grated onion
2 eggs, beaten separately
⅛ teaspoon dried thyme
1 teaspoon garlic powder
3 dashes Tabasco sauce
½ teaspoon pepper
¼ cup Parmesan cheese
½ teaspoon salt

1. Preheat oven to 350°.
2. Cook spinach according to directions on the package. Drain well and combine with the remaining ingredients.
3. Pour into greased 2-quart casserole and bake at 350° for 30 minutes.

❧ **Makes 6–8 servings**

Spinach Pie

This makes two pies and that you'll need both of them when you're making these for "take-out." The smoked pork chops add a perfect taste to the spinach and cheese.

3 tablespoons oil
2 large onions, chopped
2 (10-ounce) packages frozen spinach, thawed and dried
4 or 5 smoked pork chops, trimmed and diced
1½ cups grated Parmesan cheese
1 cup ricotta cheese
4 eggs, slightly beaten
2 deep-dish pie crusts

1. Preheat oven to 425°.
2. Sauté onion and spinach in oil for 2 minutes. Add remaining ingredients and pour into unbaked pie shells. Bake 35 minutes or until done.
3. Cool 10 minutes and cut into serving wedges. Can be cut into smaller wedges for appetizers.

❧ **Makes 12–16 servings**

Spinach Rings

This recipe only makes 6 to 8 servings, so when making this for a party, you might want to double the recipe. These would also be good with a white cream sauce.

½ cup chopped onion

1 egg

½ teaspoon salt

⅛ teaspoon black pepper

1 (10-ounce) package frozen spinach, thawed and drained

8 strips of bacon, uncooked

1. Sauté onion in pan sprayed with vegetable cooking spray.
2. In mixing bowl, beat together egg, salt, and pepper. Add spinach and onions. Mix well.
3. Grease bottoms of standard muffin tins and line sides with bacon. Cut to fit. Place spinach mixture in lined tins. Bake at 350° for 15–20 minutes.
4. Remove from tins and serve.

❦ **Makes 6–8 rings**

Curried Rice

Curried Rice is gently seasoned, and the perfect complement to everything from roasted chicken to Curried Pork (page 221).

3 cups vegetable stock

2 cloves garlic, minced

1½ cups long grain white rice

2 teaspoons curry powder

1 tablespoon butter

2 teaspoons dried parsley flakes

⅛ teaspoon pepper

½ teaspoon salt

½ cup sliced almonds, toasted

1. In small saucepan, bring stock and garlic to a simmer. Pour into 2-quart slow cooker. Add remaining ingredients except almonds. Stir and cover. Cook on low for 4 hours.
2. Turn off slow cooker and add almonds. Let stand for 5 minutes, then fluff to incorporate almonds and mix the rice.

❦ **Makes 6–8 servings**

Garlicky Green Beans

When cooked for a long time at low temperatures, garlic becomes tender, mild, and nutty. It adds a wonderful spark of flavor to green beans.

3 (16-ounce) packages frozen whole
    green beans
1 onion, chopped
6 cloves garlic, minced
½ teaspoon salt
⅛ teaspoon pepper
1 cup water
2 tablespoons butter

1. Combine all ingredients except butter in 4-quart slow cooker. Cover and cook on low for 4–5 hours or until beans and onions are tender.
2. Drain off water and return ingredients to slow cooker. Add butter, cover, and cook for 30 minutes longer. Stir and serve.

❦ **Makes 10–12 servings**

Herbed Brown Rice Pilaf

Rice pilaf goes with everything: chicken, beef, pork, and fish. And brown rice, besides being good for you, cooks to perfection in the slow cooker.

1 tablespoon olive oil
1 tablespoon butter
1 onion, chopped
2 cloves garlic, minced
2 cups long grain brown rice
2 cups water
2 cups vegetable broth
1 teaspoon dried thyme leaves
½ teaspoon dried marjoram leaves
½ teaspoon salt
⅛ teaspoon pepper

1. In medium skillet, heat olive oil and butter over medium heat until butter melts. Add onion and garlic; cook and stir for 3 minutes. Add rice; cook and stir until rice is slightly toasted, about 5–6 minutes longer.
2. Transfer rice mixture to 2-quart slow cooker. To the skillet, add water, broth, and remaining ingredients; bring to a simmer. Pour into slow cooker.
3. Cover and cook on low for 6–7 hours or until rice is tender. Stir well and serve.

❦ **Makes 6 servings**

Asparagus and Pasta

Asparagus is not quite as economical to use as other frozen vegetables. So if you're making this casserole and want to cut costs a little, try frozen broccoli or spinach.

8 ounces uncooked spaghetti, broken
    into thirds

2 tablespoons margarine

3 tablespoons flour

2 cups milk

1 cup shredded mozzarella cheese

Dash pepper

1 (16-ounce) package frozen asparagus spears,
    thawed

1 (13.25-ounce) can sliced mushrooms,
    drained

2 tablespoons Parmesan cheese

1. Cook spaghetti to desired doneness. Drain. Keep warm.
2. Preheat oven to 400°.
3. Grease 9" pie pan.
4. Melt margarine in medium saucepan and stir in flour until smooth and bubbly. Gradually add milk with wire whisk. Blend well. Cook over medium heat 6–10 minutes, stirring constantly, until mixture thickens. Add mozzarella and pepper.
5. Spoon spaghetti into greased pie pan. Top with asparagus, then mushrooms and pour white sauce on top. Sprinkle with 2 tablespoons Parmesan cheese.
6. Bake 20 minutes or until mixture is bubbly.

❧ **Makes 6–8 servings**

Potluck Pointer

To keep small batches of an entreé or a side dish warm, use an insulated ice bucket instead of a slow cooker. Food will stay warm for about 1 hour.

Baked Ziti

Looking for a meatless entrée? The pasta and cheeses combine to delight even the picky eaters.

1 (16-ounce) package ziti, cooked
2 cups cottage cheese
1 (32-ounce) jar spaghetti sauce
1 teaspoon oregano
1 teaspoon garlic powder
½ teaspoon onion powder
8 ounces shredded mozzarella cheese

1. Mix all ingredients except mozzarella.
2. Spread in a greased 9" × 13" baking dish. Sprinkle with mozzarella cheese.
4. Bake at 350° for 30–45 minutes.

❧ **Makes 8–10 servings**

Take wheat and barley, beans and lentils, millet and spelt; put them in a storage jar and use them to make bread for yourself.

—Ezekiel 4:9

Risi Bisi

Risi bisi, or rice with peas, is a classic Italian side dish. A little sour cream and cheese make it decadent and delicious.

2 tablespoons butter
1 onion, chopped
2 shallots, finely chopped
2 cups long grain rice
4 cups water
1 vegetable soup bouillon cube
1 teaspoon dried Italian seasoning
⅛ teaspoon pepper
1½ cups frozen baby peas, thawed
½ cup sour cream
¼ cup grated Parmesan cheese

1. In small saucepan, melt butter over medium heat. Add onion and shallots; cook and stir for 4 minutes. Add rice; cook and stir for 3 minutes longer. Place into 2-quart slow cooker.
2. Add water, bouillon cube, Italian seasoning, and pepper. Cover and cook on low for 5–6 hours or until rice is almost tender.
3. Stir in peas; cover and cook for 30 minutes. Then add sour cream and cheese; cover and cook for 30 minutes longer. Stir and serve immediately.

❧ **Makes 8 servings**

Clara's Creamed Corn

Corn combined with two kinds of cheese makes one delicious side dish. Try this one alongside a baked ham.

2 (16-ounce) packages frozen corn

2 (15-ounce) cans creamed corn

1 cup mascarpone cheese

2 (3-ounce) packages cream cheese, cubed

1/3 cup butter

2 tablespoons honey

1 cup whole milk

1/4 teaspoon white pepper

1 teaspoon dried thyme leaves

1. In 4-quart slow cooker, combine all ingredients and mix well. Cover and cook on low heat for 3 hours.
2. Stir gently to combine. Serve or hold on low heat for 2 hours, stirring occasionally.

❦ **Makes 12 servings**

Potato Apple Gratin

In French, apples are *pommes*, while potatoes are *pommes de terre*, or apples of the earth. These two foods combine beautifully in a rich casserole.

1 cup whole milk

1 cup heavy cream

1 (10-ounce) can condensed cream of potato soup

4 egg yolks

1/8 teaspoon white pepper

1/8 teaspoon nutmeg

3 cloves garlic, minced

1 onion, finely chopped

2 pounds small red potatoes, unpeeled, thinly sliced

3 Winesap apples, peeled, cored, and thinly sliced

1 cup shredded Havarti cheese

1/4 cup grated Parmesan cheese

1/2 teaspoon paprika

1. In medium bowl, combine milk, cream, soup, egg yolks, pepper, nutmeg, and garlic; mix well. In 4- to 5-quart slow cooker, layer 1/3 of the onion, potatoes, and apples, sprinkling some Havarti cheese over each layer. Repeat layers.
2. Pour milk mixture over all. Sprinkle with Parmesan cheese and paprika. Cover and cook on low for 7–8 hours or until potatoes and apples are tender and gratin is bubbling. Serve immediately.

❦ **Makes 10–12 servings**

Wild Rice Salad

Wild rice and brown rice cook well in the slow cooker. This salad can be made into a main dish salad with the addition of 3–4 cups chopped cooked chicken, made according to the instructions on page 413.

2 cups wild rice

2 cups brown rice

2 onions, chopped

2 cups water

4 cups vegetable broth

2 cups apple juice

1 teaspoon salt

1/8 teaspoon pepper

1 teaspoon dried thyme leaves

1 cup mayonnaise

1 cup plain yogurt

1/2 cup sour cream

1/4 cup tarragon vinegar

2 tablespoons sugar

2 red bell peppers, chopped

2 green bell peppers, chopped

2 pints grape tomatoes

1. In 4-quart slow cooker, combine wild rice, brown rice, onions, water, broth, and apple juice. Add salt, pepper, and thyme; stir.
2. Cover and cook on high for 3–4 hours or until liquid is absorbed and the rice is tender.
3. In large bowl, combine mayonnaise, yogurt, sour cream, tarragon vinegar, and sugar; mix well. Add bell peppers and tomatoes.
4. Drain rice mixture if any liquid remains, and stir into mayonnaise mixture. Cover and chill for 3–4 hours. Stir gently before serving.

❦ **Makes 12 servings**

Every third year you shall bring out the full tithe of your produce for that year, and store it within your towns; the Levites, because they have no allotment or inheritance with you, as well as the resident aliens, the orphans, and the widows in your towns, may come and eat their fill so that the Lord your God may bless you.

—Deuteronomy 14:28–29

Gemuse

This is an old favorite handed down through generations, beginning in 1911. Pronounced *guh-meese*, which is the German word for "vegetables," it works with any vegetables; just mash them separately and mix them in with prepared mashed potatoes. As the song goes, "Memories are made of this"!

5 pounds potatoes

½ pound carrots

3 stalks celery, chopped

4 onions, peeled and diced

1½ sticks butter

½ cup milk

1 cup sour cream

1. Peel potatoes and cut into bite-size pieces. Cover with water in 5-quart pan.
2. Add carrots, celery, and onions, and cook over medium heat until vegetables are tender. Drain vegetables, separating carrots, and mashing them in separate bowl.
3. In large bowl, mash potatoes, celery, and onions by hand. Add butter and milk and beat with electric mixer. Beat in sour cream. Put into greased 9" × 13" baking dish. Top with ½ stick of butter and keep warm at 250°.

❦ **Makes 8–10 servings**

Garlic-and-Herb Mashed Potatoes

First cook the potatoes to tender perfection in the slow cooker, then mash them with delicious ingredients to make some of the best mashed potatoes anywhere!

6 pounds red potatoes, peeled

6 cloves garlic, minced

2 (5") sprigs fresh thyme

1 cup vegetable broth

1 cup butter, cut into cubes

1 teaspoon dried thyme leaves

1 (8-ounce) package cream cheese, cubed

1 cup mascarpone cheese

1 cup whole milk

1 teaspoon salt

¼ teaspoon white pepper

1. In a 7-quart slow cooker, combine potatoes with garlic, thyme, and vegetable broth. Cover and cook on low for 7–8 hours or until potatoes are tender.
2. Drain potatoes and return to hot slow cooker. Remove thyme stems, leaving leaves with the potatoes. Add butter and dried thyme leaves; mash until smooth.
3. Beat in remaining ingredients until potatoes are fluffy. Cover and cook on low for 2 hours longer, stirring once during cooking time. You can hold the potatoes on low for another hour before serving.

❦ **Makes 12–14 servings**

Matha's Best Crunchy Sweet Potatoes

Since the granola is added at the end of cooking time, it stays crunchy. This recipe has a wonderful combination of flavors and textures.

6 sweet potatoes, peeled and cubed

½ cup brown sugar

½ cup pineapple juice

1 teaspoon cinnamon

2 tablespoons honey

1 teaspoon salt

⅛ teaspoon pepper

2 tablespoons butter

½ cup coconut

1 cup granola

1. In 4- to 5-quart slow cooker, combine cubed sweet potatoes, brown sugar, pineapple juice, cinnamon, honey, salt, pepper, and butter. Cover and cook on low for 7–9 hours or until potatoes are tender.
2. Using a potato masher, partially mash the potatoes; stir well. In small saucepan over medium heat, toast coconut, stirring frequently, until browned, about 5–7 minutes. Sprinkle over potatoes, then top with granola.
3. Cover and cook on high for 20–30 minutes longer until hot, then serve.

❧ **Makes 8–10 servings**

Mashed Sweet Potatoes

Looking for a change from all the super-sweet sweet potato recipes with marshmallows and lots of brown sugar? What a pleasant change this is. Use extra butter when serving.

2 (15-ounce) cans yams, drained

4 tablespoons butter

½ cup hot cream

2 tablespoons dry sherry or bourbon

1 cup dry bread crumbs

½ teaspoon paprika

2 teaspoons butter

1. Place yams in a large mixing bowl and begin mashing. Add 4 tablespoons butter, cream, and sherry. When fully mashed, remove yams from bowl and place in a greased 8" square casserole.
2. Mix together bread crumbs, paprika, and 2 teaspoons butter and spread on top of potato mixture. Bake at 350° until crumbs are brown.

❧ **Makes 8 servings**

Fruity Sweet Potatoes

You'll love the pairing of apricots and sweet potatoes along with the buttery apricot sauce. This is fantastic!

2 (23-ounce) cans yams, drained

1 (23.5-ounce) can apricots, drained and with liquid reserved

1¼ cups brown sugar

1½ teaspoons cornstarch

1 teaspoon grated orange rind

⅛ teaspoon cinnamon

1 cup apricot juice from can apricots

2 tablespoons butter

½ cup pecan

1. Mix yams and apricots in greased 9" × 13" baking dish.
2. In saucepan, mix brown sugar, cornstarch, orange rind, cinnamon, and apricot juice. Bring to a boil, stirring constantly until thickened. Add butter and pecans. Pour over potatoes and apricots. Bake at 375° for 25 minutes.

❦ **Makes 8–10 servings**

Creamed Peas and Onions

Creamed peas are a classic side dish. Add two kinds of cheese, onions, and garlic, and you have a side dish fit for company.

2 (16-ounce) packages frozen green peas

2 onions, finely chopped

4 cloves garlic, minced

1 (16-ounce) jar four-cheese Alfredo sauce

1 (10-ounce) container refrigerated Alfredo sauce

½ cup light cream

1 (8-ounce) package cream cheese, cubed

2 cups shredded Muenster cheese

1. Combine all ingredients except cheeses in a 4-quart slow cooker and stir gently to blend. Cover and cook on low for 4 hours.
2. Uncover, add cheeses, and stir to blend. Cover and cook on high for 30–40 minutes longer, or until peas are hot and sauce is blended. Serve immediately.

❦ **Makes 10–12 servings**

Mom's Green Bean Casserole

Red peppers and mushrooms add great flavor to this updated casserole. And the topping, toasted in butter on the stovetop, is just superb.

2 (16-ounce) packages frozen cut green beans

2 onions, chopped

6 cloves garlic, minced

2 red bell peppers, chopped

1 (8-ounce) package fresh mushrooms, chopped

1 (16-ounce) jar Alfredo sauce

2 (10-ounce) cans golden cream of mushroom soup

¼ cup butter, melted

1 cup heavy cream

1 teaspoon dried thyme leaves

¼ teaspoon white pepper

¼ cup butter

2 cups soft bread crumbs

1 cup crumbled canned French-fried onions

1. In 5-quart slow cooker, combine green beans, onions, garlic, bell peppers, and mushrooms; mix well.
2. In large bowl, combine Alfredo sauce, soup, melted butter, heavy cream, thyme, and pepper; mix well. Pour into slow cooker.
3. Cover and cook on high for 4–5 hours or until mixture is bubbling.
4. In large saucepan, melt ¼ cup butter. Add bread crumbs and crumbled onions; cook and stir until toasted and golden brown.
5. Uncover slow cooker and turn heat to high. Sprinkle with bread crumb mixture and cook for 30 minutes longer.

🍲 **Makes 12–14 servings**

Then he lay down under the broom tree and fell asleep. Suddenly an angel touched him and said to him, "Get up and eat." He looked, and there at his head was a cake baked on hot stones, and a jar of water. He ate and drank, and lay down again.

—1 Kings 19:5–6

Wild Rice Amandine

Wild rice has such a nutty flavor. You could substitute brown rice for the white rice in this recipe. Be sure to double this recipe when taking out.

¼ cup white rice

¾ cup wild rice

¼ cup margarine

2 tablespoons chopped onion

2 tablespoons dried chives

2 tablespoons finely chopped green pepper

2½ cups chicken broth

¼ cup finely chopped almonds

1. Mix white rice with wild rice; wash and drain.
2. In heavy saucepan, heat margarine and stir in chopped onions, chives, and rice. Cook over gentle heat, stirring until rice begins to turn yellow.
3. Remove from heat and add green pepper. Stir in chicken broth and add almonds. Put into greased 8" square baking dish and cover. Bake at 300° for 1 hour and 15 minutes.

❦ **Makes 6–8 servings**

Wild Rice Pilaf

Wild rice cooks to perfection in the slow cooker. You could add another container of Alfredo sauce if you think the dish needs it. Pilafs should be rather firm, not soupy.

2½ cups wild rice

1 onion, finely chopped

1 cup orange juice

4 cups vegetable broth

1 teaspoon salt

¼ teaspoon white pepper

1 (10-ounce) container refrigerated Alfredo sauce

⅓ cup chopped parsley

1 teaspoon grated orange rind

1 cup chopped pecans

1. Combine all ingredients except Alfredo sauce, parsley, orange rind, and pecans in 3-quart slow cooker. Cover and cook on low for 5–7 hours or until rice is almost tender.
2. Stir in Alfredo sauce, parsley, and orange rind. Cover and cook on high for 1 hour, then stir and add pecans. Cover, turn off heat, and let stand for 10 minutes. Stir again and serve.

❦ **Makes 8–10 servings**

Broccoli Rice Casserole

In our "hurry and wait" world of today, recipes that are as easy as this one are welcomed by most cooks. Short on time? You can also buy celery and onion already chopped in small containers or packages in your grocer's produce department.

4 tablespoons butter

½ cup chopped celery

½ cup chopped onion

1 (10.75-ounce) can cream of mushroom soup

1 soup can milk

1 cup mushroom stems and pieces

½ cup sliced water chestnuts

1 (10-ounce) package frozen chopped broccoli, thawed and drained

2 cups cooked rice

Salt and pepper to taste

1 (8-ounce) jar Cheese Whiz

½ cup bread crumbs

1. Coat 9" × 13" baking dish with cooking spray.
2. Melt butter in skillet and sauté celery and onions for 2 or 3 minutes over medium heat. Stir in the soup and milk, blending with a whisk. Heat until warm.
3. Remove from heat and add mushrooms, water chestnuts, broccoli, rice, salt, and pepper. Put the mixture in the prepared 9" × 13" baking dish. Cover with the Cheese Whiz. Top with bread crumbs. Bake at 350° for 30–45 minutes.

☙ **Makes 12–15 servings**

Ye shall eat nothing leavened; in all your habitations shall ye eat unleavened bread.

—Exodus 12:20

Carol Sue's Broccoli and Carrots

Broccoli and carrots are cooked to perfection in a cheese sauce, and topped with butter-toasted bread crumbs.

1 (16-ounce) package frozen chopped broccoli

1 (13-ounce) package frozen broccoli florets

1 (16-ounce) package frozen sliced carrots

1 tablespoon olive oil

1 tablespoon butter

1 onion, chopped

4 cloves garlic, minced

2 (16-ounce) jars four-cheese Alfredo sauce

½ cup heavy cream

2 cups shredded Swiss cheese

2 tablespoons cornstarch

⅓ cup butter, melted

2 cups soft bread crumbs

½ cup grated Parmesan cheese

1. Spray a 4- to 5-quart slow cooker with nonstick cooking spray. Combine broccoli, broccoli florets, and carrots in slow cooker.
2. In large skillet, heat olive oil and 2 tablespoons butter over medium heat. Add onion and garlic; cook and stir until tender, about 6 minutes. Stir in Alfredo sauce and heavy cream and stir well.
3. Pour onion mixture into slow cooker. Cover and cook on high for 3–4 hours or until vegetables are hot and tender.
4. Toss cheese with cornstarch and stir into slow cooker. Cover and cook on high for 20 minutes.
5. In large skillet, melt ⅓ cup butter over medium heat. Add bread crumbs; cook and stir until toasted, about 6–8 minutes. Stir in Parmesan cheese and sprinkle over mixture in slow cooker. Serve.

Makes 10–12 servings

Crispy Broccoli Casserole

This recipe is great as it is, but since if you're a cauliflower lover, try using 1½ pounds broccoli and 1½ pounds cauliflower.

3 pounds frozen broccoli florets, thawed

4 eggs, slightly beaten

2 cups cottage cheese

2 tablespoons minced onion

2 teaspoons Worcestershire sauce

3 cups shredded Cheddar cheese

¼ cup butter, melted

2 cups bread crumbs

1. Spray 9" × 13" baking dish with vegetable cooking spray.
2. Drain broccoli and pat dry with paper towel.
3. In large bowl, mix together eggs, cottage cheese, onion, Worcestershire sauce, and Cheddar cheese.
4. Line baking dish with broccoli. Pour cheese mixture over broccoli.
5. Add bread crumbs to melted butter and stir with fork. Spoon this over top of casserole and pat down. Cover broccoli flowers so they are not exposed to the heat. Bake at 350° for 30 minutes.

🍂 **Makes 8–10 servings**

Cauliflower Casserole

Cauliflower is a delicious vegetables, cooked or raw. You can substitute cream of mushroom soup or cream of chicken soup in this recipe for a little variation.

1 medium head cauliflower, broken into florets

1 cup sour cream

4 ounces shredded Cheddar cheese

1 (10.75-ounce) can cream of celery soup

½ cup crushed cracker crumbs

½ cup Parmesan cheese

Paprika

1. Place cauliflower and a small amount of water in a saucepan. Cover and cook for 5 minutes or until crisp-tender. Drain.
2. Combine cauliflower, sour cream, cheese, soup, and crumbs and put into greased 8" × 8" square baking dish. Sprinkle with Parmesan cheese and paprika. Bake at 325° for 30 minutes.

🍂 **Makes 6 servings**

Laura's Cauliflower Gratin

For those of you who don't have a food processor, try substituting regular bread crumbs. Make this recipe often; it's a keeper.

Bread Crumb Topping

4 slices sandwich bread with crust, cut into quarters

2 tablespoons unsalted butter, softened

1/4 teaspoon salt

1/8 teaspoon ground black pepper

Filling

4 quarts water

1 tablespoon salt

3 pounds cauliflower florets

2 tablespoons unsalted butter

2 tablespoons minced shallots

1 minced garlic clove

1 tablespoon flour

1/2 cup heavy cream

Pinch nutmeg

Pinch cayenne

Salt

1/8 teaspoon ground black pepper

1/2 cup + 2 tablespoons grated Parmesan cheese, divided

1 teaspoon fresh thyme leaves, minced

For the topping:

In a food processor, pulse bread, butter, salt, and pepper in 10 1-second pulses until the mixture resembles coarse crumbs. Set aside.

For the filling:

1. Heat oven to 450°.
2. Boil 4 quarts of water and add 1 tablespoon of salt and the cauliflower. Cook 3–4 minutes until outsides are tender but inside is crunchy. Drain cauliflower, rinse in cold water, and drain again.
3. Heat butter in a large skillet about 2 minutes. Add shallots and garlic and cook about 30 seconds until fragrant. Stir in flour until combined. Whisk in cream and bring to boil. Stir in nutmeg, cayenne, 1/4 teaspoon salt, pepper, 1/2 cup Parmesan, and thyme until it is blended.
4. Turn off heat and combine cauliflower with sauce. Transfer mixture to greased 2-quart baking or gratin dish. Sprinkle the remaining 2 tablespoons of cheese then the bread crumb topping over the top.
5. Bake 10–12 minutes at 350° until golden brown and the sauce bubbles around the edges.

Makes 6–8 servings

Orange Cauliflower

Orange adds a nice spark to cauliflower, especially when it is used in three forms! This is a good side dish to serve with a ham or pork chop dinner.

4 heads cauliflower

½ cup orange juice

1 cup orange marmalade

1 tablespoon chopped fresh tarragon leaves

1 teaspoon salt

⅛ teaspoon white pepper

1 tablespoon grated orange zest

1. Remove florets from cauliflower, trimming ends. Discard stems and center of cauliflower.
2. Place cauliflower in 5- to 6-quart slow cooker. In small bowl, combine remaining ingredients. Pour over cauliflower in slow cooker.
3. Cover and cook on low for 5–6 hours, or until cauliflower is tender when pierced with a knife, stirring once during cooking time.

❧ **Makes 10–12 servings**

Copper Pennies

This carrot recipe's ingredients may look strange, but the dish created from them is sure to become a favorite. It's great for any take-along event.

2 pounds carrots, thickly sliced

1 (10.75-ounce) can tomato soup

½ cup oil

1 cup sugar

1 tablespoon Worcestershire sauce

1 teaspoon dry mustard

1 onion, sliced in rings

1 green pepper, sliced in strips

1. Cook carrots in saucepan just covered with water until tender. Drain.
2. In medium bowl, mix all remaining ingredients. Add carrots to bowl. Cover and marinate overnight.
3. Bake at 350° for 30–45 minutes.
4. Can be served warm or cold.

❧ **Makes 10 servings**

May God give you the dew of heaven, and of the fatness of the earth, and plenty of grain and wine.

—Genesis 27:28

Creamy Spicy Carrots

This simple dish can be kept in the slow cooker on low or warm for 2 hours after it's finished. This is perfect for a buffet lunch before Christmas caroling.

3 (16-ounce) bags baby carrots

2 onions, chopped

2 cups vegetable broth

1 teaspoon salt

¼ teaspoon pepper

1 tablespoon curry powder

½ cup heavy cream

3 tablespoons butter

1. In 4-quart slow cooker, combine carrots, onions, broth, salt, pepper, and curry powder. Cover and cook on low for 5–7 hours or until carrots are tender.
2. Uncover and add cream and butter. Turn off slow cooker; using a potato masher or immersion blender, mash the carrots until smooth. Cover and cook on low for 1 hour longer until hot. Serve immediately.

❧ **Makes 10–12 servings**

Vegetable Quiche

Quick to prepare, this vegetarian entreé is a welcome addition to any buffet table.

1 (16-ounce) package frozen broccoli, thawed or cooked

⅓ cup chopped onion

¼ cup chopped green pepper

1 cup shredded cheese

1½ cups milk

¾ cup Bisquick

3 eggs

1. Spray 9" pie plate with vegetable cooking spray.
2. Mix broccoli, onion, green pepper, and cheese in pie plate. Beat remaining ingredients until smooth. Pour over vegetable mixture.
3. Bake at 375° for 45–60 minutes until golden brown.

❧ **Makes 6–8 servings**

He brought me to the banqueting house, and his intention toward me was love.

—Song of Solomon 2:4

Barb's Best-Ever Potato Salad

The use of bottled salad dressing offers you endless variety in this potato salad. Try the French or Italian suggested here, or experiment with your own favorite—Caesar, honey-mustard, even blue cheese!

7 medium potatoes, cooked in jacket, peeled, and sliced

1/3 cup clear French or Italian dressing

3/4 cup sliced celery

1/3 cup sliced green onions, including tops

4 chopped hard-cooked eggs

1 cup mayonnaise

1/2 cup sour cream

1 1/2 teaspoons prepared horseradish

1 teaspoon mustard

1. In medium bowl, pour dressing over hot, cut-up potatoes. Marinate several hours or overnight in refrigerator. When ready to serve, add celery, green onions, and eggs to potatoes.
2. In small bowl, combine mayonnaise, sour cream, horseradish, and mustard and stir together. Pour over salad and toss well.

❦ **Makes 8–10 servings**

Potato Salad

Cook your potatoes so easily in the slow cooker. They turn out tender and moist, with practically no effort on your part, perfect for potato salad.

5 pounds russet potatoes

2 onions, chopped

6 cloves garlic, minced

1 1/2 teaspoons salt

1/4 teaspoon white pepper

1 cup water

1 1/2 cups mayonnaise

1 cup whipped salad dressing

1/2 cup plain yogurt

1/3 cup yellow mustard

2 tablespoons Dijon mustard

1/3 cup whole milk

1 cup chopped green onions, green and white parts

1 cup thinly sliced radishes

1. Peel potatoes and cut into cubes. Combine in 5- to 6-quart slow cooker with onions and garlic. Sprinkle with salt and pepper, then pour water over.
2. Cover and cook on low for 8–9 hours or until potatoes are tender. Drain potato mixture.
3. In large bowl, combine remaining ingredients and mix well. Add hot potato mixture and stir gently to coat. Cover and chill for 4–5 hours until cold. Stir gently before serving.

❦ **Makes 10–12 servings**

Cheesy Tater Tot Casserole

This delicious recipe uses Tater Tots to make a rich and creamy side dish. Serve this with fried chicken, some cooked carrots, and a gelatin salad.

2 (16-ounce) bags frozen Tater Tots, thawed

2 (16-ounce) jars four-cheese Alfredo sauce

1 (12-ounce) can evaporated milk

⅓ cup chopped fresh chives

¼ teaspoon white pepper

3 cups shredded Cheddar cheese

½ cup grated Romano cheese

1 teaspoon paprika

1. In 5-quart slow cooker, combine all ingredients except Romano cheese and paprika; mix well. Sprinkle with Romano cheese and paprika.
2. Cover and cook on low for 5–7 hours, stirring twice during cooking time, until mixture is hot and potatoes are tender. Serve immediately.

❧ **Makes 12–14 servings**

Tater Tot Casserole

The addition of smoked sausage to this casserole adds a burst of flavor while increasing the protein. I double the sausage for the "big" meat eaters when we go to summer picnics.

2 (16-ounce) cans green beans, drained

1 (10.75-ounce) can cream of mushroom soup

1 (10.75-ounce) can cream of celery soup

1 cup diced onions

16 ounces smoked sausage

1 (16-ounce) bag frozen Tater Tots, thawed

1. Mix green beans, soups, and onions in bowl and place mixture in greased 9" × 13" baking dish.
2. Dice smoked sausage into small pieces and place on top of green bean mixture. Top with tater tots. Bake at 350° for 1 hour.

❧ **Makes 8–10 servings**

Grandma's Peas and Carrots

Carrots take a long time to cook in the slow cooker, while peas just a brief period, mainly to heat through. They both turn out perfectly in this simple recipe.

10 carrots, sliced

2 onions, chopped

4 cloves garlic, minced

1 cup vegetable broth

⅓ cup butter

2 tablespoons honey

1 teaspoon salt

¼ teaspoon white pepper

1 teaspoon dried marjoram leaves

4 cups frozen baby peas

1. In 4- to 5-quart slow cooker, combine all ingredients except peas and mix well. Cover and cook on low heat for 7–8 hours or until carrots are tender.
2. Stir gently and turn heat to high. Add frozen peas and stir again. Cover and cook on high for 15–25 minutes or until peas are hot and tender. Serve immediately.

❧ **Makes 12 servings**

Zucchini with Stuffing

Everyone who has a summer garden seems to have an overabundance of zucchini and they're nice enough to share with those of us who don't have gardens. Chop the zucchini extra-fine so your finicky eaters don't know it's in this recipe.

6 cups chopped zucchini

¼ cup chopped onions

1 (6-ounce) box stovetop dressing

½ cup margarine, melted

½ cup shredded carrots

1 (10.75-ounce) can cream of chicken soup

1 cup sour cream

1. Put zucchini and onions in saucepan just covered with ¼ cup water and bring to boil. Simmer for 3 minutes. Drain well.
2. Combine stovetop dressing with ½ cup melted margarine.
3. Layer half of dressing mix on bottom of greased 9" × 13" baking dish.
4. Mix zucchini and onions with carrots, soup, and sour cream.
5. Put zucchini layer on top of dressing.
6. Top with the remainder of dressing.
7. Bake at 350° for 25 minutes.

❧ **Makes 8–10 servings**

Squash and Apple Bake

This delicious side dish is perfect for the holidays, or anytime you want to serve a ham or turkey. Peel the squash using a sharp knife, then scrape out the seeds with a spoon. Save the seeds to roast for snacks, if you'd like.

1 (3-pound) butternut squash

1 (2-pound) acorn squash

4 Granny Smith apples, peeled, cored, and cubed

2 onions, chopped

6 cloves garlic, minced

¼ cup butter

½ cup brown sugar

2 teaspoons salt

¼ teaspoon white pepper

1 teaspoon dried tarragon leaves

⅓ cup apple cider vinegar

½ cup water

1. Peel, seed, and cube both types of squash. Combine with apples, onions, and garlic in 5-quart slow cooker.
2. In small saucepan, melt butter over medium heat. Add sugar, salt, pepper, and tarragon; remove from heat. Stir in vinegar and water until blended.
3. Pour this mixture into slow cooker. Cover and cook on low for 7–9 hours or until squash is tender when pierced with a fork. Using a potato masher, partially mash the ingredients, then stir to combine.

❦ **Makes 10–12 servings**

Sandwiches

⚜

Yes, you can make sandwiches in the slow cooker. It's the perfect place to cook tender fillings that you can use with everything from tortillas to hoagie buns to popovers. You can also transform classic sandwich recipes into stratas and casseroles that are perfectly suited to this appliance.

Sandwiches are ideal for youth gatherings and for casual potlucks. You'll create an air of community when you involve the congregation in meal preparation. And having parishioners make their own sandwiches makes the whole event easier on you!

It's easy to prepare a few different fillings in several slow cookers, then just put out different types of rolls and buns, along with toppings such as shredded cheese, sliced tomatoes, lettuces, mustard, mayonnaise, ketchup, pickle relish, and various vegetables, and let everybody make their own sandwiches.

By using the broiler in the oven, you can easily toast or brown bread slices, English muffins, or cut sandwich buns to use with these fillings. Toasting the bread will help give the sandwich more texture and character.

Also think about using leftover meats from any of the previous chapters to make your own favorite sandwiches or sandwich fillings. Even a rice pilaf or leftover vegetables can be combined with some cheeses and condiments to make a delicious wrap with lettuce leaves or flour tortillas.

—*Linda Larsen*

Alice's Crunchy Apricot-Ham Wraps

This recipe is ideal for a Ladies' Guild luncheon. Place a pretty slow cooker on the table, along with a selection of homemade rolls and some lettuce leaves for those on a low-carb diet.

3 pounds fully cooked ham, cubed

1 (10-ounce) jar apricot preserves

2 onions, chopped

3 cloves garlic, minced

1 cup chopped dried apricots

2 tablespoons prepared mustard

2 green bell peppers, chopped

1 cup sour cream

2 tablespoons cornstarch

1 cup chopped pistachios

1. In 5-quart slow cooker, combine ham, preserves, onions, garlic, apricots, and mustard; mix well. Cover and cook on low for 8 hours.
2. Add bell peppers to slow cooker. Cover and cook on low for 1 hour. In small bowl, combine sour cream and cornstarch. Stir into ham mixture. Cover and cook on low for 30 minutes.
3. Stir mixture and add pistachios. Serve in homemade buns, tortillas, or lettuce wraps.

❦ **Makes 10–12 servings**

Christine's Best BBQ Sandwiches

Combining beef and pork makes a rich and savory sandwich filling. Use tortillas to make wrap sandwiches.

1 (3-pound) boneless beef chuck roast

1 (1½-pound) boneless pork loin roast

2 onions, chopped

6 stalks celery with leaves, chopped

½ cup barbecue sauce

½ cup chili sauce

½ cup ketchup

¼ cup brown sugar

2 tablespoons apple cider vinegar

12–16 onion buns, split and toasted

1. Cut beef and pork into 2" cubes. Place onions and celery in bottom of 5- to 6-quart slow cooker and top with meat. In bowl combine remaining ingredients except onion buns; stir well. Pour into slow cooker. Cover and cook on low for 8–9 hours or until meat is very tender. Stir well, using a fork if necessary, to help break up meat.
2. To serve, spoon some barbecue on the onion buns, making sandwiches.

❦ **Makes 12 servings**

Sloppy Joe in the Round

You do have to bake the bread for this fun sandwich, but that only takes a few minutes. The filling is rich and flavorful, just right for a picnic. You can serve this filling in plain hamburger buns too.

4 pounds 90% lean ground beef

4 onions, chopped

6 cloves garlic, minced

3 carrots, chopped

1 (8-ounce) can tomato sauce

1 (6-ounce) can tomato paste

¼ cup tomato juice

1 tablespoon chili powder

¼ cup Worcestershire sauce

2 tablespoons cornmeal

4 (11-ounce) cans refrigerated French bread dough

2 tablespoons olive oil

1 teaspoon dried thyme leaves

1. In large skillet, cook ground beef until browned, stirring to break up meat. Drain thoroughly, but do not wipe out skillet. In a 6-quart slow cooker, combine cooked beef with onions, garlic, and carrots; mix well.

2. In skillet that you used for the beef, combine tomato sauce, paste, juice, chili powder, and Worcestershire sauce. Bring to a simmer over medium heat, stirring until a sauce forms. Pour into slow cooker.

3. Cover and cook on low for 8–9 hours. Meanwhile, preheat oven to 350°F. Grease two large cookie sheets and sprinkle with cornmeal. Open dough; do not unroll. Place the four rolls on work surface, seam side down.

4. Form two large rings with the dough by attaching the ends of two rolls together; pinch the ends thoroughly to seal. Place on prepared cookie sheets. Cut ¼" slashes diagonally across the top of the dough rings. Drizzle with oil and sprinkle with thyme. Bake for 25–35 minutes, rearranging cookie sheets in oven once, until loaves are golden brown.

5. Remove loaves from cookie sheet and cool on wire rack. Then store, covered, at room temperature. When ready to eat, cut each loaf in half crosswise to make two rings. Spoon the ground beef mixture onto bottom half of loaf and top with the other half. Cut into wedges to serve.

❧ **Makes 16 servings**

May God give you the dew of heaven, and of the fatness of the earth, and plenty of grain and wine.

—Genesis 27:28

Pulled Pork Sandwiches

Pulled pork from Pulled Pork Burritos (page 224) combines with flavorful coleslaw in these fabulous sandwiches.

6 cups pulled pork (page 224)

2 cups shredded cabbage

1 cup shredded carrots

½ cup chopped green onions, green and white part

½ cup mayonnaise

2 tablespoons yellow mustard

1 teaspoon celery seed

12 onion rolls, cut in half

¼ cup butter

1. Shred and moisten the pulled pork with cooking liquid according to recipe directions.
2. In large bowl, combine cabbage, carrots, green onions, mayonnaise, mustard, and celery seed; mix well.
3. Spread cut sides of rolls with butter and place, cut side up, on broiler pan. Broil until golden brown.
4. Make sandwiches with the pulled pork and the cabbage mixture. Serve immediately.

🍃 **Makes 12 servings**

BBQ Chicken Sandwiches

Chicken thighs cook perfectly in the slow cooker while staying moist and tender. These flavorful sandwiches are delicious served with potato salad and apple wedges.

4 pounds boneless, skinless chicken thighs

1 teaspoon celery salt

1 teaspoon seasoned salt

½ teaspoon pepper

2 onions, chopped

6 cloves garlic, minced

1 (18-ounce) bottle barbecue sauce

1 (6-ounce) can tomato paste

¼ cup honey

1 teaspoon dried Italian seasoning

12–14 sandwich rolls

1. Sprinkle chicken with celery salt, seasoned salt, and pepper. Place onions in bottom of 5- to 6-quart slow cooker and top with chicken and garlic.
2. In medium bowl, combine barbecue sauce, tomato paste, honey, and Italian seasoning; mix well. Pour over chicken.
3. Cover and cook on low for 8–9 hours or until chicken is cooked. Using two large forks, shred chicken in the sauce. Serve on split and toasted sandwich rolls.

🍃 **Makes 12–14 servings**

Beef and Bean Wraps

These are burritos made in the slow cooker. The refried beans add a rich flavor and smooth texture to this hearty filling. If the filling isn't thick enough at the end of cooking time, thicken with cornstarch as directed.

2 pounds ground beef

2 onions, chopped

5 cloves garlic, minced

1 (15-ounce) can refried beans

1 (15-ounce) can kidney beans, drained

2 (10-ounce) cans enchilada sauce

1 (4-ounce) can chopped green chiles, drained

1 tablespoon chili powder

1 teaspoon cumin

1 teaspoon salt

1/8 teaspoon pepper

12–14 (6") corn tortillas

2 cups shredded Cheddar cheese

1 cup sour cream

2 cups chopped tomatoes

2 cups shredded lettuce

1. In large skillet, cook ground beef with onions and garlic over medium heat, stirring to break up beef, until beef is thoroughly cooked.
2. Combine beef mixture with refried beans, kidney beans, enchilada sauce, green chiles, chili powder, cumin, salt, and pepper in 4-quart slow cooker; mix well.
3. Cover and cook on low for 8–9 hours until mixture is hot and blended. If necessary, thicken with a mixture of 2 tablespoons cornstarch and 1/4 cup water.
4. Serve mixture with tortillas, cheese, sour cream, tomatoes, and lettuce, and let people make their own wraps.

Makes 10–12 servings

Veggie Submarine Sandwich

Vegetables cook to tender perfection in the slow cooker to save you time and energy. Then make a buffet and let everybody create their own masterpiece!

2 onions, chopped

3 red bell peppers, sliced

2 zucchini, sliced

3 yellow summer squash, sliced

1 pound fresh green beans, trimmed

2 (8-ounce) packages sliced mushrooms

5 cloves garlic, minced

1½ teaspoons salt

¼ teaspoon white pepper

1 cup water

½ cup mustard

⅓ cup honey

1 cup mayonnaise

14–16 hoagie buns, split

2–3 cups shredded Cheddar cheese

1. Combine all vegetables in 5- to 6-quart slow cooker. Sprinkle with salt and pepper; toss. Pour water into slow cooker. Cover and cook on low for 5–7 hours or until vegetables are tender.
2. Drain vegetables and place in large bowl. In medium bowl, combine mustard, honey, and mayonnaise; mix well.
3. Lay out the split buns, cheese, mayonnaise mixture, and vegetables. Let people make their own sandwiches.

❦ **Makes 14–16 servings**

Flaky Tex-Mex Braid

If you have a couple of events on the weekend, or around the holidays, plan on serving Tender Pot Roast one day, and make these sandwiches the next!

3 cups shredded leftover Tender Pot Roast (page 176)

3 (4-ounce) cans chopped green chiles, drained

3 red bell peppers, chopped

4 (8-ounce) cans refrigerated crescent rolls

1 (15-ounce) can refried beans

3 cups shredded pepper jack cheese

1. In large bowl, combine pot roast with drained chiles and red bell peppers; mix well.
2. On work surface, unroll crescent roll dough. Divide into eight 14" × 9" rectangles. Spread a 12" × 3" rectangle of refried beans on each dough rectangle. Divide beef mixture on top of beans and sprinkle with cheese.
3. Using a sharp knife, make cuts 1" apart on the 14" sides of the dough almost to the filling. Cross the strips alternately over the filling, pressing gently to seal, to create a braided appearance.
4. You can refrigerate the sandwiches, unbaked, for up to 2 hours at this point. To bake, preheat oven to 350°F. Bake the sandwiches for 30–35 minutes or until crust is deep golden brown. Cut into slices to serve.

❦ **Makes 18–20 servings**

Turkey Enchilada Sandwiches

You can use this filling to make enchiladas, too. Just roll up flour or corn tortillas with the filling and some cheese, place in a greased baking dish, top with more cheese, and bake until hot.

2 onions, chopped

6 cloves garlic, minced

3 jalapeño peppers, minced

2 (10-ounce) cans enchilada sauce

3 (15-ounce) cans black beans, drained

1 (16-ounce) jar salsa

1 teaspoon cumin

¼ teaspoon cayenne pepper

2 (2-pound) turkey tenderloins

1 (8-ounce) package cream cheese, cubed

16–18 (8") flour tortillas

3 cups shredded CoJack cheese

4 cups shredded lettuce

2 cups chopped tomatoes

1. In 5-quart slow cooker, combine the onions, garlic, jalapeño peppers, enchilada sauce, black beans, salsa, cumin, and cayenne pepper. Mix well and place the turkey on top.

2. Cover and cook on low for 8–9 hours or until turkey is thoroughly cooked. Remove turkey from slow cooker and, using two forks, shred it. Stir back into slow cooker along with cream cheese.

3. Uncover and cook on high for 20–30 minutes or until mixture is thickened. Serve with tortillas and remaining ingredients to make wrap sandwiches.

❧ **Makes 16–18 servings**

Grandmother's Best Chicken Salad Sandwiches

You could serve this salad on split and toasted English muffins, in pita breads, or with lettuce to make low-carb wraps.

8 Poached Chicken Breasts (page 413), cubed

3 cups seedless red grapes, cut in half

6 stalks celery, chopped

1 cup golden raisins

1 cup dark raisins

1 cup broken pecans

1 cup mayonnaise

1 cup vanilla yogurt

1 teaspoon salt

1/4 teaspoon white pepper

1 teaspoon paprika

1/2 cup heavy whipping cream

32 slices raisin bread or other breads, toasted

1. In large bowl, combine cubed poached chicken breasts, grapes, celery, golden and dark raisins, and pecans; toss gently.
2. In bowl, combine mayonnaise, yogurt, salt, pepper, and paprika. In small bowl, beat cream until stiff peaks form. Fold into mayonnaise mixture.
3. Fold mayonnaise mixture into chicken mixture. Cover and chill for 1–2 hours. Use to make sandwiches with toasted raisin bread, other breads, or sandwich buns.

❦ **Makes 16–20 servings**

Thai Chicken Wraps

Use the preshredded carrots you can find in the produce aisle of your supermarket to make these flavorful wrap sandwiches.

3 pounds ground chicken

2 onions, chopped

6 cloves garlic, minced

2 tablespoons minced fresh gingerroot

1 cup chicken broth

2 tablespoons Worcestershire sauce

2 tablespoons soy sauce

2/3 cup peanut butter

1 tablespoon sugar

1/4 teaspoon pepper

3 tablespoons cornstarch

1/3 cup lime juice

3 cups shredded carrots

1 1/2 cups chopped cashews

24–30 large lettuce leaves

1. In large skillet, cook chicken in two batches until almost done, stirring to break up meat. Drain chicken and place in 4-quart slow cooker.
2. Add onions, garlic, gingerroot, chicken broth, Worcestershire sauce, soy sauce, peanut butter, sugar, and pepper; stir.
3. Cover and cook on low for 4–5 hours or until chicken is thoroughly cooked and mixture is hot and blended. In small bowl, combine cornstarch and lime juice and mix well. Stir into slow cooker.

(continued)

(Thai Chicken Wraps—continued)

4. Cover and cook on high for 20–25 minutes or until mixture thickens. To serve, set out filling, shredded carrots, chopped cashews, and lettuce leaves to use for wraps.

❦ **Makes 18 servings**

Mu Shu Turkey Wraps

Mu Shu Pork is traditionally served in pancakes with hoisin sauce. This updated version substitutes turkey and flour tortillas, and is delicious.

2 (2-pound) turkey tenderloins, cubed

2 onions, chopped

2 red bell peppers, chopped

2 (8-ounce) packages sliced fresh mushrooms

2 (4-ounce) cans bamboo shoots, drained

½ cup hoisin sauce

¼ cup soy sauce

¼ teaspoon pepper

1 cup chopped green onions

4 cups hot cooked rice

2 teaspoons sesame oil

14 flour tortillas or lettuce leaves

1. In 5-quart slow cooker, combine all ingredients except green onions, rice, sesame oil, and tortillas or lettuce leaves. Cover and cook on low for 8–9 hours or until turkey is thoroughly cooked and vegetables are tender.

2. Stir in green onions and turn slow cooker to high. Cover and cook on low for 20–30 minutes until hot; drain and return to slow cooker.

3. Stir in sesame oil, then set out tortillas and/or lettuce leaves and offer the filling to add and roll up.

❦ **Makes 14 servings**

Roast Beef Wraps

You can combine lots of leftover slow cooker recipes to make wrap sandwiches. Just use your imagination and what you have on hand!

1 (12-ounce) tub soft cream cheese

1 cup sour cream

6 cups shredded leftover Italian Roast Beef (page 180)

½ cup thinly sliced green onions

2 cups leftover Wild Rice Pilaf (page 303)

12 (10") flour tortillas

2 cups shredded Swiss cheese

1. In large bowl, beat cream cheese with sour cream. Stir in beef, green onions, and pilaf.
2. Place tortillas on work surface. Spread with the beef mixture and sprinkle with cheese. Roll up tortilla, fold in ends, and roll to enclose filling. Cut in half diagonally and serve.

☙ **Makes 12–14 servings**

In response to his people the Lord said: I am sending you grain, wine, and oil, and you will be satisfied.

—Joel 2:19

Monte Cristo Sandwich Strata

Monte Cristo sandwiches are layered chicken and ham sandwiches that traditionally are deep-fried. This method, using two slow cookers, makes a bunch and is much easier.

1 (1-pound) loaf sourdough bread, cubed

3 cups chopped cooked chicken

2 cups shredded Havarti cheese

2 cups shredded Swiss cheese

2 cups chopped cooked ham

12 eggs

2 cups whole milk

1 cup heavy cream

1 teaspoon salt

¼ teaspoon pepper

1 teaspoon dried oregano leaves

⅓ cup cider vinegar

⅔ cup currant jelly

⅓ cup water

2 tablespoons honey

½ teaspoon paprika

2 tablespoons butter

½ cup powdered sugar

1 cup crisp rice cereal crumbs

1. Spray a 6-quart slow cooker with nonstick cooking spray. Layer cubed bread, chicken, cheeses, and ham in slow cooker.

(continued)

(Monte Cristo Sandwich Strata— continued)

2. In large bowl, combine eggs, milk, cream, salt, pepper, and oregano; beat well. Pour into slow cooker. Let mixture stand for 20 minutes, pushing bread back down into the egg mixture as necessary. Cover and cook on low for 4–5 hours or until egg mixture is set.
3. In 2-cup slow cooker, combine vinegar, jelly, water, honey, paprika, and butter. Cover and cook on low for 2–3 hours, stirring twice during cooking time, until sauce is blended and slightly thickened.
4. To serve strata, scoop out of slow cooker and drizzle with currant jelly sauce. Sprinkle with powdered sugar and cereal crumbs, and serve immediately.

☙ **Makes 12–14 servings**

The one who sows sparingly will also reap sparingly, and the one who sows bountifully will reap bountifully. Each of you must give as you have made up your mind, not reluctantly or under compulsion, for God loves a cheerful giver.

—2 Corinthians 8:6–7

Ham and Veggie Wraps

You can add just about any vegetable to this hearty wrap sandwich. Think about using different colors and flavors of tortillas to add interest to the spread.

2 onions, chopped
5 carrots, sliced
4 potatoes, peeled and cubed
1 teaspoon dried basil leaves
2 cups chicken broth
2 green bell peppers, chopped
4 cups cubed cooked ham
1½ cups mayonnaise
3 cups shredded Cheddar cheese
18–20 flour tortillas

1. Place onions, carrots, potatoes, basil, and chicken broth in 5-quart slow cooker. Cover and cook on low for 6 hours or until vegetables are almost tender.
2. Add bell peppers and ham to slow cooker. Cover and cook on low for 2–3 hours longer or until ham is hot and bell peppers are crisp-tender.
3. Drain mixture and place in large bowl. Add mayonnaise and cheese, and mix well. Make wraps with flour tortillas; serve immediately.

☙ **Makes 18–20 servings**

Meatloaf Sandwiches

You could substitute two pounds of frozen precooked meatballs for the meatloaf if you'd like. But this is an excellent way to use up any kind of leftover meatloaf.

1 recipe Mom's Meatloaf (page 187), cubed
1 (26-ounce) jar spaghetti sauce
1 (6-ounce) can tomato paste
1 (15-ounce) can tomato sauce
1 teaspoon dried oregano leaves
1 teaspoon dried Italian seasoning
3 cups cubed mozzarella cheese
16–18 hoagie buns, split and toasted
16–18 slices American cheese

1. In 4-quart slow cooker, combine cubed meatloaf and remaining ingredients except for mozzarella cheese, hoagie buns, and American cheese.
2. Cover and cook on high for 2–3 hours or until mixture is hot, stirring once during cooking time. Stir in mozzarella cheese.
3. Place American cheese on bottom half of each toasted hoagie bun. Top with some of the meatloaf mixture, then the bun tops. Serve immediately.

❦ **Makes 16–18 servings**

Cranberry-Turkey Sandwiches

All of the flavors of Thanksgiving are contained in this easy-to-make sandwich. And the cream cheese spread is the perfect finishing touch.

2 onions, chopped
6 cloves garlic, minced
1 envelope onion soup mix
2 (2-pound) turkey tenderloins, cubed
1 teaspoon salt
1/8 teaspoon pepper
1 teaspoon dried sage leaves
1 (16-ounce) can whole berry cranberry sauce
1/2 cup chicken broth
1/3 cup butter, softened
10–12 hoagie buns, split
1 (12-ounce) container soft cream cheese

1. Place onions, garlic, and onion soup mix in bottom of 4- to 5-quart slow cooker. Sprinkle turkey with salt, pepper, and sage, and place in slow cooker. In medium bowl combine cranberry sauce with chicken broth; mix well. Pour into slow cooker.
2. Cover and cook on low for 6–8 hours or until turkey is thoroughly cooked.
3. Spread butter on split hoagie buns and toast in the oven under the broiler. Spread cut sides with cream cheese, and make sandwiches with the turkey mixture. Serve immediately.

❦ **Makes 10–12 servings**

Greek Pita Turkey Sandwiches

Greek flavors include lemon, feta, yogurt, oregano, and olives. This easy sandwich is simple to make and fun, too.

1 pound spicy bulk turkey sausage

2 onions, chopped

6 cloves garlic, minced

¼ cup flour

2 cups chicken or turkey broth

3 pounds turkey tenderloins, cubed

1½ teaspoons salt

½ teaspoon lemon pepper

1 teaspoon dried oregano leaves

2 cups plain yogurt

1 cup grated Parmesan cheese

3 cucumbers, peeled, seeded, and chopped

1 teaspoon dried oregano leaves

2 tablespoons lemon juice

1 cup sliced black olives

1 cup crumbled feta cheese

24 whole wheat pita breads

1. In large skillet, brown sausage with onions and garlic over medium heat, stirring to break up meat. When done, sprinkle with flour; cook and stir for 1 minute.
2. Add chicken or turkey broth; cook and stir to loosen pan drippings. Bring to a boil.
3. Pour into 4- or 5-quart slow cooker. Sprinkle turkey with salt, lemon pepper, and 1 teaspoon oregano; add to slow cooker. Cover and cook on low for 6–7 hours or until turkey is thoroughly cooked.
4. Meanwhile, combine remaining ingredients except pita breads in large bowl; cover and refrigerate.
5. When turkey is done, use a slotted spoon to remove the mixture from the slow cooker. Make sandwiches with the pita breads and the yogurt filling; serve immediately.

Makes 24–30 servings

Shredded Beef Tacos

Use a mild salsa for children, and a spicy hot one for adults. This can be part of a taco buffet. For toppings, set out shredded lettuce, guacamole, fresh chopped tomatoes, salsa, cilantro, and shredded cheese.

4 pounds beef sirloin tip, cubed

3 onions, chopped

8 cloves garlic, minced

1 (10-ounce) can condensed tomato soup

1 (16-ounce) jar salsa

⅓ cup apple cider vinegar

1 (16-ounce) can tomato paste

2 (4-ounce) cans chopped green chiles, drained

24 taco shells

1. Combine beef, onions, and garlic in 6- to 7-quart slow cooker. In large bowl, combine soup, salsa, vinegar, tomato paste, and chiles; mix well. Pour into slow cooker.
2. Cover and cook on low for 7–8 hours or until beef is tender. Stir vigorously to break up meat.
3. Heat taco shells as directed on package. Serve beef mixture in taco shells and offer the lettuce, guacamole, and such as toppings.

❧ **Makes 20–24 servings**

Canadian Bacon Pitas

Pineapple and green bell peppers combine with Canadian bacon to make a hearty and flavorful sandwich that's a bit like Hawaiian pizza.

3 onions, chopped

1 (20-ounce) can pineapple tidbits in juice, undrained

1 (16-ounce) can crushed pineapple in juice, undrained

6 carrots, sliced

2 green bell peppers, chopped

4 (4-ounce) packages sliced Canadian bacon, chopped

¼ cup cornstarch

½ cup chicken broth

20–24 pita breads

1 head butter lettuce

1 head green lettuce

1. Combine onions, both kinds of pineapple, and carrots in 5-quart slow cooker. Cover and cook on low for 6–7 hours or until carrots are tender. Stir in green bell peppers and Canadian bacon.
2. In small bowl, combine cornstarch with chicken broth; mix well. Stir into slow cooker. Cover and cook on high for 20–25 minutes or until sauce thickens.
3. Cut pita breads in half and gently open. Line with lettuce leaves and spoon Canadian bacon mixture into each bread. Serve immediately.

❧ **Makes 18–20 servings**

Sloppy Janes

What do you call a Sloppy Joe filling made from turkey? Sloppy Janes, of course! Serve a choice of beef or turkey fillings for your next youth gathering.

3 pounds ground turkey

3 onions, chopped

4 cloves garlic, minced

3 stalks celery

3 carrots, chopped

1 (8-ounce) can tomato sauce

1 (6-ounce) can tomato paste

½ cup tomato juice

1 teaspoon dried basil leaves

1 teaspoon poultry seasoning

¼ cup white wine Worcestershire sauce

12 slices American cheese

12 hamburger buns, split

1. In skillet, cook turkey until browned, stirring to break up meat. Drain thoroughly, but do not wipe skillet. In a 5-quart slow cooker, combine cooked turkey with onions, garlic, celery, and carrots; mix.

2. In skillet that you used for the turkey, combine tomato sauce, paste, juice, basil, poultry seasoning, and Worcestershire sauce. Bring to a simmer over medium heat, stirring until a sauce forms. Pour into slow cooker.

3. Cover and cook on low for 8 hours. Place one slice American cheese on each split hamburger bun, and make sandwiches with the turkey filling.

☙ **Makes 12 servings**

Just for Kids

✤

I remember being a picky eater. I didn't even like sandwiches as a child because there were too many flavors all bunched together. And I sat for a long time at the kitchen counter as my Brussels sprouts and cauliflower got very, very cold.

Getting kids to eat can be one of the biggest challenges of parenthood. Here are a few tips. Kids usually like mild foods, and foods they are used to. It takes as many as 20 introductions of a new food before a child will try it! So keep adding new foods to your child's diet; he or she will eventually try it, and may even like it!

One of the tricks to getting children to enjoy new foods is to introduce them slowly. Don't add too many foods to their diet at once. And make sure they see you eating fruits, vegetables, and other healthy foods with relish and enjoyment.

When you're feeding a crowd of kids, the simpler the better. Children generally do not like complicated recipes, with lots of different flavors. Every parent has the experience of a sweet little toddler refusing to touch her peas because they are touching the mashed potatoes.

And you have to be extra careful with food safety when you're cooking for kids. Never serve them undercooked eggs or meat, and strictly follow the 2-hour rule; refrigerate foods that have been left out at room temperature for 2 hours.

Best of all, these recipes are prepared using a slow cooker, so they're no-fuss.

—*Linda Larsen*

Mini Meatloaves

Kids love this recipe. The mini meatloaves are like large meatballs, but shaped differently. They are easy to serve at a buffet.

1½ cups soda cracker crumbs

2 eggs, beaten

½ cup ketchup

2 tablespoons brown sugar

2 tablespoons yellow mustard

⅛ teaspoon pepper

3 pounds 90% lean ground beef

3 tablespoons vegetable oil

1 (26-ounce) jar pasta sauce

½ cup ketchup

¼ cup honey

2 tablespoons apple cider vinegar

1. In large bowl, combine crumbs, eggs, ½ cup ketchup, brown sugar, mustard, and pepper; mix well. Add ground beef and mix gently but thoroughly with hands.
2. Scoop out individual balls, using a ¼-cup measure. Form into an oblong shape. When all the meatloaves are formed, heat oil in a large skillet over medium heat. Brown the meatloaves on both sides, turning once, about 4–6 minutes total. As they are cooked, place in 5- to 6-quart slow cooker.
3. In medium bowl, combine pasta sauce, ½ cup ketchup, honey, and vinegar; mix well. Pour over meatloaves. Cover and cook on low for 8–9 hours until meatloaves are tender and internal temperature reaches 165°F. Stir gently and serve.

❦ **Makes 12–14 servings for kids**

Potluck Pointers

Worried about diluting your beverage when trying to keep it cold with ice? Save your plastic snack-size yogurt, pudding, and applesauce containers. Wash them, fill with punch or another beverage, and freeze. When headed to your potluck, use these supersize ice cubes to chill your beverage. No worries about watered down drinks!

Slow Cooker Lasagna

Lasagna is everyone's favorite. You can omit the onions and garlic if you're serving very young kids, but add another ¾ pound of ground beef to keep the volume the same.

2 pounds lean ground beef

3 onions, chopped, if desired

4 cloves garlic, minced, if desired

1 (28-ounce) jar pasta sauce

1 (6-ounce) can tomato paste

1 cup tomato juice

1 teaspoon dried Italian seasoning

1 (8-ounce) package cream cheese, softened

¾ cup milk

1 tablespoon cornstarch

1 (15-ounce) package ricotta cheese

2 eggs

1 (16-ounce) package regular lasagna noodles

4 cups grated mozzarella cheese

⅓ cup grated Parmesan cheese

1. Spray a 6- or 7-quart slow cooker with nonstick cooking spray and set aside. In large skillet, cook ground beef until partially cooked, stirring to break up meat. Add onions and garlic, if using; cook and stir until beef is browned. Drain thoroughly.
2. Add pasta sauce, tomato paste, tomato juice, and Italian seasoning to beef mixture, and bring to a simmer. Simmer, stirring frequently, for 10 minutes.
3. In medium microwave-safe bowl, combine cream cheese and milk. Microwave on 50% power for 1 minute, then stir. Microwave on 50% power for 2 minutes longer; then remove and stir until smooth sauce forms. Stir in cornstarch, ricotta cheese and eggs.
4. Break lasagna noodles into irregular pieces. In prepared slow cooker, layer noodles, beef mixture, cream cheese mixture, and mozzarella cheese. Continue layering until slow cooker is ¾ full. Top with Parmesan cheese.
5. Cover slow cooker and cook on low for 4–5 hours or until noodles are tender and lasagna is bubbling around the edges. Let cool for 15 minutes, then serve.

❦ **Makes 12 servings for kids**

But the fruit of the Spirit is love, joy, peace, patience, kindness, goodness, faithfulness, gentleness and self-control. Against such things there is no law.

—Galatians 5:22

Penne Pasta Pizza

Pasta and pizza combine in a fun layered casserole. Serve with a gelatin fruit salad and small dinner rolls.

1½ pounds pork bulk sausage

1 onion, chopped

1 (8-ounce) package mushrooms, sliced

1 (26-ounce) jar pasta sauce

1 (10-ounce) can condensed tomato soup

1 (16-ounce) package penne pasta

1 (10-ounce) can golden cream of mushroom soup

1 cup ricotta cheese

1 cup shredded mozzarella cheese

1 cup shredded Cheddar cheese

1 (4-ounce) package sliced pepperoni

1. Spray a 6-quart slow cooker with nonstick cooking spray and set aside. Bring a large pot of salted water to a boil. In skillet, cook pork sausage until partially cooked, stirring to break up meat. Add onion and mushrooms; cook and stir until sausage is cooked. Drain thoroughly, then add pasta sauce and tomato sauce and bring to a simmer.

3. Cook penne pasta for half of the time directed on package; drain. Combine in bowl with cream of mushroom soup and ricotta cheese; stir to blend.

4. In prepared slow cooker, place half of pork mixture, half of pasta mixture, half of mozzarella and Cheddar cheeses, and half of the pepperoni. Repeat layers. Cover and cook on low for 4 hours or until pasta is tender and casserole is bubbling. Let cool for 15 minutes, then serve.

❧ **Makes 8–10 servings for kids**

They feast on the abundance of your house, and you give them drink from the river of your delights.

—*Psalms 36:8*

Hot Pizza Dip

Heat some bakery focaccia in the oven until hot and crisp, then cut into small wedges to serve with this dip for the ultimate pizza experience!

1½ pounds ground beef

1 onion, chopped

4 cloves garlic, minced

2 red bell peppers, chopped

1 (16-ounce) jar pizza sauce

1 teaspoon dried oregano

1 tcaspoon dricd basil

½ teaspoon dried thyme leaves

¼ teaspoon pepper

1 (8-ounce) package cream cheese, cubed

1 cup diced mozzarella cheese

1½ cups diced Cheddar cheese

2 cups sliced pepperoni

¼ cup grated Parmesan cheese

20 breadsticks

4 cups pita chips

1. In large skillet, cook beef with onion and garlic until beef is browned, stirring to break up meat. Drain well. Add bell peppers to mixture along with pizza sauce, oregano, basil, thyme, and pepper; stir and remove from heat.
2. In 4-quart slow cooker, layer beef mixture with cream cheese, mozzarella cheese, and Cheddar cheese. Top with pepperoni and Parmesan cheese.
3. Cover and cook on low for 3–4 hours or until cheese is melted and dip is bubbling. Serve with breadsticks, hot pizza crust, and pita chips.

❀ **Makes 10–12 servings for kids**

Cheeseburgers

If you don't want to add onions to this recipe, add another half-pound of ground beef. But for authentic cheeseburger flavor, you need to use the processed cheese spread.

2 pounds ground beef

2 onions, chopped, if desired

2 (10-ounce) cans condensed tomato soup

1 (6-ounce) can tomato paste

1 cup water

2 tablespoons yellow mustard

1 teaspoon dried basil leaves

1/8 teaspoon pepper

10–12 English muffins, split and toasted

1 (8-ounce) jar processed cheese spread

10–12 tomato slices

1. In large skillet, cook ground beef until done, stirring to break up meat. In 4- or 5-quart slow cooker, combine beef, onions, tomato soup, tomato paste, water, mustard, basil, and pepper; stir well.
2. Cover and cook on low for 6–8 hours until blended. To serve, spread processed cheese spread thinly on both cut halves of each English muffin. Top half with a tomato, then the beef mixture. Cover with second half of English muffin and serve.

❀ **Makes 10–12 servings for kids**

Chicken Tenders with Mustard Dip

Children love chicken tenders; they're so easy to eat. And because they are mild, they can be seasoned any way you'd like.

3–4 pounds chicken tenders

1/2 cup honey

1/3 cup yellow mustard

1 teaspoon salt

1/8 teaspoon pepper

1 cup sour cream

1 cup mayonnaise

1/3 cup honey

1/4 cup yellow mustard

1 teaspoon onion salt

1. In 3- to 4-quart slow cooker, combine chicken tenders with honey, 1/3 cup mustard, salt, and pepper; mix well. Cover and cook on low for 6–7 hours or until chicken is thoroughly cooked.
2. While chicken is cooking, in medium bowl combine sour cream, mayonnaise, 1/3 cup honey, 1/4 cup mustard, and onion salt; mix well.
3. Drain chicken and let cool on wire racks for 5–7 minutes. Serve the tenders with sour cream dip.

❀ **Makes 8–10 servings for kids**

Tater Tot Hot Dish

Kids of all ages adore Tater Tots. These crunchy little cubes of potato combine easily with other ingredients in the slow cooker. They won't be crunchy, but they'll be delicious!

2 tablespoons butter

2 (12-ounce) packages brown-and-serve breakfast sausage

3 cups sliced carrots

1 cup sour cream

1 cup ricotta cheese

1 (16 ounce) jar four cheese Alfredo sauce

1 (2-pound) package frozen Tater Tots, thawed

2 cups shredded Colby cheese

¼ cup grated Parmesan cheese

1. Melt butter in heavy skillet over medium heat. Add sausages; cook until brown and hot. Drain sausages on paper towels.
2. Add carrots to skillet; cook and stir for 3–4 minutes or until carrots are glazed. Add sour cream, ricotta cheese, and Alfredo sauce to skillet; heat through.
3. Cut sausages in half. Layer the sausages, Tater Tots, and Colby cheese in 5-quart slow cooker. Pour carrot mixture over all and stir gently to mix. Top with Parmesan cheese.
4. Cover and cook on low for 5–7 hours or until casserole is hot and blended. Serve immediately.

❧ **Makes 8–10 servings for kids**

Cheesy Mini Sloppy Joes

Kids love anything that's small. These tiny sandwiches are fun to make and easy for small children to eat.

3 pounds ground beef

2 cups finely grated carrots

1 (10-ounce) can condensed tomato soup

1 (10-ounce) can condensed Cheddar cheese soup

1 cup ketchup

½ cup grated Parmesan cheese

24 mini sandwich buns, split

12 slices American cheese, quartered

1. In large skillet, cook ground beef until done, stirring to break up meat. Drain well.
2. Combine all ingredients except Parmesan cheese, buns, and American cheese in 4-quart slow cooker. Cover and cook on low for 5–6 hours or until mixture is hot. Stir in Parmesan cheese until blended.
3. Split the sandwich buns in half and place one-quarter of a slice of cheese on each half. Using the meat mixture, make sandwiches and serve immediately.

❧ **Makes 24 servings for kids**

Easy Spaghetti

Carrots not only sneak in some nutrition, but they help keep the sauce thick. The pasta will be very soft, kind of like canned pasta, but that's what kids like!

1 pound ground beef

1 cup shredded carrots

1 (16-ounce) package mini frozen meatballs

2 (10-ounce) cans condensed tomato soup

2 (8-ounce) cans tomato sauce

1 cup tomato juice

1 (16-ounce) package spaghetti pasta

1 cup grated Parmesan cheese, divided

1. In medium skillet, cook ground beef until done, stirring to break up meat. Drain well. Combine in 4- to 5-quart slow cooker with all remaining ingredients except ½ cup of the Parmesan cheese.
2. Cover and cook on low for 6–7 hours or until pasta is tender and meatballs are hot. Sprinkle with remaining ½ cup cheese and serve.

Makes 12–14 servings for kids

Chicken-Potato Casserole

Tater Tots make another appearance in this chicken casserole. You could add or subtract vegetables that you think the kids would/would not like.

6 boneless, skinless chicken breasts, cubed

½ teaspoon salt

⅛ teaspoon pepper

2 tablespoons butter

1 (16-ounce) package baby carrots

2 cups frozen corn

1 (2-pound) package frozen Tater Tots, thawed

1 cup sour cream

1 cup whole milk

2 (16-ounce) jars four-cheese Alfredo sauce

1 cup shredded Muenster cheese

1 cup shredded Cheddar cheese

¼ cup grated Parmesan cheese

1. Sprinkle chicken cubes with salt and pepper. Melt butter in heavy skillet over medium heat. Add chicken; cook and stir until almost cooked through.
2. Place chicken in 6- to 7-quart slow cooker. Add carrots, corn, and Tater Tots; mix gently.

(continued)

(Chicken-Potato Casserole—
continued)

3. Add sour cream, milk, and both jars of sauce to skillet and bring to a simmer. Add Muenster and Cheddar cheeses, stir, and remove from heat. Pour into slow cooker. Sprinkle top with Parmesan cheese.
4. Cover and cook on low for 6–7 hours or until chicken is thoroughly cooked and casserole is hot and blended. Serve immediately.

❦ **Makes 12–14 servings for kids**

Pretzel Snack Mix

Sweet and salty is a wonderful flavor combination. This mix has lots of fun ingredients and textures; the kids will love it.

1 (16-ounce) package pretzel sticks
4 cups pecan halves
4 cups crisp square corn cereal
4 cups salted cashew halves
1 cup butter, melted
1 cup powdered sugar
½ cup brown sugar
2 teaspoons cinnamon

1. Combine pretzels, pecans, cereal, and cashews in 6-quart slow cooker. Melt butter in medium saucepan over low heat. Stir in both kinds of sugar and cinnamon; stir until blended.
2. Drizzle over mixture in slow cooker. Cook, uncovered, for 2–3 hours on high, until mixture is glazed. Cool on paper towels. Store, covered, in airtight container.

❦ **Makes 16 cups;** ❦ **Makes 32 servings for kids**

*But grow in the grace and
knowledge of our Lord and
Savior Jesus Christ.*

—2 Peter 3:18

Flying Mom

Ever fly with a toddler? It can be quite an experience! More than 30 years ago, my husband, Larry, our 1-year-old son, Tim, and I set out on a memorable commercial airline flight from San Francisco to Indianapolis. Our son was allowed to sit on our laps during the flight, thereby saving us the cost of a third passenger fare. Thus, we took two of the three seats next to the aisle, with the third seat being occupied by an elderly woman sitting by the window.

Although caring for and entertaining a toddler can be a challenge under any circumstances, it is especially taxing some 5 miles high in cramped quarters. During the 4-hour flight, our son slept some, squirmed some, stood up on our laps and played some, and tried to grab our co-passenger at every opportunity whenever she was within reach. Notwithstanding this tense and tiring situation, everything went fine until it was time for the passengers to be served their meals. (Remember those long-ago years when three-course meals were even part of the economy flight package?) Tim, now fully alert and not missing any opportunity, was able to upset my salad on the lap of the passenger in the window seat. Horrors!

I immediately apologized and tried to help clean up the mess, noticing that French salad dressing was now part of the passenger's dress. After it was all said and done, the lady was quite calm and exceptionally understanding. She mentioned that she was on her way to visit her children and grandchildren, and that as accidents go, this was a very minor one. She refused our offer to reimburse her for any cleaning costs and took a turn holding Tim while he bounced in her lap. In the end, a near disaster turned into a pleasant and heartwarming experience.

–Susie Siegfried

Simple Cheesy Tomato Soup

American cheese melts beautifully into a mild tomato soup in this delicious and healthy recipe.

2 (28-ounce) cans stewed tomatoes

3 shallots, minced

4 stalks celery, including leaves, chopped

1 teaspoon salt

1/8 teaspoon white pepper

2 tablespoons sugar

2 (16-ounce) jars four-cheese Alfredo sauce

1 cup heavy cream

3 cups cubed processed American cheese

1. In small batches, in blender or food processor, purée the tomatoes with shallots and celery. Place in 5-quart slow cooker along with salt, pepper, sugar, and Alfredo sauce.
2. Cover and cook on low for 6–7 hours or until soup is hot and blended. Stir in heavy cream.
3. Place some cheese in the bottom of each bowl, and ladle hot soup over the top. Serve immediately.

❧ **Makes 14–16 servings for kids**

Mom's Mac and Cheese

This macaroni and cheese is pure, simple, cheesy, and rich. Make sure to check it at the minimum cooking time so the pasta doesn't overcook.

1 (16-ounce) container cottage cheese

2 (12-ounce) cans evaporated milk

1 cup heavy cream

3 cups cubed processed American cheese

2 cups shredded Colby cheese

1 (16-ounce) box elbow macaroni

1/4 cup butter

1. Spray a 6-quart slow cooker with nonstick cooking spray. In food processor, process cottage cheese until smooth. Pour into prepared slow cooker and stir in milk and cream; mix well.
2. Add remaining ingredients and stir. Cover and cook on low for 5–7 hours or until macaroni is tender. Stir gently and serve.

❧ **Makes 12–14 servings for kids**

May the Lord give you the dew of heaven, and of the fatness of the earth, and plenty of grain and wine.

—Genesis 27:28

Chicken Noodle Soup

The shredded carrots will melt into the soup, adding a sweet flavor. This hearty soup is healthy and delicious.

6 boneless, skinless chicken breasts
2 (10-ounce) cans condensed cream of
  chicken soup
1 cup shredded carrots
2 cups baby carrots
2 (32-ounce) boxes chicken broth
2 cups water
3 cups baby frozen peas
1 (12-ounce) package egg noodles

1. In 7-quart slow cooker, combine chicken, condensed soup, both types of carrots, chicken broth, and water. Cover and cook on low for 5–6 hours.
2. Remove chicken from slow cooker and chop. Return to slow cooker along with frozen peas and noodles. Cover and cook on high for 30 minutes or until noodles are tender.

❦ **Makes 14–16 servings for kids**

Taco Soup

Use the smaller amount of taco seasoning mix if the kids are picky. If they like it spicy, add more spices!

2 pounds ground beef
2 (15-ounce) cans tomato sauce
1–2 envelopes taco seasoning mix
3 (15-ounce) cans kidney beans, drained
3 cups tomato juice
3 cups water
4 cups frozen corn
6 cups corn chips
3 cups shredded Colby cheese

1. In large skillet, brown ground beef, stirring to break up meat. Drain thoroughly.
2. In 7-quart slow cooker, mix beef with remaining ingredients except corn chips and cheese. Cover and cook on low for 4–5 hours or until soup is hot and blended.
3. Serve with corn chips and cheese.

❦ **Makes 12 servings for kids**

Pizza Fondue

Sausage and pepperoni combine in a cheesy tomato sauce for a wonderful dip. You can also serve this with breadsticks.

1½ pounds pork bulk sausage

2 (16-ounce) jars Cheddar cheese pasta sauce

3 (10-ounce) cans pizza sauce

1 (4-ounce) package thinly sliced pepperoni

1 cup heavy cream

2 cups diced processed American cheese

2 cups shredded mozzarella cheese

3 (12-ounce) rolls refrigerated pizza dough

1. In large skillet, cook sausage until browned, stirring to break up meat. Drain well and place in 5-quart slow cooker. Stir in remaining ingredients except for pizza dough.
2. Cover and cook on low for 3–4 hours or until cheese is melted, stirring once during cooking time.
3. Preheat oven to 400°F. Roll out pizza dough onto cookie sheets as directed on package. Bake for 15–20 minutes or until crust is golden brown. Immediately cut into small rectangles and serve with fondue.

❧ **Makes 18–20 servings for kids**

Burger Ravioli Casserole

You can leave out the onion if you think the kids won't like it, but it does get soft and sweet when cooked this way.

2 pounds ground beef

1 onion, chopped

1 cup shredded carrots

2 (26-ounce) jars pasta sauce

1 (15-ounce) can tomato sauce

1 cup tomato juice

1 cup beef broth

1 (25-ounce) package frozen cheese ravioli

2 cups shredded mozzarella cheese

⅓ cup grated Parmesan cheese

1. In large skillet, cook ground beef with onion and shredded carrots, stirring to break up beef. When beef is done, drain thoroughly.
2. Combine beef mixture in 7-quart slow cooker with pasta sauce, tomato sauce, tomato juice, and beef broth. Cover and cook on low for 7–8 hours.
3. Uncover and stir in ravioli, making sure ravioli is well distributed in the slow cooker. Cover and cook on low for 20–30 minutes longer or until ravioli is hot and tender. Sprinkle with cheeses, cover, and let stand for 5 minutes, then serve.

❧ **Makes 12–16 servings for kids**

Oatmeal Fruit Cookie Crisp

Apples and cherries combine in this simple crisp, which gets extra texture from crumbled oatmeal cookies.

4 apples, peeled, cored, and chopped

2 tablespoons lemon juice

½ cup sugar

2 (21-ounce) cans cherry pie filling

2 cups brown sugar

2 cups rolled oats

1 cup flour

2 teaspoons cinnamon

1 cup butter, melted

12 oatmeal cookies, crumbled

1. Sprinkle apples with lemon juice. Place in 5-quart slow cooker and stir in ½ cup sugar and both cans cherry pie filling.
2. In large bowl, combine brown sugar, oatmeal, flour, and cinnamon. Add butter and stir until mixture is crumbly. Stir in crumbled oatmeal cookies.
3. Sprinkle oatmeal mixture over fruit mixture in slow cooker. Cover and cook on low for 5–6 hours or until apples are tender and topping is hot.

❧ **Makes 18 servings for kids**

Mini Chicken Cheese Sandwiches

If the kids will eat them, add other vegetables to this simple recipe. Chopped green bell peppers, chopped celery, or mushrooms will add more nutrition.

6 boneless, skinless chicken breasts

1 teaspoon salt

⅛ teaspoon white pepper

2 cups chicken broth

2 cups shredded carrots

1 cup mayonnaise

½ cup plain yogurt

2 cups diced processed American cheese

18–20 mini sandwich buns

1. Cut chicken breasts in half and sprinkle with salt and pepper. Place in 4- to 5-quart slow cooker and add chicken broth.
2. Cover and cook on low for 6–7 hours or until chicken registers 165°F on a meat thermometer.
3. Remove chicken from slow cooker and shred; place in large bowl. Add enough broth from the slow cooker to moisten. Stir in carrots, mayonnaise, yogurt, and cheese; mix well.
4. Cover and refrigerate for 2–3 hours before serving. Make sandwiches with split mini buns.

❧ **Makes 18 servings for kids**

Sweet Things

✠

Ah, dessert. Many people feel that no meal is complete without it. I have a great sweet tooth, and have fond memories of many bake sales at church in which I both prepared offerings and was a consumer.

At any church gathering, dessert is mandatory—whether as simple cookies or candy or an elaborate cake or pudding. And yes, you can make dessert in the slow cooker. Cakes turn out moist and tender, pudding is creamy and sweet, and the gentle heat is perfect for melting chocolate for candies.

You may need to use an insert or cake or bread pan for some of these recipes. There are special molds and pans you can buy that are made for the slow cooker, but many recipes will work just fine in ordinary pans and molds. Just be sure to fill the pan about half full, and be sure that there is a small space between the pan and the slow cooker sides so heat can circulate.

Fondue is a natural for the slow cooker. The appliance should be used as the serving container as well; it will keep the mixture at the correct temperature. As with appetizers, think about crisp, cool, and crunchy accompaniments to these recipes. For fondue, crisp cookies, cool fruit, and tender cake make great dippers. Serve warm cakes with ice cream, warm puddings with whipped topping, and poached fruits with cakes and crushed nuts.

—Linda Larsen

Three-Layer Dessert Bar

These dessert bars are deliciously grand, and terribly easy to make and take. Everyone will rave about them.

First Layer

5 tablespoons sugar

¼ cup cocoa

1 egg, beaten

½ cup melted butter

1 teaspoon vanilla

2 cups crushed graham crackers

1 cup fine coconut

½ cup nuts

Second Layer

3 tablespoons milk

2 tablespoons vanilla instant pudding

¼ cup butter melted

2 cups powdered sugar

Third Layer

4 squares semisweet chocolate

1 tablespoon butter or margarine

For the first layer:

Mix together all ingredients and press into greased 11" × 15" jelly roll pan and chill for 1 hour.

For the second layer:

Combine all ingredients and beat with electric beater for 2 minutes. Spread on top of first layer and then chill for 1–2 hours.

For the third layer:

3. Melt chocolate and butter together in microwave for 1 minute. Remove and stir. Microwave for 30 seconds more if necessary. Spread on top of second layer. Refrigerate for 3–4 hours or overnight.

❦ **Makes 36**

Butter of kine, and milk of sheep, with fat of lambs, and rams of the breed of Bashan, and goats, with the fat of kidneys of wheat; and thou didst drink the pure blood of the grape.

—Deuteronomy 32:14

Cherry-Almond Treats

Holiday cookie trays are a welcome treat as a hostess gift or to share with friends and family. These yummy cookies will add something special to your goodie tray.

1 cup margarine or butter

½ cup sugar

1 egg yolk

½ teaspoon salt

2½ cups flour

4 egg whites at room temperature

¼ teaspoon cream of tartar

10 tablespoons sugar

¾ cup ground almonds

1 cup cherry preserves

1. Cream together margarine and sugar. Stir in egg yolk. Add salt and flour to creamed mixture. Put dough mixture into 15" × 10" × 1" greased baking dish and bake for 20 minutes.
2. Beat egg whites until stiff, adding in cream of tartar. Gradually beat sugar into egg whites.
3. Combine almonds with cherry preserves and spread over dough. Spread egg white mixture on top of preserves, and bake 10–15 minutes or until lightly browned. Cut when cool.

❧ **Makes 24**

Caramel Turtle Brownies

This is such a popular recipe that I'm sure you've had it at many of your church carry-ins.

1 (18.25-ounce) package German chocolate cake mix

¾ cup melted butter

⅔ cup evaporated milk

14 ounces Kraft caramels

1 cup chocolate chips

½ cup pecan pieces

1. Mix together cake mix, melted butter, and ⅓ cup of the evaporated milk. Put half of this mixture in greased 9" × 13" baking dish. Bake 6 minutes.
2. Melt caramels with remaining ⅓ cup evaporated milk on low heat, stirring while melting.
3. While cake is still hot, pour caramel mixture on top of cake. Sprinkle chocolate chips over caramel and then top with nuts.
4. Spread remaining cake mixture on top of nuts.
5. Bake at 350° for 20–25 minutes.
6. If desired, frost with chocolate icing.

❧ **Makes 24**

Date Pinwheels

Take these pinwheels with you, and you'll be sharing the recipe with all who taste them.

1 pound of pitted dates, chopped

½ cup water

½ cup granulated sugar

½ cup butter

½ cup brown sugar

½ cup granulated sugar

1 egg, well beaten

½ teaspoon vanilla

2 cups sifted flour

½ teaspoon baking soda

1½ cups chopped pecans

1. Combine dates, water, and ½ cup granulated sugar. Cook until thick (2–3 minutes), stirring constantly. Cool.
2. Cream together butter and sugars. Add egg and vanilla and beat well.
3. Sift dry ingredients and add to creamed butter mixture. Stir until smooth. Chill while making the date mixture.
4. Divide dough in half. Roll one part on lightly floured surface till ¼" thick.
5. Combine date mixture and nuts. Spread half of filling evenly over dough and roll like a jelly roll. Wrap in waxed paper with open edge of roll on bottom. Repeat with remaining dough and filling. Chill rolls till firm.
6. Cut in ¼" slices and place on lightly greased baking sheet. Bake at 400° for 8–10 minutes.

❧ **Makes about 3 dozen**

Hast thou not poured me out as milk, and curdled me like cheese?

—Job 10:10

Oatmeal Carmelitas

The addition of caramel topping to oatmeal and chocolate chips makes a cookie bar that will become a most-requested treat.

1 cup flour

1 cup quick-cooking oats

½ teaspoon baking soda

¼ teaspoon salt

½ cup packed light brown sugar

¾ cup butter or margarine, melted

1 (6-ounce) package chocolate chips

½ cup chopped nuts

¾ cup caramel ice cream topping

3 tablespoons flour

1. Preheat oven to 350°.
2. Grease bottom and sides of 9" square baking dish.
3. Combine flour, oats, baking soda, salt, brown sugar, and margarine in large bowl and mix to form crumbs. Press half of mixture into bottom of greased 9" square baking dish. Bake at 350° for 10 minutes.
4. Remove from oven and sprinkle chocolate and nuts over crumb mixture.
5. Microwave caramel topping for 10–20 seconds. Mix caramel topping and flour together well. Drizzle over chocolate and nuts. Sprinkle remaining crumbs over caramel topping. Bake at 350° for 15–20 minutes until golden brown.
6. Chill bars for easy cutting.

Makes 9–12 bars

And he said unto her, Give me, I pray thee, a little water to drink; for I am thirsty. And she opened a bottle of milk, and gave him drink, and covered him.

—Judges 4:19

Peanut Butter Squares

Few things are better than peanut butter and chocolate! These squares will disappear quickly, so keep the ingredients on hand to whip up a batch for your next occasion.

½ cup light corn syrup

½ cup brown sugar

1 cup peanut butter

2 cups Rice Krispies

¼ cup butter or margarine, melted

2 tablespoons vanilla

2 tablespoons milk

2 cups confectioners' sugar

1 (3-ounce) package instant vanilla pudding (not sugar-free)

¼ cup butter or margarine

1 cup chocolate chips

1. In saucepan over medium low heat, combine corn syrup, brown sugar, and peanut butter until peanut butter is melted. Remove from heat and add Rice Krispies. Press into a 9" × 13" baking dish. Refrigerate while making the middle layer.
2. In bowl, combine melted butter with vanilla, milk, sugar, and instant pudding. Spread evenly over the base layer. Refrigerate for 15 minutes or until firm.
3. In a saucepan over medium heat, melt margarine and chocolate chips and mix together. Spread evenly over middle layer. Refrigerate until chocolate layer is firm.
4. Set the cookies out for about 10 minutes before cutting. Cut into 48 small pieces. These cookies do not have to be stored in the refrigerator.

❧ **Makes 48**

And he gathered up all the food of the seven years, which were in the land of Egypt, and laid up the food in the cities: the food of the field, which was round about every city, laid he up in the same.

—Genesis 41:48

Toffee Bars

These Toffee Bars could be called candy bars and they satisfy almost anyone's sweet tooth. A good treat to take along anytime.

2 cups firmly packed brown sugar

2 cups flour

½ cup butter or margarine, softened

1 teaspoon baking powder

½ teaspoon salt

1 teaspoon vanilla extract

1 cup milk

1 egg

½ cup semisweet chocolate chips

1 cup Symphony candy bar, broken into pieces

½ cup chopped unblanched almonds

1. Preheat oven to 350°. Grease a 9" × 13" baking dish.
2. In a large mixing bowl, mix together brown sugar and flour. Using a pastry cutter or two knives, cut in the butter until mixture resembles crumbs. Remove 1 cup of mixture and set aside.
3. To mixture in large bowl, add baking powder and salt. Using a whisk, lightly beat in vanilla, milk, and egg. Continue beating until a smooth batter forms. Pour batter into prepared baking dish. Sprinkle reserved crumb mixture over top of batter in pan. Sprinkle with the chocolate chips, broken candy bar pieces, and almonds.
4. Bake bars for 35 minutes, or until a toothpick inserted in center comes out clean. Cool bars before cutting.

❧ **Makes 24**

And take with thee ten loaves, and cracknels, and a cruse of honey, and go to him: he shall tell thee what shall become of the child.

—1 Kings 14:3

Pecan Puffs

You form these into rolls and chill them. Then slice them and they become Mexican wedding cookies. Carry them wherever you go. They travel well.

4 tablespoons powdered sugar

½ cup shortening

1 tablespoon water

2 teaspoons vanilla

2 cups flour

1 cup pecan pieces

Powdered sugar

1. Cream together sugar and shortening. Mix in water and vanilla. Add flour and nuts; chill.
2. Form into small balls and bake at 250° for 40–50 minutes.
3. Remove from oven and roll twice in powdered sugar.

 Makes 36

I have fed you with milk, and not with meat: for hitherto ye were not able to bear it, neither yet now are ye able.

—*1 Corinthians 3:2*

No-Bake Cookies

Yes, you can make cookies in the slow cooker! This excellent recipe could be varied several ways. Use white or dark chocolate chips, or dried blueberries or currants instead of the dried cranberries.

4 eggs

⅔ cup sugar

1 cup brown sugar

¼ cup butter, melted

⅛ teaspoon salt

1½ cups finely chopped dates

1 teaspoon vanilla

3½ cups crisp rice cereal

1 cup chopped dried cranberries

1 cup powdered sugar

1. Spray a 1½ quart slow cooker with nonstick cooking spray. In medium bowl, beat eggs with sugar, brown sugar, butter, and salt. Stir in dates. Pour into prepared slow cooker.
2. Cover and cook on high for 3–4 hours, stirring twice during cooking time, being sure to scrape the sides of the slow cooker. You may need to turn the slow cooker to low if the edges get too dark.

(continued)

(No-Bake Cookies—continued)

3. When the temperature reaches 160°F, empty the mixture into a large bowl. Stir in vanilla, then add cereal and cranberries.
4. Let the mixture cool for 10 minutes, then drop by teaspoons into powdered sugar. Shape into balls, then place on waxed paper. Store, covered, in refrigerator.

❀ **Makes 48**

Cream Cheese Finger Cookies

These are great to take to a Christmas cookie exchange.

½ cup butter (no substitutes), softened

4 ounces cream cheese, softened

1 teaspoon vanilla extract

1¾ cups flour

1 tablespoon powdered sugar

Dash salt

1 cup finely chopped pecans

Powdered sugar

1. In a mixing bowl, cream together butter and cream cheese. Beat in vanilla.
2. Combine the flour, sugar, and salt and gradually add to cream cheese mixture. Stir in pecans; dough will be crumbly. Shape tablespoonfuls into 2" logs. Place 2" apart on ungreased cookie sheets.
3. Bake at 375° for 12–14 minutes or until lightly browned. Roll warm cookies in powdered sugar.

❀ **Makes 24**

Double Chocolate Chip Cookies

You'll find that adults as well as children will love these cookies, so you may want to make two batches to take.

1 (18.25-ounce) box devil's food cake mix
1 stick butter
1 teaspoon vanilla
2 eggs
½ cup chopped pecans
1 cup semisweet chocolate chips
1 package mini M&Ms
Walnut pieces

1. Heat oven to 375°.
2. In a large bowl, using a mixer, beat half the dry cake mix with the butter, vanilla, and eggs. Beat in remaining cake mix. Stir in nuts and chocolate chips. Drop dough by rounded teaspoonfuls or use a small cookie scoop. Top with a few mini M&Ms and walnut pieces.
3. Bake for 10–12 minutes on ungreased cookie sheets until edges are set. Centers will be soft.
4. Cool on wire rack for 1 minute before removing from cookie sheet.

Makes 60

White Chocolate–Oatmeal Cookies

Welcome a neighbor with these wonderful white chocolate–oatmeal cookies. The white chocolate and oatmeal combination is sure to satisfy anyone's taste buds.

2 sticks butter
1 cup sugar
1 cup brown sugar
2 large eggs
2 teaspoons vanilla
3 cups flour
1 teaspoon baking soda
1 teaspoon baking powder
1 teaspoon salt
1½ cups regular Old-Fashioned oats
2 cups white chocolate chips

1. Cream together butter, sugars, and eggs. Beat and add vanilla.
2. Mix together dry ingredients and combine with creamed mixture. Add white chocolate chips. Bake at 350° for 8–10 minutes.
3. Cool for 2 minutes before removing from cookie sheet.

Makes 36

Fruit and Nut Bars

These California fruit bars are so delicious that they're gone almost as soon as they're served.

½ cup white flour

1 cup oats

¾ cup firmly packed brown sugar

¼ cup whole wheat flour

1 stick butter, softened

2 teaspoons vanilla

1½ cups chopped walnuts

1 cup golden raisins

1 cup chopped dried apricots

1 14-ounce can sweetened condensed milk

1. Preheat oven to 350°.
2. In a large bowl, combine flour, oats, sugar, wheat flour, butter, and vanilla. Mix until crumbly.
3. Reserve ½ cup of crumb mixture and set aside. Press remainder on bottom of greased 9" × 13" baking dish.
4. In a large bowl, combine walnuts, raisins, apricots, and milk. Spoon evenly over crust. Top with reserved crumb mixture and press down firmly.
5. Bake for 25 minutes or until edges are lightly browned. Cool before cutting into bars.
6. Can be stored covered at room temperature for 3–4 days.

❦ **Makes 32**

Pecan Bars

These yummy pecan bars are a knockout. Add them to your cookie tray for a real crowd pleaser.

Crust

3 cups flour

½ cup sugar

1 cup butter

Dash salt

Filling

4 eggs

1½ cups dark Karo syrup

1½ cups sugar

3 tablespoons butter, softened

1½ teaspoons vanilla

1½ cups roasted salted pecans

1. For crust, mix together flour, sugar, butter, and salt. Press mixture into a greased and floured 9" × 13" baking dish. Bake at 350° for 20 minutes.
2. For filling, combine eggs, dark Karo syrup, sugar, butter, vanilla, and pecans. Pour on crust. Bake at 350° for 25 minutes.

❦ **Makes 24**

Fresh Apple Cookies

The glaze used on these cookies makes this recipe stand out. Try them for your next carry-in, and they'll stand out there as well. Dig in!

Cookies

½ cup vegetable shortening

1⅓ cups firmly packed brown sugar

½ teaspoon salt

1 teaspoon cinnamon

1 teaspoon nutmeg

1 egg

2 cups flour

1 teaspoon baking soda

¼ cup milk

4 peeled, cored, and finely chopped apples

1 cup chopped walnuts

Vegetable cooking spray

Vanilla Glaze

1½ cups powdered sugar

1 tablespoon butter, melted

⅛ teaspoon salt

3 tablespoons milk

½ teaspoon vanilla

Nonstick vegetable cooking spray

For the cookies:

1. Preheat oven to 400°.
2. Cream the shortening, brown sugar, salt, cinnamon, nutmeg, and egg in a large bowl. Add the flour and baking soda and mix well. Stir in the milk until well blended, then stir in the apples and walnuts. Drop by teaspoonfuls onto cookie sheets that have been coated with vegetable cooking spray. Bake 11–14 minutes or until golden brown.

For the glaze:

1. Combine all glaze ingredients in a small bowl and mix until smooth while cookies are baking.
2. Remove cookies from cookie sheets and, while still hot, spread on vanilla glaze.

❦ **Makes 48**

And kept the feast of unleavened bread seven days with joy: for the LORD had made them joyful, and turned the heart of the king of Assyria unto them, to strengthen their hands in the work of the house of God, the God of Israel.

—Ezra 6:22

Almond Glaze Sugar Cookies

You'll fall in love with these cookies the first time you try them. This is another wonderful recipe that's been passed from friend to friend through the years.

Cookies

1 cup Land O'Lakes soft baking butter with canola oil

¾ cup sugar

1 teaspoon almond extract

2 cups flour

½ teaspoon baking powder

Granulated sugar

Glaze

1½ cups powdered sugar

1 teaspoon almond extract

4–5 teaspoons water

Sliced almonds

For the cookies:

1. Heat oven to 400°.
2. In a large mixing bowl, combine butter, sugar, almond extract, flour, and baking powder. Beat at medium speed until creamy. Drop dough by rounded spoonfuls onto greased cookie sheets. Flatten to ¼" thickness with bottom of buttered glass dipped in granulated sugar. Bake 7 to 9 minutes or until edges are very lightly browned. Cool 1 minute and remove from cookie sheets to cool completely.

For the glaze:

1. Stir together all glaze ingredients except almonds with wire whisk in a small bowl.
2. Decorate cooled cookies with glaze and almonds as desired.

❦ **Makes 36**

And it shall come to pass in the increase, that ye shall give the fifth part unto Pharaoh, and four parts shall be your own, for seed of the field, and for your food, and for them of your households, and for food for your little ones.

Genesis 47:24

Chocolate-Raspberry Brownies

Who doesn't like chocolate and raspberry together? This would also be good with white chocolate chips in place of the milk chocolate chips.

1 (18.25-ounce) package devil's food cake mix

¾ cup melted butter

1 cup chopped nuts

⅓ cup evaporated milk

1 cup milk chocolate chips

1 (16-ounce) bag of frozen raspberries, thawed

1. Preheat oven to 350°.
2. Combine cake mix, melted butter, nuts, and evaporated milk, and stir by hand until dough holds together.
3. Press half of dough into 9" × 13" baking dish coated with vegetable spray and bake for 6 minutes to make crust.
4. Sprinkle chocolate chips over baked crust then place raspberries over chocolate chips. Crumble remaining dough over raspberries and bake for 15–18 minutes. Cool and refrigerate for 30 minutes.
5. Cut into squares before serving.

❧ **Makes 24**

Forgotten Meringues

Meringues are very easy to make. Eating them is like putting sugar in your mouth.

2 egg whites

Pinch of salt

⅔ cup sugar

1 teaspoon vanilla

1 cup mini semisweet chocolate morsels

1. Beat egg whites until foamy. Add salt and continue beating until whites stand in soft peaks. Gradually add the sugar, beating until very stiff peaks form. Add vanilla and sprinkle chocolate morsels on top. Fold In.
2. Preheat oven to 350°.
3. Drop by teaspoon onto lightly buttered cookie sheets. They may be placed close together–they will not spread. Place in the heated oven and immediately turn it off.
4. Let the cookies dry overnight in the cooling oven.

❧ **Makes 24**

Loaded Cookies

These cookies are loaded with so many good things—a mouthful of tasty treats all rolled into one cookie.

½ cup butter

½ teaspoon vanilla

1 egg

¼ cup sugar

½ cup packed brown sugar

1½ cups flour

¾ teaspoon baking soda

¼ teaspoon baking powder

½ cup chocolate M&Ms

½ cup rolled oats

½ cup crisped rice cereal

½ cup white chocolate chips

⅓ cup chocolate chips

1. In a large bowl, cream together butter, vanilla, and egg. Add remaining ingredients and stir until well blended.
2. Place teaspoon-size dough balls onto an ungreased cookie sheet. Bake at 350° for 10–12 minutes until lightly browned.

❦ **Makes 48**

Mounds Cookies

If you're a coconut lover, you're sure to love these Mounds cookies. With the addition of almonds to this recipe, it's like an Almond Joy and Mounds rolled into one.

1¼ cups flour

½ teaspoon baking soda

½ teaspoon salt

½ cup margarine, softened

¾ cup sugar

1 egg

1 cup Mounds candy bars, broken into small pieces (approximately 2 bars)

½ teaspoon vanilla

½ cup chopped roasted almonds

1. In medium bowl, sift together flour, baking soda, and salt.
2. Cream margarine and sugar in separate bowl. Beat in egg. Add flour mixture to creamed butter mixture and add candy bars and almonds. Stir in vanilla. Refrigerate dough for 30 minutes.
3. Drop by half-teaspoonfuls onto greased cookie sheet.
4. Bake at 350° for 10–12 minutes.

❦ **Makes 36**

Crisp Oatmeal Cookies

Here's an old-fashioned cookie recipe that's sure to be a hit, and you can make the cookies large or small.

6 tablespoons milk

1 teaspoon vinegar or lemon juice

¾ cup light brown sugar

¾ cup dark brown sugar

¾ cup vegetable oil

½ teaspoon salt

¾ teaspoon baking soda

¾ teaspoon vanilla

1½ cups flour

3 cups quick oats

¾ cup finely chopped walnuts

1. Combine milk and vinegar in bowl and let stand 10 minutes.
2. In large bowl, combine all the remaining ingredients in the order given.
3. After 10 minutes, stir in milk mixture. You may want to use an electric mixer to mix dough.
4. Roll into balls the size of walnuts, or larger if you like big cookies.
5. Place on cookie sheet and flatten to ⅛" with a fork dipped in milk.
6. Bake at 375° for 8–10 minutes.
7. Leave on pan for 2–3 minutes before removing from pan.

❧ **Makes 36**

Potluck Pointer

Almost everyone loves ice cream, but it can be a challenge to serve to a large number of diners. For a pretty and practical presentation, line muffin tins with multicolored muffin papers; scoop ice cream into each paper and freeze. Once frozen, you can place the individual servings into a zipper-top bag for traveling.

Deliciously Easy Brownies

Brownies are always a hit. These can be made with or without the white chocolate glaze—they're delicious either way.

1 (19.8-ounce) box of fudge brownies

¼ cup water

½ cup vegetable oil

2 eggs

3 tablespoons margarine, softened

½ cup packed brown sugar

½ cup pecan pieces

½ cup white chocolate chips

1 teaspoon milk

1. In medium bowl, combine brownie mix, water, oil, and eggs until well blended.
2. In small bowl, combine margarine and brown sugar, creaming together. Mix pecans into brown sugar mixture.
3. Spread brownie batter into greased 9" × 13" baking dish. Distribute nut mixture evenly over the brownie batter. Bake at 350° for 28–30 minutes.
4. While they are cooling, melt the chocolate chips in a microwaveable bowl for 1 minute. Remove and stir.
5. Place in microwave again for 15 to 30 seconds and remove. Stir until melted.
6. With whisk, combine milk with white chocolate. Drizzle over brownies. Cool.

❦ **Makes 24**

Behold, therefore I will deliver thee to the men of the east for a possession, and they shall set their palaces in thee, and make their dwellings in thee: they shall eat thy fruit, and they shall drink thy milk.

—Ezekiel 25:4

Chocolate–Cream Cheese Brownies

Rich, moist brownies that start with a mix—a great time-saver and oh so good.

Bar

1 19.8-ounce box of fudge brownie mix

¼ cup water

½ cup vegetable oil

2 eggs

Filling

1 8-ounce package of cream cheese, reserving 2 ounces, softened

½ cup sugar

1 egg

2 tablespoons flour

½ teaspoon vanilla

¼ cup margarine

½ cup chopped pecans

2 cups chocolate chips

Frosting

¼ cup margarine

1 square unsweetened chocolate

2 ounces cream cheese (reserved from above)

1 teaspoon vanilla

¼ cup milk

1 pound powdered sugar

For the bar:

In medium bowl, combine brownie mix, water, oil, and 2 eggs until well blended, then pour into a greased and floured 9" × 13" baking dish.

For the filling:

Mix together 6 ounces cream cheese, ½ cup sugar, 1 egg, flour, ½ teaspoon vanilla, ¼ cup margarine, and pecans and spread over bar mixture. Top with chocolate chips. Bake at 350° for 25–35 minutes.

For the frosting:

Mix together ¼ cup margarine, unsweetened chocolate, 2 ounces cream cheese, 1 teaspoon vanilla, milk, and powdered sugar. Spread on top of brownies. Refrigerate when cool.

❧ **Makes 24–36**

Potluck Pointer

Use a pizza cutter instead of a knife to cut a cooled pan of brownies. They'll be ready to serve in a jiffy.

Snowy Nutballs

These little confections are full of nuts and flavor. They are dusted with lots of powdered sugar, so make sure to serve napkins with them. They're finger-licking good.

1 cup butter or margarine

½ cup powdered sugar

1 teaspoon vanilla

2¼ cups flour

¼ teaspoon salt

¾ cup finely chopped nuts

1. Preheat oven to 400°.
2. In medium bowl, combine all ingredients. Drop in small spoonfuls onto ungreased cookie sheet. Bake 10–12 minutes.
3. While warm, roll in powdered sugar.
4. Cool and roll in powdered sugar again.

Makes 36

Chocolate-Peanut Brownies

Snickers are a favorite in most families, so these brownies that remind us of them will be a big hit with everyone. This is a great dessert to take along to a family gathering. Enjoy.

1 (14-ounce) package of caramels

¾ cup condensed milk

1 (18.25-ounce) package German Chocolate cake mix

1 cup chopped peanuts

¾ cup melted butter

1 (6-ounce) package chocolate chips

1. Melt caramels and ⅓ cup of milk in pan over hot water and set aside, keeping warm.
2. Combine cake mix, peanuts, butter, chocolate chips, and remaining milk and stir until crumbly. Press half of mixture in a greased and floured 9" × 13" baking dish. Bake at 350° for 6 minutes. Remove and cool slightly.
3. Sprinkle chips over dough. Quickly spread caramel mixture on top. Spread remaining crumbs, pressing down lightly with spoon.
4. Return to oven at 350° for 14–18 minutes. Cool 30 minutes and refrigerate until firm and set.

Makes 24

Surprise

A few years ago, my sister Lois turned 70 years young. Aside from the birthday anniversary itself, the real story lies in the behind-the-scenes family preparation for that event. For starters, anyone who knew Lois was aware that she was not one to willingly come to a big birthday bash in her honor. Rather, we worried that if she found out about it in advance, she would find a way not to come at all! Therefore, our planning had to be covert, and we promised each other that none of us would spill the beans. This was more than just a family challenge: Lois's friends and coworkers were also to be invited, and just one person could easily and inadvertently spoil the surprise.

Since Lois lives in northern Indiana, we schemers traveled to Indianapolis and met at the local IHOP, about 75 miles from her hometown. The planning then began. After resolving the questions of when, where, and how to celebrate, and who to invite, we sprang into action. We were able to obtain a large activity room in a church that her son Ed and his wife Marilyn attended. Now the question was: How were we going to get Lois to the church activity room on a Saturday afternoon? The answer was to tell her that her grandson had a display project set up there, and she was invited to see it.

During the hours before the surprise party, we carried in food and more food—a bountiful banquet of food, fit for any VIP. Some of us decorated the room with balloons and other birthday trimmings while the rest of us set up the buffet. As Lois's friends and other family members arrived, they went into the activity room to prepare for the big surprise.

We all remained silent as Ed drove Lois into the church parking lot and entered the entrance hallway with her. Then Lois entered the activity room and we let loose with our shouts of "SURPRISE!" She *was* surprised—not a hint had been dropped to give us away. And there was no escaping for Lois now—Ed was right behind her to block the doorway.

As it turned out, she had a great time; and I know she was really pleased that all of her friends and family came together to show her how much she meant to us. Plan a party for one of your friends or relatives. Even shy and modest people like to be feted. Use some of the recipes in this book to keep things easy and delicious. ❧

—Susie Siegfried

Ritz Supreme Dessert

This recipe will satisfy anyone's sweet tooth and it's a hit even with picky eaters.

3 egg whites

1 cup sugar

1 teaspoon baking powder

20 Ritz crackers, crushed fine

¾ cup chopped pecans

1 (8-ounce) container frozen whipped topping, thawed

Hot fudge sauce

1. Beat egg whites until stiff. Add sugar gradually, and fold in baking powder. Continue beating until batter forms stiff peaks. Fold in cracker crumbs and pecans.
2. Pour into a greased 9" pie pan and bake at 350° for 25 minutes. Cool.
3. Top with whipped topping and drizzle with hot fudge sauce when ready to serve.

🖤 **Makes 8 servings**

Bananas Royale

Looking for variety in your desserts? Try this rich and creamy banana-based dish.

1 cup sour cream

1 (12-ounce) container frozen whipped topping, thawed

2 cups milk

2 (3.4-ounce) packages instant vanilla pudding mix

1 (11-ounce) box of vanilla wafers

5–6 large bananas

1. In a large bowl, mix sour cream and whipped topping. Add milk. Stir in both puddings and beat with electric mixer for 2–3 minutes.
2. In a greased and floured 9" × 13" baking dish, place a layer of vanilla wafers on the bottom.
3. Cut up bananas and place half of bananas on top of wafers. Place a thin layer of pudding mixture over the bananas. Repeat layers and end with pudding mixture.
4. Crush some of the vanilla wafers in a plastic bag and sprinkle over the top.

🖤 **Makes 18–20 servings**

Black and White and Red Fondue

Fondue is such a wonderful communal dessert. Strawberries are the best choice for dipping into this creamy and sweet mixture.

2 (14-ounce) cans sweetened condensed milk

3 (12-ounce) packages semisweet chocolate chips

4 (1-ounce) squares unsweetened baking chocolate, chopped

1/3 cup unsweetened cocoa powder

1/4 cup honey

2 teaspoons vanilla

2 (12-ounce) packages white chocolate chips

2 (8-ounce) bars white chocolate with almonds, chopped

60 strawberries

Long wooden skewers

Mini marshmallows

1. In 4-quart slow cooker, combine condensed milk, semisweet chocolate, baking chocolate, cocoa, and honey; mix well. Cover and cook on low for 1–2 hours or until chocolate is melted and mixture is smooth. Stir well and add vanilla.

2. Add white chocolate chips and the chopped candy bars. Stir just to combine, then cook on low for 10 minutes. Do not stir; serve immediately with skewered strawberries.

3. To serve a crowd, choose large strawberries. Wash and hull berries; then place one strawberry on each long wooden skewer and hold in place with a mini marshmallow. Everyone can dip to their heart's content, but only use each skewer once!

❧ **Makes 12–14 servings**

Potluck Pointer

To keep your frosting on the cake and not on the wrapper, spritz your foil or plastic wrap lightly with nonstick cooking spray. Try this when transporting frosted cupcakes, too.

Chocolate-Caramel Fondue

Serve this dip with cookies, pieces of pound and angel food cake, and fresh fruits such as strawberries, pineapple, and apple slices.

1 (12-ounce) package semisweet chocolate chips

1 (12-ounce) package milk chocolate chips

1 (8-ounce) bittersweet chocolate bar, chopped

1 (14-ounce) can sweetened condensed milk

1 (13-ounce) can dulce de leche sweetened condensed milk

14 caramels, unwrapped and chopped

1. In 3-quart slow cooker, combine semisweet chocolate chips with milk chocolate chips, chopped chocolate bar, and both kinds of sweetened condensed milk. Stir to combine.
2. Cover and cook on low for 1 to 1½ hours or until chocolate is melted and mixture is smooth. Stir in caramels; cover and cook on low for another 30 minutes to melt caramels. Serve immediately.

❦ **Makes 8 servings**

Peanut Butter Fondue

If the fondue is too thick, you can stir in more evaporated milk. This can also be served as a sauce over ice cream or pudding.

2 cups peanut butter

1 (14-ounce) can sweetened condensed milk

1 (13-ounce) can evaporated milk

1 (11-ounce) package peanut butter–flavored chips

⅓ cup butter

Sliced bananas

Sliced cored apples

Marshmallows

1 cup chopped peanuts

1. In 3-quart slow cooker, combine peanut butter, both kinds of milk, chips, and butter; mix well. Cover and cook on low for 3–4 hours or until mixture is smooth, stirring once during cooking time.
2. Arrange dippers on a platter around the fondue, and provide forks, skewers, or toothpicks. Dip fruits into the fondue and roll into peanuts. Remind people to use each fork or skewer only once.

❦ **Makes 8–10 servings**

John Mike Dessert

This dessert became the favorite recipe of a young boy, so it was named after him. His name was John Michael.

55 Ritz crackers, crumbled

1 stick margarine, melted

1¼ cups powdered sugar

2 packages Dream Whip whipped topping mix

1 (6-ounce) can pink lemonade

1 cup sweetened condensed milk

1. Mix crackers, margarine, and sugar, reserving ⅛ cup of mixture for topping. Place in greased and floured 9" × 13" dish.
2. Prepare Dream Whip according to directions on package.
3. Mix together lemonade and milk and fold mixture into Dream Whip. Put on top of cracker mixture.
4. Sprinkle with reserved topping and refrigerate for at least 6 hours.

❦ **Makes 12–15 servings**

Easy Éclairs

Easy, yummy, and fabulous. The already prepared icing works like a dream with this dessert and makes it a snap to prepare.

3 cups milk

2 (3-ounce) packages instant French vanilla pudding

1 (8-ounce) container frozen whipped topping, thawed

1 (16-ounce) box graham crackers

1 (16-ounce) container chocolate icing

½ cup roasted and salted chopped peanuts

1. In large bowl, combine milk with both puddings and beat with electric mixer for 2 minutes. Fold in whipped topping.
2. In bottom of greased 9" × 13" dish, place a layer of whole graham crackers. Place entire pudding mixture on top of the graham crackers. Add another layer of graham crackers on top of pudding mixture.
3. Frost graham crackers with canned chocolate icing and sprinkle with nuts. Refrigerate overnight.
4. Cut into squares before serving.

❦ **Makes 20–24**

Angel Squares

Angel squares is a fitting name for these heavenly bars.

Squares
1 cup butter or margarine
2 cups brown sugar
1 teaspoon baking soda
1 cup hot water
2 eggs
3 cups flour
1 teaspoon cinnamon
1 teaspoon baking powder
3 cups chocolate chips

Icing
4 cups powdered sugar
1/3 cup milk
1/2 teaspoon vanilla

For the squares:
1. Cream butter and sugar.
2. Dissolve baking soda in hot water. Mix in all remaining ingredients except chocolate chips with the butter mixture. Mix well. Stir in chocolate chips.
3. In a greased 11" × 17" cookie sheet with sides, bake at 350° for 20 minutes.

For the icing:
1. For icing, mix powdered sugar, milk, and vanilla until smooth and thin.
2. Top with icing while warm.

❦ **Makes 36**

Butter Pecan Bars

Mix it up and drizzle these pecan bars with melted chocolate chips, white or milk chocolate. Either way, they'll be delicious.

2 eggs
1 cup brown sugar
1 cup sugar
1¼ cups flour
¾ cup stick butter, melted
1 teaspoon vanilla
1 cup chopped pecans

1. Beat eggs for 1 minute. Add sugars and flour and mix together. Add melted butter, vanilla, and pecans.
2. Spray a 9" × 13" baking dish with vegetable cooking spray and pour batter into pan. Bake at 350° for 35 minutes.
3. Cut into squares while still warm. Store in a tightly sealed container.

❦ **Makes 24**

And Melchizedek king of Salem brought forth bread and wine: and he was the priest of the most high God.

— Genesis 14:18

Peachy Pizza

If fresh peaches are available, they can be substituted for the frozen peaches. Be sure to serve this with whipped cream.

1 refrigerated pie crust, at room temperature for 5 to 10 minutes
1 (16-ounce) bag of frozen peaches, thawed
1 teaspoon cinnamon
½ cup sugar
¼ teaspoon nutmeg
¾ cup flour
½ cup sugar
½ cup butter
½ cup pecans

1. Unfold pie crust and place in greased pizza pan.
2. Cut up peaches into small pieces and put on top of pie crust.
3. Mix together cinnamon, sugar, and nutmeg and put on top of peaches.
4. Mix together flour, sugar, butter, and pecans and put on top of peaches.
5. Bake at 425° for 20–25 minutes.

❧ **Makes 20 pieces**

Frosted Strawberry Squares

This is especially good during the summertime, but it's a welcome treat any time of the year.

1 cup flour
¼ cup brown sugar
⅓ cup chopped pecans
½ cup butter, melted
2 egg whites
2 tablespoons lemon juice
⅔ to 1 cup sugar
1 (10-ounce) package of frozen strawberries, thawed
1 cup whipped cream

1. Mix flour, brown sugar, pecans, and butter until crumbly. Place in baking dish and bake for 20 minutes at 350°, stirring occasionally. Remove from oven, and let cool.
2. Beat egg whites, lemon juice, sugar, and strawberries with mixer until standing in peaks. Fold in whipped cream. Pour over crumb mixture. Place remaining crumbs on top.
3. Place in freezer for 6 hours or overnight.

❧ **Makes 12**

Carrot Cake Pudding

Serve this excellent pudding, which tastes like carrot cake, with Hard Sauce (page 378), or butter pecan ice cream.

1 (14.5-ounce) can sliced carrots, drained

1 (8-ounce) can crushed pineapple in juice, undrained

½ cup heavy cream

¾ cup brown sugar

⅓ cup flour

¼ teaspoon salt

½ teaspoon baking soda

½ teaspoon cinnamon

⅛ teaspoon cardamom

2 beaten eggs

2 tablespoons butter, melted

2 teaspoons vanilla

½ cup coconut

½ cup chopped pecans

¼ cup brown sugar

3 tablespoons butter, melted

1. Spray 3½-quart slow cooker with nonstick baking spray containing flour and set aside. Place carrots in large bowl and mash with potato masher until smooth. Stir in the undrained pineapple and cream; mix well.
2. Add brown sugar, flour, salt, baking soda, cinnamon, and cardamom; mix. Stir in eggs, 2 tablespoons melted butter, and vanilla. Mix well.
3. Pour batter into prepared slow cooker. Cover and cook on low for 6–7 hours or until pudding is set when lightly touched.
4. About half an hour before pudding is done, place coconut and pecans in a small dry skillet. Toast over low heat, stirring frequently, until light brown and fragrant. Stir in ¼ cup brown sugar and 3 tablespoons butter. Cook and stir until sugar melts and coats coconut and pecans.
5. Sprinkle coconut mixture over pudding and serve warm.

❧ **Makes 6 servings**

Date Pudding

The brown sugar sauce really complements this recipe. And if you're a date lover, you'll love the combination.

Pudding

1 cup pitted dates

1 cup boiling water

½ cup sugar

½ cup brown sugar

1 egg

2 tablespoons melted butter

1½ cups flour

1 teaspoon baking soda

½ teaspoon baking powder

½ teaspoon salt

1 cup chopped walnuts

Brown Sugar Sauce

1½ cups brown sugar

1 tablespoon butter

½ cup boiling water

For the pudding:

1. Combine dates and water.
2. In large bowl blend sugars, egg, and butter.
3. In medium bowl, sift together dry ingredients; add to sugar mixture.
4. Stir walnuts and cooked date mixture into sugar mixture.
5. Pour into greased 8" × 8" baking dish.

For the sauce:

1. Combine brown sugar, butter, and boiling water.
2. Whisk together and pour over date pudding. Bake in oven at 375° for 40 minutes.

❧ **Makes 9–12 servings**

Chocolate Steamed Pudding with Hard Sauce

This decadent recipe is comforting and delicious. The Hard Sauce melts into the warm pudding as you eat it. Yum.

Pudding

½ cup butter, softened

½ cup sugar

½ cup brown sugar

⅓ cup unsweetened cocoa

2 eggs

1 teaspoon vanilla

1½ cups flour

½ teaspoon salt

1 teaspoon baking powder

1 teaspoon baking soda

½ cup mascarpone cheese

¼ cup heavy cream

1 cup semisweet chocolate chips

Hard Sauce

⅓ cup butter, softened

½ cup powdered sugar

Pinch salt

1 teaspoon vanilla

For the pudding:

1. Spray a 6-cup mold or 2-pound coffee can with nonstick baking spray containing flour. In large bowl, combine butter, sugar, and brown sugar; beat well.

2. Add cocoa, eggs, and vanilla; beat until fluffy. Sift together flour, salt, baking powder, and baking soda. Add alternately to the butter mixture with mascarpone cheese and heavy cream, beginning and ending with dry ingredients. Stir in chocolate chips.

3. Pour mixture into prepared mold or can. Place a rack or crumpled foil in bottom of 4-quart slow cooker. Place the mold on top of the rack. Cover and cook on high for 4–5 hours or until pudding is set. Remove the mold from slow cooker, then cool for 30 minutes.

For the hard sauce:

1. In medium bowl combine ⅓ cup butter, powdered sugar, pinch salt, and 1 teaspoon vanilla. Beat until fluffy.

2. Unmold pudding and serve warm with Hard Sauce.

❧ **Makes 8–10 servings**

Marlene's Apricot Rice Pudding

Rice pudding is wonderful comfort food. When flavored with apricot nectar, cardamom, and nutmeg, it becomes a gourmet dessert.

1 cup medium grain white rice

1 cup sugar

¼ cup butter

¼ teaspoon salt

⅛ teaspoon cardamom

⅛ teaspoon nutmeg

2 cups apricot nectar

2 cups whole milk

2 teaspoons vanilla

½ cup finely chopped dried apricots

1 cup chopped canned apricots in juice, drained

1. Combine all ingredients except canned apricots in 3½ quart slow cooker. Cover and cook on low for 2 hours, then remove lid and stir.
2. Cover and continue cooking on low for 2–3 hours longer, until rice is tender and pudding is desired thickness. Stir in canned apricots, cover, and cook for another 30 minutes. Serve warm or cold.

❀ **Makes 8–10 servings**

Butterscotch Dessert

Get out the ice cream and whip up a treat! This scrumptious dessert will be welcome for any occasion.

30 Ritz crackers, crushed

1⅓ cups margarine, melted

1 (12-ounce) jar hot fudge topping

6–8 Heath bars, crushed

1 quart vanilla ice cream

2 (3-ounce) packages instant butterscotch pudding

1 cup milk

1 (12-ounce) container frozen whipped topping, thawed

1. Mix together crackers and margarine.
2. Spray 9" × 13" dish with vegetable cooking spray and press cracker mixture on bottom.
3. Warm hot fudge sauce in microwave for 10 to 12 seconds so it will spread more easily. Spread fudge sauce over cracker crust, then sprinkle crushed Heath bars onto fudge topping.
4. Beat together ice cream, pudding, and milk for 2 minutes with electric mixer. Pour over cracker crust and refrigerate for 4–6 hours. Top with whipped topping.

❀ **Makes 15 servings**

Butterscotch Pears

This delicious combination can be served alone, with sweetened whipped cream, or as a topping for ice cream or angel food cake.

8 large, firm pears

2 tablespoons lemon juice

½ cup dark brown sugar

⅓ cup butter, softened

¼ cup flour

½ teaspoon cinnamon

¼ teaspoon salt

1 cup chopped pecans

1 cup pear nectar

¼ cup honey

1. Cut pears in half and remove core; do not peel. Brush pears with lemon juice. In medium bowl, combine brown sugar, butter, flour, cinnamon, and salt; mix well. Stir in pecans.
2. Fill the pear halves with the brown sugar mixture, mounding the filling. Place, filling side up, in 3½ to 4-quart slow cooker; layer the pears. In small bowl, combine nectar and honey; stir to blend. Pour around pears.
3. Cover and cook on high for 2–3 hours or until pears are tender. Serve immediately.

🍲 **Makes 16 servings**

Fruit Salad

You can whip this dessert up in 5 minutes, and it will be ready to serve in less than an hour. Add a teaspoon of almond flavoring and it will be irresistible.

1 (3.4-ounce) box vanilla instant pudding

1 (3.3-ounce) box white chocolate instant pudding

1 (20-ounce) can pineapple, crushed, not drained

1 (20-ounce) can pineapple chunks, not drained

1 (29-ounce) can fruit cocktail, drained

1 (15-ounce) can mandarin oranges, drained

2 (8-ounce) containers frozen whipped topping, thawed

1 cup pecan pieces

1. Mix puddings and pineapple. Refrigerate for 30–40 minutes.
2. Add remaining ingredients and refrigerate until ready to serve.

🍲 **Makes 10–12 servings**

Kathi's Bread Pudding

This hand-me-down recipe is an old-fashioned one passed down through many generations. Make it with leftover bread. The sauce really makes this recipe—it's delightful.

Bread Pudding

2 cups dry bread crumbs

2 cups scalded milk

6 tablespoons sugar

Pinch salt

2 eggs, slightly beaten

2 tablespoons butter, softened

½ teaspoon vanilla

1 cup raisins

Whipped cream

Vanilla Sauce

1 cup water

½ cup sugar

2 tablespoons cornstarch

2 tablespoons butter

1 teaspoon vanilla

Whipped cream

For the bread pudding:
1. Put bread crumbs into greased 8" x 8" greased baking dish. Pour 1 cup scalded milk over bread crumbs and soak for 30 minutes.
2. Mix together sugar, salt, eggs, and 1 cup scalded milk. Add butter, vanilla, and raisins. Pour mixture over soaked bread crumbs and bake for 40 minutes at 350°.

For the vanilla sauce:
1. Cook water, sugar, and cornstarch until thick. Remove from heat and add butter and vanilla. Whisk together.
2. Serve with whipped cream.

❧ **Makes 9 servings**

And he pressed upon them greatly; and they turned in unto him, and entered into his house; and he made them a feast, and did bake unleavened bread, and they did eat.

—Genesis 19:3

Curried Fruit

This fragrant sauce can be served over pound cake or angel food cake, or spooned on top of ice cream for a summertime treat.

½ cup butter

1 cup brown sugar

1 tablespoon curry powder

1 (16-ounce) can sliced pears

1 (24-ounce) jar mango slices

2 (15-ounce) cans mandarin oranges

2 (15-ounce) cans apricot halves

1. Combine butter, brown sugar, and curry powder in a 4-quart slow cooker. Cover and cook on high for 1 hour or until butter melts.
2. Drain all of the fruits. Add all of the fruits to the slow cooker and stir very gently.
3. Cover and cook on high for 1–2 hours longer, or until fruits are hot but not falling apart. Serve as a compote or as a topping for cakes or ice cream.

❀ **Makes 12 servings**

Carol's Chocolate Marshmallow Dip

Sweetened condensed milk is the creamy basis for this velvety dip. Use your imagination when choosing dippers. This is a great way to use up leftover angel food cake or plain cookies.

2 (14-ounce) cans sweetened condensed milk

1 (12-ounce) package semisweet chocolate chips

1 (11-ounce) package milk chocolate chips

2 (1-ounce) squares unsweetened baking chocolate, chopped

1 (7-ounce) jar marshmallow crème

2 cups miniature marshmallows

Sugar cookies, graham crackers, gingersnaps, angel food cake

1. In 3-quart slow cooker, combine milk, both kinds of chocolate chips, and baking chocolate. Cover and cook on low for 2 hours, then stir.
2. Cover and cook on low for another 1–2 hours, as necessary, until chocolate melts and mixture is smooth.
3. Stir in marshmallow crème and miniature marshmallows to blend. Serve immediately with sugar cookies, graham crackers, gingersnaps, or angel food cake for dipping.

❀ **Makes 12–14 servings**

Apple-Caramel Dessert

This mouth-watering dessert will get rave reviews. Share it at your next neighborhood picnic.

Caramel Sauce
½ pound light caramels
½ cup evaporated milk

Crust
3 cups flour
¼ cup sugar
½ cup butter
¼ cup cooking oil
1 egg, unbeaten
¼ cup cold water

Filling
8 cups peeled and sliced apples
1 cup sugar
⅓ cup flour
2 to 4 tablespoons lemon juice

Topping
1 8-ounce package cream cheese, softened
1 egg
⅓ cup sugar
½ cup chopped walnuts

For the sauce:
> Melt caramels with milk over boiling water. Keep over hot water and set aside.

For the crust:
> Sift together flour and sugar and cut in butter until fine. Add oil. Blend egg and water together into flour mixture. Roll mixture out to fit a jelly roll pan.

For the filling:
> Combine apples, sugar, flour, and lemon juice and blend well. Place in pastry-lined pan. Drizzle caramel sauce over apples.

For the topping:
> Beat together cream cheese, egg, and sugar until smooth. Add walnuts and spoon topping on top of apples. Bake at 375° for 30–35 minutes.

❦ **Makes 36 servings**

Until I come and take you away to a land like your own land, a land of corn and wine, a land of bread and vineyards.

—Isaiah 36:17

Creamy Cream Puffs

These cream puffs are so easy to make. They are particularly delicious when filled with French vanilla pudding

1 stick butter

1 cup boiling water

1 cup flour

¼ teaspoon salt

4 eggs

2 (6-ounce) servings cook-and-serve French vanilla pudding

3 cups milk

1 (12-ounce) container frozen whipped topping, thawed

1. Mix together butter, water, flour, and salt in medium saucepan. Cook over medium heat, stirring until mixture forms a soft ball that does not separate.
2. Remove from heat and cool slightly. Add eggs one at a time. Beat after each egg is added.
3. Beat until mixture is smooth.
4. Drop batter onto greased cookie sheet.
5. Bake at 450° for 15 minutes, then lower oven to 325° for 25 minutes.
6. Cut off tops of puffs and pull unbaked dough out and toss away.
7. In medium saucepan, mix together the pudding and the milk. Cook according to package directions.
8. Remove from heat and cool, but keep stirring. Combine with the whipped topping and fill cream puffs.

❦ **Makes 12**

Pistachio Dessert

Add chopped pistachios on top of this easy-to-make dessert for an especially good treat.

1 stick butter or margarine

2 stacks Ritz crackers, crushed

3 tablespoons powdered sugar

2 (3.4-ounce) packages pistachio pudding mix

1½ cups milk

½ gallon vanilla ice cream, softened

1 (8-ounce) container frozen whipped topping, thawed

1. Melt butter and add crushed crackers and sugar, mixing well.
2. In a greased 9" × 13" dish, line the bottom with cracker mixture, saving some for top.
3. Beat together pudding mix and milk with electric beater for 2 minutes. Add ice cream then add whipped topping. Fold together and spread in pan. Sprinkle crumbs on top.
4. Can be refrigerated or frozen. If frozen, soften to room temperature to serve.

❦ **Makes 15–18 servings**

Dried-Cherry Bread Pudding

Dried cherries are tart and delicious. It's best to chop them and examine them carefully before stirring into the topping, because they may still contain pits.

9 cups French bread cubes

3 cups dried cherries, chopped

1½ cups chopped pecans

4 eggs, beaten

2 cups heavy cream

2 cups whole milk

1¼ cups sugar

⅓ cup butter, melted

1 tablespoon vanilla

½ teaspoon salt

1 cup caramel ice cream topping

1. Turn oven to 300°F. Place bread cubes on cookie sheet. Toast in the oven for 30 minutes or until dry to the touch. Place in 4-quart slow cooker along with cherries and pecans; mix gently.
2. In large bowl, combine eggs, cream, milk, sugar, butter, vanilla, and salt; beat until combined. Pour into slow cooker. Let stand for 15 minutes, pushing down on bread mixture occasionally so it absorbs the sauce.
3. Cover and cook on high for 1 hour, then reduce heat to low and cook for 5–6 hours longer until pudding is fluffy and set. Spoon into dessert bowls and top with a drizzle of caramel ice cream topping.

❀ **Makes 10–12 servings**

Old-Fashioned Bread Pudding Dessert

Here's another recipe for bread pudding. Five simple steps and it's ready to go. No wonder it's a favorite of many.

2 cups milk

4 cups bread crumbs

½ cup butter, melted

½ cup sugar

1 cup golden raisins

2 eggs, beaten

1 teaspoon cinnamon

1. Heat milk to scalding.
2. Put bread crumbs into 1½ quart buttered baking dish. Pour milk over bread crumbs. Cool.
3. Mix rest of ingredients with bread mixture. Bake at 350° for 40–45 minutes or until toothpick inserted comes out clean.

❧ **Makes 8 servings**

Banana–Graham Cracker Icebox Dessert

The term "icebox dessert" may be old-fashioned, but this classic dessert never goes out of style.

1 cup graham cracker crumbs

½ cup vegetable shortening

½ cup butter or margarine, softened

4 cups powdered sugar

2 teaspoons vanilla

2 eggs

3 large bananas

1 (12-ounce) container frozen whipped topping, thawed

1. Place graham cracker crumbs (reserving some for topping if desired) in 9" × 13" dish pan sprayed with vegetable cooking spray.
2. Combine the shortening and softened butter; cream together using electric mixer.
3. Beat in sugar until smooth.
4. Add vanilla and eggs. Beat well.
5. Put dollops of mixture on top of crumbs. Spread evenly with spoon.
6. Slice bananas and place on top of frosting mixture.

(continued)

(Banana–Graham Cracker Icebox
Dessert—continued)

7. Top with whipped topping.
8. Sprinkle with graham cracker crumbs,
   if desired.
9. Refrigerate for 4–6 hours before
   serving.

☙ **Makes 12–14 servings**

Frozen Strawberry Tarts

Freeze these longer when you want to take
them to a party.

1 (10-ounce) package strawberry halves,
   thawed
1 envelope Dream Whip whipped topping
   mix
½ cup cold milk
½ teaspoon vanilla
1 (15-ounce) can sweetened condensed milk
½ cup lemon juice
½ teaspoon almond extract
10 tart shells

1. Drain strawberries and reserve juice.
2. Prepare Dream Whip with milk and
   vanilla.
3. Mix condensed milk, lemon juice,
   almond extract, and strawberries with
   3 tablespoons of reserved juices.
4. Blend in prepared Dream Whip.
5. Spoon in tart shells and freeze at least
   4 hours.

☙ **Makes 10**

Raspberry-Pineapple Strata

There are lots of fruity flavors in this pudding-like strata. You could use dark chocolate chips instead of the white. Serve with chocolate ice cream topping.

14 cups cubed white bread

½ cup butter, melted

½ cup sugar

2 cups fresh raspberries

2 cups white chocolate chips

1 (13-ounce) can evaporated milk

1 (8-ounce) can crushed pineapple in juice, undrained

3 eggs

1 cup heavy cream

1 (6-ounce) container frozen lemonade concentrate

1. Preheat oven to 400°F. Place cubed bread on two cookie sheets. Drizzle with butter and sprinkle with sugar; toss. Bake for 10–15 minutes or until bread is lightly toasted. Remove from oven and let cool.

2. Layer cooled toasted bread, raspberries, and chocolate chips in 5- to 6-quart slow cooker.

3. In food processor or blender, combine evaporated milk and crushed pineapple. Add eggs and process or blend until smooth. Pour into large bowl and add remaining ingredients. Stir until blended.

4. Pour into slow cooker. Let stand for 15 minutes, pushing bread back into liquid as necessary. Cover and cook on low for 6 hours or until pudding is set. Serve with chocolate sauce and fresh raspberries.

❦ **Makes 12–14 servings**

Potluck Pointer

If your apple dumplings are always a hit, don't disappoint friends and family. Bring them! No one will think that it's the only recipe you've mastered. They'll simply enjoy it. And don't forget to bring copies of the recipe for sharing.

Pineapple Dessert

This easy dessert will become a favorite of yours if you like pineapple.

1 11-ounce box vanilla wafers, half of them crumbled

1 cup butter, softened

3 cups powdered sugar

4 whole eggs

2 envelopes Dream Whip whipped topping mix

1 cup crushed pineapple

1. Layer the intact cookies on bottom of a greased 9" × 13" dish.
2. Cream together butter and powdered sugar. Beat in eggs one at a time.
3. Make Dream Whip according to package directions. Then fold in powdered sugar mixture and beat with electric mixer for 2 minutes. Stir in crushed pineapple. Top with crumbs.
4. Refrigerate for 4–6 hours.

❦ **Makes 12–15 servings**

Apple Dumplings

Apple dumplings are reminiscent of old-fashioned comfort cooking. Bring a little comfort to those you love by whipping up a batch of these simple dumplings.

1 (8-ounce) tube refrigerated crescent rolls

2 large tart apples, peeled and quartered

1 cup sugar

1 cup orange juice

½ cup butter or margarine

½ teaspoon cinnamon

1. Unroll crescent dough and separate into 8 triangles.
2. Roll up one apple wedge in each triangle pinching edges to seal. Place in greased 8" square baking dish.
3. In small pan, bring sugar, orange juice, and butter to a boil. Pour over dumplings. Sprinkle with cinnamon and bake uncovered at 350° for 20–25 minutes.
4. Serve warm with whipped cream or ice cream.

❦ **Makes 8 servings**

White Chocolate–Cherry Cobbler

White chocolate is a fabulous contrast to sour pie cherries in this excellent cobbler. It adds sweetness and a great melting texture. This is also delicious with vanilla ice cream or sweetened whipped cream.

2 (15-ounce) cans sour pie cherries

1½ cups sugar

⅓ cup flour

1½ cups reserved cherry juice

¾ cup butter

1½ cups rolled oats

1½ cups brown sugar

½ teaspoon salt

1 teaspoon cinnamon

2¼ cups flour

1 teaspoon baking soda

1 (11.5-ounce) package white chocolate chips

1. Drain cherries, reserving juice. In large saucepan, combine sugar and flour; mix with wire whisk. Add 1½ cups reserved cherry juice and stir. Cook over medium heat until mixture thickens and boils. Stir in cherries and remove from heat.

2. Spray a 4-quart slow cooker with nonstick cooking spray. Place cherry mixture in bottom of slow cooker.

3. In skillet, melt butter over medium heat. Add oats; cook and stir until fragrant and lightly toasted. Remove from heat and add brown sugar, salt, and cinnamon; mix well. Stir in flour and baking soda until crumbly. Stir in white chocolate chips.

4. Sprinkle skillet mixture over cherry mixture in slow cooker. Cover and cook on low for 5–6 hours. Serve immediately with ice cream or whipped cream.

❦ **Makes 12 servings**

Hot Coffee

Way back in my high school days, my girlfriend Patsy's parents owned a catering business. They were doing a big sit-down dinner and needed some extra help serving. They asked me and some other friends if we would be willing to help. It sounded like fun, so we were given some instructions on serving etiquette and off we went.

Everything seemed to go well until dessert time. As I was pouring coffee for one gentleman, making sure to pour on the correct side as I had just learned to do, a couple of drops of coffee splashed on his hand. He became very angry. I apologized profusely and asked him if he was burned. Fortunately, he wasn't, as the coffee was not that hot. I then decided to make sure I still had enough coffee in the coffeepot to continue serving. As I stood behind him, instead of opening the lid to see, I shook the coffee pot to see how full it was. I guess I must have done it vigorously because some coffee came out and splashed the back of his suit. Well, young and foolish as I was, I quickly looked to see if anyone had noticed, especially him. Since he seemed to be completely unaware of it, I quickly retreated to the kitchen, keeping my mouth shut and deciding to let him find out on his own. I stayed in the kitchen and didn't come out until all the guests had left. Needless to say, I never served coffee again. ❧

—*Susie Siegfried*

Excellent Chocolate Dessert

There's a reason why this recipe is named Excellent Chocolate Dessert—because it is excellent! Give it a whirl and see how you like it.

1 cup flour

1 stick margarine

½ cup pecans

1 (12-ounce) container frozen whipped topping, thawed

1 cup powdered sugar

1 (8-ounce) package cream cheese, softened

1 (6-ounce) package instant chocolate pudding

3 cups milk

1. For the first layer, cream together flour and margarine and add pecans.
2. Bake at 350° for 15 minutes in a greased 9" × 13" baking dish. Cool thoroughly.
3. For the second layer, mix half of whipped topping with powdered sugar and cream cheese.
4. Spread over first layer.
5. Chill for 30 minutes.
6. For the third layer, mix pudding with milk and beat with electric mixer for 2 minutes. Spread on top of cream cheese mixture.
7. For the final layer, spread remaining whipped topping on top.

❦ **Makes 12–15**

Caramel Apple Crisp

Caramels melt together with apples in this delicious recipe, and the topping melts into a candy-like mixture. Serve with sweetened whipped cream or vanilla ice cream. Yum!

¼ cup butter

½ cup chopped pecans

1 cup rolled oats

½ cup brown sugar

1 teaspoon cinnamon

⅛ teaspoon cardamom

½ teaspoon salt

2 cups granola cereal

4 cups cored, peeled apple slices

14 unwrapped caramels, chopped

3 tablespoons flour

¼ cup apple juice

1. Spray a 3-quart slow cooker with nonstick cooking spray and set aside. In large skillet, melt butter. Add pecans and rolled oats; cook and stir until toasted and fragrant. Stir in brown sugar, cinnamon, cardamom, and salt.
2. Add granola cereal; stir and remove from heat. Place apple slices and chopped caramels in prepared slow cooker. Sprinkle with flour and top with apple juice. Top with granola mixture.
3. Cover and cook on low for 6–7 hours or until apples are tender and topping is set. Serve with ice cream or whipped cream.

❦ **Makes 8 servings**

Peach Crisp

Peach crisp is perfect for carry-in events. And there is never any left over to take home. Use frozen peaches—they are almost as good as fresh peaches, and they let you enjoy this wonderful dessert any time of the year.

Peach Crisp

½ cup sugar substitute

½ cup brown sugar

2 tablespoons cornstarch

1 teaspoon cinnamon

¼ cup low-fat margarine, melted

¼ cup water

2 (16-ounce) bags frozen peaches

Topping

½ cup quick cooking oats

6 to 9 large rectangles cinnamon graham crackers, crushed

½ cup sugar substitute

1 egg white

2 tablespoons low-fat margarine, softened

For the peach crisp:

1. Preheat oven to 350°.
2. Spray a 9" × 13" baking dish with vegetable cooking spray.

3. In a large bowl, mix together sugar substitute, brown sugar, cornstarch, cinnamon, margarine, and water.
4. Put peaches into mixture and toss, then place in prepared pan.

For the topping:
In a medium bowl, combine ingredients for topping, blending them together. Sprinkle over peaches. Bake for 30 minutes or until bubbling and firm.

Makes 12 servings

And she gave the savoury meat and the bread, which she had prepared, into the hand of her son Jacob.

—Genesis 27:17

Toffee Peach Crisp

Peaches and toffee are a wonderful combination. The toffee melts in the topping, adding a sweet burst of flavor, while the peaches become soft and tender. Serve with ice cream or whipped cream.

8 peaches, peeled and sliced

3 tablespoons lemon juice

1 teaspoon cinnamon

½ cup caramel ice cream topping

2 cups rolled oats

1 cup brown sugar

1 cup flour

½ teaspoon salt

1 teaspoon cinnamon

½ cup butter, melted

1 cup granola

1 cup crushed toffee

1. Spray 4-quart slow cooker with nonstick cooking spray. Place peaches, lemon juice, and cinnamon in slow cooker and mix. Drizzle with caramel ice cream topping.
2. In large bowl, combine oatmeal, brown sugar, flour, salt, and cinnamon; mix well. Add melted butter; stir until crumbly. Stir in granola and toffee.
3. Sprinkle over peach mixture in slow cooker. Cover and cook on low for 4–5 hours or until peaches are tender and topping is hot. Serve with ice cream or sweetened whipped cream.

❦ **Makes 8–10 servings**

Peachy Dessert

This dessert will appeal to peach lovers. You may use fresh peaches in place of frozen peaches if desired.

¾ cup flour

1 (3-ounce) package white chocolate cook-and-serve pudding

1 teaspoon baking powder

1 egg, beaten

½ cup milk

½ cup sugar

3 tablespoons melted margarine

1 (16-ounce) package frozen peaches, thawed and drained

1 (8-ounce) package cream cheese, softened

⅓ cup half-and-half

½ teaspoon cinnamon

4 teaspoons sugar

1. In a medium bowl, stir together flour, pudding mix, and baking powder.
2. In another bowl, combine egg, milk, ½ cup sugar, and melted margarine. Add to flour mixture. Spread in greased 8" square baking dish.
3. Chop peaches and place over batter.
4. Beat together cream cheese and half-and-half and pour over peaches.
5. Combine 4 teaspoons sugar and cinnamon. Scatter over peaches.
6. Bake at 350° for 40–50 minutes.

❦ **Makes 9 servings**

Lemon Cheese Pie

This cheese pie is easy to make and has a great lemon flavor.

1 (8-ounce) package cream cheese, softened

2 cups milk

1 (3-ounce) package lemon instant pudding mix

1 (9") prepared graham cracker crumb crust

1. Place cream cheese in a bowl and mix with electric beater.
2. Add ½ cup milk, a little at a time, blending until mixture is very smooth. Add remaining 1½ cups milk and pudding mix. Beat with electric mixer for about 2 minutes.
3. Pour into crust.
4. Chill until set.

❦ **Makes 8 servings**

Madolin's Peanut Pie

Isn't everyone's favorite candy bar a Reese's Peanut Butter Cup? This pie will remind you of a peanut butter cup with chocolate and peanut butter all mixed together.

1 (8-ounce) package cream cheese, softened

9 ounces of peanut butter, chunky or creamy

1 (14-ounce) can sweetened condensed milk

12 ounces frozen whipped topping, thawed

1 (10") prepared graham cracker crust

4 Reese's Peanut Butter Cups, chopped

1. With electric mixer, mix together cream cheese and peanut butter until smooth.
2. Add condensed milk and half of whipped topping, reserving some for the top. Mix well and pour in pie shell.
3. Top with remaining whipped topping and candy bar pieces.
4. Put in refrigerator to chill for at least 2 hours.

❦ **Makes 8 servings**

Pauline's Strawberry Pie

Make this pie in the summer when strawberry season is at its peak. You'll have everyone asking for seconds.

1 quart strawberries

1 cup sugar

1/4 cup water

1/4 teaspoon salt

3 tablespoons cornstarch

2 teaspoons lemon juice

Red food coloring

1 baked (8" or 9") pie shell

1 (8-ounce) container frozen whipped topping, thawed

1. In medium saucepan, mash 1 cup of the strawberries. Set remaining whole berries aside.
2. Add sugar, water, salt, and cornstarch to berries and mix with wire whisk. Cook over medium heat until thick. Remove from heat and add lemon juice and red food coloring. Cool.
3. Add remaining whole berries to mixture in saucepan and pour into pie shell. Top with whipped topping.

🐞 **Makes 8–10 servings**

Give Us S'More Pie

A cool confection just perfect for a hot summer day, or any time you crave that S'mores combination of flavors.

1 (12-ounce) Hershey's chocolate candy bar

30 regular marshmallows

3/4 cup milk

12 ounces hot fudge sauce

1 (9") prepared graham cracker crust

1 (8-ounce) container frozen whipped topping, thawed

1. Break candy bar into pieces.
2. In saucepan, stir broken candy pieces, marshmallows, and milk until all is melted and well blended. Remove from heat and cool.
3. Spread hot fudge sauce over bottom of graham cracker crust.
4. When candy mixture is cool, blend it with 1½ cups of the whipped topping and pour over hot fudge sauce.
5. Spread with remaining whipped topping.
6. Refrigerate for 3 hours.

🐞 **Makes 8–10 servings**

Sky-High Pie

Strawberries and whipping cream just go together. This is a keep-it-simple recipe that has an elegant taste.

2 egg whites

1 cup sugar

1 (10-ounce) package frozen strawberries, thawed slightly

1 tablespoon lemon juice

3/4 cup whipping cream

1 teaspoon vanilla

1 (9") prepared graham cracker crust

1. Beat egg whites with electric mixer at high speed until they peak. Add sugar gradually, beating with electric mixer, until egg whites are stiff.
2. Mix together strawberries and lemon juice.
3. Fold whipping cream into strawberry-lemon juice mixture and add vanilla. Pour into graham cracker crust.
4. Refrigerate for 4 hours.

❦ **Makes 8 servings**

Delightful Pumpkin Pie

Anything with a can of frosting and whipped topping in it has to be good. Make this during the holiday season. It'a quick to assemble and delicious.

1 (16-ounce) can sour cream frosting

1 cup sour cream

1 cup canned pumpkin

1 teaspoon cinnamon

1/2 teaspoon ginger

1/4 teaspoon cloves

1 (8-ounce) container frozen whipped topping, thawed

1 (10") prepared graham cracker crust

1. Mix together all ingredients except whipped topping and crust. Beat for 2 minutes with electric mixer on medium.
2. Fold in 1 cup of whipped topping.
3. Pour into pie crust.
4. Spread remaining whipped topping over pumpkin mixture.
5. Refrigerate for 4 hours.

❦ **Makes 8–10 servings**

Pecan Pie

This pecan pie will warm your body and your soul. It's the ideal dessert any time of the year.

4 eggs
1 cup sugar
1 cup light Karo syrup
½ tablespoon flour
¼ teaspoon salt
1 teaspoon vanilla
¼ cup butter, melted
½ cup pecans
1 (10") prepared pie crust, unbaked

1. In medium bowl, beat eggs well. Beat in sugar and syrup with whisk or electric mixer. Beat in flour, salt, and vanilla. Add melted butter and stir in pecans.
2. Pour mixture into pie crust and bake at 350° for 50–60 minutes until almost set in center.

❦ **Makes 8–10**

German Chocolate Pie

Even if you're too full for dessert, when you feast your eyes on this, you'll want some.

⅓ cup margarine or butter
⅓ cup brown sugar
⅓ cup pecans
⅓ cup coconut
1 99") graham cracker crust
1 (6-ounce) serving vanilla cook-and-serve pudding
4 ounces sweet chocolate, broken up
2½ cups milk
Whipped topping
Coconut

1. Combine margarine, brown sugar, pecans, and coconut in saucepan and cook until margarine is melted. Pour into pie crust.
2. Combine pudding, chocolate, and milk in saucepan and cook until mixture boils. Remove from heat; if needed, beat to blend. Cool for 5 minutes then pour into pie shell. Chill for 4 hours.
3. Spread with whipped topping and garnish with coconut.

❦ **Makes 8 servings**

Lemon Pie

This luscious lemon pie combines sweetness and tartness in just the right amounts. If you don't want to make the meringue for the top, use whipped topping.

1 (4-serving) package lemon pie filling, not instant

2/3 cup sugar

1/4 cup water

3 egg yolks

2 cups water

2 tablespoons lemon juice

2 tablespoons butter

1 (9") pie crust, baked

3 egg whites

6 tablespoons sugar

1. Combine filling, sugar, and 1/4 cup water in saucepan. Mix in egg yolks. Add 2 cups water and cook and stir to a full boil, about 5 minutes. Cool 5 minutes.
2. Blend in lemon juice and butter. Pour into cooled baked pie crust.
3. Beat egg whites until foamy. Gradually beat in sugar, beating to stiff peaks. Bake at 425° for 5–10 minutes or until lightly browned.

🌿 **Makes 8 servings**

Coconut Cream Pie

Try adding toasted coconut flakes to the top of the whipped topping. It's a nice garnish and gives it a luscious flavor.

2 (3-ounce) packages French vanilla instant pudding

3 cups cold milk

1 (12-ounce) container frozen whipped topping, thawed

1 teaspoon coconut flavoring

1 cup flaked coconut

1 (9") prepared graham cracker crust

1. In large bowl, combine pudding with milk. Beat with an electric mixer for 3 minutes. Fold in half of the whipped topping. Add flavoring and coconut. Pour into crust.
2. Spread remaining topping over pudding mixture.
3. Refrigerate for 3–4 hours.

🌿 **Makes 8–10 servings**

Picture-Perfect Peach Pie

If you love peaches, this will become a real favorite.

1 (3-ounce) package peach gelatin

⅔ cup boiling water

1 cup French vanilla ice cream

1 cup sliced fresh peaches or frozen peaches, thawed (plus extra for garnish, if desired)

1 (8-ounce) container frozen whipped topping, thawed

1 (9") graham cracker crust

1. Dissolve gelatin in boiling water. Add ice cream; stir with whisk until smooth. Blend in fruit and whipped topping. Spoon into crust.
2. Chill 3–4 hours.
3. Garnish with fresh peaches.

❦ **Makes 8 servings**

Split Pie

This banana split pie has all the toppings of a banana split minus the hot fudge. Make this on a moment's notice, and you'll be sure to please your family and friends.

1 (10") graham cracker crust

2 (8-ounce) packages cream cheese, softened

2 cups confectioners' sugar

2 sliced bananas

1 (2-ounce) can crushed pineapple, drained

½ cup sliced fresh strawberries

1 (12-ounce) container frozen whipped topping, thawed

1. Mix cream cheese and confectioners' sugar and spread on crust. Arrange sliced bananas over cream cheese. Spread can of drained crushed pineapple on top. Add fresh strawberries.
2. Top with whipped topping.

❦ **Makes 8–10 servings**

Large Quantity

⚜

In the elementary parochial school I attended, those wonderful ladies would make a hot lunch for us every day. The food was simply delicious—tender meatloaf, fried chicken, mashed potatoes, cooked vegetables, fruit salad, pies, and cakes—yum. I have nothing but admiration for those who cook every day for schoolchildren.

Church ladies have to be ready to tackle quantity cooking. When you're cooking a lot of food in several slow cookers, it's important to remember the 1/2 to 3/4 rule, as explained in the Introduction (page ix). Use enough slow cookers so the food fills them to the proper amount. It may help to place a timer next to each slow cooker so you can keep track of when each one started cooking, or use timers with multiple functions.

It's also important to follow food safety regulations when you're cooking in quantity. Check with your local extension service that's part of the University near you for the latest laws and rules. Use a food thermometer to make sure that meat is thoroughly cooked, and that casseroles reach a temperature of 165°F.

These recipes may also inspire you to use your slow cookers in different ways. I love the idea of making a large quantity of each ingredient for, say, a salad, in different slow cookers, then combining them with a dressing in several very large bowls. You can cook rice, meats, vegetables, and even fruits this way in the slow cooker.

Enjoy these recipes, and let them help you cook for your church family.

—Linda Larsen

Apple Pies

Use apples that are best for cooking in this recipe: Granny Smith, Jonathan, McIntosh, and Winesap are good choices. This recipe assumes that the pie crust holds 3 cups.

16 medium tart apples, peeled, cored, and sliced

3 tablespoons lemon juice

1 cup brown sugar

1½ cups sugar

2 cinnamon sticks

2 teaspoons cinnamon

1 teaspoon nutmeg

¼ teaspoon cardamom

1½ teaspoons salt

2 cups applesauce

2 cups apple juice

¾ cup cornstarch

1 cup apple cider

4 premade vanilla wafer pie crusts

2 cups heavy cream

½ cup powdered sugar

2 teaspoons vanilla

1. In 6- to 7-quart slow cooker, combine apples with lemon juice and toss to coat. Add cinnamon sticks.
2. In large bowl, combine remaining ingredients except cornstarch, apple cider, pie crusts, cream, powdered sugar, and vanilla; mix well. Pour into slow cooker.
3. Cover and cook on low for 5–6 hours or until apples are tender when pierced with a fork, stirring once during cooking time. In small bowl, combine cornstarch with apple cider and mix well. Pour into slow cooker.
4. Cover and cook on high for 20–30 minutes or until mixture thickens. Remove and discard cinnamon sticks. Pour filling into the pie crusts and refrigerate immediately.
5. When filling is set and pies are cold, whip cream with powdered sugar and vanilla in medium bowl. Spoon cream on top of apples and serve.

❧ **Makes 4 pies;** ❧ **Makes 32 servings**

Southwest Potato Salad

Cook the potatoes for this spicy salad in the slow cooker. If you don't like spicy food, leave out the jalapeño peppers.

10 pounds russet potatoes

4 onions, chopped

1 head garlic, peeled and minced

5 jalapeño peppers, minced

3 tablespoons chili powder

2 teaspoons cumin

3 teaspoons salt

1 teaspoon white pepper

6 cups frozen corn

2 cups water

3 cups mayonnaise

1 cup plain yogurt

1 (15-ounce) can creamed corn

3 (4-ounce) cans diced green chiles, undrained

2 tablespoons chili powder

2 teaspoons salt

¼ teaspoon cayenne pepper

4 cups cubed pepper jack cheese

1 cup grated Cotija cheese

1. Peel potatoes and cut into cubes. Combine in two 5- to 6-quart slow cookers with onions, garlic, and jalapeños. Sprinkle with chili powder, cumin, salt, and pepper; then pour 1 cup water into each slow cooker.

2. Cover and cook on low for 8–9 hours or until potatoes are tender. Drain potato mixture.
3. In two or three large bowls, combine remaining ingredients and mix well. Add hot potato mixture and stir gently to coat. Cover and chill for 5–6 hours until cold. Stir gently before serving.

❧ **Makes 24–26**

Potluck Pointer

When making potato salad for a large group, mix together all your dressing ingredients. Then take one-third of the potatoes and gently toss with one-third of the dressing. Transfer this batch to your serving bowl. Repeat with the remaining two batches. Mixing smaller portions reduces the chance of crumbling the potatoes.

Smoked Turkey Strata

This is a great recipe for using leftover turkey after Thanksgiving or Christmas. Or you could use ham or cooked chicken instead.

3 (16-ounce) packages frozen Tater Tots, thawed

4 onions, chopped

5 cloves garlic, minced

2 pounds plain cooked or smoked turkey breast, chopped

6 carrots, sliced

2 cups shredded Swiss cheese

2 cups shredded provolone cheese

2 (13-ounce) cans evaporated milk

18 eggs

⅓ cup yellow mustard

2 teaspoons dried basil leaves

2 teaspoons salt

½ teaspoon pepper

1. Spray two 6- to 7-quart slow cookers with nonstick cooking spray. Layer Tater Tots, onions, garlic, turkey, carrots, and cheeses in both slow cookers, making three layers of each.
2. In large bowl, combine remaining ingredients and beat until blended. Pour into slow cookers.
3. Cover and cook on low for 8–10 hours or until casseroles are set. Serve immediately.

❧ **Makes 24 servings**

Chicken à la King over Seasoned Wild Rice Pilaf

This concept, of making food in two slow cookers and serving one dish over another, saves time and makes feeding a crowd simple.

12 chopped raw chicken breasts

3 onions, chopped

2 (8-ounce) packages fresh mushrooms, chopped

2 (16-ounce) jars Alfredo sauce

2 (10-ounce) cans condensed cream of chicken soup

2 cups whole milk

2 teaspoons dried thyme leaves

1 teaspoon dried sage leaves

½ teaspoon white pepper

1 (16-ounce) bag frozen baby peas

1 recipe Seasoned Wild Rice Pilaf (page 411)

1. In two 5-quart slow cookers, combine chicken, onions, and mushrooms; stir to mix. Divide Alfredo sauce, soup, milk, thyme, sage, and pepper between the slow cookers; do not stir.
2. Cover and cook on low for 7–8 hours or until chicken is cooked. Have the Wild Rice Pilaf cooking at the same time the chicken is cooking.
3. When chicken is done, stir in the frozen peas. Uncover and cook on high for 20–30 minutes or until peas are hot and tender.
4. Serve the chicken mixture on the Seasoned Wild Rice Pilaf.

❧ **Makes 24 servings**

Cranberry-Cherry Pies

These tart pies aren't too sweet. For a nice finish, add some cocoa powder and powdered sugar to the whipped cream you dollop on top.

2 (15-ounce) cans whole berry cranberry sauce

3 (21-ounce) cans cherry pie filling

1 (16-ounce) bag fresh cranberries, chopped

1 cup brown sugar

½ cup sugar

¼ cup lemon juice

1 teaspoon salt

2 teaspoons cinnamon

¼ cup butter

3 (1-ounce) envelopes unflavored gelatin

1 cup cranberry juice

4 (9") pie crusts, baked and cooled

2–3 cups frozen whipped topping, thawed

1. In 5-quart slow cooker, combine cranberry sauce, pie filling, cranberries, brown sugar, sugar, lemon juice, salt, cinnamon, and butter. Cover and cook on low for 7–8 hours or until cranberries are soft.
2. In small bowl, combine gelatin and cranberry juice and let stand for 5 minutes. Stir into slow cooker until gelatin dissolves.
3. Turn off slow cooker and let mixture stand for 30 minutes. Spoon into pie crusts and refrigerate immediately. When pies are set and cold, top with thawed frozen whipped topping or sweetened whipped cream and slice to serve.

❧ **Makes 4 pies;** ❧ **Makes 32 servings**

Roasted Corn Stew

This thick and rich chowder starts with roasted corn for wonderful caramelized sweetness and chewy texture.

18 cups frozen corn

½ cup olive oil

1½ teaspoons salt

½ teaspoon white pepper

½ cup butter

6 onions, sliced

1 head garlic, peeled and sliced

6 tablespoons flour

1 (32-ounce) box chicken broth

4 cups water

3 (15-ounce) cans cream-style corn

4 (16-ounce) jars four-cheese Alfredo sauce

2 cups heavy cream

3 cups shredded Muenster cheese

1. Preheat oven to 400°F. Place frozen corn on three cookie sheets. Drizzle with olive oil and sprinkle with salt and pepper. Roast for 20–30 minutes until corn begins to turn brown around the edges.
2. Divide corn between two 6- or 7-quart slow cookers. In each of two large skillets, melt ¼ cup butter over medium heat. Add onions and garlic, and cook and stir for 5–6 minutes.
3. Divide flour between the skillets and cook and stir until bubbly. Add half of chicken broth to each skillet and bring to a simmer. Pour into both slow cookers. Add half of water, canned corn and Alfredo sauce to each slow cooker; stir gently.
4. Cover and cook on low for 6–7 hours or until soup is blended and thick. Stir 1 cup of heavy cream and 1½ cups cheese into each slow cooker. Uncover and cook on high for 15–20 minutes or until cheese melts. Serve immediately.

❧ **Makes 32–36 servings**

Whoever has a bountiful eye will be blessed, for he shares his bread with the poor.

—Proverbs 22:9

Mom's Goulash

Wow—this goulash has a fabulous blend of flavors and textures. The combination of sausage with ground beef makes it rich and delicious. It will satisfy any hearty appetite.

1 (16-ounce) package bacon

3 tablespoons butter

3 onions, chopped

1 head garlic, peeled and minced

2 pounds pork bulk sausage

2 pounds ground beef

½ cup flour

2 teaspoons salt

½ teaspoon pepper

3 tablespoons sweet paprika

2 (32-ounce) boxes beef stock

⅔ cup red wine vinegar

4 carrots, sliced

2 (8-ounce) packages fresh sliced mushrooms

6 potatoes, peeled and cubed

30 cups hot cooked noodles

1. In large skillet, cook bacon in batches. Drain bacon in paper towels, crumble, and set aside. Remove all but 2 tablespoons bacon drippings from skillet. Add butter.
2. Cook onions and garlic in skillet until crisp-tender, about 5 minutes. Remove with slotted spoon and place in large bowl.
3. Add sausage and beef to skillet in batches and cook until almost browned. Remove meat with slotted spoon and place in large bowl. Add flour, salt, pepper, and paprika to skillet; cook and stir until bubbly.
4. Add 1 box of beef stock and the vinegar to the skillet, and bring to a simmer. Combine carrots, mushrooms, and potatoes in two 6- or 7-quart slow cookers. Add bacon, onions, garlic, and meat on top of vegetables.
5. Pour skillet mixture into both slow cookers and top with remaining box of beef stock. Cover and cook on low for 8–9 hours or until vegetables are tender and goulash has thickened. Serve over hot cooked noodles.

❀ **Makes 30–32 servings**

On this mountain the Lord of hosts will make for all peoples a feast of rich food, a feast of well-aged wines, of rich food filled with marrow, of well-aged wines strained clear.

—Isaiah 25:6

Best Pot Roast

Pot roast cooks to perfection in the slow cooker. The vegetables give great flavor and texture to the gravy. Yum!

3 (4-pound) tri-tip beef roasts

¾ cup flour

1 tablespoon salt

2 tablespoons paprika

2 teaspoons pepper

6 tablespoons butter

6 onions, chopped

1 head garlic, peeled and minced

9 carrots, sliced

3 (8-ounce) cans tomato sauce

2 (6-ounce) cans tomato paste

2 cups beef broth

2 tablespoons sugar

1. Trim excess fat from roasts. On cookie sheet, combine flour, salt, paprika, and pepper. Dredge roasts in this mixture.
2. In large skillet, melt 2 tablespoons butter. Add one roast; brown on all sides, about 6–7 minutes. Remove from heat. Add 2 more tablespoons butter and brown second roast; repeat with third roast.
3. Add 2 onions to skillet; cook and stir until crisp-tender, stirring to loosen pan drippings.
4. Divide remaining onions, garlic, and carrots among three 6- or 7-quart slow cookers. Top each with one browned roast. Pour one can tomato sauce over each roast.
5. Add tomato paste and beef broth to skillet; add sugar and bring to a boil, stirring to dissolve tomato paste. Divide among slow cookers.
6. Cover slow cookers and cook on low for 8–9 hours or until beef is very tender. Remove roasts from slow cookers; cover to keep warm. Turn off slow cookers; using an immersion blender, blend vegetables in the slow cookers to make a sauce. Serve with beef.

❧ **Makes 36 servings**

Now the manna was like coriander seed, and its color was like the color of gum resin. The people went around and gathered it, ground it in mills or beat it in mortars, then boiled it in pots and made cakes of it; and the taste of it was like the taste of cakes baked with oil.

—Numbers 11:7–8

Simmered Beef over Potatoes

Apple juice adds a wonderful slightly sweet taste to this savory recipe. It can also be served over cooked pasta or four recipes of the Herbed Brown Rice Pilaf (page 294) rather than the potatoes.

5 pounds beef chuck roast

3 onions, chopped

2 (16-ounce) bags baby carrots

1 head garlic, peeled and chopped

1 (32-ounce) box beef broth

2 cups apple juice ·

2 (6-ounce) cans tomato paste

2 teaspoons salt

½ teaspoon pepper

1 recipe Rich and Creamy Potatoes (page 412)

1. Cut the roast into 6" pieces and trim off excess fat. Place onions, carrots, and garlic into two 6-quart slow cookers. Place beef on top. Pour half of beef broth into each slow cooker.
2. In large bowl, combine apple juice with tomato paste, salt, and pepper; stir with wire whisk until tomato paste dissolves and mixture is smooth. Divide among slow cookers.

3. Cover and cook on low for 8–9 hours or until beef and vegetables are tender. Have the Rich and Creamy Potatoes cooking at the same time. Serve the beef mixture over Rich and Creamy Potatoes, hot cooked pasta, or rice pilaf.

❧ **Makes 24 servings**

Chicken-Barley Casserole

This recipe uses two large slow cookers to feed a crowd. With such a large quantity, it's important to stir once during cooking time so the food cooks evenly.

2 (16-ounce) boxes medium pearl barley, rinsed

2 (32-ounce) boxes chicken broth

2 cups water

4 onions, chopped

2 (16-ounce) bags baby carrots

2 (8-ounce) packages sliced fresh mushrooms

14 chicken breasts, chopped

2 teaspoons seasoned salt

½ teaspoon pepper

2 teaspoons dried thyme leaves

4 cups shredded Havarti cheese

1. Drain barley and place one box in each 6-quart slow cooker; add half of chicken broth and water to each. Divide onions, carrots, and mushrooms among slow cookers.
2. Chop chicken into 1" pieces and sprinkle with seasoned salt, pepper, and thyme. Add to slow cookers. Cover and cook on low for 7–9 hours or until barley is tender and chicken is thoroughly cooked, stirring twice during cooking time.
3. Stir cheese into the slow cookers until melted, then serve.

Makes 30–34 servings

Seasoned Wild Rice Pilaf

This simple side dish can be served under a meat mixture, or all by itself as a side dish. You could substitute sliced carrots or mushrooms for the onions if you'd like.

4 cups wild rice, rinsed and drained

3 onions, chopped

12 cups chicken or vegetable broth

¼ cup butter

2 teaspoons seasoned salt

1 teaspoon dried marjoram

1 teaspoon dried oregano

½ teaspoon pepper

Combine all ingredients in a 6-quart slow cooker. Cover and cook on low for 7–8 hours or until wild rice is tender. Stir and serve.

Makes 24 servings

If your enemy is hungry, give him bread to eat; and if he is thirsty, give him water to drink.

—Proverbs 25:21

Rich and Creamy Potatoes

Frozen hash brown potatoes are a fabulous timesaver when you're serving a crowd. There are several types; this recipe uses the potatoes cut into small dice.

2 (32-ounce) bags southern-style hash brown potatoes, thawed

4 onions, chopped

12 cloves garlic, chopped

2 (10-ounce) cans cream of potato soup

1 (16-ounce) jar four-cheese Alfredo sauce

2 cups whole milk

½ teaspoon white pepper

1 teaspoon dried basil leaves

1 teaspoon dried thyme leaves

1. In 7-quart slow cooker, combine potatoes with onions and garlic. In large bowl, combine soup, Alfredo sauce, milk, and seasonings; stir until blended.
2. Pour soup mixture into slow cooker and gently stir. Cover and cook on low for 6–8 hours or until potatoes are tender, stirring twice during cooking time.

❦ **Makes 24**

Apple Chutney

If ladies in your church know how to can food, you can make this delicious recipe and sell it at a fundraiser. Make sure you follow your local extension agent's instructions for safe canning.

¼ cup butter

9 cups chopped, peeled and cored apple

2 onions, chopped

¼ cup water

¼ cup lemon juice

¼ cup apple cider vinegar

½ cup brown sugar

1 cup golden raisins

1 cup dark raisins

1 cup dried cranberries

2 teaspoons cinnamon

¼ teaspoon cardamom

1 teaspoon salt

1. In 4- or 5-quart slow cooker, combine all ingredients and mix well. Cover and cook on low for 6–7 hours, stirring once during cooking time, until apples start to fall apart and mixture has thickened.
2. Spoon into sterilized jars and seal. These should be processed in a hot water bath for long-term storage. The chutney can also be frozen in freezer containers, or refrigerated and used within 1 week.

❦ **Makes 10 cups**

Poached Chicken Breasts and Broth

Sometimes you need a lot of cooked chicken, perhaps for a salad or a casserole or just sandwiches. This is an excellent way to cook a bunch with almost no work.

4 onions, chopped

5 carrots, chopped

4 stalks celery, chopped

24 boneless, skinless chicken breasts

8 cups chicken broth

2 teaspoons dried thyme leaves

¼ teaspoon pepper

1. Layer onions, carrots, and celery with chicken breasts in two 6- or 7-quart slow cookers. Pour half of chicken broth over each and sprinkle with thyme and pepper.
2. Cover and cook on low for 5–7 hours or until chicken is thoroughly cooked. Refrigerate chicken until ready to use. Strain and freeze the broth for another use.

❀ **Makes 24 breasts**

Super-Simple Mashed Potatoes

Dried potato flakes are actually made from real potatoes. When reconstituted in this recipe, they are rich and creamy, with hardly any work.

½ cup butter

1 onion, finely chopped

3 cloves garlic, minced

2 cups water

2½ cups milk

1¼ cups ricotta cheese

⅓ cup grated Parmesan cheese

½ teaspoon seasoned salt

4½ cups dried potato flakes

Pinch nutmeg

1. In medium skillet, melt butter over medium heat. Add onion and garlic; cook and stir until tender, about 6 minutes. Add water; bring to a boil.
2. Pour into 4- or 5-quart slow cooker. Add remaining ingredients, mixing well. Cover and cook on low for 1 hour, then stir potatoes. Cover and cook for 30–40 minutes longer, until potatoes are hot and thick. Can be kept on low for 2 hours, stirring occasionally to maintain texture.

❀ **Makes 14–18 servings**

Beef Tacos

Tacos are easy to make and eat. Set out a couple of batches along with all the taco fixings you like, and stand back!

3 pounds ground beef

2 onions, chopped

6 cloves garlic, minced

2 jalapeño peppers, minced

1 teaspoon salt

½ teaspoon pepper

8 plum tomatoes, chopped

2 (15-ounce) cans kidney beans, drained

2 tablespoons chili powder

2 (15-ounce) cans refried beans

18–20 taco shells

3 cups lettuce

2 cups sour cream

4 cups shredded Cheddar cheese

4 avocados

¼ cup lime juice

1. In large skillet, cook beef until almost done, stirring to break up meat. Drain thoroughly.
2. In 6- or 7-quart slow cooker, combine beef with onions, garlic, jalapeño peppers, salt, pepper, plum tomatoes, kidney beans, chili powder, and refried beans. Cover and cook on low for 7–8 hours.
3. Heat taco shells as directed on package. Peel and chop the avocados and sprinkle with lime juice; place in bowl. Arrange a buffet with the hot filling, the taco shells, and remaining ingredients. Let people assemble their own tacos.

❧ **Makes 18–20 servings**

Then the king gave a great banquet to all his officials and ministers, "Esther's banquet." He also granted a holiday to the provinces, and gave gifts with royal liberality.

—Esther 2:18

Classic Slow Cooker Stuffing

Adding condensed soup to stuffing makes it a bit creamy as well as moist. Be sure to stir the stuffing very well before you put it in the slow cooker. Have three or four of these slow cookers going at once to feed a crowd.

14 cups cubed whole wheat bread

½ cup butter

3 tablespoons olive oil

3 onions, chopped

6 cloves garlic, minced

2 (8-ounce) packages sliced fresh mushrooms

1 (10-ounce) can golden cream of mushroom soup

2 cups chicken broth

2 eggs, beaten

1 tablespoon chopped fresh sage

1 tablespoon chopped fresh thyme

1 teaspoon celery salt

½ teaspoon seasoned salt

¼ teaspoon pepper

1. Preheat oven to 300°F. Place the bread cubes on two cookie sheets. Bake for 20–30 minutes or until the bread cubes are very dry and slightly toasted. Let cool.
2. In large skillet melt butter with olive oil over medium heat. Add onions and garlic; cook and stir for 5 minutes. Add mushrooms; cook and stir for another 5–7 minutes until vegetables are tender. Set aside.
3. In very large bowl, combine soup, broth, eggs, sage, thyme, celery salt, seasoned salt, and pepper; mix well. Stir in onion mixture. Then add bread cubes, 3 cups at a time, stirring well to incorporate everything.
4. Spray two 4-quart or one 7-quart slow cooker with nonstick cooking spray. Add the stuffing mixture, cover, and cook on low for 5–7 hours, stirring once during cooking time.

❧ **Makes 12–14 servings**

Roasted Root Vegetables

Roast root vegetables in one slow cooker, and cook Roasted Tender Vegetables (page 416) in another so they all cook to perfection. After they're done, you can mix them, or serve them separately as a choice in a buffet line.

8 potatoes, peeled and cubed

3 sweet potatoes, peeled and cubed

8 carrots, cut into chunks

2 parsnips, peeled and cubed

3 onions, chopped

6 cloves garlic, minced

2 cups vegetable broth

2 teaspoons salt

½ teaspoon pepper

1 teaspoon dried oregano leaves

½ teaspoon dry mustard powder

1. In 6- or 7-quart slow cooker, combine all ingredients and mix well. Cover and cook on low for 7–9 hours or until vegetables are tender when pierced with a fork.
2. Stir gently to combine, then serve, or hold on low heat for 2 hours, stirring occasionally.

❧ **Makes 24–26 servings**

Roasted Tender Vegetables

These delicate vegetables turn sweet when they cook. They do not cook for a very long time, so stagger your cooking times accordingly to be sure everything finishes at the same time.

4 green bell peppers, sliced

4 red bell peppers, sliced

2 (8-ounce) packages whole fresh mushrooms

2 (8-ounce) packages sliced fresh mushrooms

3 onions, chopped

6 cloves garlic, minced

2 cups vegetable broth

2 teaspoons seasoned salt

½ teaspoon pepper

2 teaspoons dried thyme leaves

In 5- or 6-quart slow cooker, combine all ingredients and mix well. Cover and cook on low heat for 3–5 hours or until vegetables are tender.

❧ **Makes 24–26 servings**

Potpourri

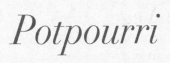

Wedding Disaster

My sister Marilyn and her husband Paul celebrated their 50th wedding anniversary in December 2004. What an accomplishment, especially when I think back to the day they were married. After the ceremony, at St. Boniface in Lafayette, Indiana, everyone came to our house for the wedding reception. Talk about good food! Marilyn, who was wearing our sister Lois's wedding dress and veil, was glowing—happiness was in the air. She came into the kitchen where all the food was being prepared to find Mom. Without realizing it, she got too close to our gas stove—the burners, of course, were on. As she turned around, my cousin Shirley was the first to see that her veil had caught fire. She quickly grabbed the crown of the veil off Marilyn's head, threw it in the sink, and ran water over it. Shirley's fast thinking saved my sister. Marilyn's eyebrows were singed, and of course she was in shock for a few minutes. Mother, of course, was a nervous wreck just thinking about what could have happened to one of her precious girls, but Dad calmed down all of his girls and the gaiety soon resumed.

What a day to remember. And 50 years later, we can still recall it as if it had happened yesterday. I can't really remember the food we had, but I know it was good, as it always was at our house. Thanks to Kodak, I can remember the cake—it was from our favorite bakery, O'Rears, which I still visit when I go back to Lafayette. ❧

—Susie Siegfried

Poppy Seed Dressing

If you would like to make this dressing sugar-free and lower the calories, try using sugar substitute in place of the sugar and applesauce in place of the oil.

1½ cups sugar

2 teaspoons dry mustard

1 teaspoon salt

½ cup vinegar

1 tablespoon grated onion

2 cups oil

2 tablespoons poppy seeds

1. Blend together sugar, mustard, salt, and vinegar. Add onion and oil and beat until thick. Add poppy seeds.
2. Refrigerate and serve.

❦ **Makes 1 quart**

Cranberry Crunch

Make this cranberry crunch especially around the holiday season. It seems that holidays and cranberries are synonymous. This is good served with ice cream and/or whipped topping.

1 (16-ounce) can whole cranberry sauce

½ cup quick-cooking oats

½ cup packed brown sugar

¼ cup flour

4 tablespoons butter

Frozen whipped topping, thawed

1. Preheat oven to 350°.
2. Spread cranberry sauce in the bottom of a 9" pie pan.
3. In a small bowl, combine oats, brown sugar, and flour. Cut in the butter until mixture is crumbly. Sprinkle mixture over cranberry sauce. Bake at 350° for 25 minutes.
4. When serving, top with whipped topping.

❦ **Makes 3 cups**

Cinnamon Pecans

You'll want to at least double this recipe so you'll have enough to share. They make great little gifts during the holiday season. Put them in a holiday tin and wish your family and friends happy holidays with these treats.

2½ cups pecan halves

2 tablespoons oil

1 cup sugar

1 teaspoon cinnamon

¼ teaspoon salt

¼ cup water

1 teaspoon vanilla

1. Toss pecans with oil and bake on a flat cookie sheet at 325° for 15 minutes. Stir often.
2. In a small saucepan, mix sugar, cinnamon, salt, water, and vanilla. Cook until at a soft boil, about 3–5 minutes. Mix with nuts and spread quickly on wax paper.
3. When cool, break apart into pieces.

❧ **Makes 3 cups**

Crab Louis Dressing

Years ago, Crab Louis was a very popular dish in California. Learn to make this wonderful salad at home using this dressing.

1 cup mayonnaise

¼ cup heavy cream, whipped

¼ cup chili sauce

¼ cup chopped green pepper

¼ cup chopped green onion

1 teaspoon lemon juice

Salt

1. Mix together mayonnaise, whipped cream, chili sauce, green pepper, and green onion. Add lemon juice and salt to taste.
2. Chill.

❧ **Makes 2 cups**

Lois's Best Dressing

Keep this dressing in your refrigerator to have it on hand for salads. This is one of the best homemade dressings and it's sure to become a real favorite in your family.

1½ cups light brown sugar

½ teaspoon paprika

½ cup ketchup

½ teaspoon salt

1 teaspoon onion powder

1½ cups vegetable oil

½ cup vinegar

½ teaspoon celery seed

½ teaspoon garlic

1. Mix sugar, paprika, ketchup, salt, and onion powder. Add oil and vinegar alternately. Then add celery seed and garlic.
2. Keep refrigerated.

❦ **Makes 1 quart**

Index

⚜